Managing
Ethnic Conflict
in Africa

Managing Ethnic Conflict in Africa

Pressures and Incentives for Cooperation

DONALD ROTHCHILD

BROOKINGS INSTITUTION PRESS
Washington, D.C.

~y of Congress Cataloging-in-Publication data:

hild, Donald S.
lanaging ethnic conflict in Africa : pressures and incentives for
peration / Donald Rothchild.
p.   cm.
cludes bibliographical references (p.) and index.
BN 0-8157-7594-6 (cloth : alk. paper) — ISBN 0-8157-7593-8
: : alk. paper)
1. Africa, Sub-Saharan—Politics and government—1960- 2. Africa,
Sub-Saharan—Ethnic relations—Political aspects.   I. Title.
DT352.8.R68   1997
323.1'67—dc21   97-4763
                                                                         CIP

9 8 7 6 5 4 3 2 1

The paper used in this publication meets the minimum requirements of the American
National Staandard for Information Sciences—Permanence of Paper for Printed Library
Materials, ANSI Z39.48—1984.

Set in Garamond Book

Composition by Harlowe Typography Inc., Cottage City, Maryland

Printed by R. R. Donnelley & Sons Co., Harrisonburg, Virginia

Foreword

Newspaper headlines about places such as Rwanda, Angola, and the Democratic Republic of the Congo suggest that conflicts between the state and ethnic groups and between rival ethnic groups are common events in Africa. It is the contention of this book, however, that such conflicts are not inevitable and that they can be avoided or at least managed.

Ethnic groups can be a creative force, providing material benefits and meeting such intangible needs as esteem and a sense of identity and purpose. It is normal for people to mobilize in an effort to gain organizational, ideological, political, and economic power. As long as they compete according to the rules of the political game and accept their opponent's right to participate, the results can be positive.

In other circumstances, however, ethnicity can be a highly destructive force. Acute tensions can be unleashed as groups struggle over territory, cultural survival, and physical existence. Also, if one group controls the state and its institutions and excludes others from positions of influence, deep resentments and hostility will often surface. In worst-case scenarios—apartheid in South Africa, the carnage in Rwanda, and civil war in Sudan—grim, hostile perceptions can result in damaging relations for all who are drawn into the confrontation. Although the examples of destructive ethnicity that Donald Rothchild has recited in this book are drawn from Africa's recent experience, encounters with collective fear, insecurity, and hostility have a long and virtually universal history.

Rothchild presents a number of cases to demonstrate how leaders can prevent harmful relations from arising and, when they occur, how diplomats and organizations can influence those involved to shift to more constructive internal systems of conflict management. Still, a breakthrough to peace will probably not result from persuasion alone. There is no alternative to sustained investment in a peace process, linking the capabilities of a responsible and responsive state with the use of pressures and incentives by mediators. The goal must be to create new institutional constraints or to facilitate the return to regularized group interactions. The analysis of noncoercive and coercive incentives in this book provides creative new options that diplomats can use to alter the strategies of groups involved in ethnic conflicts.

The book was edited by Nancy D. Davidson. Christopher Dall, Maya A. Dragicevic, Gary I. Gordon, and Cynthia M. Iglesias verified the factual content of the manuscript. Ellen Garshick provided proofreading services, and Mary Mortenson prepared the index.

Brookings gratefully acknowledges support for this project from the Rockefeller Foundation and the Rockefeller Brothers Fund.

The views expressed here are those of the author and should not be ascribed to the persons whose assistance is acknowledged or to the trustees, officers, or staff members of the Brookings Institution.

Michael H. Armacost
President

July 1997
Washington, D.C.

Acknowledgments

This undertaking, simultaneously dealing with regularized and unregularized relations and cutting across the fields of comparative politics and international relations, could not have been completed without generous help from many sources. I wish to dedicate this book to those whose encouragement and backing made this project realizable: Edith Rothchild, I. William Zartman, and my graduate students. Edith Rothchild's sense of perspective and idealism and I. William Zartman's sage advice, sense of purpose, and commitment to the study of mediation and negotiation were sustaining and inspiring. I also received indispensable support from Maria Courtis, Kathleen Fitzgibbon, Michael Foley, E. Gyimah-Boadi, Caroline Hartzell, Matthew Hoddie, Letitia Lawson, Lisa Sharlach, and Lako Tongun while they were at the University of California, Davis.

In addition to the funding received by Brookings for this project, I received funding from the University of California, Davis, and the United States Institute of Peace. I wish to express my deep appreciation to these institutions for their generosity and their confidence.

In addition to those thanked above, I would especially like to thank Thomas J. Johnson, Christopher Mitchell, Timothy D. Sisk, and two anonymous reviewers who read the whole manuscript and made keen comments on its development. I am also indebted to others who read parts of the manuscript and offered very helpful insights, including Robert Collins, Alexander Groth, Lloyd Jensen, Bruce Jentleson, Edmond Keller, David A. Lake, Susan Collin Marks, Miroslav Nincic, Steven Stedman, Saadia Touval, Nicolas van de Walle, and Larry Wade. Nigel Quinney, at the United States Institute of Peace, gave me encouragement and wise counsel; Francis M. Deng, John D. Steinbruner, and Richard N. Haass at the Brookings Institution and Joseph Klaits, the director of the Jennings Randolph Program for International Peace at the United States Institute of Peace, were steady and invaluable supporters. Jan deProsse proved herself to be a careful and understanding editor. I am deeply grateful to all these friends and colleagues for their invaluable backing.

Among the many helpful people I was able to interview, I particularly want to acknowledge the following for their keen insights: R. H. F. Austin, Jimmy Carter, A. M. Chambati, Herman Cohen, Chester A. Crocker, Jeffrey Davidow, Steven Friedman, Dawit Wolde Giorgis, Philip Habib, James Kamusikire, Henry A. Kissinger, E. Gibson Lanpher, Colin Legum, Stephen Low, Martin Lowenkopf, Donald F. McHenry, Roger J. A. Martin, George Moose, R. Murapa, Leopoldo J. Niilus, Olusegun Obasanjo, Robin Renwick, William Rogers, and Lloyd Vogelman. I have benefited enormously from the shared experiences and wisdom of these people.

I also received enormous assistance from sympathetic librarians and archivists at the World Council of Churches, Princeton University Library, American Friends Service Committee, National Security Archives, Public Record Office, Gerald R. Ford Library, Hoover Institution Archives, John F. Kennedy Library, Lyndon Baines Johnson Library, Harry S. Truman Library, U.S. National Archives, Nixon Presidential Materials Project, and the Columbia University Library.

Donald Rothchild
Davis, California

Contents

Tables

Figures

Managing
Ethnic Conflict
in Africa

1

African State Management of Ethnic Conflict

The threat of pain or the promise of reward may tip the balance among decisionmakers within a government at a particular moment.

CHESTER A. CROCKER

Grim scenarios notwithstanding, there is nothing inevitable about destructive conflict between African states and their culturally distinct identity groups. Deep social cleavages and highly injurious encounters have occurred in many countries where peoples and groups disagree over basic rules, yet a comprehensive picture also shows accommodation, reciprocity, and negotiation. Regularized political interactions among state and ethnic leaders over time are likely to facilitate their cooperation.[1] But how are leaders to structure relations to promote predictable interactions and thereby avoid mutually damaging encounters? And, when conflict becomes intense and linkages break down, how are they to encourage a return to more positive interactions?

I have shown that negotiations among ethnic leaders at the political center can lead to cooperation in certain circumstances: for example, direct bargaining occurred during the approach to Kenya's independence and was later followed by tacit bargaining.[2] To be sure, the bargaining relationship was asymmetrical: some equity was given up to ensure economic growth, and, as Mancur Olson has commented, "the costs of the policies [that ensued] fell disproportionately on the unorganized."[3] In addition, the same Kenya study showed successful negotiations among African ethnic groups to be possible in some contexts, though on an ad hoc basis and with no assured or predictable results in terms of equitable outcomes.[4]

1

Having shown ethnic bargaining to be a reality, I now ask a related question: under what circumstances will it be possible to promote negotiation and cooperation between states and ethnic groups or between ethnic groups themselves by rechanneling interactions among these leaders and changing the preferred outcomes at the national and international levels? In domestic affairs, how can state leaders utilize structural or policy incentives to encourage elites to alter their preferences and, therefore, to cooperate? Here it is important to recognize that the term *conflict management* has two somewhat different implications. Analytically, the conflicts between state and ethnic groups are conflicts between institutions of state and segments of those governed; in such situations, the state is an actor and may attempt to direct or negotiate with a societal group. But ethnic conflicts can also entail a clash of interests between two or more segments of society, with the state acting as mediator. This book will examine the state's role as both negotiator and mediator in its relations with ethnic interests.

Because of the intensity of ethnic claims, not all conflicts lend themselves to state negotiation or mediation. When recurrent patterns of relations break down and conflict intensifies, it is difficult for third-party mediators to use diplomatic incentives to alter the preferences and calculations of rival actors in order to facilitate negotiations and regularized, positive interactions leading to cooperation.[5] It is important not to overstate the influence that mediators can bring to bear on rival parties. Mediatory skill is not likely, in and of itself, to prove sufficient to bring about routinized politics. Skill must be complemented with leverage in order to overcome the mutually hurting stalemates that plague many a conflict situation and to push the process of peacemaking toward a conclusion.[6] The leverage required in each particular encounter is a function of the difficulty of the problem to be dealt with. Leverage will allow the mediator to exert some influence over the behavior of the various actors, encouraging them to alter their preferences over outcomes. The question at issue, then, is how might third-party intermediaries use noncoercive or coercive incentives (or mixes of those incentives) to help bring the dialogue within the bargaining range and thereby promote cooperation?

Mediating ethnic-related confrontations is distinct from mediating disputes between sovereign states. Because ethnic struggles involve internal conflicts between communal groups—or between such groups and the state—mediation by a single actor or coalition of actors necessarily entails the intervention of third parties in the domestic affairs of a sovereign entity. States frequently react strongly to any seeming interference by private or official intermediaries in what they perceive as their domestic jurisdiction—which complicates, but does not preclude, the process of managing ethnic or intergroup conflict. As shown in the cases of Angola (chapter 5) and Sudan (chapter 8), when the costs of violent and protracted conflict rise and there is no apparent alternative to a continuation of civil war, external actors may acquire considerable leverage, which creates new and important opportunities for the accommodation of differences between state and society.

In proceeding with this analysis, I will advance three basic propositions:

—Although mediatory skill and determination are indispensable to a negotiated solution, even greater emphasis must be placed on the context in which a mediator or coalition of mediators operates and the leverage that individual, organization, or combination of actors can bring to bear.

—Conflict management is an interlinked process that includes prenegotiation, negotiation, and implementation stages.

—It is possible in some situations to advance the process of "ripening" (advancing to the point where joint problem solving becomes possible) through the effective use of pressures and incentives by a mediator or facilitator.

The Ethnic Group

Interactions between state and society assume a constant engagement of rival interests in the contemporary political arena among various groups that have mobilized to secure public resources from those in authority at the political center. These groups—formed along ethnic, racial, religious, regional, or class lines—can have distinct origins and appeals, but they do share common features: they are socially constructed identities whose leaders advance demands upon the state, encountering each other in a dynamic interplay of interest-inspired competition and collaboration.[7] Only in worst-case situations, where groups feel physically or culturally threatened by a state dominated by an ethnic adversary, does this pattern of competition alter and intense conflict emerge. Particularly as uncertainty over the intentions of others leads to a dangerous shift in the ethnic balance of power, the leaders of the threatened group may have an incentive to launch a preemptive strike to restore the balance (what I discuss in chapter 9 as a "security dilemma").[8] Identity group members, fearing exclusion from their com-

munity more than the risks of violent action, coalesce around their leaders to struggle to achieve collective goals.[9]

Ethnicity acts as a pole around which group members can mobilize
and compete effectively for state-controlled power, economic resources,
positions, contracts, awards, and constitutional protections. *Ethnicity*, as
used in this context, refers to a subjective perception of common origins, historical memories, ties, and aspirations; *ethnic group* suggests
organized activities by people who are linked by a consciousness of a
special identity, who jointly seek to maximize their corporate political,
economic, and social interests. Ethnicity, or a sense of peoplehood, has
its foundation in combined remembrances of past experience and in
common inspirations, values, norms, and expectations. The validity of
these beliefs is less significant to an overarching sense of affinity than
is the people's ability to symbolize their closeness to each other.

The origins of a people may be imaginary, but as political memory
interacts with the experiences of the past, new socially constructed
identities emerge and become the basis of a consciousness that in some
instances can prove very destructive. In Burundi, as a side effect of the
Tutsi repressions of 1972, a sense of shared fate emerged among the
organizationally distinct Hutu of the North-Center, uniting them with
the Hutu of the South-Imbo. This process was described by one observer
as "enforced ethnicity."[10] The Hutu and Tutsi use the same language and
institutions and are often very similar to each other in appearance, leading some social scientists to deny that they do, in fact, represent separate
ethnic groups. Belgian colonial rule did much to foster a sense of difference and eventually led to the emergence of a sense of separate consciousness that has gained political expression in collective competition
and conflict—sometimes very violent conflict. The comments by one
reviewer on the Hutu-Tutsi confrontation in neighboring Rwanda are
equally applicable to the situation in Burundi: "To argue that the [eth-
nic groups] thus manufactured are artificial is to miss the point . . . it
is impossible to interpret recent events without recourse to [ethnic]
labels, and they are the labels used by the people themselves. Above
all, people kill each other because of them."[11]

It is important to stress that in most cases ethnic groups are not unitary actors for negotiating purposes. Each of them also includes a coalition of competing and cooperating interests that, in turn, make a variety of demands both upon the members of their coalition and upon
each other.[12] Insofar as ethnic groups interact with other ethnic, eco-

nomic, and social interest groups, they promote the salient interests of the membership. In a process that can be likened to a two-level game, leaders must negotiate a common position within the group and continually act to maintain the unity and strength of the heterogeneous unit at one level before they can engage in meaningful bargaining encounters at the top of the system.[13] No matter how successful these nation-building efforts may prove, intragroup differences are likely to persist, allowing political entrepreneurs the option of interacting with rival factions on separate bases.

Patterns of African Conflict Management

Political regimes are defined here as the patterns of behavior accepted by the dominant state coalitions and the general public to be the legitimate local formula for the exercise of political power. Different regimes seek various kinds of stability to mitigate the destructive consequences of intense ethnic conflict. To be sure, stability can have the effect of preserving inequities, but this can sometimes be justified on the grounds that all parties are better off when they avoid mutually hurtful behavior. In contemporary Africa, efforts to reconcile state and communal claims have been positioned along a broad continuum, from hegemonic systems (that is, hierarchical military- or civilian-led, one-party or no-party systems that concede minimal scope to ethnic or national autonomy) to a number of partial or full power-sharing systems.

For heuristic purposes, I envisage two broad patterns of coping with Africa's ethnic-related conflicts in postcolonial times: normal forms of regularized state-society relationships in which conflicts are manageable, or, in situations in which relations have broken down, domestic state negotiations and international third-party mediation attempts to bring about an equilibrium. Each pattern embodies different assumptions and rationales about what is desired and possible in state-society relations. Such differences largely reflect historical evolution, diverse bases of state legitimacy, and different styles of intergroup encounters. Because these patterns form part of an interconnected political process, in such conflicts as those in Sudan, I will analyze them in terms of a progression from colonial regimes—which form the backdrop against which modern-day stages are played out—to regularized patterns of domestic relations in postcolonial times and then to patterns of direct negotiation and international mediation.

The Colonial Inheritance

In middle Africa, a region that includes countries between the Sahara and South Africa, where societies continue to be horizontally stratified—that is, segmented but "unranked," accepting the moral equality of various identity groups—the modern-day problem of interethnic conflict is very much a product of historical experience.[14] To be sure, variations in natural resources, climate, cultural values, social and educational contacts, and proximity to markets and transportation centers contributed to ethnoregional disparities (at the nexus between the subregional unit and ethnic people).[15] In addition, contextual variables—such as the number and size of groups, the distribution of wealth, rates of modernization, and the pattern of group recruitment into the economy and polity—also affected the nature of interethnic relations. But no single factor proved to be more significant in shaping the configuration of group interactions than a territory's experience with colonial rule. Such an externally radiated hegemonic system concentrated bureaucratic, military, educational, commercial, industrial, communications, and other modern-sector activities within a small, privileged, white-led urban core. Different rates of contact with Western technology as well as administrative practices and values affected the various peoples and regions of a territory in distinct ways, resulting over time in cleavages between an expanding urban-based core and a relatively disadvantaged periphery.[16] Thus the imperial powers facilitated the growth of centralized institutions that were able to secure stability in the short run—but at a high political cost in terms of learned patterns of intergroup relations. In doing this, the colonizers structured core-periphery relations in a way that has survived despite later programs of corrective equity in several countries.[17]

 Colonial systems, procedures, and values could be imposed upon Africans, despite their determined resistance in various cases, because the indigenous inhabitants lacked the necessary technical and organizational capacity to halt the spread of European power. What emerged, for the most part, were transitional administrative superstructures, more remarkable for their organizational efficiency and their low decision costs than for their effectiveness in penetrating the hinterland.[18] Ironically, these "command structures" had sufficient capacity to override local opposition to their rule but lacked the ability to regulate rural subgroups effectively. In this respect, the colonial hegemonic regime established a "soft" state—one low on legitimacy and deficient in the ability to implement policies on a countrywide basis.[19]

Although a tiny cadre of administrators, recruited largely from the metropole, exerted formal regulatory powers over large territories and numerous peoples, it is important not to overstate the colonial power's actual day-to-day control. The power of these officials rested more on African acquiescence than on acceptance, more on indirect rule than on meaningful local participation. In Senegal, for example, the colonial regime achieved its considerable stability by working closely with the rural Muslim religious leaders (the *marabouts*), who were prepared to play a critical role in mediating between state and society. "The ties of these very popular religious leaders—and peanut producers—to the colonial system," writes Christian Coulon, "were strong enough to act as a kind of safety valve."[20]

For administrative convenience, the colonial officials did promote a sense of unity among a number of fluid and disunited peoples whose affinities were based on coresidence in a region and similarities of culture, traditions, and legal and economic practices, including the Karamojong of Uganda, the Sukuma of Tanzania, the Yoruba and Igbo of Nigeria, and the Kikuyu and Luhya of Kenya. The consequence was to foster ethnic consciousness, from which emerged an increasingly elite-organized competition for state-controlled resources and opportunities. At times, however, the colonial rulers went beyond this level of influence to pursue more active policies that widened the cleavages among groups. An awareness of separate districts' diverse interests in Kenya and Uganda followed logically from the practices of indirect rule and, in Kenya in the mid-1950s, led to a governmental ban on the formation of national political parties.[21] As Crawford Young asserts: "One need not assume a Machiavellian master plan of deliberate division for economical hegemony"; nevertheless, the effect of encouraging these socially constructed identities was to create an incentive among elites to mobilize support along ethnic lines, which thereby "reinforced a process of primordialization already in course."[22]

In Nigeria, the policies of the colonial power insulated the relatively disadvantaged and culturally distinct northern region from the economic, political, and social progress that marked the more developed southern territory. Such policies could be justified as protecting the two regions' distinct social and cultural ways of life, but they also had the effect of tolerating and accentuating their differences. Chief Obafemi Awolowo, the former leader of the Unity party of Nigeria, observed that British colonial policies—the closure of the North to Christian missionary influences, the "fossilization" of northern political institutions under the aegis of indirect rule, and the treatment of the North and South as distinct political and administrative units—created severe problems for subsequent regimes.[23] A similar heritage blighted the relations between the culturally distinct northern and southern regions of colonial Sudan. There, indirect rule, intended to preserve traditional authority systems and to limit change, also (whether purposely or not) did little to stop the different rates of subregional modernization. Such compartmentalization allowed Sudan's South to slip behind the extensively Arabized and Islamized North in terms of educational, infrastructural, and economic development.[24]

Colonialism, therefore, had something of a mixed impact. Though it did radiate a set of institutions and practices to Africa—some useful and some not—that became frameworks for the new polities, it also undercut Africa's autonomy from the developed West and implanted new values and identities. Colonial hegemons rarely used the opportunities at their disposal to build modern economies or infrastructures, to transform political practices, or to create the social and political linkages necessary for the transition to the future "democratic" societies envisaged in the independence constitutions. An authoritarian management style, which often emphasized the differences rather than the similarities between groups, made it difficult to mobilize the populace for united political action. Moreover, the economic and social disparities resulting from different rates of ethnoregional modernization widened as colonial development progressed. Thus former Zambian President Kenneth Kaunda was on solid ground when he warned Zambians that they faced "the danger of creating two nations within one," not along capitalist class lines but between the urban and rural areas or, in local terms, between the line-of-rail provinces and those off the line of rail.[25]

The consolidation of external hegemony brought with it an entrenchment of administrative control, economic dominance, and social and cultural patterns that, consciously or unconsciously, distinguished the relatively advantaged urban core from the relatively disadvantaged periphery. In time, something of a core political culture became manifest.[26] The ascendant state elite (largely expatriate, with significant indigenous infusions in the late colonial era) felt justified in making authoritative decisions on allocative matters for the territory as a whole. These decisions, which often benefited the urban elite at the expense of the remaining population, became the source of the grave imbalances among ethnoregional units that have since marked the contemporary period. As a consequence, an economically privileged and politically powerful center emerged, buttressed by an asymmetrical exchange relationship with the majority of peasants in the rural areas. Enclave values and lifestyles became evident among the relatively privileged in the core, linking them more closely to the bourgeoisie in the former colonial metropole than to the relatively disadvantaged rural and urban dwellers in their own country.[27]

The Postindependence Era

With this colonial experience as background, I now turn to the two broad patterns of African conflict management in postindependence times. Pattern 1 looks inward at the state, focusing on direct bargaining relationships between state and societal elites, while pattern 2 concentrates on bargaining in the international context, defined and exposed to view by external mediation of intrastate conflicts (see chapter 4).

While the main concern of the book is with bargaining and its ability to contain interethnic conflict, it is also important to keep in mind that some pattern 1 internal encounters ended in failure; the record is even bleaker for pattern 2 externally mediated efforts, however, many of which failed at either the negotiation or implementation stages. Some insight on the costs of these failures can be seen in the collected estimates of deaths in the main ethnic or nationality-related conflicts dealt with in this book (see table 1-1). The absence from the table of Rwanda and Burundi only underscores the terrible toll ethnic violence has exacted in recent years.

Regularized State-Society Relationships

In the late 1950s, as the colonial scaffolding was being partly dismantled, the former rulers created constitutions to replace their alien hegemonic (hierarchically ordered) systems with institutions intended to promote reciprocity, bargaining, and sharing. The goal of these pattern 1 encounters was to make stability and conflict coextensive: to build up institutions of efficient governmental control—the bureaucracy, military, and police—and at the same time to erect a series of checks aimed at safeguarding political and social minorities. In the latter regard, elaborate guarantees for multiparty elections, second chambers, federalism, regional autonomy, bills of rights, judiciaries, and rigid amendment clauses became commonplace in the basic laws immediately following independence.

TABLE 1-1. *Politically Related Deaths with an Ethnic or Nationality Component in Selected Sub-Saharan African Countries, 1945-94*[a]

	Number of deaths		
Country and conflict	Civilian	Military	Total
Angola			
1961-75: independence versus Portugal; Soviet, South African intervention	30,000	25,000	55,000
1975-91: civil war; Cuban, South African intervention	320,000	21,000	341,000
1992-94: renewal of civil war: UNITA versus Angolan government	150,000	n.a.	150,000– 500,000
Nigeria			
1967-70: Biafrans versus government; famine	1,000,000	1,000,000	2,000,000
1980-81: fundamental Islam versus government	n.a.	n.a.	5,000
1984: fundamental Islam versus government	n.a.	n.a.	1,000
South Africa			
1984-93: political violence	n.a.	n.a.	20,000
Sudan			
1963-72: South versus government; UK, Egyptian intervention	250,000	250,000	500,000
1983-93: South versus government	n.a.	n.a.	1,300,000
Zaire			
1960-65: Katanga secession; UK, Belgian intervention	n.a.	n.a.	100,000
Zimbabwe			
1972-79: Patriotic Front versus government	n.a.	n.a.	40,000
1981-82: Shona-Ndebele clashes	1,000	n.a.	1,000

SOURCES: Ruth Leger Sivard, *World Military and Social Expenditures, 1991*, 14th ed. (Washington: World Priorities, 1991), p. 25; Roy Licklider, ed., *Stopping the Killing: How Civil Wars End* (New York University Press, 1993), p. 161; Michael E. Brown, "Introduction," in Brown, ed., *The International Dimensions of Internal Conflict* (MIT Press, 1996), p. 4; Norma J. Kriger, *Zimbabwe's Guerrilla War: Peasant Voices* (Cambridge University Press, 1992), p. 4; "Synopsis and Update," *Race Relations Survey 1993/94* (Johannesburg: Institute of Race Relations, 1994), p. 27; Millard Burr, *Quantifying Genocide in the Southern Sudan 1983-1993* (Washington: American Council for Nationalities, October 1993), p. 9; "Angola: The Military Takes Centre Stage," *Africa Confidential*, vol. 34 (February 5, 1993), pp. 1-2; and "Angola: The Worst War in the World," *Africa Confidential*, vol. 34 (August 27, 1993), pp. 1-2.
n.a. Not available.
a. All figures should be considered approximate and best estimates.

For many African leaders, these entrenched provisions represented the price they had to pay for progress toward self-rule. In Kenya, for example, Jomo Kenyatta's incoming government reluctantly accepted a highly rigid constitution, including plans for a centralized federal arrangement (*majimbo*), out of fear that the colonial authority would use the minority issue to delay a transfer of political power. Similarly, during independence negotiations, Ghana's president, Kwame Nkrumah, reluctantly accepted certain general Ashanti demands for regional assemblies and autonomous regional powers to smooth the way to Ghanaian independence. However, these limitations upon state authority, imposed from the outside and perceived as an impediment to strong central leadership, were soon jettisoned when Kenyatta and Nkrumah had consolidated political power in their own hands.[28] The focus on regime types below is meant to explicate the logic and dynamics of each general category of conflict management.

Polyarchical Regimes: Cooperative Strategies

As organizing patterns of behavior, regimes play a key role in structuring the way that individuals and groups participate in the political selection and decisionmaking processes. Such a structuring of opportunities can act as an incentive or disincentive for cooperative behavior. I start by analyzing Africa's experience with polyarchical regimes, which are the most explicit about emphasizing the values of participation, competition, and sharing.

A significant number of African regimes did act to discard or transform the departing colonial powers' hastily erected constitutional restraints upon their control and to establish one- or no-party systems; however, polyarchical regimes survived in a limited number of African countries and became a preferred form of governance in many others in the early 1990s. Broadly speaking, polyarchy involves relatively low state control over the political process and extensive societal participation through political parties, civil associations, and the decisionmaking institutions of government. It establishes a basis for legitimate and effective governance, linking vibrant and active civil associations with dynamic and relatively secure states. Although majoritarian democracies stand out for their ability to mobilize and articulate group demands and require state accountability and responsiveness, other polyarchical regime variants, such as consociational democracy, combine a relatively high degree of state-society interaction with low to medium levels of public participation and a medium to high degree of state control.

Majoritarian democracies are in a favorable position to encourage a long-term (but not necessarily a short-term) sharing of purposes across party lines by allowing for a reasonably open articulation of claims and supplying the means for electoral accountability and monitoring.[29] The various actors' perceptions of each other remain pragmatic, and their demands tend to be negotiable, creating the most propitious circumstances for conflict management. From the 1960s to 1990s, the ruling coalitions in Mauritius, Botswana, Gambia (until the 1994 coup), and Senegal (with the 1976 reforms) did preserve constitutional processes guaranteeing competitive elections. With the exception of Mauritius, these elections represented no fundamental challenge to the entrenched party machines. They did, however, allow various political and social identities a degree of autonomous expression in a context that permitted a limited amount of competition and conflict. Moreover, Ghana (under the Busia and Limann administrations) and Nigeria (under the Shagari administration) made use of representative institutions for years. In all of these contexts, differences between groups tended to be reconcilable because competition was limited, for the most part, to distributional concerns and did not generally encompass matters of basic belief or principle. The politics of constructive competition and sharing generally involved establishing formal or informal norms of political negotiation and reciprocity that avoided adversarial behavior and instead channeled group interactions along controlled yet cooperative lines.

In the late 1980s and early 1990s, as the general public perceived authoritarian regimes to be repressive, corrupt, and unable to overcome economic scarcity, a new wave of societal demands for regime change swept the continent. Encouraged by the example of Eastern Europe and abetted at times by the external conditionalities set by donor countries and institutions, a largely urban, middle-class coalition of church leaders, civil associations, lawyers and other professionals, lecturers and students, businessmen, trade union officials, and some elements within the dominant political party itself called for concrete measures of political liberalization.[30] The impact of this internally generated opposition was enormous: in the 1990s a large proportion of the countries in sub-Saharan Africa were either scheduled for or had already pledged themselves to some form of democratic governance. In the ultimate test of party competition, Zambia has seen one president replaced by another in a hotly contested but peaceful election, and the ballot box was also used to change eleven regimes in the 1989–94 period, including those in Benin, Niger, Burundi, Malawi, and South Africa.[31]

Although the trend toward political liberalization is encouraging in terms of regularized state-society relations, the process nonetheless seems incomplete and somewhat brittle. This can be explained in part by the constraints facing these regimes: the difficulties in reversing Africa's economic decline, the continuance of clientelistic networks, the lack of widespread agreement on the rules of the game, the inadequacy of the channels of political communication, the difficulty of establishing responsive political institutions, the problems associated with too many competitors and too intense a conflict (involving religious fundamentalism, ethnic nationalism, and class antagonism), and the obstacles to maintaining a dynamic civil society. Moreover, even with elections, there is also the strong possibility that political minorities will be shut out of the political process well into the future. With political institutions overburdened and public demands and expectations high, it is not surprising that some African elites are also examining the possibility of political alternatives, such as elite power-sharing regimes, which combine moderate levels of public participation with moderate levels of state control.

Elite Power-Sharing Regimes: Mixed Strategies

The various elite power-sharing regimes of hegemonic exchange and limited democracy accept lower thresholds of participation and contestation than do polyarchies in order to achieve political stability in ethnically pluralistic societies. Like polyarchies, they select leaders through some form of election process; unlike polyarchies, however, they involve inclusive political coalitions at the political center that substantially restrict public participation, competition, and access to information. These elite power-sharing regimes represent amalgams of authoritarian control and consociational democracy (in particular, the principles of broad-ranging coalitions, balanced recruitment, and proportional allocations). Elite interests in the political arena, as well as the civil service and the military, fearful that full democracy will generate a surge of demands from ethnic and class interests in society, may opt for a partial democracy in an effort to contain and manage conflict.[32] Rather than guaranteeing certainty, however, such hybrid regimes can unravel as interelite tensions emerge, particularly with the beginning of new elections. Elite power-sharing regimes are weak and transitional forms of governance with only a moderate capacity for encouraging pragmatic perceptions (as opposed to the extremist claims of flanking parties) and for maintaining group demands at manageable levels, depending as they do on interactions within an elite circle of interest group and ethnic-based patrons, as well as powerful members of the government and bureaucracy.

Elite power-sharing regimes can be either moderately authoritarian (as in the old African hegemonic exchange regimes of the 1960s, 1970s, and early 1980s) or moderately democratic systems that provide for regular, contested elections. Either way, such regimes unite the competing thrusts of political control and bargaining among the state and various societal notables. Relying on the elite's acceptance of informal codes of procedure, these state and interest group leaders (often communal patrons) engage in an ongoing process of tacit or formal negotiations within the cabinet, the legislature, or high party organs.

Because the hegemonic exchange regimes have tended to lack popular legitimacy, to have inadequate access to information, to severely limit full and meaningful participation, and to do little to reduce the incompatibility between value and interest in society, their continuance seems to depend on the survival of the elite contract and the ability of the group intermediaries to renegotiate the terms of the original bargain.[33] Such regimes can be described as a form of state-facilitated coordination, in which a somewhat autonomous central-state actor and several considerably less autonomous ethnoregional interests engage—on the basis of commonly accepted procedural norms, rules, or understandings—in a process of mutual accommodation over shared values.

During the 1970s and 1980s, African leaders in countries such as Kenya, Cameroun, Côte d'Ivoire, and Zambia made efforts to temper single-party rule by including powerful ethnic notables in the central cabinet and legislature and the party national executive. These state leaders chose to give representation to ethnic leaders rather than face the possibility of their defection. The African countries varied in their willingness to legitimize the political role of those ethnoregional intermediaries in national politics, but their strategies of including the main patrons and allowing a limited bargaining to take place within the central political machine had roughly similar consequences.

In former president Felix Houphouët-Boigny's Côte d'Ivoire and Paul Biya's Cameroun (and previously in Kenyatta's Kenya), a more publicly countenanced system of balanced inclusion and interelite reciprocities and exchanges became evident. In the 1960s and 1970s, for example, Houphouët-Boigny accepted ethnic-based fears as part of the country's political reality and sought to demobilize major ethnic challengers by carefully distributing tangible benefits to key players in the ruling coalition and coopting important patrons into his one-party government.[34] The resulting cabinet included all the major ethnic interests, roughly in proportion to their numbers in the National Assembly.

In the Cameroun Republic, former president Ahmadou Ahidjo, despite his heavy-handed and secretive tendencies, prudently used his ministerial appointments to balance ethnoregional, linguistic, religious, and economic interests. His successor, Paul Biya, a Catholic from the South-Central region, has been even more committed to the principle of ethnic and religious proportionality, upholding the North-South balance in high executive appointments and ensuring that a northern Muslim would eventually succeed him as president. The effects of these ongoing interelite bargaining practices have often proved to be inequitable to some ethnic and regional groups; nevertheless, as long as the major actors perceive they are receiving minimal benefts from a mixed-strategy approach, conflicts within this dominant class fraction can be kept at manageable levels.

Democratic, elite power-sharing regimes share many of these tendencies; however, because these arrangements allow for a somewhat broader participation among group representatives, they are likely to gain greater staying power, at least during a transitional period. In South Africa, Timothy Sisk noted that the "control of violence through pacts such as the National Peace Accord [were] an essential pre-condition to further democratization."[35] By establishing common rules and allowing for "bargaining about bargaining," the elite power-sharing arrangement creates the basis for persistent and stable relationships.[36] Experience outside of Africa also indicates that where the state remains weak, clientelism endures and the configurations of group power remain substantially in place (as is the case in Lebanon), some form of elite power sharing is likely to gain support as a conflict-regulating mechanism. And to the extent that African leaders view majoritarian democracy as either divisive, conflict producing, or a hindrance to governmental effectiveness, they may opt for forms of governance that appear to allow limited participation but that actually rely on civilian-military elite coalitions to stabilize the regime and ensure governmental effectiveness.[37]

In Nigeria, proposals for sharing significant power between the military and publicly elected civilians—referred to locally as a "diarchy"—have received support from various political analysts intent on moderating conflict and protecting the new constitution from future military interventions.[38] Those negotiating such interelite power-sharing agreements hope that bringing the military within the ruling coalition will reduce its doubts about the transition to full democracy and lower its incentives to intervene again. Clearly, such mixed strategies run the risk of weakening democratic governance because the political legitimacy of the regime is compromised.[39] Nevertheless, such temporary arrangements may possibly provide a momentary balance between participation and control during the transition to political liberalization—albeit, in this case, largely within the elite itself.

Hegemonic Regimes: Noncooperative Strategies

Although strategies of limited and extensive compromise have been evident in many African states since independence, there have also been numerous instances of rigid, uncompromising strategies, frequently in the form of hierarchically ordered one- or no-party regimes. Firm in their determination to retain power and advance the interests of their clique or group, hegemonic regimes adopt a rather inflexible attitude regarding compromise with opponents, thus raising the cost and intensity of conflict to high levels. Despite being "soft" states with limited fiscal or regulatory capabilities, these African hegemonic regimes nonetheless attempt to preserve the outward appearance of political stability by relying on various mechanisms of coercion, ranging from inequitable recruitment and allocation policies to disenfranchisement, rigged elections, press control, and crude forms of police repression. For a time, such measures may succeed in stifling the outward manifestations of opposition, but when political legitimacy proves elusive, the ruling coalition inevitably encounters conflict within its membership or between itself and a counterelite.[40]

These postcolonial authoritarian regimes resemble each other, in principle at least, in their emphasis on centralized decisionmaking and state control; they differ extensively, however, in the degree of public participation they permit and in their norms of interelite relationships and accompanying institutions. Most commonly, the bureaucratic-centralist types (Guinea under Sékou-Touré, Ghana under Nkrumah) built on the colonially transmitted administrative institutions to enhance the elite's capacity for control. They expanded their executive branches, civil services, military, and police forces—all with an eye toward strengthening state capacity—while limiting the autonomy and authority of civil society and the constitutional checks on the state's authority for dealing with those civil associations. One-party and no-party systems replaced constitutional provisions for open electoral competition, although in some cases a limited electoral competition was allowed within the one-party framework.

In the 1970s and 1980s, some African countries (Ethiopia, Angola, Mozambique) experimented with socialist vanguard regimes, reflecting their preference for such systems and their expectations of support from the Soviet-bloc countries. Placing heavy emphasis on state control and guidance according to the tenets of Afro-Marxist ideology, these socialist vanguard regimes tended to exceed their capabilities, which became particularly apparent as the cold war waned in the mid-1980s. Their emphasis on political orthodoxy led to an extreme inflexibility toward their opponents, resulting in a lack of information and a tendency to opt for military suppression rather than accommodation.

Finally, personalistic regimes (Amin's Uganda, Chad), which rested heavily on neopatrimonial ties in society, round out the picture of state control and low public participation. These personalistic regimes represented the raw power of an individual or small clique intent on imposing its will forcefully upon society, while the bureaucratic centralist and socialist vanguard regimes attempted, in some instances, to restructure their inherited institutions to establish a new basis for effective regulation. Such personalistic systems gravely complicated the task of establishing linkages across their societies, making conflict management an extremely difficult process. These various hegemonic-type regimes, brittle and often transitory in nature, frequently resulted in stalemate and paralysis, surviving only until overwhelmed—in many cases, forcibly—by their opponents.

Regardless of its form, even the most determined and authoritarian of African regimes has lacked the capacity to impose its programs on ethnic and nationality groups demanding autonomy, especially those living in the hinterland. The weakness of state institutions has acted as something of a constraint on ruling elites, placing limits on their abilities to transform ethnic ties or clientelistic patterns in the postcolonial period. Moreover, the Afro-Marxist regimes' ideological inflexibility on the issues of including major interests in the ruling coalitions and granting regional autonomy has given their opposition an incentive to resist. And given the weakness of African state institutions, the outcome has been low legitimacy, low information, state-society alienation, and friction—even hostility and civil war. Ethnic and nationality groups have suffered destructive actions at the hands of authoritarian leaders, but they have not been crushed. Former Uganda president A. Milton Obote adopted tough tactics in his dealings with the province of Buganda after his return to power; in practice, however, he proved unable to cope with the fragmented political situation in his country, and his ethnically heterogeneous army lacked the necessary weapons and training to defeat the three guerrilla armies in the field.[41]

In Angola (and Ethiopia), where the socialist vanguard regimes showed a disdain for the politicization of ethnic and nationality interests, an insensitive and heavy-handed policy of centralization and refusal to negotiate with these groups promoted intense opposition. Thus the Popular Movement for the Liberation of Angola (MPLA) regime rejected ethnicity as a legitimate basis for political action and underrepresented the Ovimbundu people in high political and party offices; the regime also fueled feelings of neglect that contributed to the capacity of the Union for the Total Independence of Angola (UNITA) to survive and wage an effective insurgency over the years (see chapter 5).

In sum, hegemonic regimes failed to enclose social conflict and tended to foster deadlocks in state-society relations. The overall effect was to complicate the tasks of conflict management, in some cases leading to protracted civil war. This is not to say that these regimes did not provide temporary respite from state-ethnic tensions nor that they did not occasionally allow the possibility of creative initiatives, but where those temporary opportunities were not used to create new routines for interelite and intergroup reciprocity, ongoing constructive relations appeared unlikely.

It is important to stress the possibility of regime shifts within and across these categories. As the state and society develop and readjust and as the nature and strength of public demands and state responses alter over time, movement within or across regimes will reflect changing relative power positions among relevant actors. The African experience in the postindependence period is one of increasingly frequent regime changes, and in light of continued economic scarcity and the interplay of political forces, there is little reason to expect stability in the future. Ghana, for example, witnessed moves toward increased state control, including periodic shifts from polyarchy to hegemonic control during the administration of Kwame Nkrumah, a decisive movement from majoritarian democracy to military autocracy in 1972, and a change from democracy to military-led populism in 1981 (which gave way to a more classical form of bureaucratic centralism by 1983 and managed general elections in 1992).

Conflict management involves regularizing the patterns of state-society and intrasociety relations (discussed in depth in part 1). The problem is to get elites to develop routines for sharing power—to facilitate a transition from zero-sum deadlock and hegemony to mixed strategies or, preferably, to polyarchy. Negotiation and mediation, the focus of this book, are not ends in themselves but means of promoting constructive conflict relations and an enabling political environment in which economic development can occur.

The Structuring of Incentives

This brings me to the central question of part 1: what incentives and guidelines can ruling state elites or internal or external mediators use to facilitate political negotiation and reciprocity? In a domestic context where recurrent patterns of relations are present, incentives consist of structural arrangements or distributive or symbolic rewards used by the state to channel individual and group choices along preferred lines and to promote regular patterns of interaction between the state and societal groups. Polyarchies consciously make use of structural incentives (electoral, formal power-sharing, and federal mechanisms), distributive inducements (fiscal programs and allocative preferences), and symbolic rewards, while elite-coordinated regimes—with their extensive reliance on face-to-face encounters—tend to utilize ad hoc, internally developed system guidelines to encourage conciliation.

By guidelines, I mean decision rules that are reasonably explicit suggestions for action but that can be adjusted pragmatically in terms of each state-subnational encounter. Guidelines are by no means inviolate markers but rather indicators for prudent state leadership. Such guides include not only positive decision rules on the application of principles of inclusiveness, autonomy, redistribution, and proportionality, but also such negative guides to action as threats, coercion, and punishment. Combinations of these—the use of carrots and sticks—may also be relevant to the practical relations between state and society. These various packages of structural, distributive, and symbolic incentives and positive and negative decision rules will be discussed in the chapters that follow.

As the examination of specific polyarchical and elite collaborative practices in part 1 shows, wherever Africa's ruling elites have encouraged inclusiveness or diffused power by means of electoral fine-tuning or territorial decentralization or have applied positive principles of proportionality and reciprocity in four key areas—political coalitions in central government politics, elite recruitment, public resource allocation, and group rights and protections—they have managed to reduce the intensity of state-ethnic conflicts. As I will show in chapter 3, the rules that work in ethnically divided societies must take account of both an individual and collective sense of worth and must acknowledge the legitimacy of claims to equitable distributions.[42] Provided the rules have an equalizing effect, they may be able to promote a perception of fairness on the part of rival interests.

The late Claude Ake observed that "political stability is the regularity of the flow of political exchanges; the more regular the flow, the more stable the polity."[43] This emphasis on the critical link between political exchange and reciprocities and a country's stability is important. However, the analysis can be extended (and will be, in this book) by probing the incentives and guides to action that the state can use to promote increased political bargaining while still maintaining stability. As I will show in part 1, some African states have been relatively effective in facilitating regularized networks of relations under conditions of frail institutions, heady expectations, and grinding economic scarcity.

What happens, however, when the networks of reciprocities weaken, the flow of bargaining relations becomes irregular, and conflicts among leaders and groups increase in intensity? Because of the fragility of the African state and the intense societal struggles for scarce resources, it is not surprising that a weakening of the regularity and persistence of interactions—even a breakdown in conflict management patterns embedded in domestic regimes—has occurred at times in postindependence Africa. Liberia and Somalia are dramatic examples of patterns of incoherence and loss of state capabilities and authority in the 1990s, but state decay has also surfaced in other countries, such as the Democratic Republic of the Congo and Sierra Leone.[44] It is therefore appropriate to turn now to methods of coping with conflicts brought on by the weakening or breakdown of domestic regimes. Note, however, that state breakdown is only one direction that change can take: the cost of damaging encounters can also lead to new opportunities for state-society compromise (Angola, chapter 5; Rhodesia/Zimbabwe, chapter 6; South Africa, chapter 7; Sudan, chapter 8). This represents the creation of or a negotiated return to regularized patterns of relationships, which I will examine in part 2.

Conclusion

In the encounter between state and society, the goal is to establish regularized, positive interactions leading to cooperation. African regimes have used a variety of strategies intended to contain conflict: persuasion, exhortation, political education, administrative control and coercion, power sharing, redistribution, and political autonomy. Some policies would deny the validity of ethnic, national, and regional identities; others would recognize those attachments while firmly regulating their expression; still others would accept their legitimacy but work, internally or externally, to mediate between the claims. Fundamental to the latter strategy is a mutual acceptance of the legitimacy and survival of the state and ethnoregional identities and a willingness to concede a degree of autonomy and participation to each party in at least certain spheres of activity.

To concentrate on achieving a creative basis for conflict relations, it will be necessary to address the practical problems of facilitating negotiations. Those concerned with establishing effective conflict management systems in Africa must examine the role of the state in defining and negotiating the terms of its relationships with ethnic groups and the role played by international actors in mediating disputes; either way, the complexity of the two-level game at work here is increased by the group's need to negotiate an agreement among its own factional interests in order to present a united face in its negotiations with the state or other ethnic groups. In the relations between state and ethnic identity groups, some conflicts have remained internal matters, because information is at hand, group (and intragroup) demands have remained moderate and reconcilable, and ethnic interests are not threatened physically or culturally; moreover, external patrons have resisted significant involvement in what is essentially domestic competition and conflict. Consequently, in part 1 of this volume, I will examine state-societal relations within countries, focusing on the processes of regularized intergroup interactions and the state's initiative in structuring incentives to build confidence and foster cooperation among distinct identities.

However, where these ties either fail to develop or prove brittle and a process of stalemate becomes evident, some form of third-party initiative becomes indispensable. Frequently, when the parties involved cannot manage the conflict on their own and civil war breaks out, it becomes necessary to bring in domestic or international intermediaries who can exert pressure and offer incentives aimed at influencing the perceptions of key actors. Hence, in part 2, I concentrate on direct or mediated negotiations as a bargaining strategy for coping with high conflict in ethnically and regionally stratified situations. I will focus mainly on the successful mediatory efforts in Angola, Zimbabwe, South Africa, and Sudan in order to evaluate the combination of pressures and incentives needed to create new options and to overcome impasses in their relations.[45]

Finally, in the conclusion to this volume, I will return to the issue of making conflict more manageable—and, in some cases, overcoming mutual defections—through changes in the distribution of benefits. I will examine the structuring of incentives in internal political relations, indicating how these can help to keep conflict bounded and constructive. Then I will ask what happens if intergroup relations become irregular and destructive: which set of international incentives holds out the greatest promise of altering the preferences of actors and even accelerating the ripe moment to overcome stalemate and forestall further civil war?

Obviously, the stakes are very high. As recent events in Somalia, Liberia, Rwanda, and the Democratic Republic of the Congo have made clear, unless relations among certain contending groups become more regular and predictable, their conflicts can escalate dangerously, causing a plunging economy and political collapse as well as an expanding confrontation that draws in external powers. The search for guidelines and incentives to promote coordinated action in the general area of Africa's interethnic relations cannot safely be avoided.

Part One

Regularized Patterns
of Relations

2

Structuring Incentives
for Internal Conflict
Management

*Probing the psychology of ethnic violence is likely to be less
helpful than trying to regulate the conditions that give
incentive for it. Seen this way, the problem ... requires
structural resolutions, resolutions that change incentives.*

RUSSELL HARDIN

To understand conflict management, it is necessary to explore the interlinked and reinforcing relations that take place between state and societal interests. Such an examination of the interconnected process should
help clarify what can and cannot be achieved through negotiations. This
comprehensive view can be achieved by relating latent grievances and
different types of societal and extrasocietal claims to regime strategies
and policy outcomes. Hence in this chapter I examine the logic of the
policy process, focusing on the possible connections between the social
and political environments and regime types. I will then discuss how
these regimes organize incentives to structure policy outcomes on intergroup relations. Clearly, differing regime choices have consequences that
increase or decrease "the probability of certain outcomes."[1]

The Systemic Conditions

Given Africa's objective circumstances in postindependence times,
the record of state-ethnic relations is, on balance, a relatively favorable
one. In terms of economic conditions, however, the performance of the
sub-Saharan African states has certainly been most disappointing: infla-

FIGURE 2-1. *A Systems Approach to State-Ethnic Relations*

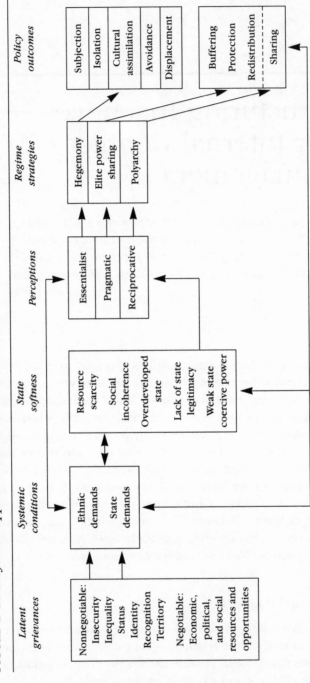

SOURCES: Raymond F. Hopkins, *Political Roles in a New State: Tanzania's First Decade* (Yale University Press, 1971), pp. 51, 55, 56; and Shaheen Mozaffar, letter, December 19, 1986.

tion and unemployment are on the rise, and in 1994 per capita income had fallen to a level 20 percent below that reached a decade earlier.[2] The share of world exports among forty-eight less developed countries (of which thirty-three are African) fell from 1.7 percent in 1970 to 0.4 percent in 1994.[3] The resulting crisis, wrote Claude Ake, "has been phenomenally harsh, tragic, and demoralizing."[4]

Moreover, the state and its institutions are in decline, unable to implement their regulations effectively throughout the territories ostensibly under their control. For example, the Niger government's weak hold over the southern Saharan areas under its control prompted a Touareg uprising in 1991 that stemmed from grievances on the issue of political autonomy.[5] In this context of economic scarcity and state weakness, state third-party actors are not always able to enforce the peace; in those cases where ethnic leaders become fearful for their group's well-being and security, such as Liberia, Somalia, Rwanda and Burundi, they may sometimes see little alternative to expropriating incoming weaponry and taking the military offensive to provide for their own safety. That regularized political routines have emerged at all under such circumstances reflects well on the political acumen of African state and societal elites.

Latent Grievances

At the outset, it seems necessary to relate the regime strategies of hegemony, elite power sharing (including hegemonic exchange and contemporary elite power-sharing arrangements), and polyarchy (both parliamentary and presidential) to the latent grievances in the environment over such concerns as insecurity, inequality, status, identity, recognition, and territory (see figure 2-1). These grievances can be tapped by political elites intent upon making demands for change as well as those wishing to maintain the status quo (that is, making counterdemands). In general, it can be argued that situations tending toward the establishment of hegemonic regimes (with their hierarchically organized one- and no-party systems) will reflect what Edward E. Azar described as "the interconnected nature of the various structural factors (political, economic, ethnic, religious, linguistic) [that] makes protracted social conflicts so devastatingly unresolvable."[6] The inability of actors to separate these issues can result in a limited bargaining range and intense (albeit, at times repressed) intergroup conflicts.

By contrast, situations tending toward elite power sharing and polyarchical regimes may largely avoid linking the structural factors mentioned by Azar and, instead, emphasize the negotiable and less complex dimension of divergent economic interests. The former frequently involve destructive, even intractable, conflicts in which group security and survival seem to be threatened in one manner or another, whereas the latter, which may bring less intense passions to the fore, allow greater scope for creative conflict procedures based on understood norms of bargaining and reciprocity. Whether an ethnically related group acts like any other interest group, competing in the marketplace for publicly controlled resources, is therefore likely to reflect the structural incentives and reciprocal perceptions that prevail in each situation.[7]

Contrary to commonly held impressions about the inevitability of zero-sum interethnic relations, Africa in fact exhibits a wide range of conflict-creating perceptions, demands, and responses.[8] Certainly, profound differences, not easily negotiable, have surfaced and led to deep chasms between distinct identity groups in the same society. The forces that produce these intense political attitudes and commitments often display both a heavy emphasis upon subjective, mainly psychological concerns and the cynical manipulation of these fears by political activists. It was hard-line leaders around President Juvenal Habyarimana of Rwanda, resentful over being denied power in the transitional government that followed the 1992–93 Arusha peace process, who played upon group fears and organized the terrible violence that shook their country.[9] The elite's manipulation of the norms of exclusion from their group does much to bring about conformity among the threatened members. Yet there may be a broad array of symbolic and psychological factors that are potentially conflict producing, including a fear of restratification and the loss of political dominance; an assertion of group worth and place; the existence of negative remembrances and images; the determination to resist the efforts of a controlling group to spread its language, culture, or religion; and evidence of a sense of superiority on the part of a politically or economically dominant minority.[10]

Where ethnic and political minorities fear the consequences of a fundamental reorganization of regime (for example, the creation of an Islamic state in Sudan) and where they remain deeply anxious over their subordination or their cultural or physical survival, intergroup conflicts are likely to be intense and, in some cases, highly destructive of lives and property.[11] Fears for their community's physical security and future well-being lead to difficulties of commitment to the regime and its norms and to the adoption of an "essentialist" perception regarding their ethnic adversaries' intentions (see figure 2-1). The distrust engendered

makes bargaining and implementation of agreements difficult and frequently ends in heavy-handed stalemates or violent outcomes.

As important as these security concerns and fears of exclusion are in
explaining high-stakes conflicts and the use of hegemonic forms of control, these factors do not by any means tell the entire story of Africa's
interethnic relations. Since Africa's decolonization, the leaders of some
polyarchies and elite-coordinated regimes have managed to avoid the
worst-case scenarios by channeling demands along predetermined
paths and developing new routines and incentives for conflict avoidance. By emphasizing the tangible or distributive side of these state-
societal relations (and playing down demands for multidimensional or
indivisible goods and the subjective sources of conflict), these elites
have defused some of the anxieties and passions of ethnic rivalry.

In societies that are scarcity-prone and have weak state institutions,
issues of recruitment and allocation among societal interests and administrative units lend themselves to "neutral" distributive principles such as
proportionality—the distribution of state resources and political and
administrative positions among ethnic peoples and regional units on the
basis of their relative numbers. Where political routines have become
widely understood and accepted and a bargaining culture has emerged,
leaders can find compromise formulas to bridge the gap between the
relatively advantaged and the disadvantaged on such basic questions as
subregional need versus derivation (the place of extraction) in allocative
policies (oil-based wealth in Nigeria), merit versus proportionality in
recruitment policies (Kenya), legislative representation based on subregional parity or population size (Nigeria), or centralization versus decentralization of power (Ghana, Zambia, Nigeria, and Sudan in 1972). The
state, however, may not always be prepared to act generously in implementing its contract, as Nigeria's repressive responses to Ogoni claims
for enhanced distributions in the 1990s show.

Although the old hegemonic exchange (interelite political negotiation
practices within a coercive one- or no-party structure) did not gain legitimacy in Zambia and Uganda in the 1970s and 1980s, their political leaders
nonetheless acted in terms of political expediency, appointing ethnic intermediaries to high positions of state in accordance with rough guidelines for
balanced representation. Such practices gained more acceptance in Jomo
Kenyatta's Kenya and Felix Houphouët-Boigny's Côte d'Ivoire; in these
countries, something tantamount to an inclusive grand coalition developed,
avoiding adversarial politics and allowing the dominant elite to negotiate
policy questions quietly among themselves. Later, under the power-sharing

compromise in South Africa, the African National Congress leadership, seeking to reassure local minorities and overseas investors about the regime's future course, included representatives of the National party and the Inkatha Freedom party on a proportional basis in the cabinet following the 1994 elections; in addition, President Nelson Mandela announced that the former military commander, Georg Meiring, would command the new South African National Defence Force for a five-year term.

Moreover, central government practices in many polyarchical and elite power-sharing regimes reveal a keen regard for maintaining balance among groups and subregions when recruiting for their civil service or allocating revenue. The ethnic composition of Ghana's senior staff members of the central government in 1972, still reflecting the recruitment values of the previous polyarchical regime, showed, with few exceptions, remarkably close parallels between the ethnic proportions in the civil service and the society at large.[12] Furthermore, an analysis of public expenditure patterns in Nigeria and Kenya indicated recurrent use of the proportionality principle in the mid-1970s to early 1980s to achieve a degree of fairness in the expenditures on roads, health, and education among these countries' subregions.[13]

In brief, distributive issues between ethnic interests that share a sense of common destiny are normally policy questions with tangible referents—such as goods, jobs, taxes, roads, and schools—and are frequently amenable to political solutions. The effect is to widen the scope for conflict management under difficult political and economic conditions. Exceptions to this generalization are readily apparent, of course. Where differential rates of modernization and political and economic practices have combined to create a profound sense of comparative group deprivation, the objective and subjective sources of conflict can reinforce each other and exacerbate latent tensions. For example, when discussing the increasing strains in North-South relations in Sudan following the 1972 Addis Ababa agreement, Dunstan Wai wrote: "A feeling of *relative economic deprivation* is growing, and the intransigent refusal of the Arab Sudanese to share real political power and revenue from within and aid from without with the Southern Sudanese will gradually erode any desires in the South to identify with the 'Sudanese state.'"[14] In this case, Southern Sudanese are inclined to view economic and political relations as part of the structure of incentives and, hence, less tractable than might be anticipated where unranked equal collectivities compete over distributable goods.

The Nature and Intensity of Collective Demands

The nature and intensity of ethnic and subregional demands have proved a pivotal factor in the development of regularized relations between the state and society. Demands made by elite representatives upon those in power at the political center "play important roles in creating conflict and in mobilizing the masses for particularistic interests."[15] Such background factors as elite self-interest, the number and distribution of ethnic groups, unequal rates of modernization among subregions, degree of social mobilization, the communications revolution, and the fragility of political institutions no doubt explain much about the collision among social forces. Yet an understanding of the interactional process at work in a particular country requires more: in particular, a probing of latent grievances, the role of ethnic entrepreneurs in the shaping of ethnic demands, the structuring of state-ethnic relations, and the responses of state elites.[16] To the extent that political leaders make negotiable demands (and this may vary with each encounter), the conflicts tend to arise over divisible goods, increasing the possibility of effective negotiation and mediation.

Clearly, the potential for conflict management is greater when group demands are reasonable and moderate (that is, negotiable) and when they accept the legitimacy of competing interests and do not challenge the integrity of the political order. Nonnegotiable (or uncompromising) demands for assimilation, restructuring of power, border rectification, population movement, and partition and territorial separation are likely to pose fundamental challenges to a state's organizing principles and informal rules of engagement and, therefore, to elicit an aggressive response from state officials. Different kinds of state and ethnic demands are influenced by rival elites' perceptions of each other; they, in turn, relate and reinforce the regime strategies put into play by those in power (see figure 2-1).

I will examine each of these types of demands and their implications for the negotiation process. Where ethnic leaders and their constituents are prepared to compete for public resources according to prevailing societal rules and where they perceive their rivals in pragmatic terms (that is, they assume a basic conflict of interest in their relationships with other groups but do not preclude the possibility of conciliatory behavior on specific issues), they may have an incentive to make moderate demands that can be satisfied within the state. Ethnic differences do not, in and of themselves, preclude the possibility of collaboration. Provided that an overarching sense of shared future exists among diverse ethnic and other interests, state and ethnic leaders may be able to live with a certain amount of uncertainty and even join forces to solve common problems.[17]

To gain insight into the demand process, it is necessary to distinguish between the public's felt dissatisfactions and the ethnic intermediary's critical role in selecting and shaping these points of discontent for presentation to state officials. The gap between grievance and its elite articulation has enormous implications for systemic stability. To some extent the problem is mitigated if demands are passed through mid-level elites and ethnic associations before going to ethnic entrepreneurs in the capital city. However, if the ethnic go-between fails to consult and therefore to display sufficient sensitivity to the constituents' feelings, the operating norms of a clientelistic relationship can become weakened, which can lead to the patron's loss of credibility.

An idea about the nature of the general public's felt dissatisfactions can be secured from the results of surveys administered in Kenya (1966), Zambia (1969–70), and Ghana (1973).[18] In all three cases, members of the general public focused upon distributive issues, expressing the most modest and restrained kinds of grievances. In Ghana, villagers in the relatively disadvantaged Northern and Upper Regions stressed the need for sanitation, market stalls, road improvements, and plumbing, while their counterparts in the more advantaged Western and Ashanti Regions and Greater Accra voiced their need for a broad array of improvements, including such costly items as modern markets, electricity, schools, and hospitals. In general, the "revolution of rising expectations" was a phenomenon most evident among the relatively advantaged; by comparison, the less advantaged, in both urban and rural areas, made essentially reasonable demands for public services and amenities.[19] Where minimal demands were evident, the effect was to reduce pressure on heavily burdened governments to redistribute scarce resources and hence to allow them to temporize or "satisfice" on key development projects, at least for a limited time.

When demands made upon the state by the relatively disadvantaged are limited in scope and intensity and are divisible, state elites are sometimes able to surmount the heavy constraints of the political and economic environment and to engage in bargaining relationships with ethnic intermediaries at the top of the political system. To the extent that societies are able to develop recurrent patterns of interaction, the result will be gains in the responsiveness and stability of the political system. However, there are limits to such relationships. Manfred Halpern predicts that where "there is no similarity whatever between the loyalties which the transforming center requires and those to which the local community adheres," then bargaining will be unable "to overcome the underlying incoherence."[20]

Nonnegotiable demands, characteristically rigid and high-wrought, tend to cluster around accurate or inaccurate threat assessments or largely emotionally laden issues such as physical and cultural survival, group status, worth, identity, territory, and subordination.[21] Profound anxieties, arising from a diffuse sense of danger, have the effect of limiting and modifying perceptions and therefore becoming the source of extreme collective reactions. Particularly where security-related issues come into play, ethnic leaders are likely to go beyond economic perspectives and stress the need to cope with a perceived threat to group survival, even if this places them at a comparative economic disadvantage.[22] To the extent that the resulting claims of rival groups are incompatible, the outcomes can include hostile, zero-sum perceptions and intense, even intractable, conflicts.[23]

Nonnegotiable demands are likely to emerge where state elites and ethnic representatives hold incompatible definitions, values, or perceptions of interests. Especially in an ethnically or racially dominated state such as Burundi or Hendrik Verwoerd's South Africa, where state leaders and other ethnic representatives disagree over fundamental principles, not tangible interests, conflict tends to be intense and frequently becomes unmanageable. For example, when Leo Kuper writes about polarizing ideologies among dominant and subordinate groups in such repressive contexts as Rwanda, Burundi, pre-independence Algeria, and postindependence Zanzibar, he describes minority domination as constituting a system that excludes reform along the lines of power sharing:

> While dominant polarizing groups see reform as a stepping stone in the reversal of power, not as a process in the sharing of power, subordinate groups consider it a delusion to hope that the State, which is the instrument of their oppression, will bring about effective change, and they see reformism as a device in the maintenance of power.[24]

The web of relations linking state and ethnic elites is therefore torn asunder, and ethnic identity groups, fearful for their future, retreat to the safety of their separate communal "containers."[25]

Clearly, intractable conflicts—involving intense demands for security as well as for power, status, and territory—were evident in both vertically and horizontally stratified societies. Because the dominant minority in colonial Zanzibar and Algeria, apartheid South Africa, and postcolonial Burundi and Rwanda denied the principle of equality and enforced inequitable practices through top-down control, a system of vertical stratification came to feature nonnegotiable claims from both the ruling (but vulnerable) minority and the excluded (and resentful) majority. Both sets of antagonists adopted essentialist perceptions toward each other's intentions and perceived acts of conciliation and compromise as indications of weakness and, consequently, a threat to their status or security. With the two actors lacking a sense of common fate, leaders can direct group demands along conflict-laden and inflexible lines. The reciprocity that does occur between group intermediaries is then negative in nature, and sometimes demands escalate so that the security or survival of one group is preserved at the expense of the other.

The violence in Burundi in 1972 revealed hard-liners within the minority Tutsi who had long voiced fears of what they regarded as the "Hutu peril."[26] The Tutsi, who controlled the state apparatus and the army, responded with extreme ferocity to initial attacks by bands of Hutu and "Mulelist" rebels in Bujumbura and some of the provinces in the South. Exhibiting a diffusion effect, Tutsi army "counter-violence" followed the Hutu majority's assumption of power in neighboring Rwanda and demonstrated acute Tutsi fears over the possibility of the rebellion spreading to engulf their country as well.[27] Violence, then, followed from relations of dominance, perceived superiority, and group insecurity. In such situations, the systemic conditions and reciprocal perceptions of group leaders are so negative that minority leaders seek a concentration of power at the political center to safeguard their group's opportunities and survival; this inevitably occurs at a heavy cost in terms of developing the kinds of legitimate routines for ongoing negotiations and joint problem solving.

Nonnegotiable demands also appear in horizontally stratified societies. The unranked ethnic system, writes Donald Horowitz, does not involve superiority and subordination; rather, "parallel ethnic groups coexist, each group internally stratified."[28] Yet, despite the parallel nature of these groups, conflicts can still become intense, especially when demands for power, status, territory, and autonomy are put forth in uncompromising terms.

Consider territorial autonomy, for example: where such demands do not raise questions about the legitimacy of the state and its normative order, they also do not threaten the political system. Where state elites perceive these ethnoregional claims as reasonable and creating scope for enhanced efficiency, they may seek to accommodate them by conceding a limited administrative responsibility. A variety of subregional councils, planning boards, district assemblies, autonomous administrative authorities, and federal relationships have thus emerged; all of these have provided a limited capacity for local initiative and action while stopping short of separatism and secession. As President Gaafar el-Nimeiry of Sudan is reported to have said, a federal system is necessary "to reconcile the country with itself."[29] (Yet he did not allow such a system to develop in the 1980s.) Where perceptions are mutually pragmatic and claims are negotiable, regional autonomy may be able to contribute creatively to state coherence.

However, where the demand for territorial autonomy is presented in a confrontational and abstract or intangible manner and this then raises questions about the legitimacy of the political order itself, conflict tends to become destructive. In general, it seems reasonable to hypothesize that the more rigid the demands, the more inflexible the state's response will be. To be sure, national or ethnoregional leaders have justified the call for territorial self-determination in Biafra, Eritrea, Katanga, the Republic of Somaliland, and Western Sahara and the claim to irredentist reunification in Somalia and among the Ewe and Bakongo by pointing to the artificiality of the colonial divisions.[30] Nevertheless, Africa's successor states, invoking the international legitimacy conferred upon them at independence by other states, have insisted upon the territorial integrity of the new states against all other claimants, internal or external.[31]

In certain cases (such as Biafra, Katanga, and Eritrea, which did not recognize its union with Ethiopia as legitimate), leaders have refused to negotiate their differences with state authorities on the basis of the status quo, instead persisting in their demands for full separation. The demand by an ethnoregional elite for a further grant of self-determination in postindependence times amounted to a radical assertion of group rights, potentially destructive of the organizing principles of the state. Such a claim precluded reform and implied that no compromise would provide sufficient guarantees of group survival within the existing political order.[32] The inevitable consequence was serious, often violent, conflict.

Under what circumstances might such a nonnegotiable stance be justified? This question, posed most poignantly during the Nigerian civil war, brought inconclusive answers. Some contended that a valid claim to national self-determination rested on the need to preserve the survival of the affected group. For Tanzania's president, Julius Nyerere, this was indeed the case. When his government recognized the state of Biafra, he argued that secession "was declared because the [Igbo] people felt it to be their only defence against extermination."[33] Yet, at the time, other observers were equally emphatic in denying that federal troops had engaged in acts of genocide against the Igbos or that Colonel Odumegwu Ojukwu had exhausted all the possible remedies under the system before breaking connections with the Nigerian state.[34] Thus Biafra's nonnegotiable demand for separation had given rise to an equally inflexible Nigerian federal government counterdemand, with deadlock and violent struggle as the logical outcomes.

Finally, it is important to stress that the nature of ethnic demands can change over time. In some situations, ethnic groups begin with negotiable demands involving modest resource costs; however, when the state does not meet these demands, they can lead to extreme, nonnegotiable demands. In others, such as the white minority demand for political control in Rhodesia and South Africa, the claim to dominance gave way as African military capabilities increased and forced white leaders to reconsider their options on negotiations.

Perceptions

It will be sufficient here to consider two main types of perceptions: essentialist and pragmatic (see figure 2-1). It is also important to note a third type of perception that ethnic leaders and their followers can have about each other: a reciprocative one. Those adopting a reciprocative perspective assume that interethnic relations can be made less threatening through conciliatory moves by the main actors in a conflict situation; this leads them to seek to transform the structure of relations, by acting in a conciliatory manner to induce a similar response. If such conciliatory moves are repeated, they can establish the basis for long-term mutual expectations of collaborative behavior. Such a perspective has been evident on occasion in contemporary Africa (for example, the redistributive policies discussed in chapter 3); nevertheless, with scarce resources and intense struggles for an advantaged share of state allocations, elites have been more inclined toward pragmatic and, in the worst cases, essentialist perceptions of each other.[35]

An Essentialist Perception

Since independence, Africa has experienced a wide range of essentialist views regarding interethnic relations, leading in worst cases to polarization, hostility, the collapse of overarching norms, and, at times, violence.[36] This can be partly explained by the expectations that actors have of their adversary's behavior and partly by the prevailing incentive structure, which furthers destructive encounters under conditions of severe economic scarcity. Interacting and escalating ethnic and class fears around the time of decolonization in Zanzibar, Burundi, and Rwanda culminated in violent attacks upon defenseless communities, in particular those regarded as the political elite or intelligentsia.[37] In these three cases, a privileged minority controlling state institutions and determined to preserve colonially inherited patterns of social stratification perceived itself as pitted against an underprivileged ethnic and class majority dedicated to bringing about a radical restructuring of social opportunities.[38] After independence, majority incentives for a preemptive attack surfaced in Rwanda, with terrifying consequences.

The common thread running through these highly intense encounters was a reciprocity of fear and aggressive behavior, which grew precipitously whenever the stereotypical images of other groups were supported to any extent by actual events. In Rwanda, the rather unstructured Hutu uprisings of November 1959 and the subsequent Tutsi reprisals substantiated each group's most negative assessments of the other. Quoting Gregoire Kayibanda's statement that, between these two communities in Rwanda, "there is no intercourse and no sympathy, [they] are ignorant of each other's habits, thoughts and feelings as if they were dwellers of different zones," René Lemarchand stresses the polarization of expectations that followed the uprising and "the all-pervasive climate of fear and suspicion which gripped the country at the approach of the [1960] elections."[39] These events in Rwanda also diffused across international borders, exacerbating latent fears in neighboring Burundi, where, according to U.S. Ambassador Thomas Melady, an "either-or mentality of dominating or being eliminated" became prevalent in the Hutu and Tutsi mindsets.[40]

Later, in 1993, as the extremist leaders among Rwanda's majority Hutu people felt threatened by the consequences of the power-sharing provisions of the Arusha accords negotiated with the Tutsi-led Rwandan Patriotic Front, essentialist thinking again became manifest. These militant Hutu leaders used Radio Mille Collines to describe Tutsis as "enemies" who should be exterminated. With the prevailing incentive structure encouraging these elites to adopt a damaging course of action, they seized the opportunity of the president's death to launch a highly destructive preemptive strike, leaving 500,000 to 1,000,000 Tutsi civilians and some moderate Hutu elites dead. Fear for their future under the Arusha accords caused a dangerous escalation of group violence. This phenomenon is not unlike the classic description of the "security dilemma" as used by international relations theorists, where the search for security and the lack of reliable information about a rival's intentions may lead to preventive action of a military nature.[41] Attempting to justify the massacres that engulfed the country, the prefect of greater Kigali, Francois Karera, argued that "the Tutsi are originally bad." He continued: "If the reasons [for the killings] are just, the massacres are justified."[42]

Other examples of essentialist thinking—for instance, the experiences with "ethnic cleansing" in Sudan and Kenya in the 1990s—could be examined, but the cases already discussed seem sufficient to highlight the existence of insecure and hostile perceptions contributing to highly destructive conflict outcomes.[43] Where group appraisals of an adversary's intentions predispose actors toward zero-sum expectations, a positively reinforcing negotiating relationship becomes difficult to initiate and sustain. As I indicate below, a change of perceptions in response to a conciliatory overture by a rival is possible in certain situations, but, more commonly, essentialist thinking sets in motion a cognitive process leading to interactions marked by fear and antagonism.

The effect is to gravely complicate the negotiation process. Where state and ethnic leaders view others as fundamentally threatening to their physical, cultural, or social survival, they tend to believe that any compromises on their part will weaken their position. Because ethnic group A assumes that group B (and any coalition partners) intend to harm A and will take advantage of any relaxation of A's defensive stance, B is regarded as untrustworthy under any circumstances. In line with this assessment, actor A considers ethnic group B's word to lack credibility; A therefore takes for granted that B will twist any concessions made at the bargaining table to A's disadvantage. Group A views any signs of cooperation on its part as likely to be misinterpreted as weakness. Conciliation would, therefore, become the basis for new demands by B, requiring A to make greater outlays of political resources to re-establish the status quo between opposing state and ethnic interests.

A Pragmatic Perception

Pragmatic perceptions are promoted when the incentive structure encourages leaders and groups to make moderate demands and abide by the rules of the game.[44] To the extent norms are shared and minorities protected, collective action can be channeled along peaceful, constructive lines. Although the pragmatists appraise their relations with other actors warily, they tend to assess their rivals' intentions in broader and less menacing terms. They harbor no illusions about basic conflicts of interest with other groups; however, because actor A perceives B to be seeking to maximize the opportunities of its own group members and not to harm A directly, some scope exists for the state to make use of existing rules to facilitate positive-sum outcomes—at least in certain issue areas.

In South Africa, for example, although President Nelson Mandela was quite firm about the need to ensure that blacks win political power, he sought at the same time to reassure the Afrikaners and others that "the African National Congress is aware of the concerns and fears of all minorities, including the whites. We have always shown an openness to understanding these fears and finding appropriate means to address them."[45] True to his pragmatic spirit, Mandela was prepared to reconcile a sense of distinct communal interests with a willingness to enter, albeit cautiously, into reciprocal understandings and negotiations with other ethnic leaders and groups on specific issues. In doing so, the pragmatist can distinguish between other people's desires to distance themselves socially and their preparedness to advance the political and economic interests of the group through conciliatory overtures.

The costs (in the sense of not having one's own way) of conciliatory behavior in certain matters have proven acceptable in many instances on the continent. Ethnic groups and their brokers have at times acted competitively and gained preferential treatment, but, as pragmatists, they have normally done this in the spirit of self-maximization, not in an effort to destroy an adversary. To the extent that the various ethnic interests share moral and functional linkages, they are likely to be encouraged to reach informal understandings on matters of mutual concern. The results of this pragmatism can be seen in the emergence of such markets of "exchange" as political coalitions and power sharing, elite recruitment, resource allocation, decentralization and regional autonomy, and political, social, and cultural group rights and protections. In these issue areas, moderate assessments of rivals' intentions have opened the way to effective bargaining relationships, for the costs of defection are perceived as outweighing those of cooperation. Hence focusing upon the tangible and narrow questions that legitimately divide ethnic groups (instead of focusing on those that raise collective consciousness about a generalized and unremitting "threat") appears crucial to regularized intergroup relations.

State Responses to Ethnic Demands and Counterdemands

Certainly, regimes (the legitimate formulas for exercising power) are critical for structuring how state elites are likely to respond to societal demands. By setting parameters on the nature of choice, regimes can have a significant impact on the management of conflict. To be sure, the regimes discussed here overlap each other in specific situations; even in hegemonic regimes, some reciprocity inevitably occurs between the rulers and the ruled, and the tendency of polyarchies to concentrate power at the political center is quite common. Yet the thrust of the organizing processes of hegemonies and polyarchies is distinguishable, with distinct consequences for state-society relations. These regime types differ in terms of their openness to the demands of interest groups, central discipline, roles of political parties, regularity of elections, and ideological commitments and preferences. They also diverge quite noticeably in their willingness to bargain with domestic class and ethnic interests and in the relative costs they are prepared to pay to achieve efficient administration.

The Hegemonic Approach

Hegemonic regimes that consolidate power at the political center and emphasize hierarchical control by government and party often tend to impose serious restraints upon the aggregation and channeling of group demands to decisionmaking elites. As resisters of ethnic and regional demands, these bureaucratic centralist regimes tend to repress the opposition, inhibit free expression, limit the arena of decisionmaking, restrict public accountability, and allow only narrow and restricted opportunities for mass participation. When communal intermediaries do manage to break through the controls to articulate their claims, state leaders in hegemonic regimes can be expected to respond slowly and reluctantly, leading to a greater likelihood of antagonistic relations.

Hegemonic regimes are not merely resisters of group claims; they also process and make demands in their own right. The authoritarian state relies upon the ability of a dominant political elite to impose its preferences on society, acting in line with its penchant for central direction and encapsulated decisionmaking and dealing with situations of intense ethnic and regional conflict by using five basic policy mechanisms (see figure 2-1).[46] These include:

—Subjection: coercive measures to assure the self-determination of the dominant (minority or majority) interests without making significant concessions to the counterpulls of subordinate political interests, for example, apartheid South Africa, Burundi, Sudan;

—Isolation: attempting to manage conflict by separating the contending groups into distinct political systems, for example, de facto autonomy (UNITA in Angola), de facto partition (Cyprus), secession through military action (Bangladesh), or full separation by means of a referendum (Eritrea);

—Cultural assimilation: the interpenetration and absorption of politically weaker identity groups into the core culture, for example, Sudan, Liberia;

—Avoidance: circumscribing and containing ethnic conflict by seeking to insulate the state from direct confrontations among social groups, for example, imposing no- or one-party systems (Ghana and Sierra Leone); and

—Displacement: endeavoring to transform the interethnic encounter by permanently moving an ethnic population from one locale to another, for example, transferring enclaves, local "regroupement," ethnic cleansing, assisted emigration, and disguised or undisguised deportations.

In hegemonic regimes, state elites, fearful that communal demands will be nonnegotiable and contribute to the "overpoliticization" of the society, tend to perceive ethnic conflict as intense and threatening to the organizing principles of the political system.[47] Therefore they use the hierarchically based controls at their disposal to either resist communal demands or attempt to structure societal relations in line with their preferences. However, this elite dominance can occasionally result in quite creative outcomes: for example, the 1975 land reforms of President Mengistu Haile Mariam in Ethiopia ended the domination of northern landlords in the South, restoring southern peasant control over the land in their own home area.[48]

But the authoritarian approach is not without heavy costs. The suppression of communal demands, if it can be achieved, may create the appearance of normality but still fail to come to grips with group griev-ances and fears festering beneath the surface. And not only are civil lib-erties repressed, but, in terms of conflict management, deterrence does little to build regularized rules of relations in the society. For good or ill, there are definite limits to the coercive and penetrative capacities of the hegemonic state in Africa. Consequently, where individuals and groups successfully defy state norms, the weak state can do little to stop them from opting for a kind of de facto autonomy (Angola's UNITA, Ethiopia's Tigray, or Eritrea under the regime of Mengistu Haile Mariam). Paradoxically, the lengths to which the more ideologically inclined hege-monic states (such as formerly Afro-Marxist Ethiopia and Angola) have gone to coerce compliance have often produced either acquiescence or devastating civil wars. Hence the tendency toward repression con-tributed to a zero-sum mentality and, ultimately, to intractable state-ethnic deadlock or confrontation.

The Elite Power-Sharing and Polyarchical Approaches

By contrast, the elite power-sharing and polyarchical regimes allow a broader range for legitimate conflict among the elite representatives of ethnic, regional, and other interests. Determined to preserve stability, their state elites have an incentive to view intergroup relations in more pragmatic terms. This inclines them to be more prepared to open chan-nels for the articulation of collective demands and to be responsive to these claims. Provided that leaders have an incentive to build and main-tain broad electoral support constituencies and that norms on partici-pation and the acceptance of electoral defeat are in place, political minorities will have less reason to fear for the future. In these circum-stances, the greater openness and flexibility of polyarchical regimes can create positive feedback; ethnic-related demands can thus be more moderate, because group leaders have reason to anticipate a greater responsiveness on the part of state officials.

However, the elite power-sharing and polyarchical regimes differ sig-nificantly in the ways they have come into being and in their organiz-ing patterns. The old hegemonic exchange regimes emerged primarily during the 1960s, 1970s, and 1980s and reflected their leaders' pre-paredness to co-opt and engage in limited bargaining relations with their country's powerful ethnoregional entrepreneurs. These were largely transitional arrangements among elites, born of the need to recognize the configurations of societal identity, clientelism, and group power after independence. Their breakdown often resulted in ethnic monopolization and loss of accountability; recently, in Gabon and the Republic of the Congo, a return to hegemonic exchange practices has occurred, building on the best of the old system. Similarly, the contemporary elite power-sharing democratic regimes (sometimes referred to as elite pacts) use a moderately open system of governance that links elite cooperation and control with competitive elections and hold out the real possibility of being a transition toward a full polyarchical arrangement.[49]

In some instances, polyarchical regimes also manifested the continuities of the postindependence process. Not feeling particularly threatened by the bargain struck with the outgoing imperial authority, leaders in Botswana, Gambia (until 1994), Mauritius, and Namibia essentially accepted existing clientelistic practices and preserved intact the basic laws and structures inherited from the colonizers. Also, during the 1970s and 1980s, leaders in Senegal shifted from hegemonic to polyarchical regimes, followed by a wave of political liberalization in most African countries in the 1990s. The middle-class elites demanding democratic changes were partly voicing their frustrations over the arbitrariness, corruption, and inefficiency of authoritarian rule, and they were partly responding to an international environment that rejected the claims of autocrats to international legitimacy.

By institutionalizing competitive elections and a degree of public accountability, polyarchies are certainly more effective than their elite power-sharing counterparts in regularizing public access to decisionmakers. Nevertheless, because the elite power-sharing regimes establish informal routines for broadly balanced and inclusive coalitions and proportional decision rules on civil service appointments, fiscal allocations, university admissions, and educational scholarships, they are responding (albeit in a less public manner) to the appeals of ethnic, regional, and other intermediaries.

More so than hegemonic regimes, then, the polyarchic and various elite power-sharing regimes are processors rather than makers of demands. They are more inclined to accept the legitimacy of autonomous social interests and, in order to promote measures necessary to make ethnic groups feel secure in their relations with the state and other ethnic interests, are also more inclined to negotiate with and accommodate these powerful social forces to achieve national unity. Much of their pragmatism, no doubt, originates in a recognition of their state's low capabilities; yet, in some cases (Mauritius, Senegal), it also demonstrates elite preferences for regulating conflict through more cooperative types of encounters. The effect of this pragmatism is to channel social conflict along predetermined paths, thus lending a sense of regularity and predictability to the routines and rules of the political system.

The contemporary elite power-sharing and polyarchical regimes' preparedness to accommodate ethnic and subregional demands follows logically from their governing elites' perception that claims on the state can generally be reconciled and therefore that the intensity of intergroup conflicts is likely to be low or moderate. A willingness to engage in political bargaining and reciprocity naturally gives rise to a proclivity to accept the need for direct negotiations with ethnoregional leaders (as in South Africa) or some form of third-party buffering between domestic ethnic interests (as in Ghana in 1994). Here, the distinction between the state as a party to conflict and the state as mediator can be important. In the first case, the state as a relatively autonomous actor seeks to advance its interests and, at times, those of the society at large; in the latter case, the state's initiatives involve the use of such tactics as good offices, conciliation, mediation, and arbitration to determine the rules for social interaction. When the state becomes a party to the conflict and gains an interest in the outcome, the costs of intransigent behavior on either side may become excessive, causing the antagonists to see other internal or external third-party actors as indispensable for facilitating a mutually beneficial agreement.

State elites can also choose to adopt policies of protection, granting constitutional and legal guarantees to minorities to reassure them of their status and safety in the political order (Nigeria in 1979, 1993). In South Africa, the 1994 interim constitution gave minority parties (not minority ethnic and racial groups as such) guarantees of inclusion in decisionmaking and provincial affairs, although the nature and composition of group influences in the Inkatha Freedom and National parties made such an inference reasonable. Moreover, despite the evident constraints of economic scarcity, state elites in Kenya, Ghana, Nigeria, Côte d'Ivoire, and Cameroun have, at times, pursued a strategy of redistributing fiscal resources to the less advantaged ethnoregions of their country, thereby increasing the likelihood that the people in these areas will have an incentive to support the state and comply with its regulations.

Finally, polyarchies and, to a lesser extent, contemporary elite power-sharing regimes can pursue policies that involve interethnic sharing in decisionmaking and implementation activities. Where the demands are moderate and groups share pragmatic perceptions of each other's intentions, a sense of common fate may prevail. Collective conflict does not then disappear but focuses largely on such negotiable issues as resource allocation and the distribution of political positions and social opportunities. As learning occurs and routines of political bargaining become accepted, informal practices of cooperation become evident in executive, legislative, and party affairs. Sharing also gains expression from time to time through formal rules, for example, those governing the application of the principle of Nigeria's "federal character" in the making of federal appointments. By means of a sequential process, bargaining can induce a series of responses that can lead over time to established organizing principles of action.[50] Acceptance of such basic principles can lay a foundation that allows for an operating consensus without the necessity of regular negotiations on each issues.

The results include an increased ability to develop elite linkages and progress toward consolidating a "self-enforcing" political system, but the political legitimacy that designates such regimes can be costly.[51] The larger number of powerful political actors participating in decisionmaking compels leaders to invest more resources in the negotiating process in order to reach agreements.[52] Moreover, the continuous political interplay that marks these regimes sometimes makes broad-ranging plans difficult to implement and can contribute to indecision, mediocre appointments, and various abuses and corrupt practices. When these possibilities are linked to an open regime's potential for demand generation or outbidding, the calculus of potential benefits and costs becomes intricate and situational.

The Interconnected Conflict Process

This chapter attempts to give the reader some insight into conflict management as a system of interactions. Collective grievances and demands are linked to the structuring of regimes and their strategies and policies. Ethnic and regional demands and state responses are seen as interwoven and reinforcing. Demands for inclusive state coalitions and proportional distributions are accepted as negotiable and legitimate and can be handled within the political order, whereas demands for group security and such indivisible goods as the separation of populations and secession are generally nonnegotiable and threatening to the political system. As such, these latter demands have potentially destructive consequences for social coherence and state legitimacy.

Because of the critical feedback effect and a variety of external pressures, the relationships between group demands and state responses are by no means inflexible. The possibility of altering both demands and state responses and therefore of developing new routines and new regime choices is apparent. Leaders in multiethnic Benin and Senegal have coordinated changes toward greater political liberalization, while those in Zimbabwe, determined to consolidate their political power over an ethnically and racially divided society, have shifted from a colonially negotiated polyarchy to one where the forms of constitutional democracy are present, but in practice the powers exercised by the ruling regime "severely limit contestation."[53]

Certainly, one can anticipate that state responsiveness to the fears of the vulnerable and the demands of the disadvantaged will have a positive, long-term impact. Not only does a responsive state encourage ethnic intermediaries to frame their demands in moderate terms, but it also facilitates action before reformist possibilities have been eclipsed by the emergence of an intransigent opposition. Also, a responsive state facilitates conflict management by giving ethnic and regional intermediaries an increased opportunity to pull back from inflexible stances without an extraordinary loss of face. State reasonableness lends an indispensable aura of legitimacy to the political system, creating time and space for potential adversaries to develop new perceptions about each other and, in the process, open up new avenues for cooperative behavior.

Moreover, the responsive state provides incentives for stable, lasting cooperative relations. In this respect, the basic regime choices of majoritarian democracy, elite power sharing, and hegemonic rule can make a critical difference. This is because regimes play a significant role in structuring the routines of encounter between the state and civil society, either organizing intergroup interactions to facilitate the channeling of demands along predetermined lines or, alternatively, blocking access and thwarting interelite and intergroup reciprocity and negotiations. Also, as Jennifer Widner notes, multiparty regimes provide politicians with incentives to form coalitions to back broad policy reforms; such incentives do not exist to such an extent in less competitive systems. Although candidates tend to form voting blocs to push national issues in a multiparty setting, Widner argues that, in a semicompetitive system, "economic policies that yield general, indivisible benefits are hard to generate because there is no clear, individual return to those who invest time and energy in building a coalition for their provision."[54]

State regimes structure intergroup encounters in different ways: allowing or forbidding scope for the aggregation of collective demands, facilitating or obstructing the channeling of these demands to decision-makers, reacting or failing to react to legitimate claims on state elites, and implementing or refusing to implement public policies along intended lines. Hegemonic systems tend to rely, to some extent at least, on the threat or actual use of coercion; they combine generally low degrees of societal participation with the repression of dissent. In Sammy Smooha's terms, control systems attempt "to buy political stability (or, more accurately, to avoid turmoil and bloodshed) at the expense of political democracy."[55] Not only do their repressive tendencies cause them to be slow in securing information and responding to legitimate demands, but their heavy-handedness is destabilizing over the long term, often provoking bitter, even violent, reactions from civil associations. The effect is to cramp social learning, thus discouraging the emergence of stable and persistent interactions over time. Authoritarian rulers can succeed for some years in suppressing the outward manifestations of ethnic antagonism or political opposition, but deterring conflict is not tantamount to providing internal incentives for cooperation. Without a common consensus over norms and values, fissures within the dominant coalition may prove fatal and allow society to overwhelm the ruling state elite.

By limiting and guiding public participation along desired lines, various partially authoritarian regimes (radical state populist, state corporatist, and hegemonic exchange regimes) are sometimes advantageously placed to impose creative policies on society. Because of the way these partially authoritarian regimes consolidate power, they insulate their elites from certain members of the public. State populism excludes many middle-class and professional members and a significant number of traditional leaders; corporatism places some groups and associations outside its sphere of concern and leaves state-linked groups with insufficient autonomy; and hegemonic exchange and other power-sharing regimes tend to be highly elitist in their organization and policies. Such regimes can enable their ruling coalitions to live with a certain amount of incoherence. They can preserve the appearance of normality while denying oppositional elements a legitimate arena in which to fight out their differences. Thus the partially hegemonic regimes offer a limited scope for bargaining and compromise among various pluralistic interests, so that such bargaining takes place within firm parameters determined in each case by the ruling state coalition.

A gradual movement from a partially hegemonic regime to greater political liberalization, even full democracy, can take place—but it is certainly not a given. As Frances Hagopian notes, regarding the experience of Brazil with pacted democracy, a civilian-military agreement that brings the armed forces into the ruling coalition can reduce the uncertainties of the officer corps about the transition to a partially democratic regime, thereby lowering military incentives to intervene again. However, such civilian-military accords run the risk of strengthening undemocratic forces at the political center.[56]

Allowing, then, for possible abuses by elites under such regimes, partially hegemonic systems nonetheless provide a setting where temporary arrangements can set the stage for future transition toward full democracy. In the scarcity-prone and soft-state conditions of contemporary Africa, such tacit and informal practices as ethnic balancing in government and civil service appointments and proportionality in resource allocations encourage agreement on bargaining outcomes, while in most cases avoiding zero-sum antagonisms among communal interests. Elite power sharing tends to make conflict more manageable by drawing the representatives of key interest groups into the decisionmaking circle. The effect of this inclusion is to encourage face-to-face encounters, thus breaking down distance and promoting reciprocity among rival group leaders. Although inclusive coalitions in semicompetitive regimes are necessarily somewhat unstable and temporary, they can contribute to conciliatory outcomes by changing the structure of incentives: reassuring political minorities regarding their security, enlarging the scope for interethnic cooperation, dispersing the conflict among different tiers of government, and encouraging the use of distributive formulas perceived as fair by a wide gamut of leaders and constituents.[57] To the extent that cooperative behavior is rewarded, such a structure of incentives can lead to the development of linkages and negotiation practices that will carry over into the phase of full political liberalization.

Democratic regimes, with their emphasis upon low state control, open party contestation, regular elections, and public accountability, provide features that can facilitate intergroup cooperation. Clearly, in the absence of an overriding agreement regarding norms and values, democratic regimes have been difficult to create and, once launched, have inevitably involved risks. Particularly under conditions of economic scarcity and weak state capacity, the uncompromising claims advanced by some regional, ethnic, religious, and ideological interests can prove highly threatening to basic system norms. The possibilities for adversarial and highly destructive politics notwithstanding, where democratic regimes have proved sustainable over time (Botswana, Mauritius, Senegal), they hold the greatest hope for developing constructive rules for managing state-society relations.[58] Such democratic regimes allow for the development of strong states and vibrant and active societies, thereby providing the basis for legitimate and well-informed governance.

In Nigeria, for example, the 1987 Political Bureau made a series of proposals regarding the lines of the new constitution, seeking to make ethnicity more manageable by creating a set of "truly integrative national institutions."[59] With this goal in mind, the Political Bureau recommended the maintenance of federalism, the enshrinement of the "federal character" (balanced recruitment) principle, the creation of additional states, a broadly inclusive two-party system, electoral provisions to ensure countrywide support for the president, and a revenue allocation system distributing significant percentages of the federation account directly to both the states and local governments. Larry Diamond appropriately points out that, in terms of facilitating cooperation among the country's many ethnic groups, such a structuring of relations "can be used to encourage cross- and transethnic forms of political mobilization."[60] The new constitutional system structured intergroup interactions to foster cooperation by encouraging the formation of broadly inclusive party systems and governmental coalitions, decentralizing administrative responsibilities, and manipulating electoral systems to promote shared transethnic concerns. Rules to encourage regular and fair elections made losing more acceptable because candidates, perceiving the shadow of the future political course, retained the hope of success in subsequent campaigns. A process was set in motion to encourage empathy among rival groups and factions, which—if it had not been subverted by elite corruption and backsliding in civilian times and then by military manipulation and the Abacha coup—might have provided incentives for political stability and for moderate and conciliatory behavior.

Majoritarian democracy, then, is distinguishable from its partially authoritarian counterparts in the determined way it structures incentives for cooperative behavior and in its increased capacity for developing norms of encounter that are likely to prove acceptable to the main societal groups. Building upon political reciprocity and negotiation, political leaders may become engaged in an extended learning process. They gain an appreciation of the high cost of mutually damaging encounters and eventually move on to create "a zone of overlapping, rather than zero-sum, agendas."[61] Seen in this light, the initial act of forging a constitution is not an end in itself but part of a larger process of confidence building that leads to repeated interactions. To the extent that state and societal elites succeed in establishing political routines of reciprocity and bargaining, inclusive cabinets and executive branches, and governance according to informal norms of proportionality and fairness, relations across groups may well become more predictable. In addition, networks of relations may emerge that will provide incentives for intergroup cooperation.

But in the real world, especially under conditions of dire poverty and evidence of elite self-interest, these positive-sum possibilities may remain logical but unrealizable. The struggle for scarce resources can take extreme forms, and ambitious politicians may make uncompromising demands and seek to outflank moderates within their own community. Moreover, majoritarian power can become the basis for a new tyranny, leading to concerns among minorities that they will be shut out of positions of power and have to endure the rule of others. Thus thoughtful observers such as W. Arthur Lewis urge West Africans to consider rewriting the rules of the democratic game to ensure that the politics of inclusiveness prevails.[62] Perhaps some such rewriting of the rules would enlarge democracy's relevance by promoting a more effective management of social conflict.

Internal Incentive Structures

Hegemonic regimes, to the extent that they rely on force and repression, offer minority leaders and groups little incentive to abide by the rules of the political game. Because political safeguards are not provided and norms are not shared, the incentive structure does little to promote cooperation and even encourages leaders to adopt damaging courses of action. The risks of association remain high, and, where conflict becomes intense, there may be no reliable domestic or international safety nets.

The possibilities for reducing insecurity increase significantly in polyarchical regimes. I see four main internal incentive (or trust-promoting) mechanisms that attempt to encourage the commitment of ethnic minorities to the social contract: constitutional guidelines for proportional allocations, electoral arrangements ensuring broad minority participation, elite power sharing at the political center, and decentralization and federalism. Although I will disaggregate these incentives, it is important to stress at the outset that to be effective, as in South Africa in the early transition period, they must be combined into a package; and it is the cumulative effect of this package that will prove critical in giving elites a reason to prefer moderate behavior.

Constitutional Guidelines for Proportional Allocations

Perceiving a connection between rules that fail to acknowledge intense ethnoregional conflicts and the equity claims that all groups make to public resources, some African regimes, such as Cameroun in the 1960s and Dahomey (now Benin) in the 1970s, have sought to promote conciliatory behavior by routinizing politics, seeking to ensure that allocations are distributed on a fair basis to all groups regardless of whether they are within the ruling coalition. Although mildly authoritarian regimes sometimes make use of formulas for proportionality to encourage intergroup cooperation, elite power-sharing and polyarchical regimes tend to be more systematic about using the proportionality principle when making their developmental allocations (which are especially easy to put into effect in such polyarchical and relatively advantaged countries as largely homogeneous Botswana). Ruling coalitions in the polyarchical regimes, knowing the social costs of mutually damaging ethnic-related conflicts, may be inclined to accept "intergroup equity as the major decision rule for the political system, superseding such alternative criteria as individual ability or social efficiency."[63] Given the potentially strong emotions surrounding the issue of resource allocation, governing elites are attracted to the proportionality principle because it represents a relatively easy and neutral decision rule to administer and is perceived to have equalizing effects.[64]

Provided ethnic demands continue to be reasonable and some adjustment is made in the proportionality arrangements to take account of demographic and other changes, it remains possible for African leaders to work within the political system to meet the guidelines of fairness. Using such guidelines will compensate ethnic minority interests and thereby encourage their confidence. Ensuring that all areas receive services and amenities, whether or not they have supported the ruling coalition, makes politics less threatening to political minorities. Indeed, redistributive policies can, on occasion, become a source of intense differences, but it seems even more certain that perceptions of discrimination in the allocation of scarce public resources will contribute to bitter ethnoregional antagonism—as the separatist actions in northern Somalia have illustrated only too clearly.[65]

Electoral Arrangements Ensuring Broad Minority Participation

In an effort to reassure ethnic minority groups that they do have a place in African society and to make politics generally less threatening, constitutional engineers have experimented with a variety of mechanisms intended to ensure at least minimal inclusion of these minorities in decisionmaking arenas. The possibility of being represented in the ruling coalition at the political center will, it is hoped, reduce the likelihood that militant flank parties will emerge and seek to outbid the dominant centrist party with uncompromising communal appeals (in South Africa, for example, the Conservative party versus the National party, or the Pan-Africanist Congress versus the African National Congress).

Inclusion, then, can be an incentive to abide by the rules of the game, encouraging moderate politicians and their supporters to play an active role in policy formulation and implementation and to behave in a generally cooperative manner. With their ethnic representatives a part of the centrist, ruling coalition, the respective memberships may come to feel that they have access to those in authority and that the power elite will be more responsive to their claims.

Two very different examples of electoral efforts to encourage inclusive politics in Africa point to the possibilities for experimentation in this respect. First, in an attempt to ensure that the president would have had the support of a broad-based constituency in Nigeria, the 1993 constitution provided that a candidate would have been deemed to have won a national election when that person had secured a simple majority of the total number of votes cast as well as one-third of the votes cast in each of at least two-thirds of the states. If no candidate met that requirement, then an electoral college consisting of all the members of the national and state assemblies, sitting in their respective houses and voting on the same day, would have elected a president on the basis of a simple majority of those present and voting.[66] Such provisions structure institutions so as to break down narrow parochialism and to build the confidence of smaller ethnic groups that the rules apply fairly to all peoples.[67]

Second, the preparedness of the major parties in Namibia and South Africa to adopt a modified system of proportional representation (PR) reflects their determination to reassure minority groups regarding their participation in the new ruling coalition. Recognizing that a "first-past-the-post" electoral system tends to polarize the society into winners and losers, the proponents of PR contend that a proportional system will be more informative about the full range of public preferences as well as more likely to enhance the prospects for including various parties in the decisionmaking bodies, since there is no expectation of a majority-take-all outcome. Such a system will also encourage the politics of inclusion because political parties will have an incentive to present lists containing representatives of all major interests and communities in order to have a chance to win at the polls.[68] The effect is to place an emphasis on diversity and moderation. Minority interests recognize that they have an opportunity to exert influence from within the dominant, centrist coalition, and they have a reason to act in a conciliatory manner and thus to avoid parochially inclined politicians' outbidding appeals to members in their own community.[69]

Commenting on the African National Congress's preparedness to opt for a PR system in South Africa, Timothy Sisk observed that "the ANC has been sensitive to a crucial aspect of electoral-system choice: the need to consider not only what is desirable [clear-cut parliamentary leadership], but also what is *possible* given the preferences of others."[70] By accepting PR, ANC leaders embraced rules that took account of the white minority's sense of personal and group insecurity and encouraged them to respond in a constructive and moderate way to the political changes taking place around them. In South Africa's case, PR is based upon the country's ethnically heterogeneous developmental regions.[71] Even so, the tendency of some identity groups to concentrate in certain areas gave an ethnic dimension to the PR arrangement adopted there.[72]

Elite Power Sharing at the Political Center

As I will note in chapter 3, where the leaders of a single ethnic group (and its allies) have captured control of state institutions and then excluded the representatives of other groups from the centers of power, the costs in terms of intense interethnic conflict have invariably proved high (apartheid South Africa, Ethiopia, Mauritania). In this respect, President Daniel arap Moi's underrepresentation of the Kikuyu in the Kenya cabinet following the 1992 election and his suspension of parliament in January 1993 (thereby denying the opposition an effective voice) may have done more to heighten ethnic tensions than his manipulation of the rules during the preelection period.[73] Those ethnic leaders remaining on the periphery feel barred from effective participation, and they often conclude, rightly or wrongly, that state policies threaten the political interests of their group and even their security.

One alternative to the dominance of a single group is the strategy of representing major ethnic and other interests in the ruling coalition. Such an approach assumes that, when the leaders of major ethnic and nationality interests are assured of participation in the governmental process, group conflict is more likely to be channeled along collaborative lines—whether this is done by formal political rules (Mauritius's "best loser" formula, South Africa's agreement to include major parties in the government under the interim constitution, or Nigeria's constitutional provisions on "federal character") or by informal rules (elite power-sharing arrangements made in Zambia, Kenya, Côte d'Ivoire, and Cameroun).[74]

In South Africa, the 1993 constitution provided that any party winning over 5 percent of the seats in the National Assembly would be included in the cabinet on a proportional basis for a five-year period. After the 1994 general election, this provision led to the establishment of a cabinet coalition of twenty-seven members: eighteen drawn from the ANC, six from the National party, and three from the Inkatha Freedom party. As Nelson Mandela said about ANC approval of this pragmatic grand coalitional arrangement, his party's stance "shows the priority we have given to national interests above that of our own."[75] Such a strategy of inclusion, compared with the majoritarian formula adopted in the 1996 constitution, sacrificed some party control over public affairs to promote a coalition of parties within the government, negotiating their interests at the center of power rather than withdrawing and failing to cooperate in the rebuilding of the country. By organizing intergroup relations to ensure routinized political participation, leaders are creating incentives for continued cooperation. As intra-elite learning takes place, empathy and confidence in each other's good intentions could well materialize. There are risks, to be sure, that opponents of this arrangement will mobilize their supporters to take political action along communal lines, attempting to flank leaders who have adopted a conciliatory position; however, those taking the path of accommodation can counter that the economic and political benefits of amicable relations for the society as a whole outweigh such risks. As Mandela has said, the South African agreement to include the representatives of major parties in the cabinet was "designed to create national unity and [was] not a simple power sharing formula."[76]

Decentralization and Federalism

Where ethnic groups are concentrated in specific areas of a country, it is possible to give expression to institutional pluralism through such mechanisms as devolution, decentralization, subregional autonomy, and federalism. The various arrangements differ significantly in the powers they assign to central, subregional, and local authorities, but they share the common objective of reducing conflict by separating groups into

distinct political units, each possessing responsibility for certain specified functions. In the past, African leaders such as Kwame Nkrumah
and Ahmed Sékou Touré, determined to concentrate political and economic power at the center, were suspicious of such autonomous
arrangements; they regarded them as creating pockets of power that
seemed likely to hinder the transformation of their countries. Early semi-
federal experiments were scuttled in Uganda, Kenya, Ghana, Sudan,
Cameroun, and Ethiopia, largely out of fear that political autonomy
would exacerbate intergroup tensions, weaken central control and, in
the worst cases, lead to secessionist activities.[77]

In recent times, however, some African leaders have become more
accepting of geopolitical expressions of ethnic identity. In Senegal,
Zambia, and Ghana, for example, decentralization measures have been
implemented that offer new scope for participation and influence in
local politics and administration. Niger's government, in an effort to bring
an end to the rebellion, signed an agreement with the Touaregs in 1994
giving them greater administrative autonomy.[78] The ruling elite in formerly Afro-Marxist Mozambique displayed increasing pragmatism regarding the symbolic role that traditional authorities will henceforth be permitted to play in the life of their country; in the 1992 peace accord, these
rulers agreed "to respect and not antagonize the traditional structures
and authorities where they are currently de facto exercising such authority." A conference on democratic governance and decentralization held in
1993 in Kampala went further, to broach the subject of giving traditional
authorities a political role by reserving seats for them on local councils.[79]

Even federalism, one of the fullest expressions of horizontally based
stratification arrangements, has won acceptance in Nigeria and in certain circles in Ethiopia and South Africa. Recommending that Nigeria
continue with a federal form of governance, the 1987 Political Bureau
described one alternative, "confederalism," as "the first dangerous step
toward the disintegration of Nigeria," and another, "unitarism," as failing
to take adequate account of "the centrifugal forces of the country's ethnic, social, linguistic, and religious pluralities and the historic experiences of uneven development among the various nationalities and geo-
graphical sections of the country which could ... seriously undermine
the growth of the Nigerian nation-state if they are not adequately contained in a political framework which is generally acceptable to all sections of the country."[80]

Federalism, therefore, was perceived by then-president Ibrahim
Babangida and key members of his administration as a political neces-

sity.[81] By dispersing limited powers to the states, it provided a minimally acceptable formula allowing the main interests to exercise at least some power and providing an incentive to act cooperatively with each other. As Donald Horowitz notes, federalism can "proliferate the points of power and so make control of the center less vital and pressing."[82] Given the overpoliticization that has long marked the struggle for power at the political center in Nigeria, this ability to spread state authority among a greater array of key actors can make politics less threatening and therefore encourage cooperation within the limited number of areas assigned to the central government. This can, however, also exacerbate conflicts if ethnically exclusivist governments that act repressively and refuse to allocate resources proportionately emerge at the subregional level.

In Ethiopia and South Africa, moves toward some form of federal structure have been in evidence, but it remains to be seen whether a consensus over this type of governance will, in fact, emerge. Since the downfall of Mengistu Haile Mariam's regime in Ethiopia, the new ruling Ethiopian Peoples' Revolutionary Democratic Front (EPRDF) has come to look more favorably on federalism as a useful confidence-building mechanism. Noting that "previous [repressive and centralizing] attempts to [unify Ethiopia] have led to wars, to fueling nationalistic tendencies," President Meles Zenawi argues that federal government is necessary to adjust to the realities of his country's ethnic character.[83] Therefore he has issued a series of proclamations declaring the right of "nations" to "administer [their] own affairs within [their] defined territory" and giving regional administrations legislative, executive, and judicial powers over all domestic matters, leaving aside such central responsibilities as defense, foreign affairs, and economic policy. Although intended to diminish conflict, such experiments with ethnic federalism could have the opposite effect, fueling secessionist movements and possibly encouraging new conflicts over territory and resources. The boundaries that the EPRDF set for the new subregions have created suspicions that might become the source of future problems, for they have favored Tigray and the Afars at the expense of the Amhara and the Somali Isaaks in the Awash Valleyland.[84]

In South Africa, the ANC and South African Communist party made major concessions on the powers of the subregions to the government, the Inkatha Freedom party, and the Afrikaner Volksfront in July 1993 to gain their support for the draft constitution. ANC representatives rejected any suggestion of an ethnically inspired federalism; even so, KwaZulu-Natal Province did come close to an ethnically based federal relationship, despite the fact that it contained a significant number of minorities. At that time, however, the autonomous powers of the subregions were increased, and ANC negotiators, recognizing federalism as an inducement for cooperative behavior, indicated that they were prepared to negotiate over additional powers and extra representation in the central legislature. Communist party negotiator Joe Slovo saw no reason to fear increasing subregional representation in the National Assembly: "This will cement a new SA rather than fragmenting it," he declared.[85]

The interim South African constitution of 1993, as finally composed, established nine provinces having both legislative and executive authorities. These authorities, subject to the constitution, were entitled to an "equitable" share of national revenues, as determined by an act of parliament, and, within limits set by parliament, they were permitted to levy taxes and surcharges. The provincial legislatures were vested with the power to make laws for their provinces in certain fields, including agriculture, health services, housing, public transport, roads, tourism, and traditional authorities.[86] Although the central government had overriding legal competence and financial capacity, the existence of relatively autonomous subregions reassured ethnic minorities about their ability to participate in decisional matters of importance to them.

In both Ethiopia and South Africa, then, reconfiguring institutions along federal lines was appealing as an incentive that well-intentioned leaders could use to advance mutual interests. Nevertheless, for all their disclaimers, the new governments in both cases appeared to fear the divisive effects of ethnically inspired federalism and to prefer strong central leadership. Federalism is viewed as recognizing and working with ethnic differences, but at a possible price of promoting ethnic insularity and losing territorywide purpose. The fiscal costs of decentralizing political power in a significant way are also a factor in the minds of the ruling elite. Hence, the dependence of these subregions upon central government transfers in these countries decreases the likelihood of establishing genuine federalism at this juncture. By one estimate, for example, some 88 percent of the money for provincial administrations in South Africa comes in the form of central government transfers.[87]

In brief, the thrust of the polyarchical regimes toward recognition of convergent interests, even a consensus on norms, acts as a general domestic incentive for intergroup cooperation. Polyarchy is not without its risks, particularly in its early period of development; where it becomes firmly established, however, it can play an important preventive role, organizing the relations between state and society so as to reduce ethnic fears and encourage amicable relations. Furthermore, where a package of structural incentives is used under such polyarchical regimes to achieve inclusiveness, administrative decentralization, electoral competition, and proportional outcomes, and where agreements on goals and values emerge, regularized patterns of relations can become accepted features of these societies.

In South Africa, for example, the 1993 draft constitution and postelection laws embraced a mix of inducements, including power sharing of cabinet positions, elections held in accordance with a system of proportional representation, subregional autonomy, and constitutional requirements on amnesty for a broad gamut of offenses. The effect was to enhance moderate politics and political stability. Rather than couch these appeals in ethnic terms and thereby outbid rival politicians within their own communities who were committed to the course of moderation, such a mix of incentives influenced African leaders to view a cooperative course as in their own best interests. These politicians perceived defection as costly to them and to their constituents and were thus swayed to work within the established system to maximize the benefits open to them under the constitutional arrangement.

The significance of this goes beyond conflict management objectives alone. Where conciliatory behavior and political stability can become accepted and create an enabling environment, political leaders will find themselves in a more advantageous position to launch far-reaching and sustained programs of economic and social development.

3

The Effect of Regimes on Conflict

Democratic governments use far less violence against their citizens than do authoritarian ones. Democracies also provide accepted channels for the expression of dissent and opposition within the system. Both government and opposition thus have fewer incentives to use violence against each other.

SAMUEL P. HUNTINGTON

The last chapter examined the various ways that Africa's state coalitions have structured their relations with society to promote positive, regularized interactions leading to cooperation. Three types of regimes—hegemony, elite power sharing, and polyarchy—have different patterns of societal interactions. But, in an environment of soft states, elite preferences will not automatically be put into effect nor will regime outcomes prove distinctive and significant. This raises the question of to what extent regime patterns of organization act as a link between strategy and both enacted policies and their outcomes. What are the consequences of these enacted policies for the management of ethnic and ethnoregional conflict?

I have already argued that the flow of negotiations and reciprocities is likely to prove critical to collaborative behavior over time. Such interactions tend to be most regular and persistent in the elite power-sharing and polyarchical regimes that accept the legitimacy of ethnic interests and allow these ethnic groups some scope for autonomous political action. The effect can be to lay a largely self-enforcing foundation for an operating consensus on the political rules. Nevertheless, the constraints imposed by economic scarcity, weak institutions, competing and conflicting demands, and political culture (clientelistic relations) make likely some sort of reliance upon a political machine and its penchant for quid pro quos across regime types in Africa. As Charles Lindblom observes: "Mutual adjustment among leaders . . . is inevitable even in a highly authoritarian system."[1] Despite such similarities, the different political thrusts of these various types of regimes propel them along somewhat dissimilar lines.

To compare and contrast the impact of regimes on ethnic conflict, I will examine how they perform in two of the main markets of internal political negotiations: political coalition formation and resource allocation.[2] By focusing on these two arenas of cooperation, I will compare what one game theorist, Martin Shubik, describes as the *core* of a cooperative solution (coalition formation) with the concept of *value* (resource allocation). Shubik regards the agreement to cooperate in the actual business of governance as more critical than the fair distribution of resources (that is, "how the proceeds of a game *should* be divided").[3] Therefore a comparison of these two cooperative forms should reveal something about the anticipated distribution of gains. Finally, I will comment upon the general consequences of regime patterns for reducing intergroup tensions and the implications of continuing high conflict for dispute settlement within states.

Before a discussion of the markets of exchange, one caveat is essential: although it may be assumed that political bargaining is likely to facilitate cooperation, efforts at domestic negotiations are not without risks. The linking of rival groups through a process of elite self-interest can sometimes lead to undesirable concessions.[4] There is a chance, as Manfred Halpern notes, that bargaining within a dominant elite over distributive resources "precludes the building of capacity—at the center or locally—to overcome the underlying incoherence."[5] Halpern's point that bargaining over tangible goods can mask incoherence, thus entrenching the status quo, is well taken. Yet, even so, bargaining may still have value. To the extent that such relationships contribute to the process of social learning, they enable ethnic and other social interests to gain understanding and sympathy for their rivals' concerns and possibly to learn to expect predictable patterns of behavior. Such learned relationships can make effective policy coordination feasible, for a sense of community emerges out of a mutual recognition of common expectations.

Forming Political Coalitions

Where the leaders of a single ethnic or nationality group and its allies have captured control of state institutions and then excluded the representatives of other groups from the centers of power (the Afrikaners in South Africa, the Amhara in Emperor Haile Selassie's Ethiopia, the Tutsi in Burundi), the costs in terms of intense interethnic conflict have invariably been high.[6] The rules of relationship create conflict because they fail to acknowledge the legitimacy of equity claims by all groups. Ethnic leaders remaining on the periphery of power feel barred from effective participation and often conclude, rightly or wrongly, that state policies threaten the political interests of their group and even their security. As Larry Diamond comments regarding the first Nigerian republic, the three ruling parties viewed the securing of state power "as essential to their survival," so that competition became intense among ethnic entrepreneurs for assured access to or, better yet, positions within, the state.[7] Excluded ethnic leaders exhibit feelings of powerlessness and comparative disadvantage that result, all too often, in ill feelings and negative group memories. In some instances, this can contribute to a loss of state legitimacy and even to the instigation of military coups and attempts at ethnoregional secession.

One alternative to the dominance of a single group is the process of representing plural interests at the political center, mainly through some form of inclusive coalition. When the leaders of major ethnic and other interest groups are assured of minimal participation in the governmental process—whether by formal or informal political rules—group conflict is more likely to become channeled along collaborative lines. Where authentic ethnic leaders are included and exert a significant amount of influence from within the ruling coalition, disagreements over the basic rules are likely to be minimized. This gives these leaders more incentive to control their constituencies and to direct their political activities along constructive channels. Moreover, inclusive coalitions involve learning within the elite about each other's concerns, thereby promoting empathy and conciliatory behavior. To the extent that regimes do operate according to widely understood formal or informal rules about involving major groups and their representatives on a proportional basis, a confidence-building (or trust-inducing) mechanism will be put in place that is likely to facilitate predictable rules of social relations, which are critical to the effective management of conflict.

By recognizing the existence of formal and informal decision rules on inclusiveness and the maintenance of an ethnic balance, observers are taking account of stable patterns of state-society relationships but by no means implying that these state leaders use some precisely calibrated formula of equity or that elite power sharing and polyarchical practices reach out to all levels of government and society. An acknowledgment of elite power sharing is not necessarily indicative of collaborative practices with nonelite interests, especially those far from the corridors of national power. As René Lemarchand notes regarding Chadian circumstances in the late 1980s, the hegemonic exchange "model obtains only at specific levels, i.e. the government and administration . . . and to a lesser extent perhaps at the UNIR (Union Nationale pour l'Independence et la Revolution)."[8] Although elite appointments can act as a rough indicator of group inclusion or exclusion, a full insight into political dynamics must also take account of "the constellation of roles and resources which define the political opportunity structure in the system"—in particular, which government or party officials hold relatively significant versus insignificant positions.[9]

Hegemonic Regimes and Limited Inclusion

How, then, have the different regime types compared in promoting interethnic cooperation through the organization of inclusive coalitions? Turning first to the African experience with hegemonic regimes, one can reasonably conclude that such regimes, in their basic reliance upon top-down, hierarchical control, make only limited use of broad-ranging coalitions to deal with the problem of integration. In Africa, the intensity of ethnic competition and conflict has at times buttressed essentialist perceptions, contributing in turn to the adoption of ethnically exclusive regimes (whether majority- or minority-dominated) intent on furthering their control and preventing a change of leadership elites (see figure 2-1). The dominant state elite, conscious of its own or its identity group's self-interests, limits effective representation in the decisionmaking process, thus blocking the access of out-groups to a large extent. This enables the government to delay raising many ethnic claims to a level requiring a political response.[10] As Donald Horowitz has observed, "Ethnic conflict has fed authoritarian tendencies."[11] In addition, the exclusivist and repressive tendencies of such regimes have further sharpened antagonisms between groups.

Clearly, hegemonic regimes vary considerably in their preparedness to apply the rule of reciprocity in any systematic manner. For the more enlightened and pragmatic, reciprocity is a political necessity born of state softness, but hardly a preference. In other instances, however, hegemonic leaders have either been scornful of the use of ethnic balancing as a matter of principle (Afro-Marxist Mozambique and Angola), or they have used state institutions to repress opposition leaders (Verwoerd's South Africa, Siad Barre's Somalia, Abboud's Sudan, Burundi, and Mauritania).

The Afro-Marxist regimes' disdain for a conscious policy of ethnic balancing was an expression of their leaders' perceptions of the primacy of socioeconomic class over ethnic patterns of stratification. Because the dominant political elites in these states did not wish to recognize ethnic identity groups as legitimate political interests, these regimes tended to play down the need for reciprocal relations with ethnic intermediaries.

In Ethiopia, the Derg, demonstrating continuity with the country's prerevolutionary past, in the late 1970s and 1980s allowed one nationality group, the Amharas, to largely dominate the decisionmaking process. In 1979 the Amharas filled fifteen out of sixteen seats on the Standing Committee and nine of the eleven remaining seats on the Derg's Central Committee. They also held thirty-one of the thirty-seven posts as government ministers and permanent secretaries, six of the seven commissioners, and thirteen of the fourteen provincial administrators.[12]

In Angola, although some important ethnic peoples (most notably the Ovimbundu and other southern ethnic groups) were not proportionately represented in the highly influential Political Bureau of the Popular Movement for the Liberation of Angola (MPLA), it is nonetheless important to recognize that efforts were made to represent other elements outside the regime's Luanda-Kimbundu support base. In 1979, for instance, the MPLA Political Bureau included six Kimbundu, three *mestiços*, one Bakongo, and two Cabindans. Increasing numbers of leaders from the Front for the Liberation of Angola (FNLA), whose Bakongo-based military forces were defeated in the 1970s, were also co-opted by the MPLA into high administrative positions.[13] The regime ruled out any compromise that would include UNITA within a governmental coalition on an autonomous basis, thus in effect excluding a large Ovimbundu constituency from meaningful participation.[14]

The Afro-Marxist regimes preferred instead to consolidate state control by means of bureaucratic agencies and party branches and, if necessary, military control. This refusal to accept the validity of ethnic interests or to include them in the political process had important implications for conflict management. Bureaucratic control mechanisms can succeed in suppressing minor conflicts and moderately intense ones, but because of state softness in Africa, these mechanisms might still be unable to cope with, and might instead even become the source of, intense and violent ethnic resistance (as with the Tigrean insurgency).

The disdain for ethnic balancing is also evident in the non-Afro-Marxist hegemonic regimes. In Mauritania, for example, the reluctance of the dominant Moorish (Arab-Berber) leaders to give the black population significant representation in the decisionmaking process led to considerable dissatisfaction and violence in 1966 and 1987. By the late 1980s, Mauritania's president, Ould Taya, exercising a rather shaky dominance over the country's black African population (including the Soninke, Tukulor, Wolof, and Peul), showed some willingness to build an inclusive coalition at Mauritania's political center. Although three relatively minor cabinet posts—involving sports, transport, and public works—were usually reserved for black Mauritanians, the power of the Mauritanian state remained concentrated in the hands of the dominant white Moorish community, particularly in the country's administrative structure. Not surprisingly, the Mauritanian government acted swiftly to squelch a coup attempt in 1987 involving Peuls in the army and to counter a clandestine black resistance movement led by the African Liberation Forces of Mauritania.[15]

Similarly, in Sudan the dominant state elite resists fully including genuine southern leaders in the main decisionmaking institutions. As I indicate in chapter 8, many southern Sudanese have complained that their region (including the provinces of Upper Nile, Equatoria, and Bahr el Ghazal) has been "neither proportionally nor adequately represented at the national level."[16] The South makes up about 30 percent of the country's population, yet it has been separated from the rest of Sudan by varying degrees of modernization, distinct colonial experiences, and different religious, cultural, and ethnic mixes. The result is that the leaders in the South are deeply suspicious of what they have perceived as the assimilationist policy thrust of the northern "Arabs" (whose 4 million people make up 39 percent of the country's total population).[17] In fact, class, culture, ethnicity, and regional identities have all reinforced one another, producing a conflict situation that has exploded into a series of bitter civil wars in the postindependence period.

Certainly, the domination of Sudan's northern politicians and military rulers and their general unwillingness to apply the proportionality principle for selecting cabinet ministers has contributed significantly to the conflict. Between 1958 and 1985, the various military and civilian governments displayed different coalition-building tendencies. The yearly average of southerners appointed to the cabinet during General Ibrahim Abboud's regime was 7.6 percent and, for General Gaafar el-Nimeiry, 7.2 percent, whereas the various civilian regimes, which tended toward a somewhat more conciliatory position on this issue, showed distinctly higher yearly averages (14.0 percent) and more inclination to appoint southerners to influential ministerial positions. During Abboud's period in office (1958-64), one southerner, Santino Deng, was retained in the cabinet, but in the relatively undistinguished post of minister of animal resources.[18] With Nimeiry's military intervention in April 1969, southerners were again appointed to less influential ministerial positions. In due course, Abel Alier was named minister for supply and internal trade and Joseph Garang, minister of state for southern affairs; the latter was depicted by southern leaders as "a Ministry without powers."[19] Although this pattern appeared to change under the military-led and fundamentalist-supported regime of Lieutenant General Omar Hassan Ahmed al-Bashir, the appointed southerners were not actually authentic spokesmen for their subregion, and all were appointed to fairly minor positions in the government.[20]

Clearly, the tendency of Sudan's various hegemonic regimes to build disproportionately representative ruling coalitions raised the level and intensity of North-South conflict. John Garang de Mabior, the commander in chief of the Sudan People's Liberation Army—in a speech following al-Bashir's intervention and 1989 suspension of the constitution—called for the establishment of a broad-based interim government of national unity. In fact, he had sound reasons to be concerned. According to one estimate, only two of the thirteen northern Sudanese in the government were "decidedly neither members nor sympathisers of the Muslim Brothers," and one of the three southerners was regarded as "an active" Islamic National Front member.[21] Thus on recruitment issues, al-Bashir remained part of the exclusivist military tradition, limiting the participation of an effective southern opposition voice and gravely complicating the process of developing effective rules and routines for political cooperation.

The link between practices of exclusion and increases in interethnic conflict in authoritarian regimes is also evident in apartheid South Africa, where the Afrikaner-dominated regime (1948-94) was a quintessential example of hegemonic repression in its relations with the black majority while being a polyarchy in its interwhite interactions. An Afrikaner political machine imposed executive power from the top down, while the predominantly Afrikaner security establishment provided support for the P.W. Botha government (less so under the subsequent government of F.W. de Klerk).[22] As a consequence of executive-military predominance, the cabinet and parliament were generally subordinated to the executive branch; even so, these centers of power, led in South Africa by the Afrikaner-guided National party, continued to exert some influence over policy choices.[23] Moreover, the parliament and cabinet illustrated the general dominance over the structures of power by the 4.6 million whites (60 percent Afrikaners) in a country of 36 million people. The House of Assembly was elected solely by the white community, the "Coloureds" and Asians voted for separate and less powerful legislative chambers, and the black community was excluded from the electoral process and lacked a separate legislative chamber of its own.[24]

Under the Botha administration, in early 1989, the cabinet for general affairs was exclusively Afrikaner in composition (although it had previously included one "Coloured" member and one Indian member as ministers without portfolio); the deputy ministers included fifteen Afrikaners, two English South Africans, and one Indian South African.[25] This situation was modified slightly under Botha's successor, de Klerk, for in September 1989, two English-speaking members of parliament were appointed to the eighteen-person cabinet; significantly, however, no one from either the Coloured or Indian chambers was included. When the principle of inclusiveness was put into effect by the government of Nelson Mandela following the 1994 elections, it contributed to an easing of intergroup tensions in the period immediately following.

Yet even authoritarian regimes have at times recognized the need to incorporate representatives of a country's major interests in high party and governmental posts. Under Nigeria's military administration in the 1970s, the government sought to avoid damaging competition and to reinforce the confidence of ethnic and other interests in the political system by making extensive use of the proportionality principle when recruiting government elites.[26] Similarly, several civilian-led hegemonic regimes sought to avoid conflict by making quiet use of the practice of "ethnic arithmetic" in selecting candidates for high political office. Guinea's Ahmed Sékou Touré provided an excellent example of the use of proportionality practices in a highly authoritarian context.[27]

In Zaire, certain proportional practices were in evidence, although these were largely symbolic in content. Some observers detected a preference for people from Equateur province when recruiting members of the government, especially in the Zairian army, but they also stressed

President Mobutu Sese Seko's tactic of co-opting people into the governmental coalition from other ethnic groups (particularly Lunda representatives from the Shaba region and Luba leaders from Kasai) in an effort to prevent any minister or group of ministers from having too much influence and thereby defusing the ethnic issue.[28] A survey of the regional origins of 212 regime ministers and high party officials who held office from 1965 to 1975, conducted by Crawford Young and Thomas Turner, revealed a relatively balanced representation of ethnic groups over time.[29] Despite the strong taboos against politicized ethnicity in Mobutu's hegemonic regime, the continuing practice of ethnic proportionality was deemed necessary to demobilize ethnic opposition. Nevertheless, minority spokespeople have often dismissed as inadequate these and other efforts by hegemonic regimes to promote national unity through the co-optation of out-groups.[30]

The Elite Power-Sharing and Polyarchical Regimes

As noted above, some elements of reciprocity and bargaining surface from time to time in hegemonic regimes; however, for the polyarchical and elite power-sharing regimes these represent the basic political logic.[31] To the extent that state elites succeed in establishing political routines of reciprocity, building inclusive cabinets, and operating according to informal norms of proportionality and fairness, outbidding practices are likely to be contained, and networks of relations may emerge that promote sustained intergroup cooperation. The hard-line Hutu reaction to the power-sharing provisions of the 1993 Arusha accords is something of an exception here.[32] In general, however, it seems fair to contend that the thrust of these regimes, particularly the more democratic variants, toward an acceptance of principles of inclusion and balanced representation acts as a general incentive for intergroup cooperation. When "all the relevant political forces find it best to continue to submit their interests and values to the uncertain interplay of the institutions," then democracy can become "self-enforcing," and stable and reinforcing rules of relationship can be said to have emerged.[33]

Partial Experiments with Polyarchy and Broad Inclusion

Certainly, some African countries have experimented briefly with selected polyarchical and elite power-sharing practices that did not culminate in stable regimes. The overthrow of Burundi's first democratically elected government after four months in office by a Tutsi-led army in 1993 underlines the fragility of polyarchical experiments in desperately poor and deeply divided societies. Where rules and procedures on such matters as competitive elections, inclusiveness, and proportionality have failed to gain the necessary adherence or the military has felt uncertain about its future under polyarchies, these experiments with constitutionalism have proved unable to set the parameters for acceptable behavior.

Independent Uganda's experience with constitutional government and power sharing has been "vigorous" and sometimes "violent."[34] To facilitate the independence negotiations with both the Baganda secessionists and the British, President Milton Obote showed effective leadership, agreeing to a constitution that provided for competitive elections and a "federal relationship" with Buganda and the Western Kingdoms and Busoga.[35] Obote also sought to reassure the Baganda leaders in September 1961 by forming a political alliance between his Uganda People's Congress (UPC) and Kabaka Yekka (Kabaka Only), a neotraditionalist movement committed to maintaining the unity and autonomy of the kingdom of Buganda.

However, it soon proved difficult to maintain a constitutional system in a highly pluralistic and intensely competitive climate, so a confrontation between the coalition partners emerged. Obote terminated the alliance with Kabaka Yekka in August 1964 and subsequently ended the federal relationships with Buganda and the Western Kingdoms. Despite the 1966 shift toward a more authoritarian style of leadership, however, Obote still found it necessary to accommodate the realities of ethnic pluralism. Although he disapproved of ethnic representation and balancing in principle, he nonetheless continued to show himself a master of informal hegemonic exchange practices, including cabinets carefully balanced along ethnic lines.[36]

Then, following Amin's fall from power, Obote's UPC was eventually restored, bringing with it considerable Langi and Acholi influence in the cabinet and army. Several Baganda and Basoga people did receive ministerial appointments, but many observers regarded these people as lacking in stature and unable to represent their constituents effectively.[37] Moreover, important elements, such as Yoweri Museveni and his Ankole-based National Resistance Army, remained outside the ruling coalition, revealing the government's failure to bring important ethnoregional leaders within the ruling circle. Widespread perception of northern dominance under Obote's rule contributed to the bitter resistance against his second administration and ultimately led to his downfall in 1985. Significantly, Museveni, as the newly inaugurated head of state in 1986, made a concerted effort to offer leadership by appointing a broad-based government, including prominent Baganda, Acholi, and Langi representatives as well as leaders of the military factions and various political parties. Inclusion was viewed as the price that a soft, no-party state must pay to ensure political stability.[38] Although Museveni's cabinets were expanded to include as many as forty-eight members by the spring of 1989, this stratagem did not work quite as well as expected, for some ministers withdrew from his cabinets over time, leaving the regime vulnerable to new divisive forces.

In Zimbabwe, tension and suspicion also marked the coalitional strains between Robert Mugabe's Zimbabwe African National Union (ZANU) and Joshua Nkomo's Zimbabwe African People's Union (ZAPU) during the early and mid-1980s. Between the pre-independence election in 1980 and the first postindependence election in 1985, ZANU's electoral strength rose dramatically; meanwhile, ZAPU's support, based largely on the Ndebele people, declined. In February 1982 Nkomo was dismissed from the coalition cabinet, and by November 1984 the last two ZAPU (but not Ndebele) members of the cabinet had been ousted from their administrative posts.[39] Zimbabwe was moving, some feared, toward becoming a de facto one-party state.

Following ZANU's victory in the 1985 general election (winning sixty-three of seventy-nine seats in the common roll election), Mugabe pursued his goal of consolidating power with renewed determination. Even so, Mugabe found his attempts to establish a united, one-party regime frustrated by his inability to win a single seat in Nkomo's Matabeleland stronghold; this disappointment was heightened by Ian Smith's hold on the white members elected in a separate vote before the general elections. As a consequence, Mugabe unleashed a "get tough" strategy.[40] He strengthened ZANU's hand by establishing an executive presidency, abolishing the Senate, and ending the practice (designed by the Lancaster House conference) of reserving twenty of one hundred House of Assembly seats for whites (see chapter 6).

Meanwhile, the ZANU-ZAPU unity talks, which appeared to be making little headway, revived in 1987 as Nkomo agreed publicly to accept Mugabe as the leader of a unified party. With this initiative, the talks started up anew and gained momentum, ultimately resulting in the December 22, 1987, unity accord. The accord clearly provided an incentive for intergroup cooperation, bringing the country's major partisan and ethnic interests within the central decisionmaking arena. As one ZAPU dissident told reporters: "We felt excluded from Government after independence. . . . The Government, however, has now offered us a chance to rebuild."[41] Nkomo himself came away from the agreement as one of two party vice presidents and, after a subsequent cabinet reshuffle, as the third most senior member of this high executive body; moreover, other key ZAPU members were allocated seats in the cabinet and in the ZANU politburo and central committee.[42] The upshot of this was a noticeable easing of ethnic tensions, in particular the decline of terrorism in Matabeleland.

Inclusiveness has also resulted in elite power-sharing regimes, where informal rules and routines serve to facilitate the representation of the major social interests on a roughly proportional basis. These pacts among dominant class interests—whether formal or informal, authoritarian or openly competitive—are unquestionably elitist in their thrust and therefore only partially inclusionary. Nevertheless, their ability to recruit relatively inclusive cabinets and party executives results in participation by the main ethnic, ethnoregional, and other interest group spokespeople in the key decisionmaking processes, albeit on an ad hoc and rather temporary basis. The preconditions for such power-sharing regimes include pragmatic elite political cultures and values, the availability of moderate material resources, and deferential clientelistic structures, all conditions that are likely to coexist only temporarily in Africa. Nevertheless, in such postcolonial regimes as those of Kenyatta in Kenya, Houphouët-Boigny in Côte d'Ivoire, Ahidjo and Biya in Cameroun, and Museveni in Uganda, the dominant leader did pursue inclusive strategies, appointing a roughly proportional representation of the main ethnic and subregional spokespeople to their cabinets and high party positions.

The effect of such informal practices is to promote cooperation and negotiations among key societal notables in their interactions at the political center. Kenya's Jomo Kenyatta accepted the need to co-opt the main ethnic and subregional strongmen into the ruling one-party coalition and was relatively open in his attempt to combine strong central leadership with limited bargaining relations within the ruling elite. The resulting state-ethnic coalition of elite spokespeople is, according to one observer, characterized "by competition and bargaining between a number of ethnic groups and more modern interest associations on the one hand, and government on the other."[43] Such national leaders seek variously to compensate for state weakness and to defuse state-ethnic conflicts by skillfully using ministerial and other appointments to balance ethnoregional and other interests in their societies. Competition for government positions and public resources can then take place within the system, undercutting rebellious types of activity, including separatism.

However, the hegemonic exchange regime lacks legitimacy in the eyes of the general public. Not only does it severely limit full and meaningful participation and access to information, but at times it even takes a destructive turn, as leaders gain an incentive to divert public resources to fulfill their essentially private purposes. Even so, where genuine democracy appears threatening to elite interests in the future, new forms of elite power sharing may emerge. In 1995, with the discussions of the future Nigerian constitution, there was an airing again of the idea of "diarchy," in which authority is shared between the military and publicly elected civilians. Also, some variant of the elite pact may well be used as a conflict-regulating mechanism in other sub-Saharan states (for example, Somalia and Liberia). Given individual and communal insecurities and the soft-state conditions prevailing in many African countries, ruling coalitions are likely to be attracted to such forms of elite power sharing as an internationally acceptable alternative to full democracy.

Polyarchies and Coalitional Politics

In the best of circumstances, where the public participates actively in the political process and the government is responsive, transparent, and accountable, there is an implied agreement in the society about the process embedded in the regime. Norms of reciprocity are likely to develop and to promote regular and frequent interactions between state and society. As such, fully democratic regimes seem uniquely well designed to manage conflict, for they combine vibrant and active civil associations with a dynamic and secure state.[44] A broad-based inclusion of the society and its leaders in the political life of the country lays a foundation for legitimate governance. Of course, polyarchies are feared in some quarters because they provide openings for ethnic mobilization, particularly through the party system and the outbidding activities of elites at the margins. The interplay among rival organizations and actors must take place within a well-understood normative order, one that assures that demands remain reasonable and that contestation proceeds according to the rules of the game. However, where this overriding agreement on democratic rules of encounter contains its own incentive for cooperation—that is, self-interest becomes the basis for acting moderately over time—the effect is likely to be stable competition and intergroup cooperation.[45] This agreement can be undercut where ethnic fears escalate and calculations of self-interest shift substantially, but short of this, polyarchies exhibit a surprising ability to absorb shocks.

As I have indicated, polyarchical experiments were launched in the postcolonial years, only to fall apart in the face of elite ambition, economic hardship, overpoliticization, and corruption. Sudan, Ghana, and Nigeria, for example, have all witnessed cycles of change, in which polyarchy was supplanted by military or civilian authoritarianism, and then, as these governments became fatigued by endless political negotiations, they have given way or even orchestrated the return to civilian rule—and a possible new cycle of regime changes. In each case, the interludes of polyarchy were briefer than the experience with civilian or military authoritarianism. In weak civil societies unable to oppose hegemonic rule effectively, polyarchy often seemed too fragile to endure.

In a few cases—Mauritius, Gambia (until 1994), Botswana, and Senegal (after 1976)—polyarchy proved sufficiently resilient to withstand the postcolonial pressures of economic decline, political inflexibility, corruption, and social malaise. The competitive party systems in these societies have survived intact, and their governments remain reasonably responsive to the demands of societal interest groups. Yet, if these four cases attest to the viability of polyarchy during the dark days of the 1970s and 1980s, they can hardly be considered a representative sample of African countries. All of them are relatively small in either size or population. Their social configurations are also somewhat unusual: examples are the support that Senegal's *marabouts* (religious leaders) have given the ruling party and, in Botswana, the stabilizing influence of the Tswana, the preponderant ethnic core group.

In the late 1980s and early 1990s, Africa's middle-class elite expressed increasing dissatisfaction with the repressive tactics, corruption, and inefficiency of the bureaucratic centralist regimes then in power and demanded decisive moves toward political liberalization. African intellectuals became increasingly vocal in dismissing the economic justification for continued authoritarian one-party rule, namely, that hegemonic regimes were a shortcut to rapid economic development. Arguing that authoritarian regimes had shown lower levels of growth than their polyarchical counterparts, Peter Anyang' Nyong'o contended that "authoritarianism has stifled development"; rather than encouraging capital accumulation, it led "to increased consumption by bureaucrats and kleptocratic politicians."[46]

The impact of this African call for political liberalization was enormous, and by the end of 1991, a large proportion of the countries in sub-Saharan Africa had committed themselves to some form of democratic governance. Although reforms in Côte d'Ivoire and Kenya were limited, those in Mali and Benin created the possibility of more thorough-going regime change.

The polyarchical model opens up real avenues for inclusion and participation. Polyarchy fosters a bargaining culture in which those who are in power can afford to lose. Even in the 1980s, the government in power in Mauritius was ready to step down following an electoral defeat. By the 1990s, such preparedness to abide by the rules of the game became more commonplace; for example, a democratically elected government in highly pluralistic Benin organized a hotly contested national election in March 1996, and when former President Mathieu Kerekou reemerged and won, outgoing President Nicéphore Soglo respected this outcome and stepped down. And not only do polyarchies create room for maneuvering (coalitions can form and reform), but this type of regime is more willing to accommodate on such issues as power sharing, decentralization, and regional autonomy, thereby giving ethnic and subregional minorities a sense of security as well as opportunities to participate in governance. For example, the local council system in Botswana is described as "the centerpiece of [its] democracy."[47]

Polyarchies in Africa also use formal constitutional provisions to ensure inclusiveness. In Nigeria, both the 1979 federal constitution and the constitution of the ruling National Party of Nigeria (NPN) sanctioned the values of inclusiveness and proportionality in their formal rules. The 1979 constitution, expressly seeking to incorporate major ethnic and state interests in the decisionmaking process, provided that the country's "federal character" must be taken into account when making federal appointments, and in line with this principle, article 135(3) stated that the president shall appoint at least one minister from each state and that person shall be an indigene of that state. The strategy of ethnic balancing became "the supreme principle of state and government business" in Nigeria.[48]

The "federal character" principle had a mixed impact. It did manage to prod those in power to close some gaps in the areas of higher education, the recruitment of minorities into cabinet positions, and public service appointments, although continuing northern control of the ministries of defense and internal affairs showed that numerical balancing could be reconciled with unequal effective control.[49] Nonetheless, some

Nigerian analysts charge it with creating a variety of other problems: heightened expectations and politicization, the use of noneconomic criteria in determining the location of industries (such as the steel industry), weakened civil service professionalism and morale, and an overloaded bureaucracy.

The centrality of Nigeria's 1979 rules on balanced representation can be seen by their capacity to survive several changes of government. Even though the constitution itself was set aside following Major General Muhammadu Buhari's 1983 military coup, the informal practices of coalition formation remained largely intact. Buhari's Supreme Military Council displayed what some called a "northern character"; it nonetheless included both Yoruba and Igbo members.[50] Moreover, the eighteeen-member Federal Executive Council contained a member from every state except Bendel, and that state was compensated by the selection of one of its own as the head of the civil service.[51]

Major General Ibrahim Babangida, who came to power during a bloodless coup in 1985, sought to adopt a more liberal posture than his predecessor. Among other things, he took a more open approach to the recruitment of southerners into high administrative positions (five of his twenty-two cabinet members were Yoruba speakers, with two appointees each from Oyo and Ogun).[52] In time, however, Babangida's commitment to representativeness seemed to wane. In January 1990, he assumed command of the defense and interior ministries, thereby removing the two leading southern members of the cabinet. This action led to complaints that the cabinet was not balanced in ethnic and subregional terms, contributing to discontent.[53] In April 1990, the country was gripped by an attempted coup led by southern army officers, who gave a radio address about the marginalization of the peoples of the South and Middle Belt and announced the temporary excision from the country of the five most northern states of Sokoto, Borno, Katsina, Kano, and Bauchi. The coup attempt was quickly crushed, but it did reveal the extent of misgivings among southern elites about their perceived loss of power at the political center.

In 1986, Babangida, beginning preparation for the return to civilian government, selected the members of a Political Bureau to identify the basic problems that had led to past failures and to make recommendations for a new constitution. Throughout the bureau's deliberations, the continuities with the 1979 constitution were evident. The Political Bureau said that "the principle of 'federal character' should be taken into consideration in the appointment of ministers and commissioners [and that] the national executive organ and the principal organs of each political party [should] reflect the federal character of Nigeria."[54]

This principle was followed in the 1992 constitution, which stated that the composition of the federal government and its agencies is to reflect the country's federal character.[55] Then, under the Abacha regime's 1995 draft constitution, the constitutional conference provided that in making appointments to the high civil service and executive, the president "shall have regard to the federal character of Nigeria and the need to promote national unity."[56] Clearly a *regime*, in the sense of understood norms of acceptable political behavior and action, had become apparent regarding the issue of federal character in Nigeria.

Allocating Resources

A political coalition represents the core of a cooperative solution, and the fair distribution of resources is a prime example of the somewhat less critical issue of value. This is not to deny that patterns of distributing scarce resources are highly important to conflict management. Ethnic groups have quite frequently mobilized behind their intermediaries to compete effectively for a proportional (even an extraproportional) share of public resources. This mobilization of group members for competition is likely to contribute substantially to the group's unity and sense of purpose over the years.[57] "Ethnic groups persist," Robert Bates asserts, "largely because of their capacity to extract goods and services from the modern sector and thereby satisfy the demands of their members."[58] In this respect, ethnic groups can be likened to the interest-defined groups that they compete with for state-controlled resources.

It is relatively easy to show that the link between hegemonic regimes and what Shubik calls the *core* issue of ethnic inclusion carries over into what he characterizes as the *value* question of equitable distribution of public resources.[59] In the case of hegemony, there is a connection between some groups' dissatisfaction over the process embedded in the regime and the outputs and outcomes of that process (the unfair distribution of resources). Unless the main ethnic groups can be satisfied as to the fairness of the means of reaching decisions about distributions as well as the fairness of the decisions themselves, the conflict management process is not likely to prove satisfactory.

To start with, it is useful to look briefly at white racial hegemony in apartheid South Africa in terms of its skewed social allocations, particularly regarding inequities in landholding and public spending on education, health, housing, and welfare.[60] A consistent pattern emerges of favoritism for the relatively advantaged white community. During the apartheid era, whites made up roughly one-eighth of the total population, yet 86 percent of the country's agricultural land was set aside for their use. This inequity was further perpetuated by resource allocation patterns: $567 million of the $700 million allocated for agricultural purposes was set aside for white farmers.[61] In the first ten years of President Botha's rule, the number of African children enrolled in school rose from 3 million to nearly 6 million, and expenditures for African education climbed from $70 million to over $350 million. Yet the government still allocated ten times as much to each white child as to each black African child; the teacher-student ratio for whites was 1 to 19.2, whereas that for blacks was 1 to 41.[62] These relative expenditure patterns improved somewhat under de Klerk's presidency. In the 1990–91 fiscal year, government expenditure for education rose by 16.1 percent, although 3.8 times as much was allocated to each white child as to his black counterpart.[63] This disregard of the majority's demands for equitable treatment inevitably produced conflict.

Further evidence of a link between a hegemonic regime and allocative values skewed in favor of a relatively advantaged group or subregion can be gleaned from Sudanese data. As in many African countries, colonial rule in Sudan resulted in different rates of subregional modernization. The colonial government's investments and social expenditures were channeled primarily into the agriculturally developed and relatively urbanized and industrialized areas to the north and south of Khartoum and parts of Northern and Kassala Provinces. Tim Niblock estimates that these areas received eight times as much public and private investment as the three southern provinces and three times as much as Kordofan and Darfur.[64] The resulting uneven development continued in postcolonial times, heightening the conflict between the relatively advantaged northerners and the less advantaged southerners. B. Yongo-Bure estimates allocations to the South from 1946 to 1951 to be 9 percent of total national investments. He gives a figure of between 3.3 and 4.4 percent for the Southern Region from 1951–56 and concludes that little was invested in the South between 1956 and 1969.[65]

Southerners, seeking to use the benefits of development to further subregional equity, complained about their share of current and long-term developmental allocations in the period that followed.[66] Thus Jacob Alier Chol writes:

> The People's Regional Assembly found that the Southern Region was allocated a sum of £s 44.4 million ... out of a total of £s 307 million for the whole country for the fiscal year 1977/78. This represented only a 14% share, when the Region ought to have got about 33% of the total development allocations, since the South is one-third of the country by population. For 1978/79, the allocation to the Southern Region was £s 33.8 million ... out of £s 332.2 million for the whole country. The Southern share here turned out to be only 11%.[67]

Although Sudan's distributions did move closer to the guidelines on proportionality by the early 1980s (with 79.8 percent of the revenue allocated to the North in 1980–81),[68] the gap between North and South in terms of quality-of-life indicators had become so wide that proportionality in itself would have been insufficient to guarantee fairness. In this hegemonic regime, then, the dominant northern coalition was able to skew allocations in favor of its own areas (in particular, the areas around Khartoum and Gezira) at the expense of the periphery (in the upper North, Darfur, Kordofan, and the South). The consequence was to intensify interregional tensions.[69]

Finally, the link between ethnic dominance in a hegemonic regime and skewed ethnoregional distribution patterns is obvious during Emperor Haile Selassie's reign in Ethiopia (1930–74). Selassie, who concentrated power in the bureaucracy at Addis Ababa, recruited an estimated 60 to 70 percent of the high central government officials and provincial governors from among the Amhara of Shoa Province for his cadre of rulers.[70] Amharic was "the language of power," and the bureaucratic elite used this power to limit public participation and play down the urgency of economic and social development in the hinterland areas.[71] Available developmental resources were used to promote growth in the predominantly Amhara provinces of Shoa, Addis Ababa, Gojjam, and Begemdir and, to some extent, Tigre and Wollega. On the eve of the Ethiopian revolution, Edmond Keller notes, some 70 percent of Ethiopia's industrial activities were concentrated in Addis Ababa and Asmara. Moreover, central allocations for such social services as health and education showed continuing neglect of the relatively disadvantaged southern provinces. "As with education," Keller observes, "the best and largest number of health care services were clustered in Addis

Ababa and other urban areas. By the end of 1973, there were only 85 hospitals in the entire country; 25 of these were in Shoa Province, and more than half that number were in Addis Ababa."[72] This neglect of the periphery helped to foment the 1974 revolution.

The revolution did represent a shift toward the value issue on more egalitarian allocations, particularly regarding education.[73] Thus the number of students in government schools and universities nearly quadrupled between 1973–74 and 1983–84, albeit at a loss in educational quality. The government sought, in principle, to establish a secondary school in every province, but it was prevented from accomplishing this by the rebellion that broke out in parts of the North and Southeast. Thus, despite the gains in distributing educational opportunities more evenly among provinces in postrevolutionary Ethiopia, insurgent movements became more determined in their opposition, suggesting that, in this case at least, the core of a cooperative solution (inclusion in the dominant coalition) may be a more fundamental objective than such value issues as the way resources are distributed.

Clearly, state elites in these and other hegemonic regimes tend to use their positions of power to skew distributive patterns in favor of their own ethnic or subregional support group, and often with conflict-producing consequences. On the contrary, state elites in the elite power-sharing and polyarchical regimes have been more prepared to allocate public resources according to the principle of proportionality, that is, the distribution of state revenue capital assets among ethnic peoples or subregions on the basis of their relative numbers. Because ethnic leaders and groups are more satisfied with the fairness of the means of reaching decisions in polyarchies than in the more elitist power-sharing regimes, however, there is a tendency for the general public to be more suspicious of distributional outputs and outcomes in the elite power-sharing regimes.

In polyarchical Botswana, where the Botswana Democratic party has an assured base among the Bamangwato and Bakwena peoples, the regime is reportedly quite evenhanded in allocating public resources among the subregions.[74] Surprisingly, in light of evident scarcities, the government has even gone beyond this on some occasions to employ the principle of extraproportionality (or redistributive equity). By putting principles of proportionality into effect, more often than not government leaders are aware of the social costs of a mutually damaging ethnic and subregional conflict and, hence, are willing to accept "intergroup equity as the major decision rule for the political system, superseding such alternative criteria as individual ability or social efficiency."[75] By benefiting all units according to their relative numbers, the proportionality principle can prove minimally acceptable as "fair" to all major ethnoregional groups. As such, it establishes rules that facilitate tacit, if not explicit, bargains over tangible goods and services, thereby promoting interethnic and interregional cooperation; in effect, it becomes an incentive for state-ethnic and interethnic cooperation.

Evidence of the use of the proportionality principle in allocations among Africa's subregions requires statistical data from an extended time period.[76] Such data are neither readily available nor reliable; so, when procured, they must be put forward most tentatively. Even so, data on budgetary allocations among subregions from Nigeria (polyarchical during part of this period) and Kenya (an elite power-sharing regime during much of this time) do indicate a tendency toward proportional allocative values in the late 1970s and early 1980s. In the Nigerian road programs, the index of variation between 1975–76 and 1979–80 decreased significantly from 1.18 to 0.48. In health, it declined slightly from 0.96 to 0.88, while in education the decline was from 0.70 to 0.51. In Kenya, between 1974–75 and 1982–83, the hospital programs index decreased from 1.01 to 0.89 and education programs from 0.53 to 0.45. However, in the Kenya road programs, the index of variation did rise from 0.44 to 0.70.

The correlation measurements between different time periods also point to some interesting changes in rank order. The road data on oil-producing Nigerian states show per capita expenditures declining by more than half in relatively advantaged Rivers and Mid-Western; Rivers (but not Mid-Western) fell significantly in rank from second in 1975–76 to eighth position in 1979–80. However, the health data show relatively disadvantaged North-Eastern rising from twelfth position to fifth, and the education data also indicate that relatively disadvantaged North-Central jumped from twelfth to fourth position. Yet, on the whole, what stands out is the general stability in the rankings for the other subregions. Although the 1975–80 plan period was a heady time of oil-based prosperity, Nigerian policymakers can be described as moving cautiously toward greater proportionality in allocations.

In non-oil-producing Kenya, several indications of increasing proportionality were also observable. In contrast with past preferences that favored predominantly Kikuyu Central Province, a somewhat greater tendency toward proportional allocation appeared in the initial period after Daniel arap Moi, a Tugan from western Kenya, acceded to the presidency in 1978. The allocations to relatively advantaged Nairobi declined from 1.16 in 1975–76 to 0.16 in 1982–83 for roads, and those to the relatively advantaged Central Province fell across the board, quite noticeably in the case of educational allocations (from 1.64 to 1.16). Meanwhile, relatively disadvantaged and largely Somali-speaking North-Eastern Province showed large increases in per capita allocations for district hospitals (0.67 to 2.44) and schools (0.21 to 0.79).[77] In the face of growing scarcities, then, Kenya's various leaders managed from 1974 to 1983 to make progress toward applying the proportionality principle in their subregional allocations.

As a standard of behavior, the principle of extraproportionality has received support in both elite power-sharing and polyarchical regimes and, in some cases, in authoritarian-inclined states. Thus former president Ahmadou Ahidjo of the Cameroun called for a policy of *developpement equilibre* among the subregions; Zambia's former president, Kenneth Kaunda, urged urban workers to restrain their wage demands to enable the government to reallocate resources to the rural areas; and Ghana's former president, Hilla Limann, promised Ghanaians that his administration would create an equitable system for the distribution of development, social services, and public facilities to help reverse the rural-urban imbalance in the country.[78]

Without attempting to overstate the commitment of these governments to extraproportional allocations, I wish to point out that, despite an evident scarcity of resources, some governments have conformed to their stated principles on redistribution. In Tanzania, Zambia, and Ghana, governments have, albeit irregularly, established priorities on the allocation of public resources that are redistributive in intention, if not in result. Statistics from Tanzania for 1969–70 to 1974–75 confirm a widespread impression of increasing subregional equity in public expenditure patterns, especially in such fields as health and education. Relative inequities in governmental expenditures declined by 30 percent during this period, from a relative deviation of 1.31 in 1969 to 0.91 in 1974 in per capita distributions of development funds to the subregions.[79]

Zambia's 1971 estimates showed considerable consistency between the government's redistributive principles and planned allocations. In such areas as authorized expenditures on health, feeder roads, and rural development by province, per capita allocations were lower for the relatively advantaged line-of-rail provinces than for the relatively disadvantaged provinces off the line of rail.[80] With per capita expenditures on rural development, the only major exception to this pattern was in the line-of-rail but less industrialized Southern Province. Because the relatively disadvantaged subregions had a limited capacity to absorb the additional allocations, 1971 expenditures in these subregions failed to keep pace with authorized capital fund expenditures. In 1971, actual expenditures in the relatively advantaged Copperbelt and Central Provinces exceeded allocations by 153 percent; expenditures in the six remaining less favored provinces were 79 percent less than authorized. This led President Kaunda to state, "The money was there but the will, the sense of urgency, the development machinery were sadly lacking."[81]

Although Ghana's economic decline in the 1970s and early 1980s worked against corrective equity programs, various Ghanaian regimes have nonetheless put measures into effect that were intended to improve the productivity and quality of rural life. The civilian-elected regime of Kofi Busia set up a national development levy in 1971 to channel resources from the urban centers into rural development schemes; however, this levy was suspended by General I. K. Acheampong following the coup. Nevertheless, the heavy-handed Acheampong military regime did seek to consolidate its shaky position by enlarging its support base through actions that were redistributive in their effects. At times, the military government favored the relatively disadvantaged North in budgetary allocations, as in the per capita capital fund expenditures for secondary schools in 1975–76.[82] Subsequently, President Limann's short-lived polyarchical regime sought to improve the terms of trade between Ghana's rural and urban areas by sharply raising the prices paid for cocoa and other export items. His successor, Jerry Rawlings, implemented a program of structural adjustment in the 1980s, establishing policies on producer prices and infrastructural support that had the effect of reversing urban-rural terms of trade in favor of the rural farmers.[83] He also limited expenditures on urban hospitals to 50 percent of the national health budget in an effort to channel resources and trained personnel to the less advantaged subregions, and he spoke of the need to establish university campuses in all of the country's subregions.[84] Even though such policies entailed a denial of resources to the urban centers, survey data show that the emphasis upon rural development enjoyed considerable support in urban elite circles.[85]

In these cases, extraproportionality represented a commitment of resources by scarcity-prone African states to promote greater interregional equity. Such an approach involved the government's attempt to convince elites in the advantaged areas that such expenditures would involve mutual gains, facilitating balanced development and reducing ethnoregional tensions. Yet, as Keller warns, redistributive policies could themselves "cause intense controversy," especially if previously advantaged elements perceived themselves to be threatened by a possible reversal of status.[86] Under these circumstances, a strong governmental effort to educate the privileged about the positive long-term consequences of redistribution seems imperative.

Conclusion

In the last two chapters, I have examined the hegemonic, elite power-sharing, and polyarchical regimes structuring Africa's intergroup relations on the basis of different underlying political logics. These organizational patterns have different ways of managing ethnic and ethnoregional conflicts. Polyarchical regimes strive consciously to structure institutions so as to promote cooperation among the various actors. By limiting the range of permissible choices (for example, Nigeria's requirements on federal character in federal appointments), they seek to provide an incentive to avoid mutually damaging behavior.[87] The intention behind such confidence-building measures was to weaken the appeals of political parochialism and encourage the development of trust across subregional and ethnic groups. Where the norms, institutions, and routines of polyarchy become accepted and where, as in contemporary Botswana, these norms, institutions, and routines are buttressed by high rates of economic growth (estimated by the World Bank at 8.8 percent per capita annually over a twenty-year period), there are good reasons for agreeing with Ted Robert Gurr that these countries are likely to be the least strife-torn.[88] There is general satisfaction in these societies with both the fairness of the means of reaching decisions and the outputs and outcomes of the system. To be sure, polyarchies sometimes create a situation of demand overload under soft-state conditions and increase the costs of arriving at decisions; at times, they can provide openings for ethnic mobilization that are uncompromising in their appeals. Yet, if the norms of constitutionalism hold and political moderation and crosscutting cleavages develop, these regimes can help to reduce the intensity of intergroup conflict, making intergroup relations more regular and predictable.[89]

The elite power-sharing regime is a more transitory phenomenon that promotes negotiations within the dominant political elite on distributional issues. These regimes can form the basis for new agreements between elite notables, including the military and civilians. In these arrangements, an authoritarian consociational variant allows reciprocity to take place among state, ethnoregional, and other intermediaries within the one-party cabinet or party organization. The more contemporary elite power-sharing variant may accept the need for competitive elections but nonetheless attempt to contain power within the dominant coalition. This type of regime may not last long following the demise of its leader or the ruling elite's belief that a system of controlled reciprocities and negotiations is necessary to preserve stability. In fortuitous cases, such pacts may facilitate the transition to polyarchy, as the experiences of South Africa and Colombia suggest.

However, in hegemonic regimes, the leadership elite is most conscious of its own fragility and most prepared to avoid uncertainty by using force to maintain the status quo. This elite fears the consequences of political and economic instability and therefore justifies the concentration of power at the political center to ward off possibly fatal challenges to its authority. The resulting system, which represses group demands and makes heavy claims of its own on society, is potentially costly, for it fails to develop either effective connections across elites or political memories of common causes, thus leaving the state exposed to internal divisions once the scaffolding of externally imposed unity is torn down. The general public questions the fairness of both the means of reaching decisions and the distributional outputs and outcomes in hegemonic regimes, making for a most unsatisfactory system of conflict management in these ethnically divided societies. Moreover, authoritarianism strengthens the group identity of the repressed, providing the basis for future escalation of conflict from protest to violence and war.[90] By containing participation, certainly the authoritarian regime can sometimes circumscribe domestic conflicts, denying ethnic activists a legitimate arena in which to fight out their differences. This capacity to act as a deterrent to internal conflict led Daniel Geller to conclude that centrist systems "suppress moderate or high levels of turmoil more rapidly than polyarchies" and "manifest less violence and for briefer durations than either polyarchic or personalistic states."[91] For a limited time, then, the "unidirectional nature" of the hegemonic regime's route of general deterrence can restrain social conflict.[92]

Where reciprocities are in evidence, a sense of security prevails, competition among interests remains regularized, information is readily available, and the regime itself is in a position to provide its own incentives for cooperation, then the possibility of building intergroup trust and a common consensus on norms and values is greatly increased. This is most likely to occur in a polyarchical or elite power-sharing regime, which explains why such regimes are relatively more successful in handling such conflicts on their own and thereby keeping them out of the international arena. Experience certainly demonstrates that polyarchies can break down because of elite political ambitions, economic malaise, intense competition, or widespread elite corruption; however, in time, as Nigeria's experience with the "federal character" principles indicates, the guidelines provided by previous constitutions seem likely to be recreated by subsequent generations and to have a moderating impact.

Nonnegotiable demands are most likely to surface in hegemonic regimes; in addition, the institutions supporting and routines guiding interactions in hegemonies tend to be least conducive to conciliation among groups. Group fears and the resulting polarization tend to be pronounced, and the incentive to launch a preemptive strike (the logic of the security dilemma) can lead to rapidly escalating violence. As a result, these regimes are most susceptible to systemic breakdown (social disengagement, rebellion, and civil war) and the reestablishment of new repressive practices.

Thus a paradox becomes evident. Hegemony, which offers the fewest incentives for conciliatory behavior, nonetheless attracts some support from elites who see it as a practical means of retaining power and suppressing destructive conflict. It may indeed be a heavy-handed form of coordination, one that lacks legitimacy and postpones the task of building the networks of reciprocities that bind a society together. Yet the appeal of these authoritarian regimes lies in their ability to impose hierarchy and to avoid the costs of negotiation with autonomous interests. This explains the attraction for Mengistu of military over political solutions to the challenge of Tigrayan or Oromo nationalism and some variant of the one- or no-party system to openly contested elections. In soft states, hegemony may be insufficient to overcome autonomous resistance (for example, UNITA in Angola, Southern Sudan, or the Isaak-controlled areas in northern Somalia), but elites may prefer ongoing state-society incoherence to the complicated tasks of sharing power and building consensus.[93]

Hegemonic regimes can, in many instances, endure a certain amount of incoherence and stalemate and temporarily succeed in shunning meaningful incentives for cooperation, especially in poor, late-developing countries. Alternatively, their leaders may come to recognize the high costs of a mutually damaging stalemate (as in Sudan in 1972) and may thus decide to cease their unwinnable efforts to impose their terms on society, by accepting the need for new approaches. This can take two forms. First, the government can take a direct initiative, such as Obote's negotiations with the Rwenzururu separatist leaders in 1982 (see chapter 4). Where the state itself is a party to the conflict, such a course is often difficult for proud leaders of sovereign states to pursue, as was the case in Nigeria-Biafra or is currently in Sudan.

Second, the government can accept a face-saving third-party intervention—by either a private or public actor or a combination of these. Hence, if the political logic of a hegemonic regime normally precludes positive incentives of its own to promote cooperation, it is still possible, if the costs of continued conflict remain high and a stalemate is unacceptable, that the ruling coalition will accede to new ideas for conflict management advanced by others. In such a situation, only local leaders can determine the legitimate rules of the game for themselves; however, international actors can at times facilitate a transition to the norms of regularized relations by providing information, reducing misperceptions, changing the game, and providing monitoring and enforcement measures. Possibly, a third party may be able to encourage the actors to alter their preferences and consequently to move from deadlock to agreements that can reduce the risks of association.

In the next section of this book, therefore, I will examine the role of external third parties in attempting to offer alternatives to leaders engaged in protracted civil wars. Regimes, for the most part hegemonic, unable to resolve societal conflicts for themselves, make use of third-party interveners to reconstruct their linkages with society, possibly enabling them to establish or return to regularized patterns of relations. In what contexts will such interventions prove feasible, and how do third-party actors structure incentives to encourage state and ethnic leaders to commit themselves to an agreement and then to abide by the terms of their bargain? I will attempt to shed some light on the creative role that external actors can play in using pressures and incentives to influence the parties locked into a high-conflict encounter to reconsider their preferences.

Part Two

Third-Party Mediation
of Violent Conflict

4

The Use of Coercive and Noncoercive Incentives

A skillful blending of inducements and pressures is central to playing the role of mediator.

WILLIAM B. QUANDT

International negotiations and mediation become necessary to establish regularized, constructive interactions in a society under severe strain. When a weak state lacks the capacity to regulate society effectively and the relations between ethnic and racial sections within a country (or between one or more ethnic groups and the state itself) become irregular and even hostile, the mechanisms of management fail, often with highly destructive implications.

One option for state elites is to attempt to either eliminate the opposition or force it to capitulate, as happened in forty-one out of sixty-eight twentieth-century civil wars tabulated by Stephen Stedman, including those in Uganda (1966, 1987), Burundi (1972), and Nigeria.[1] Another option is to attempt to institutionalize conflict management by negotiating with the partly autonomous state and subnational interests, as happened in twenty cases tabulated by Stedman, including Zaire (1965), Sudan (1972), Angola (1975), Zimbabwe (1979), Chad (1987), and Namibia (1989). Cooperation is a preferred objective to the extent that both sides perceive that they benefit from a joint problem-solving effort.

In some instances of intense interethnic conflict, the internationalization of the conflict can be avoided and the African state can itself act to reduce tensions with ethnoregional elites through a process of direct, bilateral negotiations. In such cases, the state is a party to the conflict, not a mediator. Direct negotiations (without the intercession of a third party) took place between the government of Senegal and the

Casamance insurgents in May 1991 and between the Ghanaian government negotiating team and the leaders of seven ethnic peoples in the
Northern Region in June 1994, and they were the preferred course
of the African National Congress (ANC) and the government of F. W.
de Klerk in South Africa. In the latter case, de Klerk spoke of an intrusion
into his country's sovereignty, while the ANC feared that a third-party
intervener might extract unwanted compromises, as happened in the
Zimbabwe independence negotiations.[2]

One African example of effective state negotiations with an ethnoregional movement is the initiative taken in 1982 by President A. Milton
Obote of Uganda in his dealings with the Rwenzururu movement. The
Rwenzururu leaders sought to separate themselves from the Kingdom
of Toro and be granted the status of a separate district within Uganda
(or, in the case of the Konjo people of the higher and more inacces-
sible Ruwenzori area, to become a separate kingdom on their own). A
violent struggle ensued between the Konjo and Amba peoples on the
one hand and the dominant Toro, and subsequently the Ugandan army,
on the other. Casualties proved high at times, especially in 1963 and
1964, when Batoro forces massacred many Bakonjo in their struggle for
control of the fertile valleys. Subsequently, Ugandan army units sought to
reestablish central control over separatist elements in the Mountains of
the Moon area, adding to the general carnage.[3] In 1979, the Rwenzururu
movement seized the opportunity accorded it by the collapse of Idi
Amin's regime to strengthen its military arm by securing significant
amounts of military equipment and supplies from that administration's
retreating soldiers. As a result of this strengthening of Rwenzururu fighting capabilities after the country's liberation, the security threat became
serious in the period from 1979 to 1982.

Following initiatives by the Obote government, a successful bargain
was struck between state and ethnoregional interests in August 1982.
The Rwenzururu leaders, unable to achieve their preferred objective of
national self-determination, ranked compromise over continued war and
deadlock. At the ceremony marking the reincorporation of the
Rwenzururu people into Uganda, the former king of the Rwenzururu,
Charles Irema Ngoma, appealed to his forces to surrender their guns to
state officials. In appreciation of this "magnanimous act," the Obote
regime offered Ngoma and several of his lieutenants a number of tangible concessions: a bus, personal cars, trucks, shops, and funds for study
abroad.[4] The Ugandan government also agreed to extend a degree of
local autonomy to the Rwenzururu area. Thus members of the
Rwenzururu elite were reconciled by a package of material payments

and administrative appointments that caused them to accept the government's offer of peaceful relations. During the negotiations, the government quite obviously preferred direct political negotiations with the secessionist leaders to the intercession of a third-party mediator, mainly because a mediator would have underscored the independent status of the Rwenzururu movement.

Of course, many conflicts between a state and ethnoregional or racial groups are too deep-seated and threatening to be resolved through direct state-ethnic negotiations, which explains why most civil wars have been terminated through victory or capitulation. In these cases, the legitimacy of state or sectional actors may be dubious, and the kinds of material incentives used to resolve the Uganda dispute may be inadequate to the task at hand. Arnold Wolfers writes on the topic of inter-country interactions that "the more relations between [autonomous political actors] degenerate toward enmity the more [they] are justified in fearing for the things they cherish and the more reason they have to make and require sacrifices by which inimical claims can be defeated."[5] Hence increasing cleavages between political interests and a negative spiral leading to more intense conflicts and even protracted civil wars make conflict resolution by means of direct, bilateral negotiations relatively unlikely.

Nevertheless, as the Stedman data indicate, third-party actions have at times played a significant role in conflict reduction. Of course, third-party mediators must operate within well-defined parameters, as I will show. When discussing third-party interventions here, I am using the term *mediation* broadly to include the extension of good offices (that is, facilitating communication between rivals); by *conciliation* I mean clarifying misperceptions and misinformation with an eye to establishing a positive environment that encourages rival actors to shift their preferences and, consequently, to facilitate reaching an agreement. *Mediation* in the formal sense means promoting agreement by helping to provide information, reduce misperceptions, develop a consensus on principles and goals, set an agenda, define the issues under contention, recommend compromises and adjustments, and manipulate pressures and incentives in order to alter the payoff structure. As Saadia Touval notes, "Mediation is the most versatile of intermediaries' roles, and may subsume the roles of good offices and conciliation."[6] In line with this assessment, in the next four chapters I will compare and contrast three types of mediation processes:

—Unofficial mediation, exemplified by the conciliation effort of Washington A. J. Okumu in South Africa (chapter 7) and of the World

Council of Churches in the Sudanese conflict (chapter 8), in which the private, nongovernmental intermediary clarifies misinterpretations and misperceptions, communicates between the antagonists, and in some instances proposes agendas. The unofficial mediators set great store by their reputation for neutrality and impartiality in the conciliation effort.[7]

—Colonial official mediation, the coercive mediation of the departing colonial power, for instance, the British in Ghana and Rhodesia/Zimbabwe (chapter 6) at the time of decolonization. The stake of the colonial power in the outcome was never in doubt.

—Third-party official mediation, which facilitates agreements by means of various pressures and incentives in addition to the functions performed by those engaged in unofficial mediation. Examples are the role of the great powers (the United States and the Soviet Union), the United Nations, and middle powers (Zaire and Portugal) in Angola (chapter 5), the Commonwealth Eminent Persons Group mission to South Africa in 1986 (chapter 7), and the UN and other international observer missions to South Africa in 1993 and 1994. In contemporary third-party official mediation, coalitions of mediators are quite commonplace, and, because these actors may have very different interests in the outcome, such alliances frequently require an ongoing bargaining relationship within the mediatory coalition in order to maintain the pressure on the target states or movements.

The possible mix of pressures and incentives that mediators can employ in these processes can make compromises more acceptable by helping the actors to change their preferences, by increasing information on which to base decisions, and by offering a way for both parties to save face.[8] To determine the range of available pressures and incentives for a third party to help narrow the differences between state and ethnic or interethnic rivals, the mediator faces several constant factors that can be subsumed under a single broad category: the conflict situation.

These factors include elite power relations, the military balance, the perceptions of both parties to the dispute (essentialist versus pragmatic), the nature of the demands (negotiable versus nonnegotiable), and timing. The conflict situation is described in terms of the preferences of each party for either making concessions, standing firm, or escalating the conflict. These preferences are, in turn, influenced by the nature of the demands being advanced and the perceptions of both parties regarding their alternatives and the likely responses of their adversaries to various possible forms of action. The nature of the conflict situation largely determines how each party will rank the alternative possible outcomes: getting one's way (unilateral concessions by the opposing party), mutual concessions and compromise, unilateral concessions and yielding, or no concessions by either party. Because of their central and not always fully recognized importance to the ethnic-related negotiating process, it is important to focus at greater length on the relationship of perceptions to demands and timing.

The Relationship of Perceptions to Demands

In a context of antagonistic encounters, a third-party actor has limited ability to exert pressure or organize incentives to change the patterns of encounter. Certainly, if both parties have totalist perceptions and non-negotiable demands (the worst-case scenario), a third-party mediator will have little scope for altering the basis of conflict; stalemate and destructive encounters are the likely outcomes. In this instance, both parties would prefer mutual defection to either unilateral concessions or cooperation. However, when both parties have pragmatic perceptions and make negotiable demands, an opening exists for bargaining, mutual concessions, and mediatory initiatives.[9] The best-case scenario would bring together reciprocative perceptions and negotiable claims; because of the intensity of competition and conflict, however, this may not be possible, making it necessary to build connections on the basis of shared interests and political expediency. In time, though, the learned relationships of pragmatism can lead to a willingness to make unilateral concessions for the sake of common interests.

Despite the tendency of state and ethnic leaders to resist making concessions (fearing that such actions would not be reciprocated), such negotiating initiatives are always possible, given that cooperation is generally preferable to mutual defection. With sufficient iterations over time, the existence of a bargaining range can create an opening for transforming an encounter through the assistance of a third-party mediator. If the mediator can help to narrow the existing differences, convincing at least one and preferably both sides to alter their preferences and make concessions in their own objectives, then cooperative actions can materialize. Stressing the role of initial misperceptions in bringing on a mutually damaging stalemate, Glenn Snyder and Paul Diesing point to the need for communication to correct the misleading signals and to facilitate bargaining and compromise.

> The usual purpose of communication is to *influence* the opponent to move toward a desirable bargaining outcome. One does this by communicating information about one's demands, about

one's power and readiness to act if the demands are not met, about the favorable consequences to the opponent if he makes certain moves, about the impossibility of his achieving certain of his apparent goals, about the availability of other desirable outcomes he may have overlooked, and so on. These communications are intended to revise the opponent's estimates of the bargaining situation in such a way that the outcome one desires seems desirable or at least unavoidable to him as well.[10]

As the case of Sudan shows (see chapter 8), a private mediator can help to promote a cooperative settlement in an intense conflict situation, partly by clarifying misperceptions among key actors. In this case, the private mediator was assisted at critical junctures by a state actor who took firm initiatives to push the peace process along. In other conflicts, such as those in Angola (chapter 5) and Rhodesia/Zimbabwe (chapter 6), official mediators not only provided information, clarified misperceptions, and communicated between the adversaries but also exerted a decisive influence on the negotiation process, using both noncoercive and coercive incentives to alter the nature of the distribution of gains. In something of a best-case scenario, the third-party actor succeeded in helping to make mutual cooperation preferable to efforts to attain unilateral concessions.

In intense encounters that display totalist perceptions and nonnegotiable demands, there is at best a narrow scope for cooperation and compromise. Such a combination of perceptions and demands makes mutual defection the most likely strategy in both cases, for it is assumed that cooperation can involve concessions that may not be reciprocated. Although both parties have little incentive to opt for a strategy that provides a less than optimal benefit, nonetheless there remains a chance that they will choose a strategy of cooperation in the expectation that their adversary will respond in a like manner.[11] One or both actors could eventually shift from their initial positions to avoid a stalemate, thereby enhancing the possibility of a genuine reciprocation, which would lead to cooperation.[12] This indeed proved to be the case in Angola, Zimbabwe, and Sudan.

In the more normal type of encounters, both parties have pragmatic perceptions and both make negotiable demands. The actors recognize that if both parties insist on achieving their main objectives war will result, so they back away, at what they consider to be the last possible moment, from a possible civil war and opt for compromise. The prospect of prolonged stalemate or war is so unpleasant that one or both antagonists would be prepared, in the final analysis, to accept the humiliation of yielding rather than face what is perceived as a worse outcome.[13] Thus the threat of civil war becomes an incentive for changing strategic choices and negotiating with an adversary. A willingness to make concessions encourages iterations aimed at accommodative outcomes. Not only may the parties reduce their demands to reach agreement, but by increasing their rival's benefit, they provide a positive incentive for cooperation. Obviously, there is considerable scope for transforming this relationship through the introduction of a third-party mediator prepared to use a variety of incentives to encourage the antagonists to alter the distribution of benefits and pull back from their original demands before it is too late.

In the bargaining between state and ethnoregional actors just before the independence of Ghana and after independence in the Uganda/Rwenzururu negotiations, relations were antagonistic, but pragmatic perceptions led to the creation of options that sweetened the deal, thereby avoiding a destructive encounter. Although the actors harbored no illusions about their significant conflicts of interest, they took care to avoid deadlock and possible military confrontation. The governments did so because of the possible delay in Ghana's independence or the likely costs of instability; the Ashanti-based National Liberation Movement did so because of the overwhelming military strength at the disposal of the state and the concessions offered on autonomy and material benefits. Late in the encounter, both sides arrived at a compromise and thus avoided a violent clash. In the Ghana case, some scope existed for a third party to encourage one or both parties to reduce their claims, to clarify misperceptions and misinformation, to offer incentives, and to communicate productively.

By contrast, mediators are much less able to provide incentives for encouraging a mutually beneficial solution in a relationship that involves totalist perceptions and nonnegotiable demands. Certainly, if neither party can induce the other side to act in a reciprocative manner, no change in mutual perceptions can be expected to take place, and a grim equilibrium is likely to result. Even when a mediator is actively engaged, it may be impossible to overcome the political logic that prevails in this type of encounter, as happened during the Nigeria-Biafra conflict. In brief, a third-party actor may be necessary but insufficient to alter the existing preference for mutual defection.

Timing

Another given that constrains the mediator is timing, probably the vaguest of the factors in a conflict situation. In at least one of my interviews with people involved in mediation, a diplomat was forthright about his adherence to what he described as "the timing school of diplomacy," that is, the belief that seizing the ripe moment is the critical point in the negotiation process.[14]

In fact, third-party interveners can often do precious little to overcome the antagonists' profound distrust; instead, they must wait on the periphery while the costs of conflict mount and the situation becomes ripe for resolution.[15] In Rhodesia (Zimbabwe), the agreement that was reached in 1979 could not have been the basis for a settlement in 1976. It was a matter of timing. However, as both sides came to recognize that the war was one of attrition—mutually damaging and unwinnable, at least in the short term—their incentives for considering a third-party mediated (or arbitrated) settlement increased.

As actor preferences shifted, the relationship changed from the grim logic of deadlock and intense and prolonged conflict to one involving possible concessions. A roughly similar sequence of events in Sudan led up to the Addis Ababa agreement of 1972. But mutual damage is surely a costly way of altering perceptions, and when third-party mediators can use other inducements to help speed up the process of change, they are fulfilling their most challenging and complex task. Such inducements open a window of opportunity through which the third-party actor can facilitate agreement by joining otherwise unrelated issues for bargaining purposes (using the strategy of issue linkage) and can thereby encourage the antagonists to "change the game simply by starting to play a new one."[16]

Even though the mediator obviously cannot move very far in advance of events (that is, rapidly accelerate the process of ripening), the decision costs are nonetheless often lower earlier in the conflict than they are later.[17] Structuring encounters in advance of independence, as happened in Malaysia, created habits of accommodation under the aegis of a third-party enforcer before the strains of competition and conflict were tested.[18] Following independence, learned norms of reciprocity can be encouraged through the use of such confidence-building mechanisms as power sharing, balanced recruitment, equitable developmental allocations, representative electoral outcomes, and measures for decentralization and federalism.

Nevertheless, it is significant that the four cases discussed here that successfully utilized third-party intervention in one form or another (Angola, Rhodesia, South Africa, and Sudan) all achieved their objectives in the later stages of the conflict. For a temporary period, the external intervener can maintain the peace by altering the balance of ethnic power and leading group leaders to moderate their demands.[19] Even so, there is no conclusive evidence to link protracted disputes and high costs to a willingness to reduce tensions or to settle differences. At earlier stages in a conflict, before positions have hardened on the various issues, it might seem easier to move closer to an antagonist's position. This logic led Inis Claude to conclude that there are in fact two periods of "golden opportunity" in the mediation process: incipiency and maturity.[20] In conflicts having an ethnic or racial dimension, when perceptions become totalist and demands are nonnegotiable, the period of incipiency can usefully be explored (as was done in Rhodesia, Angola, and South Africa), but the parameters within which the third-party intermediary must work, in practice, often leave only limited scope for an effective intervention at this stage. Certainly, poorly conceived initiatives at the incipient stage can prove counterproductive, because once rejected, these overtures can set precedents for the future.

Incentives Available to Mediators

Although mediators must operate within some well-defined parameters in an ethnically or racially related conflict, they may still be able to influence the sequence of events in certain situations through personal experience and qualities and the effective employment of noncoercive and coercive incentives. Experience and personality clearly count in all aspects of the mediatory process. The advantages of being able to relate to people and to gain their confidence and respect are well documented in the annals of political diplomacy.[21] The skillful diplomat, Lord Carrington, in the Lancaster House negotiations on Rhodesia in 1979, made a significant difference by surrounding himself with a team of able people; setting an effective agenda; adopting a phase-by-phase approach, leaving the issues of the ceasefire and transition for the later stages of the conference; timing his conciliatory and threatening moves appropriately; understanding the values and preferences of the disputants; practicing patience and tact; and formulating options imaginatively. Lord Carrington, as the foreign secretary of the colonial power in Rhodesia, was certainly anything but neutral regarding the outcome of the deliberations. However, his perceived interest in securing a settlement enabled him to gain leverage over the more conservative politicians around him; by using that influence to alter the pattern of demands, Carrington gained credibility with the militant nationalists and thereby increased his capacity to shape the agreement along the lines of his predetermined agenda.[22]

What options, then, do mediators, whether acting alone or in a coalition with other mediators, have at their disposal to change the distribution of gains and bring the rival parties from stalemate and possible war to a negotiated agreement, or even to speed the process to avoid extensive mutual damage? Does the structure of conflict allow for the possibility of hastening the ripe moment? The challenge, states Jeffrey Rubin, "is to *create* [the] favorable conditions rather than wait for them to appear."[23] To analyze how new options might be created that could alter the strategies of the disputants, I now turn to the mix of noncoercive and coercive incentives at the disposal of third-party actors.

In mixed-motive conflict situations, where lack of trust, temptation to compete, and the possibility of mutually beneficial cooperation are present, self-interest suggests a strategy using various kinds of incentives.[24] In this context, when recurrent patterns of relations are weak or absent, diplomatic incentives consist of material and nonmaterial goods offered by a mediator to persuade actors to modify their preferences and, consequently, their behavior. Incentives are designed to influence adversaries' strategies along predetermined lines. The incentives used by a third party may range along a continuum of intensity from noncoercive to coercive or be combined in a "carrot-and-stick" fashion. Finally, incentives may well involve a time element (for example, deadlines).[25]

As shown in table 4-1, the incentives available to third-party mediators to promote cooperation with or between antagonistic parties can be disaggregated into six types. These incentives are grouped in terms of the relative ease or difficulty of employing an inducement and its anticipated effects on both giver and recipient. Although noncoercive incentives can make an important contribution in moving the adversaries toward a peaceful outcome, in certain situations there may be no alternative to coercive international action. As I. William Zartman and Johannes Aurik conclude, threats are useful in making stalemate more painful, but "what is crucial to making the deadlock productive is the positive exercise of power to provide incentives to a better alternative, the prospects of requitement, and a formula for a way out of the costly conflict."[26]

Inevitably, the conflict-regulating schema outlined here has some intersecting and overlapping features. This typifies any dynamic process that brings together initiators and recipients with varying mixes of material and nonmaterial incentives. In fact, the carrot-and-stick approach entails a conscious strategy of packaging incentives to include

TABLE 4-1. *Costs and Benefits for Third-Party Mediator and Recipients*[a]

Incentives	Costs and benefits	
	Third party	Recipient
Noncoercive		
Purchase	+	+
Insurance	+ +	+ +
Legitimation	+ + +	+ + +
Coercive		
Pressures	−	−
Sanctions	− −	− −
Force	− − −	− − −

a. Pluses and minuses indicate the levels of benefits and costs of each strategy to both third party and recipients. Noncoercive incentives are positive-sum games because they involve benefits for all actors; coercive incentives, however, imply raised costs for the targeted actors.

both noncoercive and coercive features. Nevertheless, avoiding overlaps is less important for my purposes than delineating the nature of alternatives. With this in mind, I will now characterize the six types of incentives that can be used to facilitate cooperation, moving from the least explicitly coercive to the most.

Noncoercive Incentives

Noncoercive incentives provide disputants with rewards for altering their perceptions and thereby acting in a cooperative manner. These incentives create new options that can alter the strategies of the rival parties, encouraging them to adopt new courses of action that can sometimes lead to the cessation of violent encounters and the building of confidence. As Louis Kriesberg observes, "reward" refers to "inducements or promises which offer the adversary something it values, and is made in anticipation of a reciprocating concession."[27] I examine three such rewards—purchase, insurance, and legitimation—in an effort to gain an appreciation of when these noncoercive incentives are likely to be used by third parties, be accepted by adversaries, and produce positive results.

PURCHASE. Because both initiator and recipient find purchase (the use of some form of fiscal or tangible incentive) the easiest to apply, it is frequently viewed as an attractive means of promoting cooperation in intense conflict situations. By "enlarging [the] pie," comments Saadia Touval, the third-party actor "may alter the payoff structure and transform the situation into a positive sum game in which a compromise, enabling gains to both sides, is possible."[28] A third-party mediator can use side payments to induce one or both parties in an ethnically related dispute to modify their demands. Examples include the U.S. efforts to promote internal accommodation in Cyprus, where a £500 million aid package for refugee assistance and development was put forward in 1985, and the financial and material promises made by the Italian government to the Mozambique National Resistance (Renamo) negotiators to sign a ceasefire.[29]

Side payments can also facilitate agreement between parties who are trapped in a blocked situation. Such interventions can expedite a decision when the parties are under time pressure to reach a resolution. Although perhaps the best example is the Camp David talks, several African examples are also pertinent. Thus, in a Saudi-backed effort to end the stalemate in the Western Saharan conflict in 1987, King Fahd reportedly shuttled back and forth between the tents of Algeria's President Chadli Benjedid and Morocco's King Hassan II along the Algerian-Moroccan border, offering financial inducements to the various parties in an effort to promote concessions.[30] Similarly, both the British and U.S. governments offered financial incentives to gain agreement on Britain's constitutional proposals in the Zimbabwe independence negotiations, attempting to move the confrontation from civil war to one involving concessions.[31] Fiscal incentives have low relative costs for both recipients and third-party mediators and are also relatively easy to offer, but, as hypothesized in table 4-1, their expected distribution of gains is limited.

INSURANCE. Guaranteeing nondefection by an opponent (if the recipient grants concessions), insurance is somewhat more difficult to apply. For certain recipients and third-party actors, insurance (or security incentives for groups) holds out the promise of more substantial benefits. Like purchase, this noncoercive incentive can also enlarge the pie and change the distribution of gains in a positive way. When pledging to "guarantee" future majority compliance with the basic rules if an accord is reached, the politically dominant party enlarges choice by agreeing to insure minority parties against possible abuses. Such promised guarantees can sometimes reassure ethnic minorities about their future and thereby discourage their defection, provided that the dominant actor continues to uphold the contract. Insurance incentives helped secure the assent of various minority groups to the Lancaster House agreement in the Rhodesian (as well as the Kenyan) independence negotiations. Given conflicting within-group pressures in the majority African community, the ability of majority group leaders to make credible commitments on such matters remained very much in question, however.[32]

By providing some form of insurance to minority interests, the mediator and certain recipients may accept greater costs than they would in the case of purchase. Clearly, both parties recognize the need for greater incentives to curtail an already prolonged and damaging encounter. But by operating on the assumption that future compliance can be guaranteed, the mediator is likely to become enmeshed in the conflict management process during the critically important implementation phase. Such interventions can ensure that the adversaries deliver on their commitments during the transitionary period after the agreement; however, the peacekeeping operations that ensue are inevitably costly and intrusive. Thus the Indian-mediated Sri Lankan peace accord of 1987, which was guaranteed by the Indian government (although Indian armed forces could come to Sri Lanka only at the request of its authorities), ultimately involved a broad commitment from the Indian military that resulted in extensive casualties and much resentment on both sides of the Tamil-Sinhalese divide.[33] Insurance, then, can require a somewhat greater undertaking on the part of the external actor than does purchase, in order to promote an agreement and guarantee compliance after an agreement has been reached.

LEGITIMATION. The literature on incentives makes scant, if any, reference to legitimacy, yet such intangible incentives as recognition and the valid exercise of regime authority have surfaced from time to time in ethnic-related confrontations. Thus the recognition factor figured in the Lancaster House negotiations, when Great Britain's Lord Carrington repeatedly asserted that his government would accept the internal Rhodesian regime (the so-called second-class solution) if the negotiations leading to an all-party solution broke down. In this instance, "negotiation [was] not *only* a decision-making process, it [was] also to some extent an unofficial game of performance and reputation."[34]

Another possible use of legitimation incentives surfaced in the Namibian independence negotiations. A position paper drawn up by U.S. Assistant Secretary of State for African Affairs Chester Crocker for the secretary of state's May 1981 meeting with South African Foreign Minister Pik Botha described the stalemate in Namibia as the main obstacle to the development of a new U.S.-South African relationship. Crocker urged Secretary of State Alexander Haig to make clear to the South

Africans the need to work with the United States to achieve an internationally acceptable agreement. Crocker's specific recommendation to induce the South Africans to cooperate on a Namibian accord was for the United States to give an indication that it "can ... work to end South Africa's polecat status in the world and seek to restore its place as a legitimate and important regional actor with whom we can cooperate pragmatically."[35]

Like purchase and insurance incentives, then, legitimation incentives are noncoercive and make agreement more attractive to a recipient by creating new options. However, these incentives tend to transform the distribution of benefits more radically than do other noncoercive incentive systems, thus significantly raising the potential costs for both the third-party intervener and the target. Had the United States attempted to end South Africa's "polecat" status, the United States would have severely damaged its relations with third world countries that remained deeply suspicious of continuing U.S.–South African ties. For the target state, South Africa, the price of conciliating the United States (that is, reaching an internationally acceptable settlement on Namibian independence) seemed high at the time, particularly to those elements in the government and army who were uneasy over the political and strategic consequences of the South West Africa People's Organization rule there.

Legitimacy is an intangible resource that is highly valued by both parties in a dispute. It can therefore be used by a third party to imply recognition of one or more of the negotiating parties or to attempt to extract concessions from them (as happened in the Mozambican negotiations in 1992 and the Angolan government's negotiations with Jonas Savimbi of UNITA in 1994).[36] Intangible issues such as legitimacy, esteem, and reputation become superimposed upon such tangible issues as financial allocations and constitutional and legal protections, thus creating an additional range of diplomatic incentives that the third party can use to facilitate internationally acceptable agreements.[37]

Coercive Incentives

As conflicts gain in intensity and can no longer be resolved by means of noncoercive incentives (rewards), it may become necessary for the intermediary or coalition of intermediaries to attempt to force movement toward a decision by using some form of coercive incentive (a threat or punishment). As James Laue cautions, however, the use of coercive means can lead to the termination of conflict but not its resolution, because it does not represent a party-based agreement and fails to address underlying issues.[38] Consequently, this falls under the rubric of conflict management, not conflict resolution.

A coercive incentive employs a mix of threats and punishments to induce a change of preferences from the target state or subnational group, leading to compliance with a proposed course of action. Clearly, a threat of punishment must be credible. A threat is unlikely to change the target's preferences or behavior unless the third party has both the will and capacity to carry out the warnings. But capacity is distinct from action. As indicated by Svenn Lindskold and Russell Bennett's study on the links between threat capabilities and conciliatory promises, "the possession of relatively unused threat capability enhances a promisor's credibility in terms of the attribution of trustworthy intentions"; such capability is the critical factor in promoting "positive affective relationships."[39]

PRESSURES. Of the three types of coercive incentives specified in table 4-1, diplomatic pressures are normally the lowest in costs and benefits for both the third party and the recipient. Such pressures threaten the target country or movement with limited punishment in order to push its leaders to reconsider their preferences regarding a given course of action. It is relatively easy, for example, for a third party or a coalition of actors to attempt to induce target states or movements to make domestic reforms by issuing mass media appeals, bringing up critical resolutions for a vote at international forums, providing warnings of impending action, and breaking off diplomatic relations. In fact, as Alexander George points out, "asking relatively little of the opponent makes it easier for him to permit himself to be coerced."[40] At the same time, the effect of such measures upon recalcitrant regimes has been limited, because some targeted actors have had sufficient alternatives to enable them to cushion the effect.

Thus, in the 1985 negotiations in Nairobi between the leaders of Uganda's warring parties—the predominantly northern Uganda Military Council and the Ankole-led National Resistance Movement (NRM)—Kenyan President Daniel arap Moi played a critical role in facilitating the appearance of compromise. Moi worked in an "untiring" manner in his capacity as chairman of the negotiating sessions, not only by communicating between the warring parties and helping to frame the terms of the peace settlement, but also threatening at one point to send the delegations home empty-handed if they did not negotiate seriously. Then, after months of negotiations and delays, President Moi gave the two parties an ultimatum: "Sign the agreement or go back home and fight."[41]

This appears to have been a turning point in the negotiations, for the two delegations agreed, after further deliberations, to sign the accord. Diplomatic pressure from an interested mediator was a critical factor in bringing about the accord (reportedly, NRM leader Yoweri Museveni feared the possibility that Kenya would link up with General Tito Okello's government, making an NRM victory less likely than ever).[42] However, given the intensity of the differences between the two parties and the ultimate military superiority of the National Resistance Army forces, diplomatic pressure soon proved ineffective in improving relations between the Okello government and the NRM. Thus the two parties were unable to share in the distribution of gains, and the conflict was ultimately terminated by an NRM military victory.

Diplomatic pressures were used repeatedly in the negotiations with apartheid South Africa. The United Nations and its members openly employed various diplomatic means to pressure the South African government to alter its policies on minority racial domination. In the United States, for example, both sides in the debate on appropriate measures accepted the need for diplomatic pressure; they differed mainly about the scope and potency of this pressure. U.S. Assistant Secretary of State for African Affairs Chester Crocker felt that "a mix of positive incentives and selective pressures," including selective sanctions, was necessary to hasten change to a free, nonracial polity.[43] Critics of Crocker's incrementalist approach favored a more determined use of political and economic sanctions, involving measures strong enough to compel a recalcitrant South African regime to negotiate seriously toward an end to apartheid. By 1986 the strategy used was diplomatic pressure backed by limited economic sanctions, but the credibility of this threat was not in doubt. Hence the expectation of more ironclad measures in the years ahead weighed heavily in President F. W. de Klerk's calculations on the need for a decisive change of approach.[44]

SANCTIONS. Economic sanctions overlap diplomatic pressures by reflecting an open and explicit disapproval of a particular regime or movement and its policies, but they exceed pressures by threatening punitive measures against the regime or movement in order to induce the elite to change its preferences and behavior. In other words, sanctions use diplomatic means to communicate actual or potentially harmful consequences if the targeted state should fail to alter its policies and practices. Clearly, full impact requires that the states imposing sanctions have sufficient power to implement their threatened measures; moreover, as noted earlier, an unutilized threat capacity may increase the likelihood of cooperation, because under such circumstances an initiative "is evidently considered more genuinely accommodative than it is when used."[45]

The enactment of the Comprehensive Anti-Apartheid Act of 1986 by the U.S. Congress was an incentive for a change of behavior as well as a limited but real threat (the provisions of the act could have been tightened up by determined legislators in the years following). The intent of its framers was to use economic pressures to induce the South African government to alter its policies and programs; if South Africa took a list of actions to become a more open and equitable society, then sanctions would be lifted. Senator Edward Kennedy declared during the debate over the bill that "it is intended to use [U.S.] leverage in South Africa to bring about a less racist system of government."[46] However, because the act covered only a number of relatively insignificant items exported to the United States, the act was not sufficiently punitive to overcome the Pieter W. Botha government's resistance to change, a problem anticipated in the literature on economic sanctions. As James Lindsay has stated, "Sanctions fail to force compliance primarily because they rarely inflict serious economic pain on the target."[47] The target state's insufficient vulnerability to external economic pressures enables it to ignore the call for change.[48]

In brief, the expected impact was high and had some material and nonmaterial consequences, but the distribution of gains was not sufficiently high to ensure a change of strategies. This does not mean that sanctions were not useful in mobilizing political support for a shift of strategies after F. W. de Klerk assumed power. Economic sanctions had an important symbolic value in South Africa: they reaffirmed values and acted as a precedent for later initiatives. Nevertheless, they tended to be difficult to employ, and their ability to induce the target state to make concessions was limited, at least in the short term.

FORCE. As illustrated in table 4-1, using force and military coercion to raise the costs of noncompliance is the most costly incentive for all concerned, yet it is often the most promising means of altering the distribution of gains and inducing cooperation. When used to that end, force can be viewed as having a constructive, ethical dimension. In Clausewitz's terms, it becomes an extension of politics. And if force is quite appropriate in certain contexts, in other contexts the refusal to use it can become a sin of omission. Thus many observers expressed grave misgivings over Prime Minister Harold Wilson's unwillingness to use British military force in 1965, when Ian Smith and his Rhodesian colleagues issued their Unilateral Declaration of Independence. Force, then, is not an abstraction. As George Kennan explains, "It cannot be understood or dealt with as a concept outside of the given framework of purpose and method."[49] If threats are inadequate for the challenge at hand, there may be little alternative to the use of military inducements to promote local actors' willingness to comply with internationally mandated standards of behavior.

Although forcible measures encompass a wide spectrum of options, it seems sufficient here to examine two important inducements in interethnic conflict situations: extending (or refusing to extend) military assistance, and military intervention. Clearly, military assistance has tipped the balance of forces significantly in some conflicts. The United States' extension of critically needed supplies and technical support to Haile Selassie's regime in Ethiopia and to King Hassan II's regime in Morocco buttressed the ruling coalitions at the center against ethno-regionalist challenges from the periphery.

However, U.S. military assistance has also been withheld from governments in power. In 1978 and 1979, U.S. representatives in Mogadishu repeatedly refused military assistance to the Somali government until it removed Somali armed forces from across the Ethiopian border, where those detachments were supporting ethnic kin in Ogaden Province.[50] And in the case of Angola (see chapter 5) in 1985, the Reagan administration attempted to exert pressure on the ruling Marxist-oriented MPLA regime in Luanda, altering statutory prohibitions on assistance to anticommunist resistance movements and supplying Jonas Savimbi's Ovimbundu- and Chokwe-supported UNITA insurgents with antitank weapons and shoulder-held antiaircraft missiles. The justification for this intervention, according to U.S. Secretary of State George Shultz, was the leverage it would give to a U.S.-negotiated settlement in the region, which could lead to parallel withdrawals of Cuban troops from Angola and South African forces from Namibia.[51] However, the effect was to make the United States part of the destabilization process in Angola, at some cost to its credibility as a third-party mediator.

Actual third-party military interventions in domestic disputes having an ethnic or racial dimension have occurred only infrequently, largely because of the high costs involved in such efforts to change choices on the ground. A third party using military inducements must not only have extensive capacity at its disposal, but it must also be prepared to employ it—as was the case with NATO's decision to bomb Bosnian Serb positions in 1995. In another application of military incentives by a coalition of third-party intermediaries—the Congo crisis in the 1960s—deployment of UN forces assumed some risks to transform actor preferences on the ground.[52] With this critical on-the-scene backing, the United Nations was in a position to use limited amounts of military force to press for the reintegration of Katanga province with the rest of the country.

Subsequently, in Somalia, the Bush administration dispatched a 25,000-person U.S. military force under UN auspices to ensure a safe environment for the delivery of relief supplies and to begin the process of national reconciliation. In essence, the problems in the country, with its clan-based rivalries and ethnoregional antagonisms (the Isaak rebellion and separatism in the North), were essentially political in nature.[53] However, as peacekeeping was transformed into peace enforcement under the expanded United Nations Operation in Somalia (UNOSOM II), confrontations between various international units and General Mohamed Farah Aidid's irregulars in south Mogadishu revealed the limits of external power in a hostile environment. Following a sharp military encounter between U.S. forces and Aidid's Somali National Alliance militia in October 1993, both U.S. and UN officials, recognizing that UNOSOM II lacked overwhelming force, returned to a "minimalist" diplomatic tack and attempted to rebuild national reconciliation through negotiations on a pacted agreement among prominent clan leaders.[54] As Ted Robert Gurr contended, "Only at relatively high levels of coercive force does strife tend to decline."[55]

Mixed Incentive Strategies

Thus far I have disaggregated incentive strategies into six types, distinguishing them according to the ways they distribute gains for both third-party and recipient actors. In real-life situations, however, packages of incentives that bring together coercive and noncoercive inducements may be necessary to overcome a stalemate.

Clearly, the prudence of such an approach depends on the situation. Crocker's contention—that movement toward negotiations in South Africa required "a mix of positive incentives and selective pressures"— might have been inappropriate at that juncture, given the determination and the capacity of the Botha regime to resist deadlines. In other contexts, a mix of incentives may be preferable to unilateral inducements of either a positive (rewarding) or negative (threatening or punishing) nature. Thus Martin Patchen concludes that "a strategy that begins with firmness—including the threat or use of coercion—in the early stages of a dispute and then switches to conciliation appears generally to be effective in securing cooperation from an opponent."[56] At times, one can argue just as plausibly for cautious moves by external facilitators in the early stages of negotiation, followed by concerted moves by mediators using the various carrots and sticks at their disposal to overcome the uncertain progress of incrementalism.[57]

Conflict theorists have developed one possible incentive scenario that uses a mix of carrots and sticks to induce cooperation: the graduated and reciprocated initiatives in tension-reduction (GRIT) strategy, an adaptation of the "tit-for-tat" or reciprocating strategy.[58] Although developed by Charles E. Osgood with an eye to reducing U.S.-Soviet competition and conflict, a GRIT strategy can also have implications for the largely stalemated ethnic-related conflicts in Sudan, as well as those in Northern Ireland and Sri Lanka.

Like tit-for-tat (a move by one party that takes place in response to a similar move by the other, leading to a possible spiral of further moves and responses), a GRIT strategy emphasizes a norm of reciprocity between the antagonistic parties, using a mix of noncoercive and coercive incentives to induce cooperation from rival interests. Also like tit-for-tat, neither of the parties relinquishes its capacity for self-defense. However, GRIT differs somewhat from tit-for-tat, because the conciliatory moves are initiated and sustained by one party without requiring explicit reciprocal responses from the target state or from a nonstate actor. A GRIT approach seeks to alter the structure of conflict by promoting trust between the antagonists through a series of limited conciliatory initiatives, which are communicated openly to the target state and its public. Each initiative and its conciliatory intention is announced separately, and reciprocal acts are invited but not demanded.[59]

The data from various experimental investigations lend some support to the contention that GRIT strategies have altered the perceptions and behavior of rival parties in a cooperative direction.[60] Mark Pilisuk and Paul Skolnick, after concluding that GRIT produces "only a marginal and contingent increase" of cooperation over tit-for-tat, suggest the possibility of linking the two strategies, using a series of limited conciliatory moves in the earlier stages and then a tit-for-tat strategy later on.[61] This perhaps offers an opening for a third party's initiatives that use both noncoercive and coercive incentives to promote a positive outcome, something that I will probe in greater depth below.

Conclusion

Disarray and disruptions in negotiations between the African state and ethnic group (or groups) can lead to severe conflict, sometimes with a great intensity fueled by bitter political memories of collective hurt, humiliation, and exploitation and by a competition for scarce state-controlled resources. Distorted information, manipulated by irresponsible politicians and spread by a mass media under their control, can also contribute very substantially to the emergence of ethnic fears. In worst cases, the result is prolonged, intrastate wars that are normally settled by military force and capitulation, but in some one-fourth of the cases the outcome is determined by negotiations and mediation.

Certainly internal mediators may have enormous advantages in dealing with conflicts within their own society, as seen, for example, in the important role played by church and other voluntary association leaders when intervening in South Africa's tense encounter. Internal mediators' ability to combine sensitivity to local cultural assumptions with insights into universal principles of conflict resolution make them important assets in the effort to develop cooperative relationships on the ground.[62] However, in highly intense conflicts, many of which have spread across international borders, strong external mediators with enormous resources at their disposal become an essential part of the conflict management process. Only these external actors have the capacity to wield the necessary pressures and incentives to encourage local rivals to reconsider their alternatives and then to enforce the peace during the postnegotiation stage. The purpose of this volume's focus on the latter aspect of the peacemaking process is to concentrate on the possibilities that are present for international initiatives in deeply conflictive ethnic encounters, while at the same time recognizing that internal actors also have an important contribution to make to the process of establishing regularized, positive interactions leading to cooperation.

The cases that follow link the state-society relationships discussed in chapters 2 and 3 with internationalized, and often violent, intrastate conflicts and conflict management processes. In order to emphasize the themes of the encounter between state and society, its breakdown, and third-party efforts to create or restore an intrastate system of conflict management, I have grouped the case studies as follows: the *nonexistence* of a societywide conflict management system at independence and the ongoing efforts to construct one (Angola); efforts to *reconstruct* a minority-dominated conflict management system, both of which relied heavily on the suppression of conflicts (Rhodesia and South Africa); and the *breakdown* of inherited postcolonial conflict management systems (Sudan).

ANGOLA

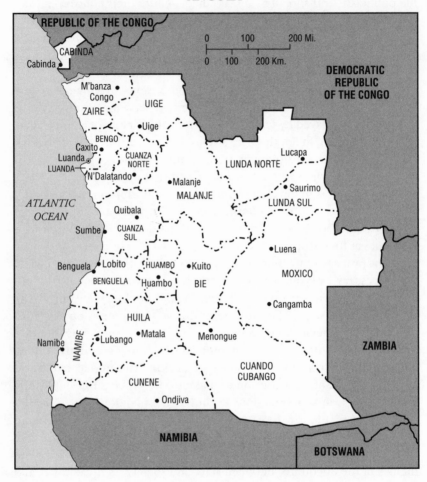

5

Constructing a Conflict Management System in Angola, 1989–97

Two parties in [a] dispute generally agree to a cease-fire
only because one is successful and happy with its gains,
while the other has lost, but fears even worse to come.

BARRY R. POSEN

Unlike Zimbabwe, where a postcolonial conflict management system was in place at the time of independence, Angola emerged from colonial rule without broadly accepted institutions for regulating state-society conflict. A military coup in Portugal in 1974 led to hasty efforts by the outgoing colonial power to negotiate a power-sharing arrangement among Angola's three nationalist movements during the transition period. However, this elite pact (the Alvor accord) was soon eclipsed by a renewal of fighting among the armies of these nationalist groups. The Alvor accord therefore failed to provide the basis for an effective

---

This chapter draws on material that appeared in three previously published essays: Donald Rothchild, "Conflict Management in Angola," *Transafrica Forum*, vol. 8 (Spring 1991), pp. 77-101; Donald Rothchild and Caroline Hartzell, "The Case of Angola: Four Power Intervention and Disengagement," in Ariel E. Levite, Bruce W. Jentleson, and Larry Berman, eds., *Foreign Military Intervention: The Dynamics of Protracted Conflict* (Columbia University Press, 1992), pp. 163-207; and Donald Rothchild and Caroline Hartzell, "Interstate and Intrastate Negotiations in Angola," in I. William Zartman, ed., *Elusive Peace: Negotiating an End to Civil Wars* (Brookings, 1995), pp. 175-203.

postcolonial conflict management system, leaving Angolans to engage each other in a civil war intensified by links between these nationalist movements and their allies inside and outside the region.

In Angola, conflict existed concurrently in both the interstate and intrastate (personal, ideological, and ethnoregional) realms. As a consequence of determined mediation efforts by U.S. Assistant Secretary of State Chester A. Crocker, backed by the Soviet Union, the interstate dimension of the conflict was ultimately settled in a tripartite agreement in December 1988, which provided, among other things, for the redeployment and disengagement of Cuban troops from Angola and for a gradual transition to independence from South African control of its close neighbor, Namibia. Meanwhile, the internal war between the government, led by the Popular Movement for the Liberation of Angola (MPLA), and the insurgent movement, the National Union for the Total Independence of Angola (UNITA), continued until 1991, when a Portuguese-mediated effort, actively supported by the United States and the Soviet Union, resulted in the Bicesse accords. This agreement proved difficult to implement, however, because UNITA leader Jonas Savimbi, after agreeing to the accords, refused to accept the outcome of the 1992 general elections and resumed the civil war.

Although UNITA initially scored a series of military victories, seizing over 70 percent of the territory of the country, the fortunes of war were reversed by 1994.[1] Angolan government forces, rearmed and supported by foreign military advisers, turned the tide of battle. In these changed circumstances, with UNITA's prospects looking increasingly bleak, insurgent leader Savimbi agreed to a United Nations–mediated agreement, the Lusaka protocol, based for the most part on the Bicesse accords.

In April 1997, two decades of civil war ended as Angolan President José Eduardo dos Santos dissolved his cabinet and installed a new government of national unity that included four UNITA cabinet ministers and seven deputy ministers. Because the two sides continue to distrust each other's intentions, however, the Lusaka protocol appears fragile and vulnerable to changes in commitment.

In this chapter, I propose to analyze the conflict management process by focusing on the efforts of a series of third parties to mediate between the Angolan government and UNITA. I will look at the roles played by the United Nations and two middle-range powers in their attempts to mediate the internal conflict and to use incentives to influence the institutions for future governance.

The Internal Incentives for Conflict

By the time of Angola's independence in 1975, what began as a struggle by Angolan nationalist movements against a colonial power had become a war characterized by both intrastate and interstate conflict. The initial indications of the emergence of such a war were a series of uprisings in Angola during early 1961. Although these rebellions were uncoordinated and lacked an inclusive national focus, they evolved into a small-scale guerrilla war against colonial domination that persisted over the next twelve years.[2] Two nationalist movements, the MPLA and the National Front for the Liberation of Angola (FNLA), were active in leading the Angolan insurgency against Portugal. These were joined by a third movement, UNITA, in 1966.

Although these three movements shared the goal of liberating Angola from Portuguese colonial rule, each movement had distinct ethnic roots, different ideological inclinations and development strategies, contrasting positions on state and party centralization, and its own ties to external actors in the international environment. The FNLA, under the leadership of Holden Roberto, was primarily uniracial and rural in background and largely supported by the Bakongo people. Its goals for Angola included ending colonialism and working toward economic development, democracy, industrialization, and pan-African unity.[3] The movement, which had close ties to President Mobutu Sese Seko's Zaire and, later, the United States, was considered to be anti-Marxist and pro-Western in orientation. Thus at a meeting between Roberto and a U.S. diplomat in 1975, the U.S. official reportedly reassured Roberto "that the US remained unflagging in its support of his and other friendly forces in Angola seeking to thwart a Soviet-backed military victory."[4]

The MPLA, headed by Agostinho Neto, was urban-based, multiracial, and committed to a Marxist worldview.[5] Although much of its leadership consisted of *mestiços* and *assimilados*,[6] it had its roots among the Mbundu people in the North-Central region, who make up some 25 percent of Angola's total population. This racial and cultural mix meant that MPLA members were inclined to take a more nationalistic or class-oriented stance on many issues than those in the other movements. The MPLA's program called for national independence, creation of a society "without distinctions based on ethnic groups, class, age, political and religious beliefs," democracy, pan-African unity, and agrarian reform.[7] The MPLA's commitment to a centralized one-party state left little room for power-sharing solutions. The MPLA had long stated that members of UNITA should be granted amnesty and integrated into Angolan politics; however, it regarded Savimbi as a "traitor" and, until the change in party and electoral rules in 1991, had called for his exclusion from the political process.[8]

UNITA found its primary base of support among the Ovimbundu people, who composed about 35 percent of the country's population. Savimbi's training in guerrilla warfare techniques and his exposure to Maoism in China failed to tie him to any particular ideology, however. By presenting himself as a leader of the black peasantry, Savimbi sought to contrast his movement to the *mestiço*-led and urban-based MPLA. Although the UNITA constitution calls for a broadly inclusive central government, Savimbi brooks no opposition within party ranks, exercising firm and rather repressive domination over the people in the UNITA-controlled areas.[9] His ambition, conclude two observers, is to become the country's head of state.[10]

The ethnoregional factor was clearly a major element in the struggle for power among the three Angolan nationalist movements. Although all the movements had multiethnic leaderships and support groups, their main bases had assumed an ethnoregional character by the time of independence. Early fears among the Ovimbundu of political and economic underrepresentation in a FNLA-led state faded as the FNLA began to disappear from the sociopolitical landscape, only to be replaced in due course by fears of MPLA hegemony.[11] The ethnic anxieties, which became increasingly evident as the civil war dragged on, became manifest during the 1992 presidential election. Presidential candidate Jonas Savimbi of UNITA won heavily in the predominantly Ovimbundu central highlands; his opponent, MPLA candidate José Eduardo dos Santos, scored equally impressive victories in the area around Luanda. Ethnicity has emerged as an increasingly significant factor in Angola's political and military life as a consequence of the way central and local leaders (and most notably, Savimbi) have played the ethnic card when mobilizing their followers for political action.[12] "Although UNITA and the MPLA did not have their roots in ethnic politics," write Thomas Ohlson and Stephen Stedman, "the last fifteen years of war have reinforced ethnic tendencies in the two parties."[13] It is now commonplace for UNITA spokespersons to accuse the government of "continuing the political and tribal genocide it initiated in 1992."[14] The tragedy of ethnic violence and killings on both sides has resulted in a negative learning process that has become a part of the contemporary scene.

The three nationalist movements suffered from military and internal weaknesses and an unwillingness to unify their forces; they were thus unable to achieve any major military successes against the Portuguese. Between 1961 and 1974, the MPLA, FNLA, and UNITA vied for control over Angola's peoples and territories and for international recognition by states and multilateral organizations and the access to resources that often accompanied such recognition. Because the FNLA had the largest army at the time, it was in the best position to challenge the Portuguese and also the MPLA and UNITA. However, the FNLA was handicapped by a lack of experienced administrators, by Holden Roberto's controlling and sometimes erratic leadership, and by an overly strong identification with Bakongo interests.[15]

The smaller size of the MPLA's armed forces limited its ability to challenge the FNLA militarily, although this was partly compensated for by its well-educated leaders and an ideological and class appeal that cut across ethnic lines. However, internal struggles for control of the movement weakened it to such an extent that by 1972 the movement had become virtually defunct as a fighting unit.[16] UNITA, which had by far the smallest military force, engaged in survival politics, and under the charismatic leadership of Savimbi, pursued political strategies directed toward consolidating power and influence.

After the coup on April 25, 1974, and Portugal's suspension of military activities in Angola, UNITA, the FNLA, and the MPLA each arranged its own separate truce with the outgoing colonial power. The three Angolan movements then followed up on these truces by jockeying for military and political positions. As I. William Zartman and Johannes Aurik assert, the prospect of independence removed "the only thing they had in common, the fight against the colonizer."[17] The FNLA, backed by Zaire and now receiving economic and military aid from the United States, moved troops into northern Angola in an attempt to gain military superiority. The MPLA, worn down by factional infighting, nonetheless sought to secure control over the Angolan capital of Luanda, a Mbundu ethnic stronghold.[18]

Sporadic violence broke out in Luanda over the next few months, as troops of the three nationalist movements clashed with each other and with some of Luanda's white population. The three main Angolan leaders made progress on the political front, however. In an effort to coordinate their approach, Roberto, Neto, and Savimbi met in Bukavu, Zaire, in July 1974, where they agreed to adopt a common position regarding negotiations with the Portuguese. At Mombasa, Kenya, on January 5,

1975, the three leaders promised to end hostilities among themselves, and they signed a tripartite agreement setting out a united approach for the forthcoming constitutional negotiations with the Portuguese government. The three leaders next met in Alvor, Portugal; there, along with the Portuguese, they held five days of talks and on January 15 signed the Alvor agreement. The Alvor agreement provided for elections to a constituent assembly in October, leading to independence on November 11, 1975. In the interim, power was to be in the hands of a Portuguese high commissioner and a transitional government composed of three ministers from each of the nationalist movements, with the comissioner acting as a third party.[19] The premiership would rotate among the UNITA, FNLA, and MPLA ministers during the transitional period. Thus Alvor created an elite power-sharing regime.

In addition, Alvor provided for the formation of a joint Angolan Defense Force, consisting of 24,000 troops, 8,000 each from the MPLA, FNLA, and UNITA. These forces were to be combined during the transition period with another 24,000 Portuguese troops. No provision was made for verification, however. This omission proved a serious flaw, for each of the movement armies soon had armed forces larger than the Portuguese, making it difficult for the latter to enforce the peace.

Still holding essentialist perceptions of each other's intentions, the three nationalist movements soon renewed fighting, which overshadowed the agreement. This conflict was fueled by the growing number of arms shipments to the three movements from abroad. Organization of African Unity (OAU) leaders, seeking to salvage the Alvor process, arranged a meeting in Nakuru, Kenya, in June, where the three movement leaders formally agreed to cooperate in implementing the peace agreement. By July, however, the fighting had escalated further, and it became clear that the postcolonial conflict management system had proved ineffectual. MPLA was able to drive the FNLA from Luanda; shortly afterward, UNITA withdrew its ministers and troops from Luanda and left for sanctuary in the southern part of the country. That process marked the final collapse of the transitional government, and following fighting in the South, UNITA declared war against the MPLA regime. Despite continuing efforts by the OAU and various African statesmen to encourage unity among the three movements, they each went their own separate way.

On November 10, 1975, Portugal quietly withdrew from Angola. By recognizing Angola's sovereignty but by failing to transfer the reins of power to any of the rival movements, the former colonial power essen-

FIGURE 5-1. *Nationalist Movements and Outside Supporters in Angola*

	MPLA supporters	UNITA supporters
Direct interveners	Cuba	South Africa
Indirect interveners	USSR	United States

tially left them all to fight it out. On that very day, the MPLA, aided by an infusion of Cuban combat forces, decisively defeated the FNLA forces (backed by direct South African intervention and U.S. covert assistance) only miles from Luanda. Then, on November 11, Angola's independence day, the MPLA proclaimed an independent People's Republic of Angola (PRA). From that time forward, the conflict in postindependence Angola definitively became a civil war, a conflict rooted in the intrastate realm. However, the nationalist movements' ties to external powers made this also a confrontation with an interstate dimension, one with implications for southern Africa and the East-West rivalry.

The relationship between regime type and engagement in the conflict in Angola is illustrated in figure 5-1. Cuba and the Soviet Union both backed the MPLA and were generally hostile toward UNITA; they both chose to intervene in Angola on behalf of the MPLA. The Soviet Union intervened indirectly (providing their allies with statements of support and economic and military assistance), and Cuba intervened directly (disbursing assistance and deploying their regular combat forces in support of their allies). UNITA was assisted by the direct intervention of South Africa and the indirect intervention of the United States, both of which were hostile toward the MPLA.

The Postindependence Conflicts

In the period following Angola's independence, the Angolan government army—the Popular Armed Forces for the Liberation of Angola (FAPLA)—bolstered by Cuban forces and Soviet-supplied military equipment, began the process of consolidating its control. The MPLA regime was fresh from victory over various guerrilla elements in the field and by February 1976 was beginning to gain widespread international legitimacy.

The military victory was far from complete, however. UNITA, the government's main internal opponent, continued to mount guerrilla attacks, primarily in the rural areas but also in urban centers. Such guerrilla activities were a challenge to the MPLA's capacity for effective control; what made these activities even more threatening to the government were their links to a powerful regional actor, the Republic of South Africa.

Generally speaking, the military challenge that internal and external antagonists posed to the Angolan government's authority between 1976 and 1980 remained manageable. The ongoing low-intensity conflict escalated in August 1981, however, when South Africa launched Operation Protea, a major incursion of its forces into Cunene province. Before withdrawing in September, the South Africans inflicted heavy damage on numerous villages and, in doing so, raised the level of world concern about events in the region. With South African Defense Forces (SADF) continuing to launch new attacks into southern Angola and FAPLA increasingly strained and reliant on Cuban troops and Soviet advisors and materiel, the Luanda regime attempted in 1983 to ease its military dilemma through negotiations and began to explore the possibility of reaching a cease-fire and disengagement agreement with South Africa.

Seeking to "end the cycle of violence in the area," "undercut Soviet influence" in Angolan affairs, bring independence to Namibia, and facilitate a Cuban troop withdrawal from Angola, U.S. diplomats responded quickly to the positive signals from the authorities in Luanda.[20] Assistant Secretary of State for African Affairs Chester A. Crocker reasoned that "our approach was aimed at improving relations with Pretoria, on the understanding that the [South African government] would move toward constructive change—in Namibia and at home—and at capitalizing on African interest in Namibian independence to lever the Cubans out of Angola."[21] In this case, initial contacts between the Angolan and South African governments and the U.S. intermediaries proved inconclusive, largely because the rivals refused to compromise on issues relating to Crocker's strategy on "linkage" (that is, tying Namibia's independence to the withdrawal of Cuban troops from Angola), particularly the timing of the South African and Cuban troop withdrawal.[22] In December 1983, though, South Africa proposed to UN Secretary-General Javier Pérez de Cuellar a one-month truce and the disengagement of forces from southern Angola.[23] The Angolans at first rejected this opening but later advised the secretary-general that they would accept the truce and disengagement proposal if these were tied to the UN Security Council's Resolution 435 regarding Namibia's independence.

The resulting Lusaka agreement of February 1984 did not represent a comprehensive settlement of regional issues but rather what some diplomats described as "a reciprocal understanding" between the two sides to disengage and desist from launching any new military engagements in the area.[24] The first stages of SADF withdrawal called for in the Lusaka agreement occurred as anticipated; the process dragged on, however. By mid-1984, then, expectations of southern African détente had largely faded. Explaining the failure to gain a wider agreement on regional issues during this period, Zartman comments that the United States "was unable to accelerate the process, unwilling to give substance to deadlines, and unready to nail down agreement already reached."[25] What appeared to some observers to be a ripe moment had passed, and the region became mired in a deadly confrontation.

The Military Climax and Stalemate

Two basic choices faced the direct interveners (South Africa and Cuba) and the Angolan government to overcome the stalemate on the ground. They could either fight on and hope to attain a military victory or seek a political settlement through negotiations. Diplomatic movement could not progress far as long as both sides still believed in the possibility of a military victory, making further military clashes inevitable.

By the summer of 1987, FAPLA, acting on the basis of Soviet advice, launched a major new offensive against the strategically important town of Mavinga. FAPLA encountered sharp resistance from UNITA and South African ground forces, supported by South African air power.[26] Another major FAPLA assault on Mavinga was turned back in October 1987; at this time, the Angolan army pulled back in an orderly manner to its support base at Cuito Cuanavale. South African and UNITA troops pursued these units to the town's perimeters and began a siege that lasted six months.

By spring 1988, the newly enlarged Cuban forces went on the offensive in southwestern Angola, concentrating their attack on the SADF contingents there. Cuban troops clashed with South Africans on June 26, near the hydroelectric dam at Calueque. In an air raid, Cuban-piloted MiG-23s reportedly bombed South African positions and the dam itself.

At least twelve white South Africans were killed, the largest number of such casualties in any battle of the war. According to a Defense Intelligence Agency assessment, "the Cuban deployment to the Southwest ended Pretoria's military dominance of southern Angola."[27]

For the South Africans, as well as the MPLA regime and the other interveners, the point had now been reached where the costs of the war in Angola exceeded its anticipated benefits. This contributed to a change of perceptions on all sides that resulted in raising negotiated peace to the status of a preferred option.

The Interstate Mediation Process

The battle of Cuito Cuanavale and the encounter at the Calueque dam represented a turning point in two respects. First, they indicated an important change in the balance of strategic forces. Cuban air superiority undermined South African pretensions to military invincibility in the region, and FAPLA's ability to hold onto the town and the airfield at Cuito Cuanavale showed them to be worthy opponents in their own territory.[28] Second, the heavy costs of the struggle had contributed to a sense of war weariness among the MPLA regime and the direct and indirect interveners. SADF losses in aircraft and manpower (including hundreds of black troops and at least sixty white soldiers) brought about a new skepticism and sensitivity in civilian circles about casualties and the financial costs of war. In Luanda, some moderate elements within the ruling coalition were fatigued by the ongoing two-front struggle that had left its economy gravely weakened and incurred thousands of war casualties.[29] When these two factors became linked to a third—increasing pragmatism in relations between the superpowers—mutual disengagement on their part became a serious possibility.

The prenegotiation process leading up to international negotiations to end the stalemate got a boost in the spring of 1987, as the Angolan government reopened discussions with the Reagan administration regarding its decision to resume sending military assistance to UNITA. In an interview in June, President dos Santos expressed hope for the establishment of diplomatic relations with the United States and described the withdrawal of Cuban troops as possible if acts or threats of aggression against his country ceased, support for UNITA ended, and apartheid in South Africa were terminated.[30] Subsequent talks with Chester Crocker in July on the question of "linkage" ended in a stalemate. In September 1987, the pace of U.S.-Angolan diplomatic contacts quickened. The Angolans reportedly accepted the U.S. position on linking a Cuban withdrawal to Namibia's independence and also proposed the redeployment of Cuban troops north of the thirteenth parallel, during the first phase, with a full withdrawal to follow.[31] However, they ruled out any compromise with UNITA and declared that they saw no solution to the problem.[32] In subsequent talks with Crocker in Luanda, the Angolans agreed, for the first time, to put the issue of full Cuban troop withdrawal on the agenda for negotiations, provided that four preconditions were put into effect: the withdrawal of South African troops from southern Angola, the cessation of South African aggression, respect for Angola's sovereignty and territorial integrity, and the implementation of UNSC Resolution 435 on Namibia's independence.[33]

Then, in March 1988, U.S. mediators met separately with the Angolans and the Cubans in Luanda and with the South Africans in Geneva. These parallel encounters showed the two sides to be far apart regarding the timetable for Cuban troop withdrawal, aid for the insurgents, and the terms for South Africa's pullback from Namibia; however, because the Angolans were prepared to accept a total Cuban troop withdrawal *in principle*, Crocker deemed the moment to be ripe for a major third-party mediation effort.[34]

The four powers began formal negotiations with exploratory talks in London. With Crocker as chairman, representatives from Angola, Cuba, and South Africa—but not the South West African People's Organization (SWAPO) and UNITA—met in secret to hold a general discussion of the Angolan proposal for a four-year withdrawal of Cuban forces: that the 20,000 troops stationed in the South would leave within eighteeen months and the 15,000 in the North would pull out in stages over a four-year period.[35] This proposal was linked to several other conditions, such as Namibia's independence and aid to UNITA; it diverged markedly from South Africa's call for a full Cuban withdrawal in one year's time. Even so, the Angolan proposal represented a useful starting point for further discussions aimed at narrowing the gaps.

During the follow-up sessions at Brazzaville and Cairo, the South Africans became more strident about the need for a quick pullout of Cuban troops and the inclusion of UNITA in Angola's ruling coalition. Even so, all sides maintained the necessary momentum at this juncture because of the quiet but persistent efforts of the two great powers. In a case of tacit cooperation, the Soviets reportedly pressed their Angolan and Cuban allies to work constructively; the United States used its influence to encourage South Africa to adopt a more pragmatic stance regarding its interests.[36] The extent of superpower influence on these partially autonomous state actors should not be overstated, but it certainly facilitated the negotiating process.

In New York, during July 1988, representatives of the Angolan, Cuban, and South African governments, with the United States acting as mediator, were able to move from uncoordinated rhetorical stances to an acceptance of general principles for a peaceful settlement in southwestern Africa. The parties deliberately postponed haggling over the details of the timetable for the Cuban troop withdrawal, the South African military pullout, the role of UNITA in Angolan politics, external assistance to the UNITA guerrillas, and possible restrictions on SWAPO and African National Congress (ANC) activities following the settlement. This agreement, for all of its omissions, was highly important because it put in place an organizing framework for the next set of negotiations.

Now that the general framework for negotiations was in place, the follow-up rounds necessarily turned to bargaining on practical issues. After a shaky beginning at the talks in Geneva in August 1988, the conferees succeeded in working out a de facto cessation of hostilities and a sequence of steps leading to peace in southwestern Africa.[37] The four parties made a commitment to reach agreement on the Cuban troop withdrawal from Angola by September 1, 1988, the very date set for the completion of South Africa's military pullout from that country. Moreover, the parties agreed to recommend November 1 as the date for beginning the implementation of UNSC Resolution 435, leading up to UN-supervised elections to be held seven months later.[38]

The momentum for peace in the region was building. Several weeks later, the three direct combatants signed an accord at Ruacana, ending the hostilities between them and setting up a Joint Military Monitoring Committee to resolve any conflicts that might arise in the course of implementing the disengagement process. Agreement on a timetable for the withdrawal of Cuban troops from Angola had now become indispensable to the success of the U.S.-sponsored peace process. The two sets of meetings at Brazzaville in August and September made some progress in narrowing the wide gaps between the South African and Cuban-Angolan positions. Moving toward a compromise, South Africa now indicated a willingness to accept a one-year time frame, and the Cubans and Angolans were reportedly prepared to accept three years.[39]

In October, during talks in New York, the four powers agreed on a twenty-four- to thirty-month withdrawal period but remained very far apart on the timing of the withdrawals. South Africa sought the withdrawal of 90 percent of the Cubans in the first year, whereas the Angolans wanted to limit the withdrawal to 50 percent. U.S. efforts to find a middle ground (75 percent of the Cuban troops leaving in the first year and the remaining 25 percent to be redeployed in the North until the deadline) were rejected by both sides.[40] The conferees did agree to hold further discussions on the matter and, accordingly, met in Geneva the following month in another effort to settle the issue. This proved a time of tense bargaining. The final product was most positive, however, for the conferees hammered out a tentative accord providing for the withdrawal of Cuban troops over a twenty-seven-month period, with two-thirds of these soldiers to be withdrawn in the first year and the remainder being redeployed by stages to the North.

The Geneva agreement was accepted by the Cuban, Angolan, and South African governments shortly afterward. It represented an important milestone in progress toward a negotiated peace in southwestern Africa. The basic agreement had by now been hammered out, although a few issues still remained on the table. The key issue of verification was left for December 22, the date that the final agreements would be signed, when it would be worked out among the UN secretary-general, Angola, and Cuba. The deal had been struck. Accordingly, the four parties gathered at the United Nations in New York for the final signing of the two accords, providing for Namibia's independence and the withdrawal of Cuban troops from Angola. The angry exchanges that marked the signing ceremony, however, revealed the essentialist perceptions that the antagonists still held about each other's intentions; it also showed that, under the right circumstances and with determined leadership, the negotiating process can sometimes surmount deeply divisive adversarial perceptions.

The achievements of this agreement were certainly very substantial. Yet several important regional matters had been consciously avoided by the negotiators or remained unresolved. These included UNITA's possible reconciliation with the MPLA regime, U.S. aid to that movement, the future of the South African–held enclave of Walvis Bay inside Namibia, the closure of ANC training camps, and the implementation of an effective monitoring process.[41] The general fragility of the accords became painfully apparent soon after the signing ceremony. President dos Santos charged that South Africa continued to aid UNITA "contrary to the signed treaty," and bitter fighting broke out in April 1989 between South African territorial forces and infiltrating SWAPO guerrillas along Namibia's northern border.[42] But the tensions accompanying disengagement did not lead to an unraveling of the settlement package; this pointed to the underlying strength of the larger process of international peace that had led up to the settlement.

The settlement also set the basis for a new effort to build a conflict management system in Angola. To be sure, a number of preconditions for an internal agreement were lacking: the parties held essentialist perceptions about each other's purposes; leaders were not yet determined to find a political solution; a mutually hurting stalemate was not present; and external pressure on their local allies was indecisive. Nevertheless, the Angola-Namibia accords of 1988 narrowed the peace agenda and showed local leaders that adversarial negotiations could prove beneficial.

Intrastate Mediation and the Construction of an Internal Conflict Management System

After the signing of the tripartite accords in December 1988 and the redeployment and disengagement of Cuban and South African military forces, the focus shifted to Angola's ongoing civil war between the MPLA-led government and the UNITA insurgents. The perceptions of the internal political actors remained relatively fixed and their confrontation intense. Angolan government leaders continued to describe Savimbi as a "traitor."[43] President dos Santos indicated that he would not negotiate directly with Savimbi, but he had not precluded other forms of contact.[44] The main antagonists found themselves locked into a mutually damaging relationship, thus making defection preferable to unilateral concessions. This left third parties very limited scope to employ incentives to alter the payoffs of the game. By 1994, however, the context of the internal encounter had changed significantly: the growing strength and capacity of the Angolan government's army raised the possibility of a government military victory over the retreating UNITA forces.

In the remainder of this chapter, I will concentrate on the internal dimensions of the conflict, comparing and contrasting the efforts by the United Nations and middle-range powers to mediate the civil war and to attempt to construct an enduring conflict management system. With a continuance of mutual distrust, it remains to be seen whether the long-term confidence-building measures of the Lusaka protocol can help promote the institutions for an enduring peace. The United Nations, which has employed its largest peacekeeping force in Angola, planned to withdraw most of its forces in mid-1997. With the international community no longer a guarantor of the peace, it will be up to the local rivals to apply the rules of relations worked out in Lusaka for themselves.

Mobutu Takes the Initiative

After the signing of the Angola-Namibia accords of 1988, the internal adversaries were increasingly left to their own devices, and a continuing struggle offered them little prospect of gaining significant benefits. Even so, the problem following the international settlement was to overcome the political stalemate and begin the search for a peaceful solution. In a highly significant initiative, President Mobutu Sese Seko of Zaire, anxious to improve his image in the region and in the West, stepped into this situation and called a meeting of the heads of state of Angola, Gabon, and the People's Republic of the Congo in August 1988.

Harsh rhetoric notwithstanding, a perceptible softening of government and insurgent positions on the issue of a political solution to their differences became apparent in early 1989. Low-level talks between the two sides in January were limited to a discussion of the government's offer of amnesty to UNITA troops who laid down their arms. This proposal was rejected by UNITA's spokesmen; however, at the request of Côte d'Ivoire leader Houphouët-Boigny, who was acting as an intermediary between the adversaries, guerrilla leader Jonas Savimbi did call off UNITA's planned rainy season offensive. In March, Savimbi extended this moratorium on offensive action; he announced the release of MPLA prisoners, declared a willingness to reopen the Benguela railway to nonmilitary traffic, and indicated a preparedness to participate in a transitional government to lead the country to free elections.[45] The MPLA-led regime responded with its own peace platform, essentially consisting of a program of amnesty for the rank-and-file UNITA soldiers.

For Mobutu, then, the peace process began in 1989, with the informal gathering of heads of state in Tokyo on February 22, the conference of regional leaders in Luanda on May 16, and separate meetings that Mobutu held on two occasions with Savimbi and Angolan President dos Santos.[46] The Luanda conference was particularly significant, because it identified national reconciliation as an objective and recognized Mobutu's legitimacy as mediator. At Luanda, eight African heads of state (from Zaire, the Congo, Gabon, Zimbabwe, Mozambique, Zambia, Sao Tomé and Principe, and Angola) endorsed a seven-point Angolan government peace plan. The plan emphasized a peace zone along the Benguela railway, an end to foreign interference, the cessation of support to UNITA, and the granting of amnesty by the government. Nevertheless, it made only limited concessions to the insurgent movement. In dos Santos's words: "We accept the voluntary and temporary retirement of Jonas Savimbi within the framework of the special handling of his case. All other Angolans would be integrated into our society within the current institutions of the People's Republic of Angola [PRA], according to their capabilities."[47]

Thus the Angolan government still made few concessions to UNITA's demands for power sharing and an autonomous existence. The government insisted upon Savimbi's temporary exile and the integration of UNITA's civilian and military components into the MPLA-led one-party state.[48] Savimbi, on his side, called for multiparty elections and a possible coalition government. He denied seeking absolute power for himself, asking only the enactment of the 1975 Alvor agreement principles regarding a transitional government of the MPLA, UNITA, and FNLA before the holding of open elections. The gap between adversaries remained wide. Even so, as Savimbi observed, fourteen years of war had shown that neither side was capable of a military victory. If they could not impose their terms on each other, a political settlement then became the only logical alternative to continued fighting.[49]

Gbadolite

Now that the war had proven to be costly and unwinnable and some signs of conciliation were in evidence, external facilitators were able to take the next step: a summit meeting at Mobutu's country residence in Gbadolite, Zaire, on June 22, 1989. This necessarily involved a meeting between the two main antagonists, dos Santos and Savimbi, which was difficult to arrange. When dos Santos received a phone call from Mobutu just before his departure from Luanda, to inform him that Savimbi might be present at Gbadolite, dos Santos reportedly reacted angrily and tried to cancel his travel plans. At this point, various African heads of state apparently interceded and persuaded dos Santos to attend the summit meeting.[50] Throughout the seven-hour, closed-door summit meeting, the two adversaries were kept apart: Savimbi was placed in a room adjacent to the main conference hall. During the day, Mobutu met with first one adversary and then the other, "cajoling and threatening" them, to extract their agreement to the summit declaration.[51]

In Mobutu's attempt to use this opportunity to pressure the adversaries to reach an agreement, he assembled an impressive array of African leaders in Gbadolite. In all, twenty countries were represented at the summit, of which eighteen were represented by their heads of state. Included in this gathering were General Moussa Traore, the current chairman of the OAU and president of Mali, President Kenneth Kaunda of Zambia, President Paul Biya of Cameroun, King Hassan II of Morocco, President Ibrahim Babangida of Nigeria, and President Robert Mugabe of Zimbabwe. Mobutu clearly intended to use this "formidable group" (as Mugabe described it) to pressure the adversaries into negotiating in earnest.[52]

In addition, both superpowers gave general support to the Gbadolite peace process.[53] Although arms shipments to the combatants continued during the Gbadolite negotiations and beyond, the superpowers nonetheless placed pressure on their clients at key junctures to keep the peace process on track. At the Gbadolite meetings in June 1989, various observers concluded that Soviet pressures contributed significantly toward wringing concessions from a hesitant and reluctant dos Santos. Similarly, U.S. officials enthusiastically welcomed the Gbadolite summit as a positive step.[54] The United States combined both negative and positive incentives to move the Gbadolite process ahead. Nonrecognition and continued military aid to the insurgents (an estimated $50 million) were both seen as means of placating key members of the Senate Foreign Relations Committee as well as pressuring the Angolan government to accept the peace process.[55] Washington also used positive incentives to promote cooperation between the MPLA and UNITA. The Bush administration held out the prospect of normalizing relations with the Luanda regime as soon as it concluded an internal settlement with the insurgent movement, and the administration also gave "tacit assurance" that, with national reconciliation, it would consider ending military aid to UNITA.[56]

What emerged from this effort, however, was not a carefully worked out peace agreement; rather, the summit at Gbadolite represented one advance in a larger negotiating process. The fact that Africans had taken the initiative and quickly produced results in the form of a communiqué that set out the principles of agreement was viewed as a heartening sign.[57] At the symbolic level, the first direct encounter between dos Santos and Savimbi and the handshake between these two adversaries signaled their willingness to search for national reconciliation by political means. In setting the framework in which this handshake could take place, Africa's leaders facilitated Savimbi's emergence from the dim shadows of unrespectability.

At the substantive level, there was confusion surrounding verbal understandings, arising from the long and turbulent negotiating session, but three principles were put forth in the text of the final Gbadolite declaration: the desire of both sides to end the war and achieve national reconciliation; the proclamation of a cease-fire to become effective on June 24, 1989; and the establishment of a commission, to be chaired by President Mobutu, to prepare the plan for national reconciliation in Angola.[58]

Clearly, the Gbadolite declaration left unresolved several issues that were important to the main adversaries; this was a major failure attributable to the intermediary's hasty action. Besides the problem that the points of agreement were not written down, the larger reality was the profound differences of perceptions and interpretation between the two adversaries. President dos Santos and his supporters came away from Gbadolite convinced that Savimbi had agreed to a voluntary, temporary exile and that UNITA's military and civilian elements would be integrated into MPLA party, bureaucratic, and military units. Savimbi, on the other hand, dismissed talk of exile, refused the proposed offer of amnesty, rejected the integration of UNITA into MPLA-administered institutions, and demanded the establishment of a multiparty system and the holding of free, open elections. Savimbi was determined to preserve UNITA's separate identity and to compete with the MPLA-led regime for power at the political center. In Savimbi's opinion, the MPLA had agreed to talk "because they have failed to wipe us out"; hence he refused to concede at the conference table what he had not lost on the battlefield.[59] In brief, MPLA viewed the Gbadolite declaration as the end of UNITA, whereas UNITA perceived the declaration as an opportunity to compete for power and to move toward power sharing at the national level.

In a situation where state softness, persistent conflict among parties, ethnic groups, and regions, and personal animosity are involved, highly conflictive negotiations such as those conducted at Gbadolite are likely to achieve only symbolic results. President dos Santos felt compelled to go to the summit meeting to demonstrate his party's commitment to peace.[60] Savimbi, for his part, was distrustful of the process from its inception and appeared to participate only to the extent that it advanced his own interests. Savimbi, the personalist and populist leader, considered himself to be indistinguishable from UNITA; thus the claims that he had agreed to his exile and the integration of UNITA into the MPLA-dominated state structure became somewhat academic.[61] "If I leave Angola," he asked, "who is going to lead UNITA into this process of national reconciliation?"[62] Each leader, then, did seek peace, but only on his own terms.

The Post-Gbadolite Constraints

The parties at Gbadolite had agreed in principle on a cease-fire, to become effective on June 24, 1989, although they failed to establish a mechanism to determine the rules of permissible behavior or resolve violations. It is not surprising, therefore, that the cease-fire never really took hold. At first, the hostilities between the MPLA and UNITA forces were limited and strategic in nature; they soon increased in intensity, however, culminating in heavy fighting around Mavinga in the winter of 1989–90.

Despite this evidence of continuing military engagements in the field, Mobutu resolutely pushed ahead with his mediatory initiative. Following the Gbadolite summit, a series of four inconclusive meetings were held in Kinshasa to work out a cease-fire agreement that would be acceptable to both sides. Then, on August 22, a second regional summit, attended by the leaders of eight African states (Angola, the Congo, Gabon, Mozambique, Sao Tomé and Principe, Zaire, Zambia, and Zimbabwe), assembled in Harare, Zimbabwe, to review the situation since the Gbadolite summit and to make recommendations on issues that had not been dealt with at the earlier summit. Significantly, UNITA was not represented at Harare; Savimbi had not been invited.

The five-hour meeting reportedly brought sharp differences out into the open. The more radical frontline leaders were highly critical of the conservative Mobutu and his handling of the earlier summit meeting. They especially criticized Mobutu's failure to secure agreement on the peace terms in writing from dos Santos and Savimbi.[63] The final Harare communiqué reflected the frontline presidents' dissatisfaction with Savimbi's behavior since the Gbadolite summit and specifically encouraged Savimbi's temporary, voluntary retirement from Angola and the integration of UNITA into the MPLA and its state institutions. As anticipated, Savimbi "violently" rejected the communiqué, and Radio UNITA warned darkly about "the plot being prepared against [UNITA] as an organization, its leader, and peace in Angola."[64]

The ongoing antagonism between MPLA and UNITA continued to poison the atmosphere in the months that followed. On September 18, eight regional heads of state met in Kinshasa for another summit. In this case, Savimbi was invited to attend, but despite pressures from U.S.

Assistant Secretary of State for African Affairs Herman J. Cohen and others, he declined to join the gathering.[65] Under these circumstances, the conferees in Kinshasa could only reaffirm their support for the Gbadolite agreement and call upon Savimbi to sign a new draft statement regarding the implementation process. Savimbi refused and countered with his own plan, proposing the creation of a multinational force to verify and guarantee the cease-fire and calling for open elections.[66]

As the memories of Gbadolite dimmed, the adversaries appeared to be more preoccupied with what divided them than with the urgent need for peace and national reconciliation. Progress had certainly been made in hammering out the technical details of a possible cease-fire; nevertheless, the adversaries remained quite unwilling to adjust their positions and to negotiate the outstanding issues.[67] Savimbi ruled out granting significant concessions on the issues of exile, the integration of UNITA into MPLA structures, multiparty elections, or power sharing, and dos Santos appeared equally unwavering on these points. Also, as time wore on, the intensity of factional differences among MPLA officials seemed to increase, thus making new conciliatory gestures even more difficult than before.[68] One Zairian diplomat reported that dos Santos was under "tremendous pressure from hard-liners in the Government." These hard-liners felt that they had been "burned" by Savimbi in the past, and they reportedly saw little to gain from developing a new cease-fire agreement at this point. Rather, they argued for a military solution to the problem of insurgency.[69] What had started at Gbadolite was now being complicated by a combination of personal antagonisms, fears for the future, schisms within a bargaining partner (the MPLA), and the character of the stakes involved in the conflict. Taken together, these variables made the costs of disagreement lower than that of agreement for the adversaries.

The Bicesse Accords

The Gbadolite process was now deadlocked, and Mobutu was unable to summon sufficient political and economic resources to bring the disputing parties to a settlement, so a new approach to the negotiations became imperative. Neither the Angolan government nor the UNITA insurgents could muster the military strength to eliminate the opposition or force its capitulation. Moreover, the conditions for a sustained military effort were less and less encouraging. Not only were Angolans weary of the protracted civil war, but their external supporters were also disengaging from the conflict. Cuban forces withdrew from Angola in advance of the schedule set forth in the Angola-Namibia accords, and South African assistance to UNITA (reportedly extended in a clandestine manner) was obviously small by comparison with former levels. Most important, the superpowers, having made the shift from adversarial to cautiously cooperative relations, were now quite anxious to reduce their involvement in Angola's internal war.

President dos Santos, recognizing that the Mobutu initiative had stalled, was forthright about the need to regain momentum in the negotiations and thus called for a new third-party intermediary.[70] Portugal, the former colonial power, rose to the occasion, and from mid-1990 onward, chaired a series of talks between UNITA and representatives of the Angolan government. U.S. Assistant Secretary Cohen, with backing from the Soviets, gave quiet support to the efforts made by Portuguese Deputy Foreign Minister Durao Barroso to work out a set of mutually acceptable principles that could serve as a framework for subsequent negotiations on a cease-fire and political settlement.[71] Cohen set out his sense of the principles that the two sides had agreed upon at their first exploratory talk in Portugal on April 24–25: he spoke of a general consensus on holding elections, the creation of a national army, the existence of political parties separate from the government, and a willingness to accept "a de facto mutual recognition."[72]

Both the Soviets and the United States continued to back their local allies with military assistance while supporting Portuguese mediatory initiatives during the period that followed. In 1990, for example, Soviet military aid to the MPLA amounted to an estimated $800 million. Meanwhile, the United States insisted upon continuing to provide support for UNITA in an effort "to convince the MPLA that a military solution is impossible and to hasten its acceptance of a mutually acceptable ceasefire and negotiations resulting in national reconciliation."[73] For U.S. Secretary of State James A. Baker III, regional conflicts such as that in Angola could be resolved through negotiations only "if both sides have the incentive to talk and compromise." U.S. aid to UNITA was important, he maintained, for persuading the authorities in Luanda that there was no alternative to a compromise.[74] As a consequence of such assistance, both the Soviet Union and the United States had considerable leverage in the final negotiations leading up to an internal settlement of the civil war.

By December, the Portuguese-initiated talks received an important boost when Secretary of State Baker met publicly with the Angolan foreign minister and Soviet Foreign Minister Eduard Shevardnadze conferred openly with UNITA's Savimbi. Then, the United States and the Soviet Union cosponsored a meeting with the two Angolan rivals and the Portuguese intermediary in Washington. With both the United States and the Soviets present, the two antagonists managed to hammer out what later became known as the Washington Concepts Paper, the basic framework for the serious negotiation sessions to follow. The elements of the conceptual framework included the following points:

—Following the signing of the cease-fire, the implementation process was to take into account the timing of free and fair elections. The Angolan government would conduct discussions with all political parties to formulate the laws that would regulate the electoral process.

—The cease-fire agreement obligated the parties to stop receiving lethal materiel. The United States, USSR, and all other countries would refrain from supplying lethal materiel to any Angolan party.

—The overall political control of the cease-fire process would be the responsibility of the Angolan parties working within the Joint Political-Military Commission (JPMC). The United Nations would be invited to provide an international monitoring force to assist the Angolan parties, at the request of the Angolan government.

—The process of creating the national army would begin with the implementation of the cease-fire and be completed by the time of elections. The international monitoring force, in charge of the cease-fire, would help the JPMC in the formation of the national army and in ensuring its neutrality.

—Free and fair elections for a new government would take place under the monitoring of international observers, who would remain in Angola until the new government was installed.[75]

Unlike the Gbadolite summit, where the great powers gave general support to Mobutu's peace initiative but displayed little urgency over the proceedings, both the United States and the USSR were now prepared to play a more active role in moving the peace process toward a negotiated agreement.[76] U.S. Assistant Secretary Cohen commented that the United States and the Soviets "both played a very important role in helping to bring about compromises under the overall jurisdiction of the Portuguese mediator."[77] In an effort in the fall of 1990 to provide an incentive to both sides to sign the Bicesse accords, Congress passed an amendment to the intelligence bill, accepted by members of the Senate at the conference stage, that promised to lower the level of lethal assistance provided to Savimbi if the Angolan government took steps toward a peaceful settlement. It was apparent to U.S. government officials that both sets of Angolan leaders heard the message and that it influenced them to sign the peace agreement.[78]

The Washington agreement on basic negotiating principles gave a new impetus to the flagging talks in Bicesse, Portugal. When the sixth round of talks took place on April 4, 1991, most of the major points of disagreement had already been resolved, so the negotiators were able to focus their attention on the remaining key issues: the formation of a unified national army, the dates for a cease-fire and for holding multiparty elections, and the international monitoring of the cease-fire. The election date proved to be the most contentious point. UNITA proposed that elections be held between nine and twelve months after the cease-fire, whereas the Angolan government proposed a waiting period of thirty-six months. Portugal recommended a waiting period of fifteen to eighteen months as a compromise. Although the MPLA indicated a willingness to accept a reduction to twenty-four months, UNITA representatives continued to insist on twelve.

This haggling over the major outstanding issues continued through the remainder of April; then, to the surprise of many, the conferees achieved a breakthrough to peace. The MPLA indicated to the Portuguese mediator that it would accept the proposed fifteen- to eighteen-month waiting period leading up to the elections. The UNITA negotiators responded positively to this concession but insisted that some additional points needed to be addressed before they could agree to this scheme. Significantly, U.S. observers on the scene reportedly concurred that these points were relevant but contended that they should not prevent the signing of an interim cease-fire accord.[79]

Because the major points of contention had been ironed out, it was now possible for Lopo do Nascimento, representing the Angolan government, and Jeremias Chitunda of UNITA to initial the various documents resulting from the interim peace accords on May 1. This preliminary agreement was made into a lasting agreement when it was signed by President dos Santos and Jonas Savimbi at a formal ceremony in Lisbon on May 31. A complex package of provisions had been settled upon, including a cease-fire, all to take effect on May 15: UNITA's recognition of the Angolan government and President dos Santos until general elections could be held; UNITA's right to take part in political activities in a multiparty democracy; free and fair elections, under the supervision of international observers; the agreement of all Angolan political forces regarding a specific timetable for elections (which were tentatively set for late 1992); and, after the cease-fire came into effect, the creation of a single national military force, composed of 50,000 troops from the current Angolan government air force and navy as well as an army evenly divided between government and UNITA forces.[80]

The accords were vague, however, about the framework for decentralization, leaving such matters as the structure of subregional and local government to be settled after the elections. The great powers that had helped to overcome the hurdles to a negotiated settlement—the United States and Russia (replacing the USSR), along with Portugal—now agreed to participate in the JPMC to oversee the transition process.

As might have been expected, the implementation of the Bicesse peace agreement proved to be troublesome and contentious. Charges and countercharges were made regarding human rights abuses, the holding of political prisoners, the hiding of war materiel, delays in troop demobilization and the integration of armies, and fraudulent voter registration.[81] The main problems with implementation arose from underfunding and the inadequate size of the UN observer team. Only $132 million was allocated, and only 480 monitors were deployed to supervise the demobilization of military forces and the creation of joint army and police units.[82] By the time of the elections, only 50 percent of the troops had been demobilized and only 10 percent of the army had been unified, thus allowing either UNITA or the Angolan army to resume military action if it chose to do so in case of an adverse election outcome.[83]

Nevertheless, for the time being, at least, an exhausted society remained intent upon giving peace a chance; Margaret Joan Anstee, in her capacity as special representative of the UN secretary-general, certified that, "with all deficiencies taken into account," the elections could be considered free and fair.[84] Both parties continued to perceive each other in grim, zero-sum terms, however, thus contributing to a breakdown in relations just as the 1992 election outcome became known. President dos Santos received 49.57 percent of the presidential vote and Savimbi 40.6 percent, so a runoff election between the two main contenders was necessary. Savimbi, accusing his opponent of electoral fraud, asserted that "it will not depend on any international organization to say that the elections were free and fair."[85] Anticipating that a cooperative relationship would lead to a loss of position, status, and an ability for self-defense, Savimbi refused to abide by the rules of the game, and a new round of fighting began.

The common interests of all sides in cooperating were undercut by the determination of UNITA's leader to play the political-ethnic card (in Savimbi's words, the Ovimbundu were 100 percent behind him and he was prepared to die for them) and resume the civil war.[86] Savimbi then withdrew the military units already integrated into the new Angolan army and ordered his troops into action.[87] Although Savimbi was no doubt a "spoiler" who had failed to make a credible commitment to the peace agreement, it is also apparent that the very structure for holding the elections, with its two-round, winner-take-all design, contributed to Savimbi's incentive to withdraw from the peace process because it made the stakes for winning exceedingly high.[88] Savimbi urged the United Nations to "take over the negotiating process," but there was little conviction, at this time, that the Bicesse accords could still be salvaged by means of third-party enforcement.[89] Full commitment required some form of power sharing, an assurance that UNITA would not be shut out of the political process after elections took place.[90]

Renewed Civil War

The nature of the military encounter between the MPLA-led Angolan government and the UNITA insurgents was a critical factor for determining their future relationship. Following UNITA's defection after the 1992 elections, the military fortunes of the two adversaries swung like a pendulum; each side was determined to take advantage of any shift in the military balance of power to achieve a military victory and, it hoped, an enduring peace.[91] By 1993, UNITA's armed forces had occupied about 70 percent of the country, although neither the capital city nor the oil-producing enclave of Cabinda was brought under its control. In 1993–94, the Angolan government army had been greatly strengthened by the purchase of $3.5 billion worth of arms and ammunition from abroad and by the retraining of its forces and critical support services in an air and land war provided by a Pretoria-based security firm, Executive Outcomes. The army then launched a sustained offensive to overrun the UNITA-held diamond mines and penetrate UNITA strongholds in the heartland.[92]

UNITA's supply of military spare parts and fuel ran low, and the UN and the international community became more and more critical of UNITA's resumption of the war, leading Savimbi to became increasingly vulnerable and isolated.[93] He had no supporter waiting in the wings and ready to come to his rescue in this "third war." Thus the growing domi-

nance of the government forces over the weakened UNITA contingents
was the major factor that induced Savimbi in 1994 to reconsider his
stance on negotiating in earnest for a return to the guidelines worked
out in the Bicesse negotiations. However, two other inducements
encouraged Savimbi to change his preferences from a bid for military
preeminence to the negotiation of new rules of relationship: the security incentives of the Lusaka protocol itself and the emergence of
mounting international and regional pressures.

The Lusaka Protocol and International Pressures

Against a backdrop of sharp military encounters, heavy casualties (an
estimated 250,000 people killed), the destruction of contested cities and
towns, and further economic deterioration, more than one year of intensive UN-mediated peace negotiations ensued in Lusaka, Zambia,
between Angolan government and UNITA representatives in 1993–94. In
these long and often frustrating sessions, the UN special representative
to Angola, Alioune Blondin Beye, was assisted by a coalition of mediators,
including U.S. special envoy Paul Hare and Portuguese and South African
diplomats. Together, they carefully crafted the Lusaka protocol of November 22, 1994. The protocol was signed by Angolan Foreign Minister
Venancio de Moura and UNITA Secretary-General Eugenio Ngolo, at a
ceremony attended by representatives from thirty countries. By reaffirming the 1991 Bicesse accords, the protocol set forth the details for
a cease-fire, a second round of presidential elections, demilitarization,
disarmament, the formation of a unified army and national police force,
and national reconciliation. The protocol's general principles emphasized the importance of reestablishing central control over the country's
security forces.

The main incentives to explain Savimbi's shift from continuing the
quest for a military victory were the military capabilities of the Angolan
government forces, the confidence-building measures set forth in the
protocol, and the pressures being applied by external actors within the
region and beyond. The changing military balance in the country was
most important in creating the political environment for launching a
new, meaningful bid for a peace agreement under UN auspices in
Lusaka. The Angolan government army was now rearmed, reinvigorated,
and making effective use of South African mercenaries to provide critically important ground and air cover and strategic bombing support:
therefore UNITA's contingents found themselves severely constrained

militarily by the fall of 1994. "Sophisticated equipment prevailed over the will of UNITA's brave soldiers," Savimbi declared. Appraising the result of this military imbalance, Savimbi candidly concluded that UNITA was "experiencing its deepest crisis since it was created 28 years ago."[94]

Savimbi now faced the prospect of a politically divided UNITA movement and a humiliating military defeat; he thus felt compelled to change strategies and negotiate a dignified truce under the aegis of the United Nations. However, the need to ease military and internal political pressures must be linked with other noncoercive incentives to fully explain both the government's and Savimbi's willingness to find a new equilibrium. One positive inducement altering the payoffs on the regime side was the assurance given the government that its activities and those of its agencies had legitimate authority over the country as a whole. Nevertheless, the protocol and the follow-up legislation carefully provided confidence-building measures (insurance incentives) that were reassuring to UNITA and its supporters. Provision was made for the termination of all offensive military actions, the repatriation of mercenaries, the release of civilian and military prisoners detained as a consequence of the civil war, and UN monitoring of the demobilization and reintegration of the armies. Only after the quartering of UNITA military forces had been concluded would UNITA generals be returned to the Angolan Armed Forces (FAA) and the selection of UNITA troops for the FAA begin. The drafters of the protocol were mindful of the need to establish a framework for a just and lasting peace, so they took pains, in their statement of general principles, to assert that the composition of the Angolan Armed Forces would reflect "the principle of proportionality between Government and UNITA military forces as provided for in the Bicesse Accords."[95]

The police force allowed considerable decentralization in its management, coordination, and monitoring activities along provincial lines, specifying that 5,500 UNITA members (including 180 officers) would be incorporated into the Angola national police and 1,200 UNITA members (including 40 officers) into the rapid reaction police force. The protocol declared that national reconciliation implied the participation of UNITA members at all levels of government and administration. In contrast with the exclusion of losing parties that marked the Bicesse accords, the Lusaka protocol emphasized the principle of power sharing in cabinet appointments at the political center as well as the granting of key governorships to the minority party. As one correspondent noted:

The agreement is premised on a power-sharing arrangement that will give UNITA enough to keep it within the government orbit but not enough in terms of regional power-bases to seek to redivide the country. That is why the negotiations over which provincial governments were given to UNITA were so protracted. It gives UNITA four ministries (Mines, Commerce, Health and Tourism), seven deputy ministries, three governorships (Uige, Lunda Sul and Cuando Cubango), some ambassadorships and control of a significant number of municipalities.[96]

Later, it was reported that Savimbi was also offered one of Angola's vice-presidential positions. Although he refused to accept this offer, he remained the head of UNITA.

Increasing pressures from the international community and the regional powers also influenced Savimbi to alter his strategies regarding military confrontation. Ohlson and Stedman's comment on the role of international pressures in conflict resolution has relevance for the negotiations leading to the Lusaka protocol: "Concessions in conflict resolution," they remark, "did not spring from political goodwill or moral reassessment; instead, they were a consequence of shrinking maneuvering space resulting from various pressures and leverages wielded by opponents and third parties."[97] In this instance, the UN Security Council passed a resolution in March 1994 singling out UNITA as the sole entity responsible for the resumption of the civil war in Angola and calling on the secretary-general to arrange a meeting between the warring parties to bring about peace along the lines of the Bicesse accords. UN Special Representative Alioune Blondin Beye worked tirelessly to carry out this UN mandate. He met with the rival parties and regional and international actors to create movement toward peace. During the negotiations leading up to the Lusaka protocol, a coalition of external mediators made extensive use of insurance incentives (promises of UN monitoring and verification) to encourage Savimbi to pursue a new course of action. The United States offered no fiscal incentives, as such. However, it may be said that a form of purchase incentive surfaced; the U.S. Agency for International Development reportedly made known its preparedness to contribute to de-mining and demilitarization activities after a settlement had taken hold, and the Clinton administration requested $100 million for the UN Angola verification mission.[98]

With respect to the diplomatic and symbolic (but important) legitimacy incentives, I should note the talks that were held between Zimbabwe President Robert Mugabe and South Africa President Nelson

Mandela in Lusaka on November 15, 1994, where their joint presence was perceived as an effort to encourage the two Angolan military delegations to reach an agreement on the proposed truce.[99] Around this time, Mugabe reportedly indicated that he was prepared to meet with Savimbi, which gave an important boost to the lonely outsider's credibility in southern Africa. Mandela was said to be on the phone with Savimbi on a regular basis, encouraging him to sign the agreement and to abide by it; he then invited the insurgent leader to visit him in South Africa. The trip did not materialize, but this initiative may nevertheless have provided an incentive to a guerrilla leader eager for acceptance. Furthermore, Zairian leader Mobutu Sese Seko, who was anxious to gain increased approval in African and Western (particularly U.S.) decision-making circles, reportedly used his advantageous position as a military equipment supplier and diamond and mineral exporter to influence Savimbi's preferences regarding a cooperative strategy.[100]

There were important differences in the political contexts surrounding the negotiation processes in Bicesse and Lusaka that raised hopes that Angola's bitter internal fighting would now come to an end. First, the change to a majority-elected regime in South Africa meant that Savimbi no longer had a powerful patron to rely upon for contacts, arms supplies, ammunition, and fuel. The southern African region was searching for a new political stability and would discourage any destabilizing influences—either a state leader such as Mobutu or an insurgent chieftain such as Savimbi—that acted to undercut smooth implementation of the protocol. Second, the provisions in the protocol on national reconciliation and power sharing gave UNITA some assurance about its future security, thereby encouraging it to adhere to the agreement. Third, the United Nations, and especially its special representative, Alioune Blondin Beye, was fully committed to the peace process in all its stages, by negotiating a return to regularized relations and then by presiding over the establishment of a self-enforcing conflict management system. In contrast to the lack of commitment that marked the Bicesse process, the UN Angola verification mission III (UNAVEM III) was determined to deploy some 7,000 peacekeepers and military observers and to oversee the implementation of the protocol.

Implementation

The Lusaka protocol represented a good foundation for constructing a stable peace. Nevertheless, the initial signs were not all positive, by any means. Deep distrust prevailed on both sides, raising serious doubts regarding the credibility of the parties' commitment to uphold the agreement. Fears that their opponent might renege or exploit the agreement contributed to the fighting that continued in the northeast, northwest, and west central provinces well after the protocol had taken effect.[101] Savimbi not only failed to appear for the signing of the protocol, but he refused at first to visit President dos Santos in Luanda, allegedly because of security concerns, and he made what could be interpreted as ominous allusions to the possibility of continuing civil war.[102] The critical factor keeping the implementation process on track was the continued commitment and leadership of the coalition of international mediators, led by UN Special Representative Beye. In light of the alternatives, implementation of the peace agreement seemed to these international actors to be a relatively low-cost investment in the stability of Angola and the southern African region.

Implementing a peace agreement following a prolonged and destructive civil war is inevitably a difficult balancing act for any third party. Those engaged in implementing a settlement must make an effort to bolster the credibility of an agreement, enabling the two sides to experience joint problem solving, to test perceptions of each other's intentions, and to reduce the risks of commitment.[103] In no area is this task more difficult than the quartering and demobilization of troops and the integration of the armed forces. Fears are widespread that a party fully complying with the agreement's provisions on demobilization and disarmament will be highly vulnerable to attack. In Savimbi's words: "No leader in history that I have known disarmed and stayed in power."[104] The result is to create an incentive to cheat, even to consider launching a preventive attack. Thus lack of information and the inability to commit credibly during a transition period contribute to a security dilemma where groups strike first in an effort to enhance their security, causing a new cycle of civil war to occur.

Because an active third-party enforcer, UNAVEM III, has been relatively serious about upholding the Lusaka protocol, the spiral of events leading to a security dilemma did not occur. In this, the peace process received important support from regional leaders; on March 1, 1996, Gabon President Omar Bongo presided over an important meeting at Libreville between dos Santos and Savimbi, where a new timetable was set on the demobilization of UNITA's military units, the withdrawal of FAA troops to stipulated assembly points, and the formation of the national army.

The two sides agreed to an army composed of 90,000 soldiers, leaving 110,000 men to be demobilized in the period ahead.[105] Nevertheless, some of the elements described above—information failure, problems of credible commitment, and the fear of cheating—continued to delay efforts to consolidate the agreement. The process of quartering and demobilizing UNITA soldiers proved slow, despite heavy U.S. pressures on Savimbi to abide by the terms of the protocol.[106] As of late March 1996, General Valery Sibanda, the commander of UNAVEM III, reported that only 17,000 UNITA soldiers had been quartered, leading to dark suspicions that Savimbi and his generals were holding back their first-line troops and their most advanced equipment.[107] The pace of demobilization and integration in the FAA quickened by the year's end. Out of 65,000 soldiers who had been confined at the assembly areas, UN Special Representative Beye reported that a total of 18,629 had been selected for the Angolan Armed Forces.[108] Despite these achievements, questions about the credibility of Savimbi's commitment to the peace agreement remained at the center of Angola's difficulties in establishing an effective conflict management system. In this respect, it is symbolically significant that Savimbi, the leader of the largest opposition party in the National Assembly, did not attend the ceremonies in Luanda to install a new government of national unity in April 1997, declaring that it was still not sufficiently safe for him to travel to the capital.

Conclusion

In this chapter, I have compared a sequence of mediation initiatives to see how the process of negotiating peace accords can lay the basis for new conflict-regulating institutions. I have examined the successful conflict management process that culminated in the negotiation of the Lusaka protocol. Three important concepts have been explored: the extent to which the incentives for external intervention changed over time, the roles of the mediators in facilitating the peace process, and the ability of the mediators to exert pressures and manipulate incentives effectively.

In the interstate negotiations, I examined movement by the four major external actors—the United States, the Soviet Union, Cuba, and South Africa—from interventionist to disengagement behaviors between 1975 and 1988 and found that the change can be explained primarily by shifts in the relative benefits (or payoff structures) for the various actors. In the late 1980s, a new cooperative relationship developed between the superpowers. As the Soviets retreated from their political, military, and ideological competition with the United States and increasingly emphasized their own domestic developmental objectives, possibilities for great-power collaboration became enhanced. The practical consequence in Angola was important behind-the-scenes cooperation in the mediation process: the Soviet Union exerted pressure on the Angolan government and the Cubans at key points, and U.S. mediators sought to influence South African preferences regarding Angola and Namibia.

The negotiation of the intrastate struggle at Gbadolite, Bicesse, and Lusaka, however, brought little fundamental change in the two local adversaries' perceptions of each other. Because the great powers and the United Nations displayed a greater involvement and sense of urgency during the Bicesse and Lusaka mediation processes than they did during the Mobutu-led initiative, however, they were able to facilitate an agreement despite the evident distrust that continued to divide the adversaries. Nevertheless, the continuing distrust between the MPLA and UNITA resurfaced in full force following the 1992 elections and in the aftermath of the Lusaka protocol, and it continues to represent a threat to the survival of the Lusaka protocol. On this topic, UN mediator Beye observed that "it is quite easy to fall into mistrust, but extremely difficult to climb back up toward a climate of trust—especially given the latest events in the field, militarily speaking, soon after the peace agreement was initialed."[109]

Regarding the roles of the mediators in promoting constructive outcomes, the situations of the third-party intermediaries differed in important ways. From the moment that Chester Crocker took office as U.S. assistant secretary of state, he showed great resolve in his search for an internationally acceptable solution to the Namibian independence issue; this, as I have shown throughout this chapter, was interconnected with events in Angola. Crocker's initial attempt to link that issue with resolution of the Angolan conflict may have made a peace settlement more difficult to obtain in the early 1980s, but once the military stalemate on the ground was recognized, linkage became a means of saving face and addressing the differences among Angolans.[110] In any event, Crocker's determined pursuit of every possible opening, his position as a representative of a global power with enormous resources at his disposal, the change in the balance of military forces, and the shift in superpower perceptions all helped to create new opportunities for a decisive move toward an international settlement.

In the intrastate negotiations, however, no comparable convergence of opportunities took place at the Gbadolite summit. The United States backed Mobutu's initiative during the Bush administration but expressed reservations about becoming a formal mediator. Mobutu lacked the diplomatic skills and determination displayed by Crocker in the earlier negotiations, and he was unable to use the resources of a great power to promote an internationally acceptable settlement; therefore, he was not able to encourage either the MPLA or UNITA to alter their preferences. Subsequently, Portuguese mediators made concerted efforts to involve the superpowers in the negotiating process, with evident success. During the final, critical weeks of the negotiations, Portugal, a medium-power mediator, was backed by the influence that the Soviet Union and the United States could exert on their allies. The importance of the superpowers' role in the mediation process was not lost on the rival Angolan leaders. Thus, Savimbi noted, when expressing his appreciation for the Portuguese effort, that "without the Americans and Soviets on their side, Durao Barroso [the Portuguese mediator] would not have gotten anywhere."[111] In the subsequent UN-led mediation effort of 1993-94 at Lusaka, the international organization had important backing from the United States and Portugal and from regional powers such as South Africa and Zimbabwe. Combined with the changing balance of military power in Angola, this left Savimbi (or his regional backer, Zaire) with little room to maneuver.

Finally, the mediators' credibility and capacity to mobilize resources had a direct bearing upon their ability to exert pressure and manipulate incentives. In both the international negotiations preceding the Angola-Namibia agreement and the internal mediation effort leading to the Bicesse accords, the successful outcomes depended substantially upon parallel U.S. and Soviet pressures exerted upon their respective clients. At various points, Crocker pressed the South Africans to cease providing military assistance to UNITA and agree to an international settlement; in the 1991 internal negotiations, American officials reassured MPLA leaders of their good intentions while also pressing UNITA (which relied heavily upon the United States for sophisticated military equipment) to make concessions on such key issues as the timetable for elections. Ironically, the use of leverage by patrons can prove a two-edged sword: a patron's commitment can give a client (such as UNITA) leverage over the patron. This may lead to domestic costs of abandoning a client who has had the foresight to build up a strong following within the patron's political system.

Similarly, the Soviet Union, which had provided the Angolan government forces with ideological support and extensive war materiel over the years, was in a position to influence its MPLA allies. During the international negotiations, Soviet diplomats were able to clarify critical points of contention and to encourage Luanda's leaders to bargain in earnest and to adopt a conciliatory position on such questions as the redeployment and withdrawal of Cuban forces. At Bicesse, the Soviets played an active part in facilitating an agreement; they met with Savimbi at the Soviet embassy in Washington, helping to shape the Washington Concepts Paper and pressing MPLA leaders to make concessions on important points of difference.

The negotiations over the Lusaka protocol involved active UN leadership in all its phases, although the United States (and, after the dissolution of the Soviet Union, Russia) did play a supporting role. Because the two internal adversaries had not repudiated the Bicesse principles after the resumption of the fighting in 1992, the UN mediator and his support team could make use of the previous agreement as a guideline for the 1993–94 deliberations. During negotiations over the Lusaka protocol, the main incentives facilitating an agreement were the Angola government's desire to restore its legitimate authority throughout the country and UNITA's need to halt the Angolan government's military offensive against its weakening positions. Other relevant factors included the insurance incentives in the protocol regarding UNITA's representation in national and subregional affairs, the provisions on proportional recruitment in the army and police forces, and the coercive diplomatic incentives involving international and regional pressures on Savimbi to sign the protocol.

Given the rising costs of military confrontation, Savimbi had little to gain from continuing the battle; he therefore agreed to what amounted to a fragile military truce, but his commitment to the agreement in 1994 seemed less than fully credible. Despite U.S. pressures to implement the agreement and to place his troops in quarantine, Savimbi appeared to hold in reserve his elite units and their modern military and telecommunications equipment. He continued to fear a future without an autonomous military force under his own command until well into the implementation period, when the UN Angola verification mission (UNAVEM III) succeeded in guiding the peace process to an apparent safe landing. Once again, the importance of investing substantial resources in the implementation process was to become evident.

Taken together, these factors show that the structures of the four mediation processes—the Anglo-Namibia accords, the Gbadolite initiative, the Bicesse accords, and the Lusaka protocol—were quite distinct, which partly accounts for the varying results from each peacemaking attempt. It still remains to be seen whether pressures and incentives mustered by the UN and its coalition that preserved the Lusaka agreement intact during the implementation phase will be carried forward and result in the establishment of an enduring conflict management system in Angola.

RHODESIA (1965–80)

ZAMBIA

MOZAMBIQUE

Zambezi R.

Lake Kariba

MASHONALAND

NORTH

Hunyani R.

Sinoia

⊛ Salisbury

MASHONALAND SOUTH

Zambezi R.

Victoria Falls

Wankie

Shangan R.

MIDLANDS

Gatooma

Marandellas

Que Que

Redcliff

Umtali

MATABELELAND NORTH

Gwelo

Selukwe

MANICALAND

VICTORIA

Fort Victoria

Bulawayo

Shabani

Mtilikwe R.

MATABELELAND SOUTH

Lundi R.

BOTSWANA

MOZAMBIQUE

SOUTH AFRICA

0   100   200 Mi.
0   100   200 Km.

6

Reconstructing a Conflict Management System in Rhodesia/Zimbabwe

A strategy... entails choices about the use of inducements by one party to the other.... The package of inducements used is critical in the fundamental aspect of creating the right time to attempt de-escalation.

LOUIS KRIESBERG

Seven years after Rhodesian Prime Minister Ian Smith made a unilateral declaration of independence from Great Britain in 1965, it was apparent that Rhodesian government forces were losing a civil war against African nationalist insurgents. However, there was no mutually hurting stalemate to force the insurgents to come to an agreement, and Rhodesian political leaders remained determined to carry on the fight against their opponents. A political solution was needed to halt the country's social and economic deterioration, but few political leaders had the will and the incentive to advocate a mutually agreeable conflict management system. Both sets of elites were deeply distrustful of their antagonist's purposes and thus viewed proposals to place their fate in the hands of their opponents as the worst possible outcome. Many local observers recognized that a strategy of mutual cooperation was in the long-run interest of the country as a whole; nevertheless, key actors on both sides feared that their adversaries would regard conciliatory gestures as a sign of weakness and would not reciprocate in kind, so they shunned accommodating overtures and instead mobilized their supporters for war.

In this situation, third-party mediation became the only alternative to continued deadly conflict. Third-party intervention held out the hope that the nature of the encounter could be changed by reducing the potential for misperception, using incentives to alter the actors' preferences, and providing monitoring and enforcement mechanisms. Britain, as the former colonial power with a long history of negotiating with Rhodesian authorities, was viewed as knowledgeable about the issues and in close contact with the main bargaining parties. Thus there were both an intermediary long active on the scene and identifiable bargaining parties, both favorable preconditions for a constructive negotiating process. Although a coalition including the United States, South Africa, Commonwealth countries, and neighboring countries Tanzania, Zambia, Botswana, and Mozambique also contributed in important ways to the mediatory process, in the end it was the British government, at the behest of its Commonwealth allies, that took the lead in exerting pressure at Lancaster House in 1979 for an agreement and a change in Zimbabwe's conflict management system.

The central issue to be probed in this chapter is, What combinations of pressures and incentives was the coalition of third-party mediators able to bring to bear to encourage the Rhodesian adversaries to accept new rules for regulating conflict? The fact that external manipulation succeeded in moving the parties toward cooperative forms of behavior will constitute evidence that, at least in certain propitious circumstances, determined mediators need not passively wait for a ripe moment to emerge. Here, the mediators cultivated ripeness by pointing out the costs of continued civil war and the ways that both sides could benefit from accommodation.

The Bargaining Parties

The Rhodesian colonial state was comparable to other settler territories in the manner in which it organized a minority-dominated conflict management system that preserved white security and prosperity. By the time the Rhodesian Front (RF) party organization was formed in 1962, many local Europeans, led by a determined element in Rhodesia's white community, exercised a commanding influence over the Rhodesian state and, after the elections in December 1962, held a firm grip on the country's political institutions. The Rhodesian white community of 249,000 people in 1971 was relatively large compared with that in neighboring countries, but it was only 5 percent of Rhodesia's total population, which included 5,220,000 Africans, 16,900 Coloureds, and 9,300 Asians. The Europeans in Rhodesia were allowed a greater measure of autonomy over domestic matters under the 1923 constitution than was the case in neighboring colonies.

The RF used this political power to provide security and to benefit its communal constituency, both economically and socially. An infrastructure was built, taxes were imposed, a security structure developed, pass laws put into effect, marketing boards set up, and the best lands reserved—all to ensure the quality of life of the resident European population, to overcome their feelings of insecurity because of the low ratio of whites in the total population, and to attract new immigrants from Europe. In line with these objectives, public allocations for health and education greatly favored the minority white community, leaving the African majority highly disadvantaged.

Thus the pre-independence Rhodesian state became an effective instrument to promote racial and class interests. Such a harsh and self-interested hegemon inevitably provoked an angry response from the resentful African majority population. Under these circumstances, a reciprocal sense of insecurity came to prevail: the African majority feared the prospect of continued social, political, and economic disadvantage; the white minority, fearing a loss of status and privileges in an African-led state, sought political power free from external control. The whites feared the shadow of the future. For them, the logic embedded in the unilateral declaration of independence (UDI) was that holding onto political power would reduce their vulnerability to the majoritarian will.

The politics of ethnicity (as well as personality, tactics, and ideology) were also consequential in colonial Rhodesia. The RF government led by Ian Smith, "playing the ethnic card," emphasized whatever differences existed between the country's two main ethnic groups, the Ndebele and the Shona. For example, the government attempted to create a constitutional order by which the Ndebele and Shona chiefs would be equally represented in the Senate and chiefs as well as commoners would gain parity in the House of Assembly. This exacerbated group tensions because the proposal greatly favored the minority Ndebele, who made up less than 20 percent of Rhodesia's population.[1] In addition, the government fomented differences and tensions along ethnic lines between the Zimbabwe African National Union (ZANU) and Zimbabwe African People's Union (ZAPU) insurgent organizations during the struggle for independence. In a divisive form of categorizing, the majority Shona became associated with the ZANU insurgents, and the minority Ndebele were linked with the ZAPU military force.[2] This division, as Jeffrey Herbst observes, had "a debilitating effect on the nationalist struggle."[3]

Shona-Ndebele tensions, of relatively recent origin, were also important in the run-up to the Lancaster House conference of 1979 and beyond. At the time of an abortive conference in Geneva that followed the Kissinger peace initiative in southern Africa in 1976, ZANU's Robert Mugabe and ZAPU's Joshua Nkomo did manage to temporarily prevail over their factional differences and unite to form a loose Patriotic Front. But this externalization effect proved short-lived. After the Lancaster House negotiations and independence, interpersonal and interethnic differences resurfaced when the Mugabe government forced ZAPU members to resign from their official positions and then used an all-Shona military unit to deal most brutally with dissident elements in Nkomo's predominantly Ndebele heartland area. Nkomo and Mugabe again managed to patch up their differences in 1987 to reach a unity accord, thus easing interethnic tensions as the Ndebele gained significant representation in the cabinet coalition (see chapter 3).

Although the unity accord made conflict between the main ethnic groups more manageable, other conflicts emerged as points of contention. Competition between the Shona subethnic groups—the Kalanga, Karanga, Korekore, Manyika, Ndau, and Zezuru—developed more slowly than between the Shona and Ndebele, but it surfaced in the 1980s as the transition to majority rule was being consolidated and as the struggle for control of scarce state positions and resources intensified. Mugabe displayed sensitivity to the problem and took care to maintain a balance between these ethnic subgroups (practicing a form of "hegemonic exchange" within ZANU's party and, in certain periods, its government coalition); disputes between these groups have nonetheless come to the fore. According to one report, "Within ZANU's Shona majority, power since independence has rested primarily in the hands of a coalition of the Zezuru and Manyika subgroups, giving the largest subgroup, the Karangas, a lesser position than many of its members feel is their due."[4]

A process of racial bargaining was evident only in the early stages of the negotiations.[5] In the 1974-75 period, four African political parties— ZANU, ZAPU, the African National Council (ANC), and the Front for the Liberation of Zimbabwe (FROLIZI)—briefly joined forces to engage in what amounted to racial bargaining with the white-led Rhodesian Front. However, by the time the Lancaster House conference took place, Europeans had no delegation of their own. They were included in the negotiating teams led by Mugabe and Nkomo for the Patriotic Front and by Bishop Abel Muzorewa for the Rhodesian government coalition. To be sure, some key negotiations did occur at Lancaster House that involved white military officers in particular; moreover, a covert form of tacit bargaining (involving the unilateral initiatives of racial interests that invited reciprocation) did play a role at the conference and in the period that followed.[6]

White Rebellion against Colonial Rule

With the election of an RF government in 1962 and an overwhelmingly favorable vote for independence two years later, the stage was set for Rhodesia's highly polarized politics. Ian Smith came to power in early 1964 and used his new position to press British authorities to agree to Rhodesia's independence along the lines of the 1961 constitution. Prime Minister Harold Wilson cautioned Smith against making any impulsive moves to reach a solution on his own terms and made Rhodesian independence conditional upon the satisfaction of five principles: unimpeded progress toward majority rule, guarantees against retrogressive amendment of the constitution, immediate improvements in the political status of the African population, progress toward ending racial discrimination, and confirmation that any proposed independence settlement was acceptable to the Rhodesian people as a whole.[7]

Last-minute efforts to negotiate the differences between Smith and Wilson's positions proved inconclusive; finally, on November 11, 1965, a determined Smith shook off the concerns of his military and civilian advisors and made a unilateral declaration of independence. He combined essentialist perceptions regarding the intentions of his African adversaries, presented uncompromising demands regarding white domination, and chose unilateral defection from Great Britain as the preferred strategy under the circumstances. Wilson was informed by his military chiefs that Britain lacked the necessary airfields in Zambia for an offensive, so he decided against a forceful intervention in Rhodesia.[8] Moreover, Wilson had only a four-seat majority in the House of Commons, and he would have felt politically vulnerable in launching an attack against a well-entrenched white-led army.

International criticism followed almost immediately; condemnatory resolutions were issued in the UN General Assembly and the Security Council. Shortly afterward, both the United Nations and the British government (with firm U.S. support) imposed selective sanctions against the illegal breakaway regime, and Great Britain banished Rhodesia from the sterling and Commonwealth preference areas. Guerrilla forays occurred into Rhodesia, and the government reacted to the threat of insurgent action by proclaiming a state of emergency. Thus a negative reciprocity, or tit-for-tat process, reinforced the mutual fears and insecurities that pitted the Smith regime against its determined opponents.

Direct Anglo-Rhodesian Talks

The British government, in an effort to manage the deepening crisis, held direct talks with white Rhodesian government authorities immediately preceding the UDI and again on three occasions between 1966 and 1971. Wilson was quite specific that only "talks," not "negotiations," would take place; the latter had been ruled out because they implied that Great Britain was negotiating with an illegal regime.[9] Britain's leverage was circumscribed, however. The British made it clear that the Wilson government would not intervene forcefully against Smith, so Britain was in a relatively weak position to influence the preferences of the white leadership in Rhodesia. The result was a process of damage control in which the imperial government responded to the increasingly exacting demands of Smith and his entourage by offering concessions on autonomy under a white minority regime. Without a hurting stalemate among Rhodesia's whites, these British concessions were unable to provide the necessary incentive to change white Rhodesian behavior; instead, they encouraged minority intransigence.

The first major Anglo-Rhodesian talks, held in December 1966, aboard the British warship HMS *Tiger*, produced a working document that set out generous terms for ending the rebellion. The document proposed that the 1961 constitution be modified to increase African representation in Parliament, thereby enabling Africans to block amendments to the entrenched clauses of the constitution and appeal any changes to a constitutional commission in Rhodesia and then to the Privy Council in London. The governor would have been given the power to appoint a broad-based interim government that could have had a majority of RF ministers (led by Smith) but would also have included three white ministers from other parties and two African ministers. Nevertheless, these beneficial terms were insufficient to change Smith's preferences and those of the hard-line Rhodesian cabinet ministers. Smith expressed strong reservations about the return to constitutionality and broad-based government.[10] His more extreme cabinet colleagues vigorously opposed the settlement, especially the provision that gave the governor the right to appoint future "broad-based" cabinets. Smith, unwilling to risk overriding a key domestic support group, consequently brushed aside Wilson's concessions.[11]

The next set of talks, aboard the HMS *Fearless* in October 1968, were equally inconclusive. Smith, with critically important backing from South Africa, remained generally responsive to his hard-line supporters and defiant toward international pressures for majority rule. Wilson cautiously sought to find a formula for political progress that did not threaten the dominant whites but yet held out the prospect of future majority rule. The *Fearless* proposals eliminated the need for Rhodesia's return to British control during the transitional period. The British draft insisted that Smith agree to a "broad-based" administration, including Africans, to carry Rhodesia through the process of introducing and implementing the new constitution.[12] Because Wilson and Smith were deeply divided over the nature and speed of the African advance to majority rule and the domestic and international safeguards that should be put into effect to block any weakening of the constitutional provisions on African participation, both sides naturally recognized at the end of the conference that "a very wide gulf still [remained] between them on certain issues."[13]

The third set of Anglo-Rhodesian talks occurred under changed circumstances: the election victory of the British Conservative party in 1970. The Heath government had close personal and business ties to Rhodesia and less sensitivity about charges of a sellout from party backbenchers and Commonwealth leaders, so they had greater scope for independent action. The result was a series of "negotiations" between Smith and a British diplomat in Salisbury that culminated in an agreement signed by Smith and Foreign Secretary Sir Alec Douglas-Home on November 24, 1971. Smith accepted the principle of eventual majority rule reluctantly to gain international acceptance (here, he was spurred by legitimacy incentives).[14] Appeals over alleged abridgment of the Declaration of Rights could no longer be made to the Privy Council, and the ability of African members of the House of Assembly to block constitutional amendments was curtailed. Moreover, under the new agreement, Africans would proceed by stages toward parity as an increasing number of African voters met the demanding educational, income, or property qualifications.

The agreement was conditional upon Great Britain's satisfaction that the proposed terms for a settlement were acceptable to the people of

Rhodesia as a whole.[15] Toward that end, the British government appointed a commission chaired by Lord Pearce, a retired appellate judge, to ascertain directly from all subsections of the population whether these proposals were acceptable as a basis for independence. The commission encountered demonstrations and bitter opposition as it traveled about the country. In the end, it found overwhelming support for the proposed settlement in the European community but concluded, in the face of heated opposition and unrest, "after considering all our evidence including that on intimidation, that the majority of Africans rejected the Proposals."[16]

Africans rejected the proposed concessions as insignificant; they also resented being left out of the negotiating process and were suspicious about the Rhodesian government's commitment to implement the provisions on majority rule (Rhodesian intelligence director Ken Flower indicated later that their fears were based on fact).[17] Smith claimed that he had come to the end of the line as far as further negotiations were concerned, and with nothing approaching a hurting stalemate in sight, the British had little room left to induce a change of preferences on the part of the antagonists.

Mediation Efforts before Lancaster House

In the early 1970s, no resolution of the conflict was feasible. From the standpoint of the dominant white minority, all signs seemed favorable: sanctions seemed bearable, many of the key African nationalist leaders were either in detention or in jail, and guerrilla warfare remained at a low level. The Smith regime was prepared to fight for continued hegemony. Meanwhile, African nationalists, insecure about their future in a white-dominated country, geared up for a new political and military push; they mobilized their constituents for internal resistance and for an externally backed guerrilla war.[18] Until the costs of continued warfare led both sides to change their preferences and perceptions, the resulting impasse could not be surmounted.

As the war with the guerrillas of the Zimbabwe African National Liberation Army (ZANLA, with military links to ZANU) widened in the area bordering on Mozambique, Rhodesia's army found it increasingly useful to cooperate with Portuguese troops in the Northeast. This proved insufficient to hold back the spread of guerrilla operations, however, which had now developed an effective support base in the countryside and were backed with weapons and training facilities by

Tanzania and the "socialist countries in Europe and Asia."[19] Rhodesian government officials began to recognize that their authority was weakening. "Things are on the decline in Rhodesia," Flower wrote in his diary in December 1974. "In spite of increased Security Force successes," he continued, "we are not keeping pace with terrorist recruiting. Indeed, we have lost the goodwill of the Africans in the forward areas and over much of the rest of Rhodesia as well."[20] The expansion of Zimbabwean guerrilla activities coincided with the 1974 military coup in Portugal, which led to Portuguese withdrawal from Africa and the independence of Mozambique. The resolve of Mozambique's new African nationalist leaders to support African self-rule in the region signaled new difficulties for the white-led regime in Rhodesia.

The Victoria Falls Conference

After the failure of both the Anglo-Rhodesian talks and internal negotiations between Smith and Bishop Abel Muzorewa in 1973, two very different regional powers, Zambia and South Africa, decided to intervene jointly in an effort to halt a further escalation of the guerrilla war. In a process that came to be known as détente, the South Africans indicated a willingness to support negotiations leading to majority rule and independence in Rhodesia, and the Zambians, prepared to overlook the source of the offer in order to advance the possibilities for a political settlement, made it clear that they would welcome these moves and "use their influence to ensure that ZANU and ZAPU desist from armed struggle and engage in the mechanics for finding a political solution in Rhodesia."[21] By 1975, several factors—the growing human and material costs of the war, the end of Portuguese colonialism, and the agreement in 1974 to unite ZAPU, ZANU, and FROLIZI with the African National Council under Muzorewa's leadership—made this a propitious time for a new international effort by Zambian President Kenneth Kaunda and South African Prime Minister John Vorster to press their respective allies to negotiate a settlement. Moreover, South Africa had extensive leverage with the Smith regime, based largely on its role in circumventing international sanctions and providing 2,000 well-armed paramilitary policemen and helicopter pilots (until their phased withdrawal in 1975-76).

Smith, responding to an initiative from the South African government for a new effort to negotiate a settlement, had little option but to react positively. A series of preliminary meetings between the Smith regime and the South African and Zambian governments followed. Under pressure from Vorster, Smith released some ANC leaders from detention in Rhodesia and allowed them to meet with their colleagues and the frontline presidents outside the country. (The frontline states—consisting of Zambia, Tanzania, Botswana, and Mozambique and later expanding to include Angola, Namibia, and Zimbabwe—shared many values and had a lot at stake if conflict spilled over borders.) Meanwhile, Kaunda exerted pressure for a united African nationalist delegation.[22]

The external pressure wielded by Kaunda and Vorster was sufficient to cajole their allies to agree to meet at the Victoria Falls bridge in August 1975. Martin Meredith reports that "both Kaunda and Vorster favoured a three to five-year transitional period before the advent of majority rule and believed that Smith and the nationalists, given enough encouragement, could be induced to accept such a plan."[23] Kaunda and Vorster also agreed on the broad outlines of a settlement: the release of political detainees, the lifting of the ban on African political parties, a common voters' roll with a limited franchise, and the appointment of Africans to cabinet and high-level civil service positions.

A high point in the détente process was reached on August 9, 1975, when Vorster, Smith, and Kaunda's personal secretary, Mark Chona, signed an agreement in Pretoria, committing the Rhodesian government and the ANC to a meeting at the Victoria Falls bridge no later than August 25. On that day, following speeches by Kaunda and Vorster, the two delegations began their deliberations in a railway car on the bridge at Victoria Falls. Both parties expressed their commitment in principle to working out a settlement but were unable to reach agreement on procedural issues. A more basic point of contention, however, remained the substantive question of majority rule. After Kaunda and Vorster left the conference room, Muzorewa forthrightly declared that majority rule was the only basis for a genuine settlement. The mediators' hard preparatory work was thus quickly canceled. Smith declared this a violation of the Pretoria agreement between Vorster and Smith and responded that Muzorewa's statement was "completely and utterly unacceptable" to his delegation because it introduced a precondition to the talks.[24] Further efforts to find an escape from this impasse found no middle ground. After two adjournments, Muzorewa indicated that the ANC would accept a draft based on the Pretoria agreement on the condition that the Rhodesian government delegation would agree to grant amnesty to its externally and

internally based members. Smith refused to accept this, and the negotiations speedily came to an end.

In sum, given the absence of perceptions of a mutually hurting stalemate, it is not surprising that the joint Zambian–South African pressures
were not strong enough to accelerate the process of "ripening" and thus
bring about a solution. The Kaunda-Vorster mediation effort had succeeded in establishing a possible framework for a settlement but had
failed to maintain sufficient pressure after the delegations began their
deliberations at Victoria Falls. Vorster, in particular, needed to impose
greater costs on the Rhodesian government for remaining intransigent.
In what was fast becoming a regional crisis, a strategy for external
manipulation was needed to overcome the stalemate.

The Kissinger Mediation Initiative

Following the collapse of the Victoria Falls talks, the situation reverted
to its former pattern. The shaky unity of the African nationalist movements under the ANC disintegrated; Smith and his more intransigent colleagues refused to accept full majority rule and prepared for a lengthy
fight; both sides became increasingly dependent on their external
patrons; the Rhodesian economy weakened; and, by 1976, with ZANLA
and the Zimbabwe People's Revolutionary Army (ZIPRA, ZAPU's military
wing) united under the joint command of the Zimbabwe People's Army
(ZIPA), the internal war had intensified. The costs of inconclusive action
on the peacemaking front were rising; significantly, however, the costs
were greater for the Rhodesian regime than for the insurgents. Mugabe,
sensing that history was on his side, prepared to bide his time and
hoped for a military victory. Smith, however, failed to take advantage of
momentary opportunities (for example, Nkomo's efforts to negotiate
with him in early 1976), and in so doing, he came to appear both intransigent and indecisive.[25]

The implications of this asymmetry of pain were not lost on U.S.
Secretary of State Henry Kissinger, who received careful briefings on the
changing correlation of military power in Rhodesia from various U.S.
and Western European intelligence agencies. Kissinger was determined
to prevent the radicalization of southern Africa with the accompanying
loss of confidence in Western capacity to stem Soviet-Cuban interventions, as seen in Angola. He sought to show that successful change could
take place in deeply divided societies such as Rhodesia by means of

negotiations.[26] Therefore, in a major speech in Lusaka on April 27, 1976, Kissinger signaled an important shift in U.S. foreign policy, which was switching from a hard-line confrontational approach to one that accommodated moderate African nationalism.[27]

Kissinger set forth a ten-point program to facilitate Rhodesian negotiations, block external encroachment, and secure "the goals of independence, self-determination, majority rule, minority rights, and peaceful change."[28] In a bid for African support, Kissinger called for the establishment of majority rule before independence, and he asserted that this must be achieved within two years after the conclusion of negotiations. He underlined his commitment to this objective by setting forth the following program of action: a warning to the Smith regime that it could not expect U.S. diplomatic or material support in its conflict with the African states or liberation movements; a communication to the Smith regime in Salisbury, stressing the urgency of reaching a negotiated settlement; a promise to press for the repeal of the Byrd amendment (which weakened international sanctions); an effort to discourage Americans from traveling to and setting up residence in Rhodesia; a willingness to help alleviate economic hardships in neighboring African countries that had closed their frontiers to enforce sanctions; a readiness to provide support during Rhodesia's transition to majority rule; and, finally, a stated interest in contributing to the creation of a constitutional structure that would protect minority rights while establishing majority rule. This agenda, Kissinger declared, was "an opportunity to pull back from the brink."[29]

There was considerable resistance in Africa to a Kissinger visit in the aftermath of the Lusaka speech, largely stemming from opposition to his earlier positions on southern African issues.[30] Nevertheless, such frontline leaders as Kaunda and Tanzanian President Julius Nyerere responded more positively to the American initiative. Smith, for his part, appeared well disposed to the proposal regarding negotiations and went so far as to cable Vorster in Zurich, wishing him "God's speed" in convincing Kissinger "that earnest discussions with the Rhodesian Government were necessary if a solution was to be found."[31] Vorster, at his meetings with Kissinger in West Germany and Switzerland in June and September, appeared to align himself with Kissinger's diplomatic strategy in Rhodesia and even with Kissinger's request to use his influence to encourage Smith to accept majority rule.[32]

Heartened by this support, Kissinger set out for Africa on September 13. He described himself, rather disingenuously, as responding to

Africa's invitation and as an interlocutor who had no special position on the issues.[33] The plan that Kissinger brought with him to South Africa for the negotiations was largely of British design, given to him by British Foreign Secretary James Callaghan. The British document elaborated on a statement Callaghan had made to the House of Commons on March 22, 1976, setting out four preconditions for negotiations, including acceptance of the principle of majority rule; elections for majority rule in eighteen to twenty-four months; no independence before majority rule; and no long, drawn-out negotiations on the terms of the constitution.[34] Kissinger described the Callaghan plan as different in some ways from American thinking, particularly regarding the foreign secretary's preference for placing either the Ministry of Defense or the Ministry of Law and Order in white hands.[35]

At Kissinger's first stop in Dar es Salaam, however, he proposed a caretaker government with a black majority and a council of state with a white majority during the transition period. Nyerere reportedly accepted the former but resisted the latter.[36] Next, in Lusaka, Kissinger met with Kaunda and outlined a similar scheme that called for majority rule in two years. Kissinger stated, "There will be a creation of an interim government by a Constitutional Conference of the liberation movements and Rhodesian authorities. There will be a black Prime Minister and a predominantly black government [and] a Council of State, which may have a white majority or be one man." Kaunda welcomed Kissinger's mission and emphasized that the "one major problem" that Zambia had with respect to Rhodesia was getting the Salisbury regime to accept majority rule.[37]

Kissinger was feeling hopeful before the critical negotiations with Smith in Pretoria on September 19. The frontline presidents supported the idea of a new approach, and Vorster indicated that he had softened Smith up for the forthcoming encounter.[38] Kissinger then held two meetings with an unnerved and rather shaky Rhodesian leader. It was clearly an asymmetrical exchange; the U.S. secretary of state, working in concert with a powerful regional hegemon, was in a more favorable position to press Smith than any previous mediator had been. At the first meeting, held at the U.S. ambassador's residence, Kissinger made skillful use of various U.S. and other intelligence briefings. He concluded that Smith could not win the war in Rhodesia without external assistance.[39] He then asked Smith three leading questions: How can Rhodesia be rescued without U.S. and South African support? If the current security situation is bleak, what will happen when the fighting intensifies in March? And, if you can last through March, what about a year from now?[40]

At this point, Kissinger presented the CIA and State Department analyses to a bewildered Smith, who was plainly upset by the foreign community's awareness of the extent of his vulnerability. Not knowing what to do next, Smith reportedly asked Kissinger what was expected of him. In response, Kissinger produced a modified version of the Callaghan plan, indicating that the documents had been cleared with the African frontline presidents. Kissinger also gave Smith a memorandum on a financial trust to be set up by the Western powers to assist Rhodesia's economic development and to reassure whites about their economic well-being. The meeting adjourned at 2:00 p.m. when Smith asked for time to think over his answer.[41]

At 5:40 that afternoon the negotiators, joined by Vorster, reassembled at the prime minister's official residence, Libertas. It was less a bargaining session than a capitulation. Smith set the tone, reportedly stating at the outset: "All I have to offer is my own head on a platter."[42] From that point on, events moved swiftly toward putting the Kissinger proposals into effect. Kissinger, in his eagerness to reach a conclusion, agreed to several demands that had not been approved in advance by the frontline presidents but that Smith regarded as essential to compensate for his concessions on the majority rule principle. These incentives included both a Council of State (with a white chairman) to be composed of equal numbers of whites and blacks and the appointment of whites to head the Ministries of Law and Order and of Defense. Kissinger's agreement to these arrangements, to be in place during the transitional period, encouraged Smith to agree to the package deal.

Smith returned to Rhodesia and carried out his part of the bargain. In a radio and television broadcast on September 24, he noted the overwhelming pressure placed on his government by Kissinger and Vorster but went on to announce his "surrender terms." His six-point plan contained the following provisions: majority rule within two years; an immediate meeting between his government and African leaders to organize an interim government to include a Council of State to enact legislation, supervise administration, and draft a constitution and a Council of Ministers to undertake executive responsibilities; enabling legislation enacted by the British government for the process leading to majority rule; the lifting of sanctions and the cessation of all hostilities following the establishment of the interim government; and the creation of an international trust fund to reassure Rhodesians about the country's economic future.

Kissinger, anxious to push his plan through to a successful conclusion, sent a telegram to South Africa, asking them to give the Rhodesians his "assurance that we will not repeat not allow new demands to be raised from the other side beyond what is agreed in Annex C" (specifically including the provisions on the composition and functions of the Council of State and the assignment of the two white ministries). In another telegram sent to Pretoria on the same day, Kissinger spoke ambiguously about surmounting the problem of appointing whites to head the two ministries but indicated that, if the whole process were threatened, he "would have no objection if this question were brought up during the negotiations for the establishment of an interim government."[43] Kissinger was, above all, determined to conclude the bargain on majority rule; he sought as best he could to exert pressure on Smith and the African nationalists, hoping that, in their search for security or power, they would decide to compromise on what he regarded as secondary issues. This risky move, which had not been approved in advance by the African frontline presidents, encouraged Smith to accept majority rule but ultimately proved fatal to the Kissinger plan.

In the face of a deteriorating military situation, Smith had little choice but to make significant concessions to Kissinger and Vorster. Smith was anxious to reduce the military pressure on his forces, so he indicated to the South Africans that he hoped Kissinger would use his good offices to bring about "an immediate de-escalation" of the guerrilla war; however, the frontline presidents were critical of Smith's summary of the agreement and were not prepared to relax the pressure.[44] The African leaders specifically denied having agreed to allow the Ministries of Defense and of Law and Order to remain in white hands, and they described as a "factual misconception" Smith's emphasis on the importance of the Council of State, especially in light of the disproportionate representation given to white interests in that body. The frontline presidents therefore refused to accept the package at it was; in particular, they rejected the procedures for a transition to majority rule as set out by Smith.[45]

The Geneva Conference

With African dissatisfaction mounting, the frontline presidents met in Lusaka and issued a statement that ruled out an end to the struggle on the basis of the Kissinger mediation initiative. The five presidents declared that acceptance of the proposals as outlined by Smith "would be tantamount to legalising [the] colonialist and racist structures of power." They therefore concluded that details relating to the structure and functions of the interim government should be delegated to a conference convened outside of Rhodesia by the British government.[46]

Although British authorities were somewhat reluctant to convene a conference in response to this request, they nonetheless put a good face on the situation and described the Kissinger proposals as "a useful basis of discussion."[47] Indicative of Britain's fundamental ambivalence about the conference and about its chances for success was the decision to nominate Ivor Richard, the British ambassador to the United Nations, rather than Anthony Crosland, Callaghan's successor as British foreign secretary, to preside over the talks, to be held in Geneva in October 1976. Callaghan, who had become prime minister, was determined on a Rhodesian outcome that involved limited commitments by Britain in the years ahead. The African nationalists, particularly Mugabe and Nkomo, were disappointed that Great Britain had failed to appoint a more senior and distinguished cabinet official to preside over the meetings. In contrast to the strong position that Lord Carrington displayed later at Lancaster House, Richard was unable to control the agenda or to use pressures and incentives to extract an agreement from the adversaries.

As the British had anticipated, the differences that emerged between the Rhodesian government and the African nationalists soon precluded hopes that bargaining would lead to reconciliation. In part, this discord can be attributed to uncertainty about what commitments the bargaining parties had made regarding the Kissinger settlement package. The militant Patriotic Front (PF), which combined sections of ZAPU and ZANU, rejected using the Kissinger proposals as a basis for the transition to independence. In this, they were joined by separate delegations led by Muzorewa of the ANC and Ndabaningi Sithole of the Zimbabwe Liberation Council (ZLC), both of whom rivaled Robert Mugabe for leadership of the African nationalist opposition.[48] They combined to demand instead that independence be granted within one year and that the liberation movement be given full powers in the interim government and control of the army and police. Ian Smith, on the other hand, expressed doubts that setting a "finite date" would be practical and maintained that the Kissinger package was nonnegotiable.[49]

The British chairperson, Ivor Richard, desperately sought ways to facilitate an accord. For example, echoing Crosland's statement, he stated that Britain regarded the Kissinger proposals as a "reasonable basis for discussion and negotiation" and not a "package deal" as seen by Smith.[50] This interpretation was supported by Kissinger himself, who admitted in front of a television audience that the frontline presidents had accepted only the basic framework for negotiations but not some of the critical details of the plan.[51] However, these details were critically important because they dominated the perceptions of the various actors regarding their future, that is, their ability to control the transition to independence and the period afterward.[52]

By December, it had become apparent that the conferees could not overcome the impasse on the date for granting independence and the structure of the interim government. Because Richard was unable to bring about a settlement, he adjourned the conference on December 14 and set January 17 as the date to reconvene. He used the interval to put forward various alternative schemes, in a last-ditch effort to accommodate the rival delegations. On a trip to Washington, D.C., on December 22, he expressed Great Britain's disinclination to be drawn into a direct administrative role or to be required to send British troops to Rhodesia during the interim period. Richard then traveled to six countries in southern Africa. He arrived in Lusaka in late December, proposing the appointment of a British resident commissioner who would take overall responsibility for the country's affairs and have a deciding vote on the Council of Ministers during the transition period in the event of a tie. He ruled out the idea of direct British administration, including the possibility of a British or Commonwealth peacekeeping force. Richard received only mild support from the PF leaders, indifference in Pretoria, and outright resistance in Salisbury, so he was compelled to retreat and rethink his proposals.

Richard made a final effort to mediate the conflict in mid-January. The situation hardened when the frontline presidents decided in the interim to recognize the PF as the only genuine liberation movement in Rhodesia. In this context, Richard suggested, rather vaguely, formation of a transitional government, headed by a British-appointed interim commissioner, that would have included equal numbers of members from each of the "political groups" represented by delegations at Geneva (ZANU, ZAPU, ANC, RF, and ZLC) and a similar number of Europeans appointed by the interim commissioner. This arrangement would have resulted in a Council of Ministers with a "substantial" African majority. Although the Council of Ministers would have had full executive and legislative powers, the interim commissioner, advised by an inner cabinet of the leaders of delegations to the Geneva conference, would have had residual responsibility for external affairs, defense, internal security, and the implementation of the program leading to independence.[53] Smith rejected these proposals as a basis for further negotiations; it was now clear that without strong support from either South Africa or the United States, Richard lacked the leverage to push back to the bargaining table either a recalcitrant Smith or a PF movement determined to intensify the guerrilla struggle.[54] Richard was left suspended in midair above the fray, doomed to watch the collapse of his diplomatic efforts.

The Anglo-American Initiative

Given that the ill-fated Geneva conference would never reconvene and the guerrilla war was intensifying, the various rivals gravitated toward two tacks to negotiate a settlement: the Anglo-American effort to resolve the Rhodesian question on a basis that would satisfy all the parties in the region, and Smith's own venture to negotiate an internal settlement with the moderate African nationalist leaders. British and American mediators were determined to use their power to accelerate the ripening process. Meanwhile, Smith, resolutely striving to keep power in white hands, was prepared to make concessions to moderate Africans on political appointments and access to land in a desperate effort to build international support for a settlement without Mugabe.

The Anglo-American coalition, which brought together newly elected U.S. President Jimmy Carter and the Callaghan-led Labour government in 1977, was determined upon a liberal solution that would accommodate black African aspirations regarding Rhodesia. The Carter team, not content with containing Soviet expansion in southern Africa, sought to get in step with black ambitions by being committed to majority rule, self-determination, and racial equality.[55] The genesis of the coalition effort began with talks between Callaghan and Carter in Washington on March 9, where the two leaders united to conduct a joint effort to overcome the stalemate. U.S. Secretary of State Cyrus Vance and the new British foreign secretary, David Owen, thereupon agreed to work toward a new conference, providing for a brief transition to majority rule, a British caretaker administration, elections open to all parties, a broadly inclusive franchise, a justiciable bill of rights, and an independent judiciary. Provision was also made for an international development fund to give economic aid to Zimbabwe during the transition period.

The Anglo-American effort to build support for a peaceful transition gained public attention with Owen's trip to southern Africa in April 1977. Despite considerable initial skepticism from African nationalists in Dar es Salaam and Lusaka regarding the new Anglo-American initiative, hopes for a political breakthrough rose as the frontline presidents indicated support for the new bid and Smith and Vorster responded positively.

To increase opportunities for "intensive consultations" with the main parties about an independence constitution and transitional arrangements, Owen announced the creation of an Anglo-American Consultative Group.[56] This group, headed by J. A. N. Graham, the deputy undersecretary at the Foreign and Commonwealth Office, and Stephen Low, the U.S. ambassador to Rhodesia, traversed southern Africa and met frequently with local leaders to develop proposals for a constitutional settlement. The importance of this endeavor is noted by U.S. Ambassador Donald F. McHenry, who remarked that "most of the work on Zimbabwe had been done by Johnny Graham and Steve Low in going back and forth, and back and forth between the various parties long before they got to Lancaster House."[57]

In contrast to Kissinger's whirlwind diplomacy, the consultative group took pains to listen to the views of the rival leaders; they sought to try to develop a framework for negotiations through a careful blending of responsiveness, material incentives, and implicit pressures.[58] The task of the mediator, Ambassador Low stated in an interview, was to reconcile the whites' concern with constitutional guarantees and the African nationalists' primary objective of securing political power through the transitional arrangements. He continued: "In specific terms, this [meant] offering the whites blocking seats in exchange for control over the electoral process, the transition period, etc. However, during the period of the Low/Graham initiative, the two sides were still [too] far apart on the future shape of the military for this to be a worthwhile subject to broach."[59]

The Anglo-American proposals began to take shape in July and were ready on September 1 for presentation to the frontline presidents, the African nationalists, the Smith regime, and South Africa. The main components of this comprehensive plan were the surrender of power by the illegal regime and a return to legality; an orderly and peaceful transition to independence during 1978; free and impartial elections on the basis of universal adult suffrage (although the constitution would provide that twenty of the one hundred seats in the National Assembly were to be elected by minority communities for a minimum of eight years); the establishment of a transitional administration by the British government, with the task of conducting the elections for an independent government; a UN presence, including a peacekeeping force, during the transition period; an independence constitution providing for a democratically elected government, the abolition of discrimination, the protection of individual human rights, protections from expropriation of property (except on specified grounds of public interest and then only on condition of prompt payment of adequate compensation), and the independence of the judiciary; and a $1 billion to $1.5 billion development fund to revive the economy of the country, which Great Britain and the United States viewed as predicated on the implementation of the settlement as a whole.[60]

Important advances from previous plans were the proposals for universal adult suffrage; the appointment by the British government of a resident commissioner to administer the country, organize and conduct the general elections, and command the armed forces during the transition; and the presence of a UN peacekeeping force to supervise the cease-fire and support civil authorities during the transition period. A learning process was clearly in evidence. By focusing on the process of implementation during the transition period, the external mediators were attempting to look ahead, seeking to develop a basis for consolidating an agreement that could endure. But the trade-offs of dealing explicitly with the delicate issue of postagreement security soon became apparent. The creation of a new, unified Zimbabwe national army that would bring together all existing armed forces and be responsible to the duly elected government was opposed by Mugabe, who wanted only PF forces to police the transition, and by Smith (and Vorster), who feared dismantling the Rhodesian army and its paramilitary units.[61] The reference to a "surrender" alienated the Rhodesian officer corps, a key element needed to ensure a smooth transition process.[62] Moreover, the appointment of a powerful British resident commissioner for Rhodesia, retired Field Marshal Lord Carver, was also seen as a sign of Owen's resolve to orchestrate a change of regime, which was regarded with apprehension by white Rhodesians.

Although the Anglo-American proposals were a logical response to the Rhodesian impasse, they were doomed in part by the mediatory coalition's inability to exert sufficient pressure to overcome the deep differences between the Smith regime and the African nationalists on such issues as constitutional protections, the unified army, and the international peacekeeping force. Owen contended that with UN ratification of the plan, penalties could be placed on any state that attempted to undermine the settlement. He also intimated that South Africa could play a leading role by exerting pressure on Smith, much as had been done in Kissinger's time.[63] This reference to Pretoria, however, showed little sensitivity to the change of attitude there following Vorster's highly charged meeting with U.S. Vice President Walter Mondale in May 1977. Mondale urged Vorster several times to press Smith to accept the Anglo-American plan, but on one occasion Vorster stated his preference for an internal settlement and reportedly "came up sharply, saying that he did not like the word 'pressure.'"[64]

The proposals were also doomed because the PF tasted military victory and the Smith regime was not ready for capitulation. In reality, beleaguered parties can absorb much more pain than theories about peace negotiations and hurting stalemates are prepared to acknowledge. As Martin Meredith remarked regarding the Anglo-American initiative, "It was an extraordinary miscalculation on Owen's part to assume that the pressures of the war, a troubled economy and declining white morale would ever have induced Smith to countenance such a plan."[65] Also, the PF's insistence that the new army be based on the liberation forces, the lack of agreed-upon constitutional guarantees for minorities, and Lord Carver's tough-minded approach to his task all compounded the threat to the still-dominant whites.

The Anglo-American negotiators, realizing their predicament, made several efforts to renegotiate some of the terms of the agreement with the PF and frontline presidents in 1978. At Malta in late January and early February, Owen and U.S. Ambassador to the UN Andrew Young secured some acceptance by PF leaders on a transitional role for a UN peacekeeping force and the creation of a Governing Council of ten members (two from each of the delegations at Geneva) to deal with criticisms of Lord Carver's "absolute control" in the interim period.[66] In April, following the signing of the internal settlement (discussed below), Owen, Vance, and Young met with the various rival parties in Dar es Salaam, Pretoria, and Salisbury, but they extracted few concessions from either side.[67] Support for the Anglo-American approach had obviously evaporated. If, as David Martin and Phyllis Johnson maintain, the plan did "add new links to the chain of events begun by Kissinger," it nonetheless lacked a basic concept that would appeal to both parties and an effective strategy for bringing sufficient pressures and incentives to bear on the reluctant actors.[68] The upshot was another setback.

The Internal Settlement

Smith was unable to achieve his first preference (an acceptable internationally negotiated settlement), so he moved by stages toward his second preference (an internally negotiated agreement). By means of the internal settlement, he modified the strategy of defection to include the political participation of moderate African nationalists but remained firm in his adversarial perceptions of his militant nationalist opponents and his determination to keep his regime's autonomy from British governmental influences.

At least three major factors led Smith to opt for an internal solution: his need for a coalition with African moderates to fulfill the demands of some insurgents for a black-led government and thus ease the pressure on his hard-pressed military forces; his hopes that, if he put the Kissinger commitment on majority rule into effect, he would gain international legitimacy and an easing of sanctions; and his recognition of a mood shift in South Africa, where Vorster, who was hostile to the Carter administration but nonetheless concerned over the security situation in Rhodesia, was increasingly supportive of an internal settlement. The decision of the frontline presidents to recognize and back the PF left the moderate African nationalists—Muzorewa, Sithole, and Chief Jeremiah Chirau (a former cabinet minister who now led the newly formed Zimbabwe United People's Organization, which sought to build support in the rural areas)—with little option but to ally themselves with Smith as a means of gaining political power. Muzorewa and Sithole, once regarded as militant African nationalists, now found themselves forging a coalition with their former enemy. They recognized that they lacked international military and political support comparable to that of the PF and therefore chose to work within the existing Rhodesian state to establish a power base for themselves. Chengetai Zvobgo also notes that it was the Anglo-American plan's recommendation to base the new Zimbabwe army during the interim period on the liberation forces that "convinced Sithole that the internal settlement plan was his only viable alternative." Such a settlement was, as Zvobgo states, a "partnership in adversity."[69]

Efforts to reach an internal settlement between Smith and the moderate African nationalists came to fruition on March 3, 1978, with the signing of an agreement providing for majority rule on the basis of universal adult suffrage, an interim government, the drafting of a constitution, and the holding of general elections. In an effort to reassure whites about their rightful place in Rhodesia, the African moderates agreed to reserve twenty-eight seats in a one hundred–member legislative assembly for whites, twenty of these to be elected on a preferential system by whites only and the remaining eight by a multiracial electorate, following their nomination by a white electoral college. This provision on reserved seats was guaranteed for a period of ten years or two parliaments, whichever was longer; at the end of that time, a commission would be appointed to make recommendations to further minority participation in the electoral process. Specially entrenched provisions were to be included in the constitution to protect the independence of the judiciary and public services board and to guarantee pensions and citizenship. These entrenched provisions could only be amended by a bill that secured seventy-eight supporting votes, thereby providing white members with a "blocking vote" for at least the next ten years.

The transitional government never gained the international legitimacy that the parties had expected. Just before the signing of the internal settlement, Owen warned Sithole that his "biggest problem [was] to get international recognition."[70] To this end, Owen listed four conditions that would have to be met before the regime's legalization would be possible: participation in the election of the president would be limited to the seventy-two Africans elected to the legislature on the basis of the common roll; Smith was not to lead the interim government; Smith was not to hold the Law and Order portfolio; and, most important, a genuine effort would be made to include Mugabe and Nkomo in the ruling coalition.[71] However, because Smith, chosen by lots, became the first chairman of the Executive Council (which also included Muzorewa, Sithole, and Chirau) and because white officials were still firmly in control of the civil service and the coercive agencies of the state, one of Owen's main preconditions was disregarded from the outset.

Nkomo and Mugabe rejected the agreement as "completely bogus," declaring that it "retains, indeed firmly entrenches, the Smith regime together with its vicious political and military structures." The PF leaders, regarding themselves as "the authentic expression of the Zimbabwean masses," declared their commitment to negotiate with Great Britain (as the colonial power) on the basis of the Anglo-American proposals.[72] On the whole, the guerrilla forces in the field paid scant attention to the offer of general amnesty, and the transitional government, which was unable to exert much influence over the insurgents, had no success in arranging a cease-fire.

The PF leaders' firm rejection of the internal settlement and subsequent constitution received broad international support. Both the frontline states and the Organization of African Unity (OAU) firmly opposed the settlement. The UN Security Council, in a vote of great symbolic importance, approved a resolution in March declaring any Rhodesian settlement made under Smith's auspices to be "illegal and unacceptable." President Carter questioned African participation in the constitutional deliberations where the voting process was worked out and continued to state his refusal to lift the sanctions then in place. To be sure, some prominent Americans and Britons were prepared to accept the internal settlement as legitimate and acceptable, and the credibility of British Prime Minister Margaret Thatcher and Foreign Secretary Lord Carrington in threatening a "second-class solution" at Lancaster House (recognition of the internal settlement) depended in part on their view of it as a possible alternative solution to the problem of governance in Rhodesia. In fact, a high point in the opposition to the Carter administration's policy on Rhodesia came when the U.S. Senate voted to end sanctions in June 1979; however, in what Stephen Low describes as a "critical moment of importance," Representative Stephen Solarz guided a House vote against the repeal of sanctions.[73] With the world community largely standing behind the PF leaders and refusing to accord the internal solution any legitimacy, the transitional regime took the face-saving choice of accepting an invitation to attend a Commonwealth-initiated all-party conference to be held in London by the British authorities. It was time now to move beyond the Anglo-American initiative to the more conclusive Lancaster House strategy.

The Lancaster House Mediation Process

In both the Kissinger and Anglo-American negotiations, the external mediators had made some intermittent progress toward a Rhodesian settlement. Kissinger's initiative used a forceful strategy, employing strong pressures and consequential incentives, that culminated in Smith's capitulation. The follow-up Anglo-American proposals represented constructive guidelines toward a solution but lacked a coherent strategy that could bring meaningful pressures and incentives to bear. As I. William Zartman has stated, the United States and Great Britain "had no leverage over the various governments of Ian Smith, no control over a deadline, no ability to demonstrate the likely catastrophe that loomed at the end of the chosen course, and no ability to block the unilateral attempts of the parties to impose a solution on each other."[74]

Prospects for a settlement improved in late 1978 and early 1979, as all sides finally became aware of the costs of continuing the war. Although the Smith-Muzorewa government was unable to secure international legitimacy, it did manage to launch punishing raids on PF positions in Mozambique and Zambia. PF leaders and their frontline state supporters never doubted that the insurgents would eventually win a military victory, but the Rhodesian raids pointed to the heavy costs such a route would entail. The new Conservative government of Margaret Thatcher (which took office following the April 1979 elections) was being pressured by its Commonwealth allies to make one more concerted attempt to hold an all-party conference on Rhodesia. The Thatcher government resisted the temptation to carry out its implicit pledges to recognize the internal settlement and end sanctions and instead committed itself to another British-led effort to complete a negotiated peace. Decisive action was achieved this time because Lord Carrington combined a coherent strategy with considerable leverage, making effective use of various pressures and incentives to gain an agreement and thereby replace the intrastate system of conflict management.

Prenegotiations

In Rhodesia, negotiations (and the mediatory activity that accompanied them) proved to be an extended and interconnected process encompassing the stages of prenegotiation, negotiation, and implementation. In this respect, the Lusaka Commonwealth conference of August 1979 was a prime example of how prenegotiations (the processes of framing the subsequent negotiations) can become critical in creating a momentum leading to a successful outcome.[75] The Lusaka conference represented an important international reiteration of the basic Callaghan principles and an agenda for reconciliation. As Jay Rothman states, the conference changed "the tone from competition to cooperation."[76]

The Commonwealth conference was preoccupied from the outset with the issue of Rhodesia. With the OAU reaffirming its support for the PF as the sole, legitimate authority in the country and the newly elected Thatcher government wavering over recognizing the Muzorewa government, a showdown among Commonwealth countries seemed likely. (Muzorewa was sworn in as Rhodesia's first black African prime minister on May 29, 1987.) A confrontation was avoided, however, because the main players adopted conciliatory stances. In this, they were assisted by Prime Minister Malcolm Fraser of Australia, who pressed Thatcher not to recognize the Muzorewa government before the Lusaka conference and proved a critically important buffer between Thatcher and both Nyerere and Kaunda at the meetings.[77]

A spirit of mutual accommodation became evident once the meetings had begun. A conciliatory speech by Nyerere observed that a democratic constitution calling for majority rule did not preclude concessions on reserved seats for minorities; following this, Thatcher spoke of the need for an internationally acceptable solution in Rhodesia. She described the constitution that had brought Muzorewa to power as "defective in certain important respects," notably, the blocking mechanism in the hands of the white minority members in parliament and the inability of the government to exercise adequate control over certain senior service appointments.[78]

The conferees adjourned with an "initial understanding" on the need for genuine majority rule and safeguards for minorities. A seven-member "contact group" met over the weekend in Kaunda's study at the State House to discuss a set of common points drawn up by Commonwealth Secretary-General Shridath Ramphal.[79] This contact group, composed of Ramphal as chair with Nyerere, Kaunda, Thatcher, Lord Carrington, Henry Adefope (Nigerian external affairs commissioner), Jamaican Prime Minister Michael Manley, and Fraser, reached an agreement that called upon Great Britain to supervise fresh elections and to convene an all-party constitutional conference. This document, unanimously approved by the thirty-nine Commonwealth heads of state or government, involved a commitment to "genuine black rule" and recognized Britain's responsibility to supervise free and fair elections (monitored by Commonwealth observers), to hold a constitutional conference, and to grant independence to Zimbabwe on the basis of majority rule.

In a concession to Thatcher, the conferees also linked the adoption of a majoritarian, democratic constitution with protections for minorities. The Lusaka Commonwealth conference was critically important to the negotiation process because it hammered out the agenda for the subsequent meetings at Lancaster House. In the words of an Australian intermediary, it provided "framework and momentum."[80] Muzorewa's secretary and Lancaster House delegate James G. Kamusikiri stressed that the Lusaka conference lent international legitimacy to the British efforts to mediate the Rhodesian dispute, which greatly strengthened Lord Carrington's well-orchestrated diplomacy in the months to follow.[81]

Phase I Negotiations: The Constitution

For different reasons, the various Rhodesian parties were all reserved in their responses to the Commonwealth plan to bring them to the bargaining table. Muzorewa evidenced distress, stating that the conference's consensus on the need for fresh elections was "an insult to the electorate and the Government of this country."[82] Smith adopted a rather hostile tone when speaking about it, and Roloef "Pik" Botha, the South African foreign minister, declared himself "deeply disturbed" by the Commonwealth plan.[83]

The largest problem was the PF's reluctance to meet Muzorewa. Mugabe and Nkomo were reportedly "incensed" that the frontline presidents had agreed to invite a Muzorewa delegation (including Ian Smith) to Lancaster House, because this undercut their claim, which was supported by the OAU, to be the sole representative of the Zimbabwean people.[84] Given this cool reaction, important African frontline presidents (of Zambia, Tanzania, and Mozambique), weary of the war and determined to deliver on the commitments they made at Lusaka, had no choice but to exert pressure on the PF leaders to deal in good faith as a united team. From the start, then, the mediation effort was not solely a British show but instead involved a coalition of mediators.

In accordance with the procedure set forth at Lusaka, the British government invited Muzorewa, Mugabe, and Nkomo to appoint a delegation of as many as twelve members to attend a constitutional conference at Lancaster House on September 10, 1979. The British also attached proposals outlining the kind of constitution that would, in their view, be an acceptable basis for independence. The proposals sought to allay African apprehensions regarding the extensive safeguards for the white community. Although only a minority of seats in the House of Assembly would be reserved for white MPs, the British government tried to eliminate the whites' ability to block bills in the legislature. The British sought to ease the advance of Africans into the senior ranks of the police, military, and public services and proposed to give the prime minister greater flexibility in making top-level appointments. Finally, in an important statement on mediatory strategy for the forthcoming conference, the government indicated that it planned to adopt a phased course of action, shifting from the comprehensive approach of the Anglo-American proposals to a step-by-step strategy that created momentum and "reduced the manoeuvring space of the participants."[85] Robin Renwick, a key member of the Carrington negotiating team, stressed in an interview that the British felt it essential to deal first with the majority rule question before tackling problems that involved a struggle for power among African parties. In Renwick's view, constitutional matters were the most basic and, if the British team could secure agreement on these, then the cease-fire and transition would likely follow.[86]

With Britain's role as mediator legitimated, the war expanding and involving heavy costs for Zambia and Mozambique, and the frontline presidents preparing to exert pressure on the PF to bring the fighting to an end, Carrington was in a strong position at Lancaster House: he could combine both leverage and strategy. Great Britain, as the colonial power, was an interested mediator, anxious, African leaders said, to make amends for the "humiliation" of the UDI.[87] While holding out the possibility of recognizing the internal settlement, the British preferred to achieve a "first-class solution," one that would bring the colony to independence, create a stable system of conflict management (including safeguards for minorities), and also preserve the unity of the Commonwealth.

For the bargaining parties, British interest in the outcome was of secondary concern: they sought a mediator who would implement the agreement fairly and would be able to use various pressures and incentives to induce the rivals to compromise on the major issues. Carrington used great skill to convince the parties involved of Great Britain's commitment to a settlement. Nevertheless, as I contended in chapter 1 of this book, mediatory skill must be placed within the political context in which it operates. Because the mediator's strategy and manipulation of pressures and incentives took place in favorable circumstances, Carrington (and his coalition of backers) was able to secure the necessary accommodations from the main players.

Carrington's determination to dominate the conference and its proceedings was evident from the outset. By seeking to achieve a breakthrough in the extended negotiating process, Carrington took an unusual stance as a mediator: he remained tough and controlling throughout the conference. Renwick described him as less a mediator than an "arbitrator." Carrington had learned from the flawed experiences of the past—in particular, the Kissinger package's assignment of key security ministries to white officials, the mediator's loss of control at Geneva, and the "unwieldy" nature of the Anglo-American proposals regarding security matters during the transition. Carrington sought to build a dynamic peace process by means of a phased approach, shaped and managed by British diplomats.[88] He pressured the delegations by writing draft proposals on the major issues, controlling the agenda, set-ting deadlines, threatening the delegations with British adoption of a second-class solution, and establishing implicit alliances, for tactical pur-poses, with the frontline presidents, the United States, and South Africa. With the clear desire to be rid of the Rhodesian problem once and for all, Carrington focused primarily on securing a settlement that would be internationally acceptable.

Carrington's opening speech at Lancaster House on September 10 based the legitimacy of his mediatory effort on the framework of gen-uine majority rule and minority safeguards that was established at Lusaka. He reiterated the importance of seeking an agreement on the constitution before deciding on the arrangements for implementing the settlement.[89] Muzorewa contended that his government had sub-stantially met Great Britain's six principles and called for British recog-nition and an end to sanctions. His desire for external acceptance left him little opportunity to challenge Carrington's plan for organizing the conference.

Nkomo, meanwhile, resisted the British scheme, fearing that a step-by-step approach would place the PF in danger, because Great Britain and Rhodesia could take advantage of the situation if the constitution were accepted and control of the armed forces left unresolved. In Nkomo's words, "The critical period leading to independence is as vital as the independence constitution itself."[90] Carrington, solidly supported by the frontline presidents, resisted any change in his phased strategy. He insisted that a comprehensive approach such as the Anglo-American plan lacked the dynamic quality that would lead to a settlement. By con-ceding that the issues raised by Nkomo and Mugabe would be discussed after the constitution had been drawn up, Carrington carried the day while still enabling the PF leaders to save face. The PF spokesmen, faced with the frontline presidents' determination to work for an honorable settlement, decided not to press the issue of procedure and said that evening that they had no intention of pulling out of the conference.[91]

Carrington then turned to constitutional matters. He tabled a sum-mary of the independence constitution that became the basis for the first phase of the discussions. His recommended constitution provided for a parliament that would include two houses, with the lower house consisting of eighty members elected on a common voters' roll and twenty elected on a white voters' roll for at least the first seven years. The whites would retain no mechanism for blocking legislation enacted by a majority in parliament and no special controls over public and security services, but they would be reassured during the transition period by the inclusion of liberal provisions on citizenship, an extensive list of fully justiciable fundamental rights for at least ten years (including freedom from deprivation of property and protection from discrimination), safeguards for pension rights, and a high court of Zimbabwe having both original and appellate jurisdiction.[92]

The Muzorewa and PF delegations reacted very differently to the recommended protections for the white minority. Muzorewa declared that the safeguards "were not really that important after all," overrode dissent on the issue within his own delegation, and accepted the British proposals.[93] Also, in a very important concession to Carrington, he indicated a reluctant willingness to hold new elections under British supervision. Muzorewa's approval of the British proposals brought on a bitter rebuttal from Ian Smith; Smith insisted that a blocking mechanism, accompanied by control of the public service commissions, was the only effective means of protecting white interests under the new constitution.[94] Muzorewa brought the matter before his delegation; the members, both white and black, voted overwhelmingly to accept the Carrington recommendations for ending the white veto.

The PF delegates, who were committed to creating a new, socialist society in Zimbabwe, expressed strong reservations about the British proposals, particularly the special parliamentary representation for the white minority, automatic citizenship for those who came to Zimbabwe after the UDI, the weakness of presidential power, and the limitations on land redistribution. The first hint of a softening of the PF position, however, came on the eve of the second week of talks, when Nkomo declared his opposition to introducing "racism" into the constitution but indicated that, if the British insisted on reserved seats for whites, "then they will have [those] seats."[95] At this point, heavy frontline pressure to reach an agreement on this issue became apparent. One frontline official reportedly told the PF leaders regarding the reserved seats that "it's only for seven years; then you can change things to suit the conditions; but if you bolt the Conference now, the UK will recognize Muzorewa and will defend his Regime."[96]

The next constitutional issue with strong PF resistance was the fundamental rights provisions regarding land redistribution. Lord Carrington warned the PF delegates that no substantial changes could be made to a document already accepted by the Muzorewa government, and he dropped hints again about accepting an internal settlement unless the PF agreed on the constitution. Yet this was no easy matter

for the PF, because the land issue went to the heart of African grievances. Because independence would inevitably lead to heady expectations, the African-led government's inability to redistribute underutilized
land to dispossessed farmers would cause widespread disappointment.[97]
Not surprisingly, therefore, the PF leaders refused to either agree or disagree with the British proposals on land rights and fair compensation,
prompting the British foreign secretary to set an October 8 deadline
for PF concurrence with the draft constitution. Still, October 8 came and
went without a firm commitment.

A potentially dangerous deadlock then became apparent. Carrington
refused the PF's offer to table the matter for the moment and proceed to
the transition questions; he did, however, extend the deadline to
October 11, but to no avail. To extricate the British and the PF from a difficult predicament, a coalition of third-party actors—including representatives from the frontline states and the United States—stepped into
the deteriorating situation. President Samora Machel of Mozambique,
responding to Carrington's appeals for support, claimed that his government was still paying the Portuguese for the costs of land redistribution and urged Mugabe to act in a conciliatory manner toward the
property owners on this issue. When the PF raised new obstacles, the
frontline leaders warned them as follows: "Since you have already publicly accepted the really *major* provisions of the constitution, you cannot threaten to break up the Conference over a minor issue like compensation. The Front-Line will *not* back you up."[98]

In a further effort to alter PF preferences on the land issue and to
keep the conference from collapsing, the frontline leaders encouraged
British and American officials in London to offer financial incentives to
enable Mugabe and Nkomo to save face. Diplomatic pressures then
became linked to purchase incentives in a most telling fashion: on
October 11, when Carrington had rejected the PF's ambiguous response
regarding the constitution, he extended an olive branch in the form of
British economic aid for land resettlement after independence.[99] Now,
the long-mooted international fund became a matter of high priority.
With the British feeling that their capacity for potential contributions
toward land resettlement was limited, the American role in backstopping the international fund became critical.

As I have previously indicated, the U.S. idea of offering financial incentives harkens back to Kissinger's 1976 proposal to provide Rhodesian
whites with what amounted to an insurance plan intended to facilitate
their agreement to a peace accord. The idea of a compensation scheme

was further refined at Geneva, Malta, and again at Lancaster House. Western diplomats feared that such a plan might destabilize the Zimbabwean economy after independence by causing a white flight; consequently, each successive discussion of the scheme narrowed its purposes and its restrictions on the levels of compensation.[100]

When the Lancaster House conference ran into grave difficulty over the land issue, Shridath Ramphal, the Commonwealth secretary-general, approached U.S. Ambassador Kingman Brewster and State Department official E. Gibson Lanpher, urging the United States to take action to break the impasse on the land question. Ramphal argued that the United States should commit itself by pledging economic assistance. President Carter responded favorably, authorizing the U.S. diplomats in London to make a nonspecific commitment to postindependence Zimbabwe.[101] This pledge, which was subject to congressional approval, was purposefully left vague regarding the amount of assistance offered; it was also made conditional upon a successful outcome at Lancaster House. Upon receiving this authorization, Lanpher first contacted Ramphal and then all the frontline representatives. Ramphal thereupon telephoned Nyerere, and word about the U.S. pledge was passed to Mugabe and Nkomo. Several days later, Ramphal indicated to Lanpher that the PF leaders were responding positively to this new initiative. Following a request to hear about the offer firsthand, Mugabe and Nkomo were assured in person that the money would be available for agricultural or educational purposes but not for a buyout of white farmers. In Lanpher's words, the financial incentive "gave them enough to save face" and enabled them to go on with the conference. President Carter, later assessing the role of U.S. financial incentives at Lancaster House, also concluded that "there's no doubt that to some degree financial promises played a role" in inducing Zimbabweans to accept the Lancaster House agreement.[102] This proved to be a very balanced assessment.

With the support of pledges from Great Britain and the United States, the PF leaders dropped their main reservations about the draft constitution. To save face, Nkomo and Mugabe declared that the Anglo-American assurances of assistance for land resettlement, agriculture, and economic development "go a long way in allaying the great concern we have over the whole land question." The conference could, therefore, proceed on to the transitional arrangements without the need to reexamine the constitutional issues in contention.[103]

Phase II Negotiations: The Transition

As the conference entered its seventh week, Carrington turned to the highly contentious subject of the transition process. At the time of the negotiations, the outgoing colonial power lacked effective control over the army and the police; thus it was in a weak position to enforce the terms of the agreement. Moreover, the terms themselves were critical in structuring the course of future power disputes. Following angry sparring between Carrington and Mugabe over Great Britain's authority to administer the elections, Carrington offered a set of recommendations regarding his country's resumption of direct rule for a limited time, the arrangements for the elections, and the agreement on a ceasefire. He proposed that the British government appoint a governor with extensive executive and legislative powers to rule Zimbabwe on the basis of the existing administrative apparatus and security forces. This governor would have the general responsibility, over a two-month period, to create conditions for free and fair elections. He would be backed by an election commissioner assisted by an election council composed of party representatives who would supervise the organization and conduct of the voting. Commonwealth observers would also be present to oversee the election.[104]

The inexplicit nature of the British proposals immediately drew criticism from both sides. Bishop Muzorewa was apprehensive that the voters might interpret his acceptance of the British proposals as weakness, so he expressed several reservations, especially regarding the need for his government to step down before new elections would be held. One week later, however, he confronted the dilemma and conditionally accepted Carrington's interim arrangements. Muzorewa was anxious to gain British support in the event that the conference collapsed and a "second class solution" became unavoidable, so he opted for a statesmanlike stance. Moreover, Lieutenant General Peter Walls, chief of staff of the Rhodesian security forces, emphasized the important role that the security forces would continue to play under the British plan and did more than anyone to convince Muzorewa of the need to resign.[105] The effect of Muzorewa's acceptance of the British plan was to increase Carrington's leverage in his dealings with the PF delegation.

The PF leaders were less conciliatory, however. They criticized the British proposals on several grounds, including the investment of the governor with considerable power during the two-month transition, the

governor's reliance upon the government's security forces and bureaucracy during the transition, the lack of a UN presence to guarantee free
and fair elections, the short length of the transition period, and the
establishment of a governing council composed of equal numbers of
PF and government members with the governor as chairman. Mugabe
and Nkomo, intensely suspicious of British intentions, challenged the
impartiality of a governor who would be wholly dependent upon existing civil service and security arms.[106] At Lancaster House, Mugabe
expressed anxiety that the Rhodesian security forces would be
entrusted with the role of ensuring the security of the state during the
transition period and asked: "Why had Britain chosen to use the institutions of the regime and to refuse equal participation by those of his
delegation?" The PF, Mugabe concluded, "could not accept a position of
inferiority in a situation where they were moving towards victory—
although victory might take time."[107]

The situation was extremely delicate. Carrington contended that the
PF leaders were looking back to the Anglo-American proposals, which
he considered too elaborate for the situation at hand. Carrington envisaged little role for the army during the transition and assumed that the
police forces, under the control of the governor, would be sufficient to
maintain the cease-fire. The gap between the British mediators and the
PF leaders remained wide. With both parties convinced that the institutions established for the transition would have a significant influence on
the election process, maneuverability was limited and a collapse of the
conference seemed highly possible.

Tensions increased on November 7, as the British government introduced an enabling bill allowing it to let part of the Rhodesian sanctions
legislation lapse. This action was not only a clear gesture of appreciation
for Muzorewa's acceptance of British proposals, but it also pressured the
PF delegation by holding out the possibility of a second-class solution.
At Lancaster House, Nkomo was sensitive to these British tactics and
declared that "the timing of the Bill was deliberate to put pressure on his
delegation."[108] The PF delegation, in a defiant mood, failed to turn up
the next day for a scheduled session at Lancaster House.

With concern deepening over the fate of the conference, various
Commonwealth and frontline state leaders again came to the rescue.
Ramphal and representatives from the Commonwealth and frontline
states met with the British mediators and PF leaders. There were reports
of "considerable disquiet" among some Commonwealth leaders over

Britain's proposal to base Zimbabwe's administration on the existing civil service, army, and police structures during the transition period; at the same time, however, a meeting of the Commonwealth Committee on Southern Africa pointedly resisted supporting PF demands for UN peacekeeping forces and also refrained from condemning Great Britain's leadership of the conference.[109]

Kaunda was invited to London by Thatcher; he pressed for changes in the British plan. At a working dinner with Thatcher and Carrington on the night of November 8, he called for concessions on the timetable for elections and for the deployment of a Commonwealth military force. Although Carrington softened his own position regarding the creation of a small Commonwealth Monitoring Force (CMF), further negotiations between Kaunda and the various parties and mediators nonetheless contributed to a breakthrough in the negotiations. In a conciliatory statement, Carrington extended the preelection period, provided that all parties would have equal status on the election council, made the military commanders on both sides equally responsible for maintaining the cease-fire, arranged that PF forces at assembly points in Zimbabwe would be properly housed and fed, and promised that the Commonwealth would take steps to set up forces to monitor the cease-fire.

The concessions regarding equal status for the opposing armies were critical to the transition compromise. The PF forces were no longer "guerrillas"; they now had a legitimate role in implementing the peace process. Mugabe, referring to the addition of a final sentence to the thirteenth point in the Carrington proposals, on the need for PF forces to comply with the governor's directions, stated on November 15 that "if you are prepared to include the Patriotic Front forces in paragraph 13 of the British paper, we are able to agree to the interim proposals, conditional on a successful outcome of the negotiations on the cease-fire."[110] Carrington concurred, and the deal was struck.

Phase III Negotiations: The Cease-Fire

To build upon the momentum created by the agreements on the constitution and the transition process, the conference now turned to the complicated question of the cease-fire. Carrington told the delegates, "You have agreed to settle your differences in elections under our authority, and we must find a way to bring peace to Rhodesia while those elections are held."[111] He was fully aware that, in situations such as that in Rhodesia, cease-fires and the separation and containment of forces are difficult to arrange because they can make the actors vulnerable.[112] Deceitful commanders may engage in cheating during the implementation process, thus shifting the balance of forces in their favor. Carrington recognized that he needed to move carefully through this possible minefield, so he set out general proposals for the cease-fire arrangements at Lancaster House on November 16.

The British proposals consciously designed a minimalist undertaking by the third party; they shunned enforcement and instead placed the responsibility for implementing the agreement on the parties themselves.[113] Carrington recommended making the military commanders responsible to the governor for the observance of the cease-fire by the troops under their command. Representatives of the two military forces were to be included on a Cease-fire Commission under the chairmanship of the governor's military advisor. The commission's functions involved ensuring compliance with the arrangements for the security of their forces and investigating actual or threatened breaches of the cease-fire. To reassure both sides that the cease-fire would be fair, the British proposed the establishment of a neutral force to monitor the cease-fire process, also to be chaired by the governor's military advisor, and invited certain other Commonwealth governments to contribute units to this group.

Initially, the PF responded to these proposals with skepticism. A separation of forces was difficult because of the number of people under arms throughout the country. Also, the small size of the Commonwealth peacekeeping force made monitoring an arduous task. Nkomo asked: If the PF and Rhodesian forces were separated, as the British proposed, "what would be done with the two armed forces by the party which won the elections? Would the winning side eliminate the other?"[114] Or would the losing side, fearful of the future, launch a preventive strike? As I discuss in chapter 4, such a "security dilemma" can apply to either side entrapped in what it perceives as a zero-sum situation.[115]

Carrington rejected the alternative PF plan, and on November 22 he submitted detailed proposals regarding the establishment and maintenance of the cease-fire. These proposals provided that, as soon as the parties reached agreement on the cease-fire, they would issue instructions regarding implementation and would cease cross-border military movements. The cease-fire commission was to be established on the day of the cease-fire, and the monitoring force was to deploy to the fifteen locations provided for the assemblage of the PF troops. Meanwhile, the government's security forces would be monitored from their existing bases.The process of assembling soldiers was to begin immediately and to take no longer than seven days.The proposals pointed up just how much this scheme relied upon the goodwill of the military leaders on both sides, by observing:

> It will be for the Commanders to ensure, with the assistance of the monitoring force, that breaches of the cease-fire are contained and dealt with. In the event of more general or sustained breaches of the cease-fire, the Governor will have to decide what action to take to deal ... with the forces which have accepted his authority.[116]

At the time these amplified proposals were presented, Carrington asked both parties to inform him by November 26 whether his ideas were acceptable. The PF spokesmen ignored this deadline. On November 26, S. C. Mundawarara, speaking for the Muzorewa delegation, declared his satisfaction with the cease-fire arrangements. He did, however, express reservations about submitting governmental forces to an external authority and about the assemblage of PF troops at points inside the country, preferring that they return instead to their initial base of operations in Zambia, Botswana, or Mozambique. One factor in Rhodesian governmental acceptance was military commander Lieutenant General Peter Walls's conciliatory attitude at this time.The British had held behind-the-scenes negotiations for two and one-half months with Walls at Lancaster House, and once he concluded that majority rule was not a threatening prospect, he was prepared to accept change.[117]

By contrast, the PF leaders angrily rejected Carrington's conduct of the constitutional conference and objected to several features of the British cease-fire plan. In essence, they demonstrated a form of "commitment problem": they did not perceive their adversary as being in a position to give a credible guarantee to fully implement the agreement.[118] In Rhodesia, this fear found expression in Nkomo's warning of a possible military coup by Rhodesian government forces in the period between the assumed PF election triumph and the installation of a PF government.[119] The requirement that PF units remain in the fifteen assembly areas was the cause of considerable resentment in PF circles. Other subjects of disapproval regarding the British proposals included the disposition of PF forces (the assembly points were located perilously between government forces placed at the country's center and on its borders), the composition and deployment of the Commonwealth Monitoring Force, and the continued presence of South African units.

At this point, both the frontline states and Commonwealth leaders played a critical role in setting parameters on the dispute. At the request of Nkomo and Mugabe, a frontline state summit was convened on November 24 and 25 in Dar es Salaam under Nyerere's chairmanship. The PF leaders declared at a news conference following the meeting that their position had the "full backing" of the frontline presidents.[120] Robert Jaster reports that Mugabe did receive strong frontline support for his opposition to British guidelines on a small CMF and the removal of government contingents from the country's borders but not for his call for a six-month cease-fire and his opposition to having PF guerrillas report to the assembly points.[121] The frontline presidents gave the impression of public support, but their statements off the record emphasized that the PF leaders could not allow the conference to collapse at this late stage.

Lobbying of Carrington by the frontline states brought concessions from him on the monitoring of Rhodesian military units, with special vigilance to be paid to the Rhodesian air force. As Stephen Stedman remarks, "This was the only time where Carrington's emphasis on arbitration had to yield to a softer approach."[122] Carrington's more relaxed leadership on the cease-fire question allowed real negotiations to take place, largely between military men such as Walls and PF military leader Josia Tongogara. These military commanders had great respect for each other, and Tongogara knew how high the costs of continued conflict would be if Mozambique made good on its threat to cease supporting his army.[123]

On November 28, Carrington showed himself to be adaptable to the new realities in the negotiating context. In response to PF demands, he spoke in a conciliatory manner about changes in the composition and size of the CMF, the future integration of the two armies, full provision for the security and accommodation of PF troops at the assembly points, and an essential role for the monitors in ensuring against breaches of the cease-fire. Mugabe replied positively to the chairman's statement and declared that "his delegation now felt that the British proposals for a cease-fire provided the basis for an agreement, and for moving on quickly to settle the details of implementation."[124] On the following day, Mugabe made clear that his delegation still did not accept the recommendations on the disposition of forces. His acceptance of the proposals was conditional, leaving some distance still to be traveled.

As a consequence, the coalition of mediators took another series of initiatives aimed at overcoming the remaining PF objections. In what

Robin Renwick describes as a risky move to begin the implementation process, the British sent Lord Soames to Zimbabwe as governor-designate. This was a precarious undertaking, because Soames was attempting to take authority over the civil and military services with no visible force behind him. This move was critical to the peace process, however, for it created a new situation on the ground. Once Soames was installed, Great Britain would be able to regain control over the institutions of state.[125]

PF leaders continued to voice resentment over the number and location of assembly points and the dispatch of the governor to Salisbury before reaching a conclusive agreement. With the governor assuming executive and legislative powers, Mugabe contended that the Muzorewa government had surrendered to the British and was therefore no longer a bargaining party at the conference.[126] There was increasing concern that the agreement reached thus far would unravel. The frontline presidents sensed the need to intervene and pressed Mugabe and Nkomo to continue the negotiations in London instead of proceeding on to New York to launch a direct appeal to the UN regarding their position. Mozambique's Machel reportedly advised Mugabe, through his London representative, Fernand Honwana, that the points of disagreement were not worth the cost of renewing the war. Under pressure from the frontline presidents, Carrington added a sixteenth assembly point and agreed to be flexible regarding the two-week deadline for the assemblage of PF troops.[127] With concessions on both sides, agreement was reached on the peace accord, and the formal signing took place on December 21, 1979.

The return to normal relations, however, did not arrive until the general elections of February 1980, when Mugabe's Zimbabwe African National Union (PF) won 63 percent of the votes cast and fifty-seven of eighty common roll seats in the new parliament. Ian Smith's Rhodesian Front won all twenty of the white seats in the communal elections; however, this was a short-term victory, for in 1990 the Zimbabwean parliament passed a constitutional amendment repealing the entrenched clauses that had provided the white community with reserved representation in the legislature. Although land ownership remained highly inequitable between the races, the Lancaster House agreement did show that insecure and distrustful ethnic and ideological interests can nonetheless negotiate a replacement of the intrastate system of conflict management.[128]

Conclusion: Credible Pressures and Incentives

Several factors explain the willingness of antagonistic parties in Rhodesia to negotiate both an end to civil war and the reconstruction of a minority-dominated conflict management system. These include the stresses of war, the fears of continued warfare, the belief that the coalition of mediators would monitor and implement the peace, and the conviction that long-term confidence-building measures would protect their vital interests. Their fears of continuing war exceeded their uncertainty about a settlement.

However, a combination of pressures and incentives used by the various coalitions of mediators also played a significant role in facilitating an agreement between ethnic and ideologically based groups in Rhodesia. The pressures brought to bear by external mediators such as Henry Kissinger and Lord Carrington influenced the behavior of the various Rhodesian actors by threatening them with punishment for defecting. By the time of the Kissinger trip, Smith realized that he was trapped in a hurting stalemate from which there was no real escape, so he shifted his position in the face of U.S. and South African pressures in order to avoid the prospect of a worsening spiral of war, isolation, and economic damage. By contrast, when South African Prime Minister John Vorster appeared reluctant to exert pressure on Smith in support of the Anglo-American plan, this initiative was unable to influence the main actors to alter their preferences.

At Lancaster House, Carrington raised the costs of PF stonewalling by controlling the agenda, issuing deadlines, and threatening to settle for a second-class solution. When these threats appeared to be insufficient, he received indispensable backing from his frontline and Commonwealth state allies. These states made it clear to Mugabe and Nkomo that they would not allow the conference to collapse over the remaining issues on the transition and the cease-fire. President Machel of Mozambique (whose country was a crucial rear base for the continued guerrilla effort) warned Mugabe that the PF's demands for an extended cease-fire deadline and additional assembly points were an insufficient basis for holding up an agreement. This amounted to an implied threat of withdrawal of support, which inevitably influenced Mugabe's decision calculus. Two main explanations for the need for increasing frontline pressures, toward the end of the negotiating process, were the PF's perception of itself as an ultimate winner in the war and the PF's sense of insecurity regarding the possibility of a preventive strike when the cease-fire was to be implemented. Consequently, only a coalition of mediators would have had the clout to reassure the warring parties during the implementation phase and bring them to a final agreement.

In pushing the negotiations ahead, the various mediators made use of multiple incentives to reach a political settlement. In Kissinger's meeting with Ian Smith in Pretoria, he discussed a plan to provide $1.5 billion to reassure whites in case it became necessary for them to leave an independent Zimbabwe. Smith responded favorably to the idea and used it, after his return to Salisbury, to gain support for a retreat from the UDI. The thrust of the Kissinger idea was quickly changed from a "buyout," with its implications of distrust, to an Anglo-American financial assistance program to encourage "a sense of confidence" among white Rhodesians and to promote Zimbabwe's development. Kissinger stated that the African nationalists were "enormously relieved" by the adoption of a more positive orientation.[129] This shift was prudent partly because there was no reason to believe that whites would want to leave an economically healthy and politically stable Zimbabwe or that the U.S. Congress would vote for such a trust fund.[130]

Moreover, Kissinger was effective in using coercive incentives, in collaboration with Vorster, to influence Ian Smith. Kissinger himself had no doubts about the expediency of using muscle in this context. He observed that no dominant community would accept a transition of the sort he proposed without an element of coercion. "Pressure" would be maintained, he assured President Nyerere, "to ensure that a real transfer takes place."[131] In his view, the main means of coercion at hand was the closing of the border with South Africa, cutting the indispensable lifeline for Rhodesian exports and imports. Vorster, as promised, did tell Smith that he would shut down locomotive traffic from South Africa to Rhodesia unless Smith agreed to Kissinger's terms.[132] These coercive diplomatic incentives had their intended effect, inducing Smith to consent to a new conflict management system. As Rhodesian intelligence chief Ken Flower wrote later, "The South African political, economic and military arm-twisting, which had been growing steadily more painful, had finally proved too much for Smith, his government and his country to bear."[133] Kissinger's use of pressures and incentives had succeeded in moving the peace process ahead, but in the end the incentives offered to Smith regarding white control of the two security ministries during the transition proved fatal to Kissinger's diplomatic initiative.

But although coercive diplomatic incentives were used to bring about a change in Smith's preferences, what incentives explain South Africa's willingness to play the "heavy" in its relations with a white-led regime to the north? In giving this support, Kissinger said, the South Africans obtained what they wanted: an open meeting with the U.S. secretary of state that would give them some legitimacy in the world community, possibly at the price of a momentary setback in the process of transforming the minority-dominated conflict management system in South Africa itself.[134]

By the time of Lancaster House, the calculus of incentives had changed somewhat. With the two delegations headed by Africans, the racial factor was still present but in a less straightforward manner than it had been in the Kissinger and Anglo-American periods. Whites certainly had misgivings over their loss of political power, but this was more than offset by the ending of the war and by their increased security regarding their future status. The proposed constitutional arrangement left whites in a leading position in the economy, civil service, and military and gave them a disproportionate share of the arable land. For the time being, at least, the whites also retained twenty separately elected seats in the parliament.

The Muzorewa delegation also responded in a conciliatory manner to Carrington's proposals, largely reflecting their determination to be supportive of the British effort in order to gain London's backing in case the conference collapsed. Because this potential collapse remained a real possibility to the very end, the British threat of a second-class solution was a substantial one. Robin Renwick insists that the British were serious about their threat to recognize Muzorewa if there was no other option. The effect was to induce Muzorewa, eager to hold on to power, to act in a supportive manner on hurtful issues such as new elections and to remain hopeful that the PF leaders would balk over the terms of the constitution or transition; it also put pressure on the PF leadership, which sought to minimize the destruction of war and to come to power as swiftly as possible.

Carrington's primary problems lay not with the Muzorewa delegation and its white members but with Mugabe and Nkomo. The PF was in a strong bargaining position as a consequence of its capacity for an extended war. PF leaders recognized that protracted war would be costly in terms of lives, property, and future economic dislocation, but Mugabe at least was prepared to make heavy sacrifices to be able to restructure the colonial system. As long as the frontline presidents continued to support the guerrilla war, Mugabe had little incentive to act in a cooperative manner. Nevertheless, as the conference gained momentum and Carrington's frontline and Commonwealth allies became committed to a successful outcome, the PF's maneuverability shrank considerably. Great Britain's exercise of its leverage through calculation, bluffs, threats, and deadlines took its toll; moreover, the use of financial incentives was critical for the land issue, enabling the PF to save face on a matter of great symbolic importance to their supporters. Given the high costs of war for all concerned, it was also apparent to the PF leaders (and particularly Nkomo) that they would lose local support if they returned from the negotiations empty-handed.[135]

As a result, the combination of pressures and incentives in the hands of various third parties contributed to keeping the negotiating process on track. Given the absence of a mutually hurting stalemate, the leverage of the coalition of mediators proved critical in both negotiating the peace and moving the society toward a majoritarian conflict management system. This demonstrated again that the use of pressures and incentives to influence the preferences of the conflicting parties is an important component of diplomatic capabilities that must not be underestimated.

SOUTH AFRICA

7

Facilitating Regime Transformation in South Africa

To make peace with an enemy one must work with that enemy, and that enemy becomes one's partner.

NELSON MANDELA

Although third-party mediation seemed a logical way of transforming South Africa's intrastate system of conflict management, both of the major parties to the dispute were most reluctant to respond to such initiatives. State president F. W. de Klerk feared that external mediation might result in unwanted concessions, particularly on issues related to minority vetoes; he talked of external mediation as an intrusion into his country's sovereignty and questioned whether a facilitator was necessary in the negotiations leading up to a new constitutional order. African National Congress leader Nelson Mandela and his ANC colleagues declared their preference for direct negotiations with the South African government, also fearing that a third-party intervener might use that person's or organization's influence to extract unwanted compromises, which they alleged happened in the Zimbabwe independence negotiations.[1] Either way, the effect was to complicate formal third-party initiatives.

Nevertheless, in the final stages leading up to elections in April 1994, an external mediator (backed up by a parallel process of state incentives) did facilitate an agreement in multilateral negotiations between the Inkatha Freedom party (IFP), the African National Congress, and the South African government's National party (NP). This agreement recognized and protected the institution, status, and role of the constitutional position of Zulu King Goodwill Zwelithini; however, the accord was narrow in scope, and Mandela agreed to it in order to smooth the way to a nonviolent election process.

Despite the general resistance to formal mediation, various types of international intermediaries nonetheless penetrated South African resistance in the 1980s and 1990s, attempting to fill a need as third-party observers, even as facilitators. In principle, observer and monitoring missions are neutral agents that verify referendums and elections, build capacity, develop democratic institutions, and monitor political violence. All of these functions are included in the dynamic of peacemaking, for fair and legitimate elections, effective party systems and civil societies, and peaceful relations are part of the ongoing process of regularized and amicable relations among different interests. In the case of South Africa, external states have funded and encouraged a variety of private and public monitoring institutions, including such diverse bodies as the Commonwealth Eminent Persons Group (EPG) or, in the 1990s, the Commonwealth Observer Group, the Carter Center, Organization of African Unity monitoring teams, the African-American Institute, the International Republican Institute, and the National Democratic Institute. In addition, the United Nations Observer Mission in South Africa (UNOMSA), which was on the scene in South Africa monitoring evidence of political violence, was active in assisting in the transition to a nonracial democracy.

Not only did the Commonwealth EPG describe its role as "facilitating a process of dialogue for change," but it enlarged on this role to put forward a "possible negotiating concept" as a starting point for the dialogue.[2] Although a significant role was played in 1992–94 by insider South African intermediaries and facilitators, particularly from church and business groups, my main concern here is with external mediation or facilitation, especially those agencies and actors able to exert significant pressures and incentives to encourage the local parties to establish a stable conflict management system. Thus UN observers actively monitored the violence, promoted democratic organizations and practices, and at times went somewhat beyond their mandate to mediate between rival interests. UN and European Community (ECOMSA) observers made recommendations to local officials on the handling of security matters immediately after the murder of Chris Hani, the former chief of staff of Umkhonto we sizwe (spear of the nation), the military wing of the ANC; before his assassination, Hani, an ANC militant himself, had provided important support for the negotiating process at difficult junctures.

Moreover, these observers urged the militant Pan-Africanist Congress to participate in the meetings of the national peace committee. By 1993 both sides had retreated from their earlier reluctance to allow external agencies a role in the negotiations leading up to a change of regimes and were welcoming an active UN presence in an effort to ensure a smooth, fair, and internationally accepted political outcome.

Driven by a need for international legitimacy, then, the main South African parties overcame their reluctance to permit external intervention and came to look positively on the confidence-building mechanisms extended by international observers. This change of heart came none too soon. With violence destabilizing the negotiations, if not the country itself, by the time the first draft constitution for a post-apartheid South Africa was issued in July 1993, the steadiness of the transition process seemed in question. Warning against "too much loose talk of civil war or the threat of it," the U.S. ambassador to South Africa, Princeton Lyman, clearly sought to alert all sides to the risk that a mutually destructive violent situation could become an established part of the country's political culture at a time when the possibility of "negotiating a transition in a timely fashion" still existed.[3]

A Unique Environment

To gain an understanding of the negotiating context of the 1980s, it is important to stress at the outset that the South African political environment was unique, making analogies to previous independence "bargains" misleading. To start with, the proportion of whites to nonwhites was considerably higher in South Africa than in most African countries, such as Ghana, Zimbabwe, and Kenya (French-ruled Algeria was a notable exception in this regard). And not only was the white community more securely entrenched, but it had abundant resources and a closely bonded relationship with the state. South Africa was both rich in natural resources and an industrialized society with transportation links by road and rail with the north and by air and sea with the world at large. Its relatively large, white middle class was locked into an intimate relationship with the Afrikaner-run state, a relationship that afforded it access, benefits, and protection. "Apartheid," noted Lloyd Vogelman of the Centre for the Study of Violence and Reconciliation in South Africa, "was designed to say we are not the minority."[4] Any major concessions made by the state to international or African nationalist demands were likely to be interpreted by sections within the white community as threatening to their collective interests, which then led, in subsequent elections, to a right-wing drift. This tendency appeared in the 1987 elections and had a hardening effect on the government and on whites in general. Hence, until the costs of the status quo rose considerably (that is, to the point where dominant elements within the ruling class perceived their interests to be threatened by isolation and effective sanctions), intergroup negotiations seemed unlikely to alter the basic rules of relationship between domestic interests as they did in more vulnerable Zimbabwe— and then only after a bitter and protracted civil war.[5]

The differences in political context between South Africa and the states to the north during the decolonization phase were compounded by the hurdles in the way of successful mediation and negotiation. Unlike Kenya and Zimbabwe, South Africa was a sovereign state, with membership in the United Nations. This gave the state, though not its government, legitimacy in the eyes of the international community. As such, the South African state was free to enter into negotiations with other states or sections within its own country as it choose to do. In Ghana, Kenya, and Zimbabwe, the British were the colonial masters and in a position to force negotiations between rival parties from above as a price of stability and independence; in South Africa, however, there was no comparable external enforcer credible in the eyes of both parties and able to maintain a momentum of ongoing negotiations. A variety of international organizations might have been able to offer some incentives to the various parties to bring them to the bargaining table, but, as I will show, this is a delicate process fraught with real difficulties and evident constraints.

In South Africa, the limitations on mediators were apparent to many observers: trust was in short supply and aims were divergent, but in addition mutual interests (that is, the avoidance of damage) were not sufficiently compelling to bring the parties to a positive-sum outcome. As Marina Ottaway remarks rather pessimistically, the bargaining coalitions were unstable, the goals were "antithetical," and the parties attached very different meanings to the purposes of negotiations.[6] Therefore, unlike colonially directed mediation in Kenya and Zimbabwe, direct mediation in South Africa, facilitated intermittently by international organizations, had to find the basis for accommodation in one of the most profoundly divided societies in the world. To the extent that the rules of the game were in contention and a sense of common fate emerging only slowly, South Africa's negotiators had to come to agreement on such sensitive issues as federalism, a shared executive, and land redistribution or face the prospect of a more deeply conflictive outcome—possibly including displacement, partition, or intensified civil warfare in the years ahead.

Failed Mediation Efforts in the 1980s

Even though the logic of some kind of political negotiations in South Africa had become apparent to many political leaders by the mid-1980s, there appeared to be a lack of opportunities for bargaining among the broad racially defined coalitions for the moment. The facilitation of direct talks among rival domestic interests was hampered by the lack of such important preconditions as a necessary degree of unity within the bargaining parties, a sufficient level of external pressure to make settlement the preferable alternative, and a mutually hurting stalemate. The lack of ripeness became especially evident in the aftermath of the extreme right-wing white victories in the elections of spring 1987.

The consequences of inaction were certainly apparent to many leaders, black and white. Averting the costs of internal violence and insecurity was clearly in the thoughts of jailed leader Nelson Mandela when, in the presence of the Commonwealth mission in 1986, he made an impassioned appeal to a South African cabinet minister, H. J. Coetsee, for direct talks between black leaders and the P. W. Botha regime to prevent a worsening of the situation in their country.[7] And, in fact, a number of current economic indicators did seem to point to increasingly difficult times. For example, gross fixed capital formation fell by 40 percent in 1985; the gross domestic product was down by 1 percent in the first quarter of 1986; voluntary disinvestment by multinational corporations was gaining momentum (the book value of U.S. investments in South Africa fell from $2.4 billion in 1982 to $1.3 billion in 1986, and the pace of disinvestment accelerated in the next year); the commercial rand declined precipitously, from $1.28 in 1980 to below 40 cents in 1986; a capital flight of $1 billion occurred between September 1985 and March 1986; and unemployment soared to 25 percent in the urban black community.[8] To be sure, relatively high gold prices and the development of a siege economy cushioned some of these effects, but future economic prospects did not look promising in 1985–86. Political indicators were equally unsatisfactory for the Afrikaner-led state. With the police and army losing control over the townships, and with administrative and educational systems in parts of the Eastern Cape degenerating, a situation of ungovernability, even "violent equilibrium," appeared to be emerging.[9]

Under these circumstances, negotiations between the government and black nationalists appeared to be a logical way of instituting a new conflict management system. Negotiations offered an opportunity for social learning and held out the possibility of avoiding a spiral into mutual destruction, with its high costs of increased social polarization, a widening repression, the development of a siege economy, and the economic and political dislocation of a broader region. The analogies of Sri Lanka, Liberia, Somalia, and Ireland came readily to mind. Unfortunately, however, intense conflicts over the rules of relationship did not easily lend themselves to rational processes of political compromise and peaceful change, especially where an entrenched racially or ethnically dominated state viewed structural transformation in deeply threatening terms.[10] In brief, although the ANC appeared stalemated in the 1980s and the South African government and the white minority were clearly hurting and anticipated (accurately) more hurt in the future, the circumstances were not propitious for the Commonwealth EPG mediation effort in 1986 because the government's fears of an agreement exceeded their fears of continued confrontation. Perceiving a change in the ethnic balance of power, the government leaders' paranoia made it "impossible to assuage [their] fears of a negotiated settlement."[11]

Despite the apparent logic of a negotiated settlement, the Commonwealth EPG mission, described by its cochair, General Olusegun Obasanjo, as an "honest broker," came away soured by its experience with an attempted mediatory effort in South Africa. The EPG mission portrayed its role as limited to facilitating a dialogue between the adversaries; yet it actually enlarged on its terms of reference and proposed a possible starting point for negotiations. The mission's negotiating concept involved a declaration of the government's intention to dismantle apartheid, the release of all political prisoners, the recognition by the state of the rights of freedom of speech and assembly, a moratorium on government and opposition violence, and an agreement between the government and the ANC on the need to "act simultaneously in fulfillment of their respective commitments."[12]

The Botha government's response to these proposals was equivocal. While raising questions regarding specific recommendations, it did nonetheless call for a continuation of the dialogue and sought to clarify the various perceptions that each party had about the nature of the conflict and its possible solution. For a brief time, some members of the cabinet, in particular Pik Botha, the foreign minister, seemed to be guardedly positive about the mission's mediatory purposes. Moreover, the ANC, under pressure from the United States, Britain, and West Germany, agreed to a "suspension" of the violence, giving the members of the mission some reason for hope of a constructive outcome.

Subsequently, however, as the Commonwealth mission came up against the hard reality of the government's nonnegotiable positions— on such points as the renunciation of violence, the preservation of group rights, and the continuance of separate education and residential areas—as well as the deliberate military raid by South African forces against three neighboring Commonwealth countries on May 19, 1986, it lost faith for the time being in a negotiated solution as a realizable objective. "The South African Government," it declared, "is not yet ready to negotiate [a nonracial and democratic] future—except on its own terms."[13]

Discussions with the Commonwealth mission had convinced the Botha regime that concessions would lead not to reduced pressure but to new demands, backed up by the threat of sanctions.[14] Three other factors are also reported to have played a part in Botha's decision to terminate the discussions: the increasing signs of unity among black African interests in South Africa, the ANC's refusal to repudiate violence, and the pressure from state security agencies against negotiations on the grounds that further success in the peacemaking venture would lead to an unraveling of the political system.[15] The upshot was as final as it was dramatic: the Commonwealth mission abandoned its mediatory effort and called upon the Commonwealth countries and their allies to implement effective economic sanctions.

Soon after the breakdown of the Commonwealth EPG mission effort, a European Community (EC) summit, under pressure from the British and West German governments (which were anxious to avoid the imposition of sanctions), endorsed a peace mission to South Africa by British foreign secretary Sir Geoffrey Howe, acting in his capacity as the president of the Council of Ministers. In endorsing the Howe mission, the EC made very clear that if South African authorities did not respond positively to Howe's appeals for a rescinding of the state of emergency, the release of political detainees, and a lifting of the prohibition on African political parties, its member states would place a ban on the importation of coal, iron, steel, and gold coins. As many had anticipated, the threat of EC sanctions was not sufficient in itself to push the Botha regime to the bargaining table. Botha resisted making any concessions to the European initiative, and the African nationalists and their supporters in neighboring states, regarding the mission as a play for time on the part of the British, generally looked upon the Howe journey as a futile effort.[16] The gap between Botha and the African leaders was clearly too large for a lone intermediary to bridge, and, after a brief encounter with a number of the protagonists, Sir Geoffrey returned to Europe empty-handed. In September 1986, Coretta Scott King, the widow of civil rights leader Martin Luther King Jr., made a further effort to start a dialogue between the contending parties; however, under pressure from the United Democratic Front, a nationwide political organization founded in 1983 to oppose the government's apartheid policies, she acted prudently and withdrew from the fray.

The depth of conflict over the basic rules of relationship in South Africa limited the middle ground and made it difficult to mediate among all the major parties. In I. William Zartman's words, the mediator lacked "the informal power to make the parties decide."[17] For the mediatory agent, involvement can also be deemed to entail a high cost, particularly where the players perceive the conflict in zero-sum terms. A defiant Botha government insisted that its bargaining opposite, the ANC, was communist-dominated and that it had to reject violence before the start of negotiations.[18] For the ANC to reject violence, however, was to surrender its main bargaining chip in advance of serious talks, a demand that the cochairs of the Commonwealth mission regarded as "unreasonable."[19] Moreover, the other nonnegotiable demands set forth by the Botha government—group rights, private enterprise, and separate education—appeared to the opposition to freeze the essentials of the status quo.

Although ANC leaders reaffirmed their willingness to enter into genuine negotiations aimed at transforming the dominant regime into a united and nonracial democracy, they nonetheless questioned the value of negotiations in the political environment of that time. ANC representatives recognized the strength of white opposition to political and socioeconomic transformation and contended that the Botha regime "relies for its survival on armed aggression within and outside South Africa.... Our people have had to accept this reality and take the only course open to them."[20] Perceiving the struggle in totalist terms, they saw their course as clear and unmistakable: to fight power with power. Their threat of an extended process of "ungovernability" leading to "people's power" limited the room for a negotiated settlement in the mid-1980s.[21]

If anything, the exiled Pan-Africanist Congress of Azania (PAC) was even more militant in its views. Rejecting negotiations as a strategy of change in South Africa, the PAC declared that "our own rejection of dialogue or negotiations rests on the unacceptability of any peace talks that cannot center on the total abandonment of the present settler-colonial political system plus the full realization of the inalienable right to self-determination by the indigenous African majority in our country."[22]

In the same vein, the Black Consciousness Movement (BCM) of Azania, which used the Azanian People's Organization (AZAPO) as its main political voice, had become openly orthodox Marxist by this time. Extremely hostile toward any proposal for a negotiated settlement, BCM leaders declared that "the Botha-Malan junta is not likely to 'negotiate' with any genuine and credible freedom fighter." BCM spokespersons also "uncompromisingly" rejected any guarantees for minority interests, a stance that ran directly counter to insistence on "visible and effective protection of minority groups and the rights against domination and for self-determination for such groups and communities."[23]

In brief, the 1986 efforts to mediate the conflict were premature. The adversaries diverged fundamentally in the mid-1980s on the rules of relations and the structures of power they viewed as acceptable. A number of factors combined to explain why the situation was not ripe for resolution: the threatening perceptions that the main groups had about one another, their divergent political and socioeconomic interests, the high power disparity in favor of white minority interests, the fragmented nature of the contending groups, and their perceptions of victory in the long term.[24] For most whites, the costs of maintaining the status quo still did not seem prohibitive; thus a policy of muddling through still seemed preferable to negotiations. "South Africa," declared P. W. Botha at the time his government launched raids against ANC bases in neighboring countries, "has the capacity and the will to break the ANC. I give fair warning that we fully intend doing it."[25] These are not the words or sentiments of a man prepared to preside over any fundamental change in regime rules and practices.

In the context of the times, moreover, there was little that mediators could do to accelerate the ripening process. This was true not only because of the constraints on mediatory efforts noted above, but also because of the mediators' own lack of credibility and ability to offer incentives. The general weakness of the mediators' position in influencing outcomes in South Africa in the mid-1980s stemmed from a number of factors. First, South Africa was not a colony in the sense normally used, ruling out the kind of directed mediation that so marked the Lancaster House conference on Zimbabwe.[26] Second, there were few possible mediators left who had credibility with both sides at that time. As the external powers took a strong stand in favor of liberation or gradual reforms, they inevitably came to identify with one set of political actors or another, thereby forfeiting the high ground from which they might have been able to facilitate no-fault negotiations.[27] Third, the weakened third-party intermediary, if one could have been found, would have had limited inducements to offer the highly principled and deeply divided opponents that would have been sufficient to alter the basis of choice. The Afrikaners, with their fear of swartgevaar (or being overwhelmed by the black majority), were hardly likely to be influenced by incentives involving side payments; the African nationalist leaders, who had already endured high costs in terms of psychological harassment and political and economic discrimination, were not likely to be attracted to the bargaining table by promises or grants of a distributive nature.[28]

More was needed, especially if a hurting stalemate were to raise the costs of continued inaction. In theory, mediators ought to have been able to provide incentives involving "insurance," that is, commitments by outsiders to guarantee compliance with the terms of the agreement.[29] However, few mediators would have wanted to become deeply involved enough at that juncture in the highly polarized South African conflict to offer the kinds of protections that the NATO powers and the United Nations later committed themselves to in Bosnia. Moreover, there was no certainty that even such an extensive involvement would have been sufficient to bring about the desired end. Because intergroup boundaries were pronounced and norms of reciprocity were weak in South Africa in the mid-1980s, the scope for bargaining seemed distinctly limited, and a third party might well have had reason to draw back from the mediatory undertaking.

The UN Initiative of the 1990s

By the early 1990s, the situation had changed significantly: the cold war had ended, Botha had been replaced by F. W. de Klerk, the economy was in recession, international determination to bring about a change in policies and outlooks was increasingly apparent, and the political costs of white minority intransigence proved inescapable. During the prenegotiation period from 1986 to 1990, a number of events took place that proved critical in bringing about de Klerk's "evolutionary conversion" regarding the need for negotiations.[30] These events included the decision in 1986 to accept the principle of a single South Africa (which in effect abandoned the notion of independent ethnic homelands); encounters between a white delegation and ANC spokespersons in Dakar and Lusaka in 1987 and 1989; meetings during much of this period between various government officials and Nelson Mandela; Namibia's peaceful transition to independence; and de Klerk's power struggle with President P. W. Botha over leadership of the party following Botha's stroke in 1989. Such a combination of learning experiences contributed to the development of trust between the adversaries, "establishing a belief in reciprocity, that good-faith concessions would be matched."[31]

In February 1990 the door was opened to negotiations for a new South Africa, as de Klerk announced that opposition parties would be unbanned, Nelson Mandela and other political prisoners released, and a moratorium placed on executions. During the initial negotiation stage that followed, the ANC and government representatives held a series of meetings, covering such critical issues as the measures to end apartheid, suspension of the armed struggle, and the holding of a multiparty conference to set up the procedural rules for an elected constituent assembly. At these bilateral talks, the negotiating teams made important progress in overcoming long-held mind-sets of distrust and hostility. Sufficient substantive agreement had also been reached on basic organizing principles by December 1991 to allow for the assemblage of the various parties at the Conference for a Democratic South Africa (CODESA). Given the strong preferences of the various leaders on all sides, this was to be an internal and direct negotiating process, with no formal mediator from the outside to act as a deadlock-resolving agent.[32]

As might be expected when a white minority government confronts a number of African nationalist parties that have long been excluded from the halls of power, the CODESA sessions revealed wide gaps between the participants on constitutional arrangements and the transition process. In response to the call for majoritarian democracy, the white establishment responded with calls for power sharing, exhibiting, as Herman Gilliomee described it, "little or no confidence in the protection of individual rights under majority rule and [expecting] civil war, anarchy and chaos if no generally accepted constitution is negotiated."[33] Despite such apprehensions, the conferees did make some progress in stating their ultimate purposes and setting up five working groups. Even so, a number of questions remained hotly contested, such as the future role of the constituent assembly, provisions on a power-sharing executive, federalism and decentralization, and the length of the transition period. The result was to prolong some deep-seated differences between the parties, leading by early 1992 to a temporary suspension of the negotiations.

By the spring of 1992, the transition process was placed under severe strain. The conferees reassembled at CODESA II in May, where sharp disagreements surfaced over such issues as a power-sharing executive, the voting majority required at the constituent assembly on such basic questions as the nature and powers of the regions, control of the security forces, and the divulgence of hidden arms caches. Meanwhile new signs of public dissatisfaction over the pace of the transition process were surfacing. The negotiations were brought to a halt in June, as South Africa faced rising violence, most notably at the town of Boipatong, where a fearsome massacre took place. Noting that 373 had died and 395 were injured during June, Mandela told the UN Security Council that in his view the violence amounted to "a cold blooded strategy of state terrorism."[34] Thus, despite evident progress on a number of constitutional issues, the ANC withdrew from the second plenary session of CODESA.

As these events were occurring and the effort to resolve political differences through direct negotiations was faltering, the international community moved cautiously into the dispute to restore confidence in the peace process. Although this chapter is primarily concerned with direct mediation, it is nonetheless important to note that in South Africa considerable indirect mediation occurred. In particular, South African church and business leaders played an important unofficial mediatory role as violence threatened the constitutional talks between the government and the ANC in May 1991. The South African Council of Churches, alarmed that a breakdown of the talks would precipitate a sharp increase in violence, led a church-orchestrated effort to intercede and to promote a dialogue between the rival parties. With the crisis continuing to worsen, de Klerk sought to promote a summit meeting, only to see this initiative end in failure. Another informal interlocutor, Louw Alberts' Liaison Committee, then stepped between the parties and successfully gained the confidence of the adversaries for the creation of a Preparatory Committee composed of members from the National party, the ANC, and the Inkatha Freedom party, who, together with church and business representatives, would attempt to facilitate a resumption of the peace effort. As Timothy Sisk observes, "This low-profile mechanism was the beginning of a process that would result in the National Peace Accord."[35]

The National Peace Accord of September 1991 sought to come to grips with the problem of violence and to promote an easing of tensions at the grassroots level by providing for subregional and local dispute resolution committees, composed of the various political parties and representatives of civil society, to settle disputes by negotiating with the various parties and recording the terms of such settlements.[36] The peace accord helped the negotiating process to move ahead, particularly by providing a structure in 1992–94, when grassroots action was possible. Yet as important as these internal mediation efforts were, it was the violence of June 1992 and the evidence of a breakdown in the CODESA negotiations that led the international community to decide that it had become necessary to intervene in the South African peace process.

Although not the only international actor to take a hand, the United Nations certainly played a key role. Urged by Mandela to intervene in the increasingly turbulent South African situation in July 1992, the UN Security Council declared itself concerned over the rising violence and its consequences for negotiations. It then unanimously adopted a resolution inviting the secretary-general to appoint a special representative "to recommend, after ... discussion with the parties, measures which would assist in bringing an effective end to the violence and in creating conditions for negotiations."[37] In accordance with this authorization, the secretary-general appointed Cyrus R. Vance, former U.S. secretary of state, as his special representative and announced that he would soon visit South Africa. Vance subsequently met with de Klerk and members of his cabinet in South Africa and then with delegations from the major political parties as well as leaders of the homelands and civil society.

On Vance's advice, the secretary-general wrote to de Klerk, Mandela, and IFP leader Chief Mangosuthu Buthelezi, expressing his concern that mass demonstrations planned for August 3 could take a violent turn. For his part, Mandela assured the secretary-general that the ANC would do all it could to avoid violence and requested that the UN consider sending observers to witness the demonstrations. Minister of Foreign Affairs Pik Botha told a national news conference that the government accepted the proposal to send thirty international observers and would even consider a marginal increase in this number; in addition, he stated that the government particularly welcomed the proposal to have the UN observer team act under the umbrella of and in coordination with South African structures (that is, the National Peace Accord).[38]

In light of this agreement, Secretary-General Boutros Boutros-Ghali did dispatch international monitors to South Africa to observe mass action throughout the country. In addition, concluding that the National Peace Accord needed to be strengthened, Boutros-Ghali recommended that the UN make available some fifty observers to function in close association with the National Peace Secretariat to further the purposes of the accord. South Africans would remain responsible for the conduct of their negotiations; however, the UN would now be on the scene in a supportive capacity. Commenting on the possible role of a mediator with muscle, Boutros-Ghali concluded that "there may well be need for CODESA to consider the appointment of an eminent and impartial person, who need not be a foreigner, to draw the strings together and to provide the impetus and cohesion that CODESA needs to accomplish its tasks."[39] The Security Council welcomed this initiative and authorized dispatching a fifty-member United Nations Observer Mission in South Africa.[40]

After arriving on the South African scene, the UNOMSA team attended political marches and rallies, observed meetings of the peace committees, and remained in close contact with the National Peace Secretariat staff. Assisting in the managing of conflicts, the team also made recommendations to local officials on the handling of security matters after the murder of African nationalist leader Chris Hani by a right-wing Polish immigrant associated with reactionary Afrikaner Weerstandsbeweging and urged active participation by the PAC and other parties in the nationwide peace commission.[41] These efforts were supplemented by other groups on the scene, including representatives of the European Community, the Commonwealth, and the OAU. The Commonwealth Group was reportedly effective in mediating between the adversaries in Natal, and the local peace committee members described the EC observers as particularly helpful. Perhaps because the EC observers were experienced as police officers themselves, the South African police were prepared to accept their advice.

In sum, the UN and other observers were important to the South African peace process as they provided a stabilizing influence and gave useful guidance to the local parties at critical junctures. By working closely with Peace Committee officials, the UN monitors strengthened the legitimacy of the Peace Accord officials and their activities. The political parties and the police could not ignore the UN officials, or what they were doing would be reported to the international community. Moreover, as the April 1994 election approached, the Independent Electoral Commission was assisted by some 5,000 international observers (1,800 of them from the United Nations) to help monitor the election process.[42]

Nevertheless, as important as this observation and advisory role was in the South African context, there were inevitably strict limits to its reach. The UN observers were circumscribed by their mandate. They could not exert pressure officially. As impartial observers, moreover, they could provide information, but they were not permitted to judge this information or intervene formally in the conflict.[43] As the secretary-general pointed out in his 1992 report, neither the UN nor any other third-party actor, domestic or international, had the capacity to break stalemates in the CODESA negotiations, something for which there was "a manifest need."[44]

Preelection Mediation Initiatives

Although the main centrist parties, the ANC, the NP, and the small Democratic party, made some progress in developing acceptable political norms in the CODESA negotiations and afterwards, they nonetheless encountered strong opposition in various quarters, including the PAC and the Azanian People's Organization (AZAPO) on the left and IFP, the Conservative party, and the new Freedom Front (FF), formed in March 1994, on the right. The FF, led by General Constand Viljoen, the former chief of staff of the South African Defence Force, called for the creation of a volkstaat or white homeland. Viljoen's FF was closely allied with Buthelezi and the IFP, increasing the bargaining power of these interests at a critical juncture. Moreover, because Buthelezi had an important power base in the KwaZulu-Natal area, IFP represented an important challenger that was best included in the political process for reasons of prudence. Buthelezi, who had split off from the ANC in the late 1970s, now demanded "Zulu self-determination" and firmly resisted ANC efforts to create a unitary South Africa with a strong central authority.[45] The ANC and NP, determined to secure an internationally recognized and legitimate outcome in the April 1994 elections and thereby prevent a possible civil war, made a concerted attempt to encourage IFP and FF's registration and participation in the election process.

Thus, with a number of issues still unresolved before the 1994 elections—the functions and powers of the subregions, IFP's call for the postponement of the elections, and the constitutional position of the Zulu king—the ANC and the NP government made a final, last-minute effort to accommodate the opposition. As far as IFP leader Mangosuthu Buthelezi was concerned, "the whole question of the sovereignty of the kingdom of kwaZulu must finally be resolved before there can be an election."[46] The center parties and government were not convinced of the need for such constitutional guarantees; however, they did seek to appease Buthelezi with an eye to encouraging as broad a participation in the election process as possible, assuring acceptance of the outcome, and containing the spreading violence and instability. At a press conference on February 16, Mandela announced six "good faith" concessions: inclusion of constitutional provisions on the notion of an Afrikaner homeland, a shift from a single- to a double-ballot system (for both the national and provincial parliaments), stipulations on financial self-management at the provincial level, provisos allowing each province to structure its own system of governance, guarantees that provincial powers would not be substantially reduced in the future, and permission to change the name of Natal province to KwaZulu/Natal.[47] Mandela's gesture of compromise was not reciprocated; instead, IFP calls for international mediation of outstanding differences gained strength.

The International Process

By early March, the Freedom Alliance (which combined white extremists with Buthelezi's IFP) pressed for an internationally mediated settlement, and an ANC national working committee raised no objections to the idea. Although the NP leader, President F. W. de Klerk, initially resisted the idea, he ultimately joined the international mediation process, viewing it as a means of surmounting the country's constitutional stalemate. With this question settled, a team of seven mediators—including former British foreign secretary Lord Carrington and former U.S. secretary of state Henry Kissinger—was selected to narrow the differences between the ANC and IFP on the remaining constitutional issues in contention.

The international mediation process was a hasty and somewhat improvised exercise. Its terms of reference were not determined before the arrival of the mediation team in South Africa, and a variety of key questions, including the date of the election, were not regarded by ANC and NP leaders to be subject to negotiation. The mediators, Kissinger said, were prepared to deal only with constitutional issues, and the implementation of any agreement arising from these efforts was to be left to South Africans.[48] With the mediators on the scene, representatives of the three parties met and concluded work on the terms of reference for the mediation, specifically excluding the election date as a matter to be discussed. From the ANC's standpoint, only constitutional issues were to be included in the mediators' terms of reference.[49] Buthelezi again sought to reopen the issue of postponing the elections, and, faced with stiff resistance from the ANC negotiating team, rejected the terms of reference. The following day, April 14, the mediators concluded that they could not help the conflicting parties to address their problems without an agreement on the terms of reference. "As mediators,"

Kissinger stated, "we refused to address the issue [of postponing the elections] on the ground that outsiders have no right to determine the date of a people's emancipation."[50] The international mediation process had collapsed before it had begun. A failure to agree on basic principles and to narrow the agenda in the prenegotiation stage proved fatal, undermining efforts to overcome Inkatha's defection and to resolve the remaining constitutional issues.

The Okumu and Government Initiatives

The breakdown of the international mediation initiative was followed by a highly focused third-party bid to end the impasse regarding the position of Zulu King Goodwill Zwelithini in the constitutional process. Professor Washington A. J. Okumu, the ambassador-at-large of FORD-Kenya (one of Kenya's opposition parties) and a special adviser to the international mediators, met Buthelezi at Lanseria Airport and urged the IFP leader to remain a part of the political process. Buthelezi thereupon asked the Kenyan professor to ascertain whether the government was interested in further discussions on IFP's participation in the elections. Buthelezi emphasized that IFP participation would be conditional on guarantees in the constitution for the Zulu monarchy.[51] Clearly, some form of insurance incentive had become critical at this juncture.

With a new possibility of IFP's participation in the elections emerging, Okumu decided to stay behind and explore the prospect of finding "an African solution" to the problems at issue.[52] On April 16, spokespersons for the Consultative Business Movement (CBM), a business community organization that acted as a secretariat during the mediation effort, met with government officials and received assurances that there were no technical difficulties in the way of an agreement. With this in hand, Okumu and CBM leader Colin Coleman drew up a draft proposal dealing with IFP participation in the election and constitutional guarantees for the Zulu king.[53] Both the ANC and IFP reacted positively to the draft proposal, and a meeting of negotiators from the ANC, IFP, and the NP government was set for April 18 in Pretoria. The next day, with Okumu acting as a mediator and with the CBM providing advice and logistical support, the parties succeeded in hammering out an agreement intended to build confidence in Inkatha circles. The "Memorandum of Agreement for Reconciliation and Peace" that emerged from these encounters involved IFP's stated willingness to participate in the national and provincial elections and an acceptance by all three parties of the need to ensure free and fair elections throughout the country.[54]

On the specific issue of the king's constitutional position, the negotiators consented to the following:

> The undersigned parties agree to recognise and protect the institution, status and role of the constitutional position of the king of the Zulus and the Kingdom of kwaZulu, which institutions shall be provided for in the provincial constitution of kwaZulu/Natal immediately after the holding of the said elections. The 1993 constitution shall for this purpose be amended before 27 April in accordance with Addendum A.[55]

Some key members of the ANC negotiating team accepted the compromise on the Zulu king's newly constituted role reluctantly.[56] Even so, the immediate consequences of the accord proved most positive in terms of a smooth transition. Having saved face, Buthelezi was able to shift his position and enter the election process at the eleventh hour to avoid exclusion from the decisionmaking arena. The mediator (part external, part internal) had facilitated a cooperative move; in the larger sense, however, the conflict appeared to be "ripe for resolution" and the mediator created a new set of options that could be seized upon by a beleaguered ethnoregional leader.

Later, during the implementation stage, the ambiguity surrounding the memorandum of agreement on various constitutional and fiscal issues set the grounds for new tensions after independence. As the negotiating parties rushed to hammer out a settlement, Steven Friedman notes, "a vital weapon in the negotiators' armoury was the ability to elevate the fudged compromise to an art form."[57] However, such fudging contributed to bitter conflict in the period that followed between the ANC and IFP. The agreement provided that "any outstanding issues in respect of the King of the Zulus and the 1993 constitution as amended will be addressed by way of international mediation which will commence as soon as possible after the said elections."[58] The ANC viewed this clause on international mediation as relevant as a necessary concession, but one they hoped they would never have to deal with, while the IFP sought to use it in their effort to wrest provincial powers from the center in the final constitution.[59] With the enactment of the new majoritarian constitution in 1996, the issue shifted and there was less impetus to underscore the international mediation question. By then, the ANC, with two years' experience in governance at the political center, was in a more powerful position; moreover, agreement in the future on a provincial constitution seems likely to clarify the powers of these authorities.

Important as the Okumu mediation effort was in providing a means for face saving, it became clear immediately after the transition to the Mandela government had taken place that this was not the sole arena for bargaining on the Zulu king's autonomous powers in the future. Third-party mediation was buttressed in this instance by a parallel process of an internal adversary providing incentives. In what two correspondents describe as "an apparent sop to the [IFP] in exchange for its partici-pation in the April poll," former state president de Klerk transferred 3 million hectares of land in KwaZulu/Natal to the Zulu king's sole trusteeship in a secret deal two days before the expiration of the old constitution and just before the elections.[60] Land that the postapartheid state might have redistributed to landless Africans was now off limits, held in trust by the Zulu king. The transfer of this land to the king's control was effected under the terms of the KwaZulu Ingonyama Trust Act, passed by the KwaZulu legislature and agreed to by de Klerk on April 25, 1994. Although de Klerk and Buthelezi both denied that the land deal represented a purchase-type inducement intended to draw Inkatha into the April elections, the timing of the land transfer seemed more than mere coincidence, and people on the scene reportedly treated these denials as a "laughable" matter.[61]

The way in which the KwaZulu land deal was handled was inevitably embarrassing to the incoming government of President Mandela. In an effort to defuse the controversy shortly after taking power, the Mandela government announced the appointment of a four-man cabinet com-mittee including representatives from the ANC, NP, and IFP to examine the background of the controversy and to make recommendations on the KwaZulu Ingonyama Trust, giving "primary consideration [to] the interests of dispossessed African people and the security of tenure of rural communities."[62] The ANC's commitment to land redistribution was in conflict with its high priority on maintaining stability, reflecting the sensitivity of the land issue in an already crisis-prone area. Clearly, further negotiations on this issue would be essential in order to find a compromise satisfactory to all sides.

Conclusion: Incentives for Change

As this discussion has shown, unofficial mediators and international bodies such as the Commonwealth EPG and the United Nations can make important (but not decisive) contributions to the process of trans-forming the intrastate system of conflict management in a deeply divided country such as apartheid South Africa. External facilitators (for example, the Vance mission and Okumu) can be most useful and effective in times of crisis, enabling the disputing parties to deal with specific issues and, in the case of Buthelezi before the elections, to rejoin the political process while also saving face. In both these cases, however, it is important to emphasize that the scope of these third-party interventions was strictly circumscribed, no doubt explaining why a direct use of incentives by the state in the form of de Klerk's ceding of state lands to King Zwelithini before the April elections was so critical.

Moreover, with respect to the mediatory activities of such multilateral bodies as the Commonwealth and United Nations, it is necessary to note that these are organizations with somewhat weak and dependent economic bases and limited military capacities. None of these international facilitators were hegemons on the South African scene. They could exhort political leaders to engage in direct bargaining, communicate between the actors, exert limited pressures, utilize certain incentives (including economic sanctions), and even set out agendas for negotiation. Rather than coerce, however, they could exert only what Joseph Nye has called "soft power," manipulating economic interdependence "to structure a situation so that other countries develop preferences or define their interests in ways consistent with [their] own."[63] Earlier experiences with sanctions in Ethiopia and Rhodesia showed how difficult it was to unite sovereign countries for concerted action; even so, the moral indignation that existed over apartheid had proven to be unique in providing a basis for the use of extensive international diplomatic pressure to break the fatal drift toward the worst possible outcome: a deadly stalemate in intergroup relations.

If their ability to provide effective side payments or to offer guarantees was limited, what kind of incentives enabled these private and public international actors and state actors to influence the preferences of political elites in the South African context? The UN, as a consequence of the broad coalition it may be able to mobilize, was able to wield economic and diplomatic incentives with some effect, creating pressures on recalcitrant elites who came to view their exclusion from the world community as extremely costly. Without question, sanctions imposed a cost on South Africans; yet it remained unclear whether the economic impact of punitive sanctions was sufficient to alter choices on apartheid. Perhaps more important had been the psychological damage of a pariah status. Thus it would seem that the ability of international bodies to hold out the possibility of "inclusion" (acceptance by the world community) may well have been the key to their acceptance as third-party interveners despite all protestations at the outset against their involvement in the country's internal affairs.[64] Hence, by offering important legitimacy incentives, the Commonwealth EPG in the 1980s and the UN in the 1990s were able to wield a degree of soft power to encourage a constructive dialogue and even to advance the internally driven negotiating process itself.

But if the use of legitimacy incentives generally moved the negotiating process forward, it should also be noted that, in the case of potential "spoilers" such as Buthelezi, the international community's conferring of legitimacy in the 1980s (by providing him with forums and, to some extent, validating his stances) created complications a decade later.[65] Thus the bestowal of legitimacy as an incentive could run in both directions. Having encouraged Buthelezi in an earlier period, it became difficult for the Americans, Germans, and British to woo a recalcitrant Inkatha back to the bargaining table in the 1990s. Rather, it was left to an unofficial Kenyan mediator in a last-ditch effort to include the IFP in the election process (backed up by a parallel process of state side payments in the form of a land transfer) who encouraged successful negotiations on the specific issue of the Zulu king's constitutional status in a future South Africa. Kenya's Okumu communicated between the parties and encouraged the acceptance of a face-saving formula on this issue. With the king's role ensured and the land transfer in place, Buthelezi had an incentive to end the election boycott and seek inclusion in the transitional government. Finally, the 1994 elections could be seen as a means of confirming the South African negotiations and beginning the transition to a new system of conflict management.[66]

Clearly, of all the incentives discussed in this volume, those involving legitimacy have had the least play in the literature on interethnic negotiations. This seems misplaced, for as the experience on direct mediation in South Africa showed, the ability of international mediators to confer constitutional legitimacy on internal parties to the dispute (for example, the Zulu king) or to hold out the possibility of political inclusion for the country as a whole (for instance, the ending of South Africa's pariah status in the world) gave powerful incentives for defection or cooperation, for psychological as well as material reasons.

SUDAN

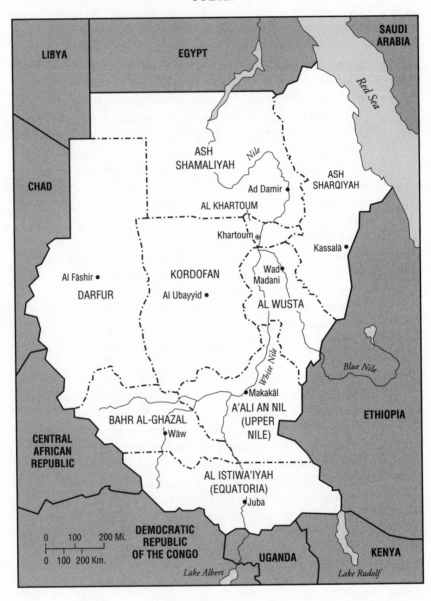

8

Coalition Efforts to Repair Internal Conflict Management in Sudan, 1971–72

One lesson of the Sudanese settlement might well be that appropriate third parties to assist in achieving such solutions frequently have to be unofficial, low profile, and, above all, private.

CHRISTOPHER R. MITCHELL

In the Sudanese peace process, the preconditions for successful mediation were all in place in the early 1970s. In addition, there was a mutually reinforcing collaboration between a state actor (Emperor Haile Selassie's Ethiopia) and a pair of unofficial mediators (the World Council of Churches and All Africa Conference of Churches) that helped to facilitate a final settlement. The unofficial intermediaries displayed great flexibility, communicating effectively between antagonistic parties, helping them to alter perceptions of their rivals, and setting agendas. When this was linked to state actors, with their capacity to exert pressure and offer incentives, it became a powerful force for changing the preferences of reluctant parties by altering the distribution of gains.[1] How-

---

This chapter expands on Donald Rothchild and Caroline Hartzell, "The Peace Process in the Sudan, 1971-1972," in Roy Licklider, ed., *Stopping the Killing: How Civil Wars End* (New York University Press, 1993), pp. 62-93.

ever, the conflict management system that emerged from the negotiations at Addis Ababa collapsed a decade later, leading to a renewal of the brutal and highly destructive civil war.

What accounts for the successful mediation of a vicious civil war by a combination of official and unofficial actors at Addis Ababa? And why did this seemingly successful effort to help the adversaries replace their conflict management system prove to be so brittle?

Before beginning my analysis, it is important to ask at the outset whether a mere decade of peace justifies the conclusion that the Addis Ababa agreement constitutes an example of successful negotiations. In particular, should the agreement be viewed as part of a cumulative process of peacemaking? Or, in light of the subsequent breakdown in state-subregional relations, should the agreement be regarded as a short respite in a long and protracted conflict? I agree with Nelson Kasfir's conclusion, put forward in the more peaceful times of 1977, that however deep the differences between northern and southern politicians or among themselves, the agreement amounted to "far more than a mere interlude in war."[2]

Support for this view can be found in the theoretical literature on negotiation and mediation, such as Saadia Touval and I. William Zartman's contention that successful negotiations and mediation cannot be limited to "the final resolution of all conflict and the reconciliation of the parties"; rather, successful negotiations should be viewed in narrower terms, as "the conclusion of an agreement promising the reduction of conflict."[3] In adopting the Touval-Zartman perspective, I look upon the Addis Ababa agreement as a case of successful mediatory action and management, irrespective of the changes in President Gaafar el-Nimeiry's policy that occurred a decade later.

The Conflict-Making Environment

In Sudan, distinct ethnic identities and histories, reinforced by cultural integration, subregional separation, and uneven economic and social development, led to grave tensions and violence as independence came and old stratifications remained between the dominant and more developed North and the vulnerable and less developed South. Class, culture, ethnicity, and subregion in Sudan all tended to overlap with and reinforce one another. In objective terms, the differential rates of subregional modernization, caused in part by colonial contacts and policies, resulted in sharp cleavages between the North and the South. In subjective terms, unmistakable evidence of uneven development became the foundation for group antagonism grounded in negative remembrances (the slave trade, Arabization policies) and current perceptions (the allocation of resources). Although these perceptions were sometimes built upon myths and stereotypes, they gained a cumulative acceptance over time, with disastrous consequences in terms of intensified North-South conflicts.

Most important, the oft-mentioned dichotomy between a homogeneous "Arab" North and an "African" and "Negroid" South was an inaccurate oversimplification that greatly distorted reality. In fact, the intermingling of peoples and cultures had been pronounced, resulting in considerable heterogeneity on both sides of the divide. In the North, 4 million Arabs made up 39 percent of Sudan's total population; the remainder included the Westerners (13 percent), the Nuba (6 percent), the Beja (6 percent), the Nubiyin (3 percent), and others (3 percent).[4] The Beja and the various African peoples of the Nuba mountains have largely held onto their own distinct cultures, while for the most part adhering to Islam.

In the South, the population of just over 3 million (30 percent of the country) was subdivided along linguistic lines into the Nilotics (including the Dinka, Nuer, Shilluk, and Anuak, living mostly in Bahr el Ghazal and Upper Nile Provinces); the Nilo-Hamitics (including the Murle, Didinga, Boya, Toposa, and Bari, who lived for the most part in Equatoria Province); and the Sudanics (including the Azande, Kreish, Bongo, Moro, and Madi, living primarily in the southwestern part of the country).[5] These southern ethnic peoples are often further subdivided into clans or subethnic peoples, thus increasing the complexity of the demographic picture in the area. Also, the South was divided further along religious lines, including a small number of Muslims and Christians and a substantial number of peoples adhering to traditional religions.

The identity of a Sudanese as a southerner or northerner, then, reflected subjective and symbolic factors at least as much as objective reality. Historical experiences with conquest, colonialism, assimilation, and exploitation combined with current perceptions of difference to create a separate consciousness. This awareness of what divided "us" from "them" gained a reality of its own as political leaders manipulated symbols to emphasize this distance. Race and ethnicity became what Karl Deutsch called a "signaling device."[6] Whether the racial or ethnic label is accurate or not, it permitted the identification of a group of people on the basis of social or economic characteristics, very quickly and cheaply and without elaborate verification procedures.

The ethnoregional divisions introduced by British administrators compounded the awareness of collective differences in group power, advantages, and opportunities. British colonial officials were determined to insulate the South from northern commercial, religious, linguistic, and educational practices and competition and so implemented special administrative policies (the "southern policy") that called for the use of English as an official language, denied trading licenses to northerners, suppressed Muslim religious activities, discouraged the use of Arab names and dress, and provided for the transfer of northern administrators to the North. The southern policy was abandoned in 1946, but not before creating and fortifying psychological and emotional boundaries between southerners and northerners that would live on after independence.[7] Commenting on the northerners' "preoccupying concern" after independence with correcting the divisive effects of the southern policy, Francis Deng writes that "the logical response was for the government to seek the unity of the country by pursuing the forced assimilation of the South through Arabization and Islamization, which, for the South, was tantamount to replacing British colonialism with Arab hegemony."[8]

The protective policy of allowing the South "to develop along its own lines" also had a variety of harmful political, economic, and social consequences. The development of a southern-based political consciousness and participation lagged behind that in the northern parts of the country.[9] In addition, relatively few southerners were recruited into the civil service: as a consequence of educational disparities and inexperience, southerners secured only 6 of the 800 senior government posts vacated by British officials just before independence. The South's relative lack of preparedness for Sudanese independence was even more apparent in terms of economic neglect. The per capita income in the South was estimated to be half that of the country as a whole and only one-fourth that of the relatively advantaged provinces of Kassala and Khartoum. As of 1970–71, 73 percent of the industrial establishments, producing 66 percent of the value of production, were located in Khartoum Province, while in the South virtually no industrial activity was reported.[10] Cotton, the country's major cash crop, was produced in Gezira, just south of Khartoum, and the country's infrastructure of railroads and communications links was heavily concentrated in the more developed areas. Well might Dunstan Wai criticize the southern policy as a cause of uneven economic modernization and conclude that the resulting deprivation left the South "dangerously vulnerable to the pursuits of the North."[11]

The consequences of a protective colonial policy were also painfully evident by their effects on social and cultural relations. The British, determined to thwart the spread of Islam to the South, assisted Christian missionaries while restricting Muslims entering the South and discouraging the use of the Arabic language by administrative personnel. Christian missions exercised a decisive control over education, thus promoting a political culture distinct from that of the rest of the country.[12] This policy inhibited nation building and did little to overcome the country's uneven development. Decades after independence, subregional imbalances in educational opportunity still persisted: in the early 1970s, for example, southern schools enrolled one-sixth as many students as in the rest of the country.[13] General Joseph Lagu, noting that the southerners were unprepared to administer their country after independence, blamed the British for offering southerners inadequate educational training.[14]

The objective aspects of uneven development coincided with the subjective factors of historical enmities, memories, and perceptions to produce a powerful conflict-making situation in Sudan. But this combined thrust toward conflict, strong and compelling as it was, did not in and of itself preclude negotiation and compromise.[15] Thus, in 1972, various key leaders did manage to prevail over stereotypes by means of an extended mediation process and display sufficient political will to find an accommodation.[16] How were northern and southern leaders both able to rise above seventeen years of civil war to reach a peaceful settlement in the early 1970s? To answer this, I turn to the processes of negotiation at Addis Ababa.

The Favorable Preconditions for Negotiations

Despite the existence of a deep and protracted conflict between the northern-led Sudanese state and the southern-based guerrillas, several general factors nonetheless contributed to a constructive negotiating process by the late 1960s. Taken together, these elements established a context for strategically placed mediators to overcome a stalemate. As a result, third-party mediators were able to help the Sudanese bargaining parties to alter their preferences and consequently to surmount their collective fears of the future—at least for a decade. The following were the main favorable preconditions that provided the framework for successful negotiations in Sudan in 1971-72.

The Emergence of Identifiable Bargaining Parties

As in many conflicts between state and ethnoregional interests, the conflicting parties were coalitions of factions, not homogeneous parties. In the state coalition, President Nimeiry had to balance diverse elements in the army and bureaucracy. The resignations of the defense minister and the chief of staff before the February 1972 negotiations (reportedly because of their aversion to meeting with the guerrilla leaders) indicated the presence of opposition elements within the northern coalition at this critical time.[17] The southern coalition was, if anything, more divided than its state counterpart. The southerners disagreed strongly among themselves about means and ends, and there were pronounced splits between the elements who remained in Sudan and those who went abroad to Uganda, London, and Ethiopia and between the various elites in Khartoum and in the South. One of the mediators noted, regarding negotiations with southern leaders: "There were many groups, and the question came up many times—who is the one to approach."[18]

As the civil war dragged on, several developments clarified the nature of the bargaining parties and their key leaders. Nimeiry crushed a military coup attempt in July 1971 and then moved swiftly to eliminate opposition elements in the army, the Muslim Brotherhood, and the political left (particularly, the Communist party). Among those eliminated was Joseph Garang, the minister of state for southern affairs. Garang, a southerner, supported subregional autonomy but expressed reservations about the Anya-Nya insurgent movement and its separatist tendencies. His demise, along with the fall of other active opponents of compromise within the army and the Muslim fundamentalists, left Nimeiry with considerable freedom to pursue a political solution to the southern problem. Much of the responsibility for handling southern affairs was immediately transferred to another southerner, Abel Alier, who played a key role in the subsequent negotiations with southern leaders.

Although the coalition of southerners never quite reached the level of cohesiveness manifested by the elite around Nimeiry, the Southern Sudan Liberation Movement (SSLM), led by General Joseph Lagu, came to represent a reasonably united party for negotiating purposes. Lagu's success in bringing together diverse southern interests was most impressive. Consolidating his base of power in eastern Equatoria, Lagu then went on to unite the various Anya-Nya forces under his command. By August 1971, Lagu had been so successful in gaining support among southern military commanders and politicians that he announced the formation of the SSLM and declared himself its leader.[19] Lagu had been greatly strengthened by the leverage gained from controlling military supplies funneled into Sudan from abroad (allegedly by Israel).[20] The result was to establish the acceptability of the SSLM among its constituents in the South and to clarify the decision structure within the SSLM. This was important to the negotiating process, for the Nimeiry regime now knew that southern leaders could deliver on the bargains that they struck.

A Mutually Hurting Stalemate

A mutually hurting stalemate, such as that reached in Sudan in 1971, is by no means an inevitable outcome of a civil war. Sudan was in many respects a soft state, with a restricted resource base and limited regulatory and coercive capacity within its boundaries. This made it difficult, if not impossible, for the government to win a military victory over the South, and the costs of attempting to do so were continually raised. After the Addis Ababa agreement had been concluded, Abel Alier was asked about the financial cost of the conflict to the Khartoum government. He replied: "It was a lot, as security alone cost £S12 million. All social and economic plans had to be suspended and administration ran at a loss of £S5 million annually."[21]

By 1971, several of the actors involved in the Sudanese conflict apparently became aware that a mutually hurting stalemate had developed between the Nimeiry regime and the southern coalition of forces. Although this stalemate involved financial and political considerations, leaders of the state and southern coalitions primarily came to recognize that a military deadlock had been reached. Neither the Sudanese state nor the SSLM possessed, nor seemed likely to muster, the resources necessary to escalate itself out of the impasse at an acceptable cost.[22] Realization that total victory for either side was out of the question provided an incentive to enter into negotiations.

In previous years, government leaders had persisted in seeking a military victory over the Anya-Nya insurgents. Ibrahim Abboud, during his tenure as president (1958–64), pursued a primarily military solution with respect to the South, seeking to quell its newly emerging guerrilla army. His failure to solve the southern problem was one reason for his downfall. Although the succeeding governments of prime ministers el-Khatim el-Khalifa, Mohammed Ahmed Mahgoub, and Sadiq el-Mahdi initially put forward political proposals to resolve the conflict, they too reverted to the use of force. Nimeiry, however, appears to have recognized that the Sudanese state was unable to achieve a military victory over the SSLM at that time. On August 1, 1969, for example, Nimeiry stated that "there is no military solution to the rebellion in the south." The period he spent (from November 1966 to December 1967) as the officer in charge of restoring order in Torit, Equatoria Province, may have helped to lead him to this conclusion.[23]

If anything, southern forces lagged behind Nimeiry in recognizing that a deadlock had been reached. The Anya-Nya had become stronger over the course of the conflict, growing from a small, nearly unarmed force of a few hundred to a unified movement under General Lagu, consisting of 10,000 to 12,000 soldiers. Although the Anya-Nya's actual control over the South remained limited, its armed strength and degree of popular support made it a force to be reckoned with.[24] Nevertheless, events in 1971 may have contributed to the Anya-Nya's realization that it could not score a final victory over government forces. Foremost among these events was a reduction in its stocks of war materiel, arising from the blocking of the channels through which Israel had previously supplied the Anya-Nya with arms. An agreement reached in November 1971 between President Nimeiry and Ethiopian Emperor Haile Selassie had closed another line of access, and one more route was cut off when President Amin expelled the Israelis from Uganda.

Nimeiry may have also found it difficult to deal with the rising political costs encountered by the Sudanese state. Among these was the sacrifice of a degree of political independence as the price of obtaining external resources. It has been alleged, for example, that the Khartoum government feared becoming too dependent on arms supplies from Egypt and the Soviet Union because such sources were unpopular with the Sudanese public.[25]

Certainly the lag between stalemate and remedial action proved hurtful to both antagonists: "The Anya-Nya had made the South virtually ungovernable," noted one observer, "but an internationally recognized secession was as far away as ever."[26] The costs for both sides of battling to an impasse were extremely high. Yet, had such a stalemate not been reached and had these adversaries continued to believe in the possibility of a military triumph, it seems unlikely that either side would have been willing to consider a negotiated solution.

Leaders Determined to Find a Political Solution

Rival leaders require political will to extricate themselves and their supporters from a mutually hurting stalemate. Their sense that time is running out and that both the conflict and their situation will worsen through inaction may often impel key leaders to begin the difficult search for a political solution. Somewhat atypically, the competing elites in Sudan did alter their political preferences at about the same time, reflecting their joint realization that the continuance of the civil war was likely to prove destructive to both parties. In other conflict situations, intransigence has seemed preferable to at least one of the parties and, as a result, the military struggle has continued and even escalated.

Political preferences for a peaceful solution to the conflict emerged on both sides for very different reasons. Nimeiry recognized that the Sudanese state was incapable of imposing its terms for peace upon the South and was therefore committed to overcoming the military stalemate by a series of conciliatory initiatives. Between 1969 and 1972, he proposed a solution that offered the South a degree of subregional autonomy within a unitary Sudanese state; replaced (and then executed) Joseph Garang as minister of state for southern affairs with a moderate southerner, Abel Alier; asked Alier to begin discussions leading to negotiations with the guerrilla spokesmen; appointed Alier to head the Sudanese delegation at the Addis Ababa negotiations; unilaterally ratified the Addis Ababa agreement; and promulgated the subsequent Southern Provinces Regional Self-Government Act.[27] Alier's appointment as head of the government delegation was taken as a positive signal of the government's seriousness of purpose regarding the negotiations; he then went on to make important contributions to the 1972 settlement, putting forth constitutional proposals on subregional autonomy that became the basis for the final accord.[28]

Within the southern coalition, the SSLM leader and Anya-Nya commander in chief, Joseph Lagu, played a critical role in the process, culminating in a settlement. Once Lagu had consolidated his position of political and military leadership within southern ranks, he was able to overcome the reluctance of some of his commanders to begin negotiations and respond positively to government overtures.[29] Lagu saw political negotiations as inevitable; thus he declared himself ready in October 1970 to enter into serious talks with government representatives: "We are not just trouble makers, we are a people struggling for a cause, and if that can be achieved by talking we see no reason why we do not accept to talk."[30]

Although Lagu agreed in principle to the talks, he nevertheless required that a variety of preconditions be met before serious discussions could begin: that the Sudanese army stop all hostilities and stay in their present positions, that southern Sudanese political prisoners be freed, and that the Anya-Nya be recognized publicly as "the only element to negotiate with in the Southern Sudan."[31] Subsequently, Lagu modified his position, indicating that if the Khartoum authorities showed themselves to be "sincere and serious," his delegation would be willing to enter into negotiations to reach a settlement of the conflict "*within the framework of one Sudan.*"[32] In taking this position, Lagu was declaring himself willing to accept Nimeiry's nonnegotiable principle on Sudanese unity. From that point on, Lagu played a central role in promoting the peace process—maintaining the unity of his delegation, responding to initiatives, and delivering on agreements. In brief, the leadership skills and commitment of Nimeiry, Alier, and Lagu to the peace process from 1969 to 1972 created a uniquely positive environment for joint problem solving.

External Pressures to Reach Agreement

As I have noted, initiating a peace process requires cooperative political decisions by rival leaders. Pressures by external actors to end a conflict are unlikely, by themselves, to bring antagonists to the bargaining table. Nonetheless, the pressures and incentives used by regional and international actors can facilitate the negotiation process. In Sudan, several external pressures were to prove significant in influencing the two contending coalitions to seek a peaceful settlement of the conflict.

Ethiopia and Uganda were two regional actors with a long-term interest and significant involvement in the Sudanese conflict. Like Sudan, Ethiopia faced what it regarded as a secessionist challenge in Eritrea. The Eritrean Liberation Front (ELF) and, after 1970, the Eritrean People's Liberation Front (EPLF) used the adjacent areas of Sudan for arms running and refuge; in return, Emperor Haile Selassie allowed military supplies to be funneled to the Anya-Nya through Ethiopia and provided training and safe haven for rebel troops. Such actions were indispensable to Anya-Nya forces and placed pressure on the Khartoum government; however, when the leaders of Ethiopia and Sudan agreed in March 1971 to cease aiding and abetting each other's secessionist movements, this had the effect of facilitating an internal settlement between the

Nimeiry regime and the SSLM. Nimeiry and the emperor were moved to reach this agreement in part because both the Anya-Nya and the Eritrean liberation movements had grown strong enough to expand, and possibly to internationalize, conflicts that still remained essentially internal wars.

Moreover, with the overthrow of Ugandan President Milton Obote in January 1971, pressures to resolve the Sudanese conflict became critical. Langi and Acholi troops opposed to the Idi Amin coup fled to the southern Sudan for safety; there, supported by the Sudanese army, they were able to regroup. During this time, plans were afoot to invade Uganda from eastern Equatoria to restore President Obote to rule. These actions were countered by Amin, who allowed the Anya-Nya a supply route through Uganda. These events came to an end when Nimeiry and Amin signed an accord in late 1971. Nimeiry agreed to terminate his support for Obote's forces in exchange for Amin's expressed willingness to curtail external access to the Anya-Nya.

These Ethiopian and Ugandan agreements effectively severed the two major supply routes to the rebels. Also, by expelling the Israeli military mission from Uganda, Idi Amin cut off one important source of military supplies for the Anya-Nya. Thus the termination of Ethiopian and Ugandan support for southern Sudanese forces greatly influenced the southern politicians to move toward an agreement with the Nimeiry regime.

Some pressures calling for an end to the protracted conflict in Sudan also emanated from other African governments. These countries were largely influenced by the economic strains that they experienced from the presence of large numbers of refugees within their borders. A study done for the United Nations High Commission for Refugees in September 1970 estimated that there were then 176,000 southern Sudanese refugees in neighboring countries, including 72,000 in Uganda, 59,000 in Zaire, 25,000 in the Central African Republic, and 20,000 in Ethiopia.[33] Criticism by African governments of the ongoing civil war, which resulted in increasing numbers of refugees being pushed over the Sudanese borders, created more pressure on the Sudanese governmental authorities, who did not wish to alienate the leaders of eastern and central Africa. This source of influence was not lost on the World Council of Churches (WCC), an international organization that had long been involved in providing aid and relief in the southern Sudan as well as to southern Sudanese refugees in neighboring lands.[34] In one memorandum, a WCC official states that "with de Garang and Wolwol we discussed the possibility...that on this trip they also try to see key OAU presidents (Nyerere, Kaunda, Kenyatta, etc.), to begin to put that sort of pressure on Khartoum."[35]

The existence of other external (including Western) pressures to settle the conflict in Sudan is less clear. Some observers allege that the U.S. government helped to push Nimeiry toward a settlement, a contention that others firmly deny.[36] Although it is uncertain what form Western external pressures took, in a meeting on October 22, 1971, Abel Alier pointed out that "since the July changes [shifts in personnel and policy made after the attempted communist coup in Khartoum], the Sudan Government has made contact with Western nations, e.g. West Germany, U.S.A., U.K." Alier went on to say that this rapprochement was expected to result in "less enthusiasm on the part of the West to embarrass the Sudan government, with whom they have cordial relations."[37]

Even though none of these external factors proved sufficient in and of themselves to move the contending parties toward an agreement, these pressures may have heightened the awareness on all sides that time was running out. Implicit in many of the aforementioned influences was the possibility that they could lead to a mutually damaging isolation: diplomatic isolation for the Sudanese government and strategic isolation for the southern insurgents (who, in the end, required external recognition to validate their "victory"). Because several of these external pressures coincided in 1971, both antagonists were made aware of the dimensions and consequences of the stalemate.

Mediators Actively on the Scene

The process leading up to the Addis Ababa agreement was also facilitated by the third-party mediators' interactions with parties involved in the conflict for several years before its resolution. Not only were the WCC and All Africa Conference of Churches engaged in refugee relief efforts, but in 1966 an AACC goodwill mission visited Sudan, seeking to evaluate the situation and to offer its services to facilitate the peace process. In 1970, after some years of exposure to the conflict, the WCC reevaluated its role in the Sudan conflict. Kodwo E. Ankrah, the African secretary of the Division of Inter-Churches Aid, Refugees and World Service of the WCC, noted that the origins of the conflict were complex and included religion, race, political, and social and economic factors. Ankrah stated that the WCC had become convinced "that we should advocate strongly that the Church leaders in Africa should approach the Sudan problem from a political angle."[38]

The presence of the WCC and the AACC at the scene of the conflict and their ongoing contacts with various Sudanese political leaders enabled them to assess the implications of changes in leadership and political will, the emergence of identifiable bargaining parties, and other shifts in the negotiating context, and thus to make the most of opportune moments to help move the parties beyond stalemate in the bargaining process. WCC representatives urged the SSLM, through its London spokesman, Mading de Garang, to create a consensus position within the Anya-Nya by resolving some of the internal problems that existed among the southern groups.[39] In addition, the mediators, because of their familiarity with actors and events, were able to react quickly to the change in government in Khartoum (in particular, the replacement of Joseph Garang as minister of state for southern affairs by Abel Alier, the former minister of public works) that followed the attempted coup by left-wing elements in the army against Nimeiry in 1971.[40]

Mediators who are familiar with the conflict and the parties involved can recognize windows of opportunity and use them to further the negotiation process. In Sudan, the WCC-AACC mediators gained the confidence of the parties through contacts with SSLM student supporters at Makerere University, Kampala, and southern Sudanese refugees in neighboring countries and through visits to the Khartoum government. As one WCC official observed, "Reconciliation efforts had to be based on a long period of preparation beforehand—perhaps five or six years. You had to nourish good relations with both sides. . . . It took time to establish our reliability and impartiality before people would 'enter into confidentiality' with you."[41]

As anticipated in the literature on negotiations, the presence of an unofficial mediator was certainly insufficient to move the conflicting parties to reach agreement. If there had been no political will on the part of the Sudanese parties to reach a settlement, no amount of effort by the mediators would have sufficed to resolve the conflict.[42] However, because an intermediary had been in Sudan for several years, it could act when the moment was advantageous to facilitate agreement between the actors and help them to overcome breakdowns.

The Process of Negotiation

In the Sudanese negotiations of 1971–72, the five favorable preconditions discussed above all combined to facilitate the constructive process of state-ethnoregional bargaining. But what happened during the peacemaking process itself?[43]

Certainly, the final agreement did not spring full blown from the minds of the men at Addis Ababa. Rather, the formula of subregional autonomy and group rights had been discussed since 1965. Following the overthrow of General Ibrahim Abboud's oppressive regime in 1964, the new prime minister, Sayed Sir el-Khatim el-Khalifa, pursued a more conciliatory approach to the South. Khalifa appointed two southerners to the cabinet, relaxed the state of emergency in the South, and invited southerners from both inside and outside the country to a roundtable conference in Khartoum. After some initial discussions on the normalization of the situation in the South and the recognition of certain human rights, the participants were unable to reach a unanimous agreement on the system of government for the South. They therefore appointed a twelve-person committee to make recommendations on a constitutional arrangement "which will protect the special interest of the South as well as the general interest of the Sudan."[44] This committee, which met for more than a year, ruled out separation and centralized unitary government and instead proposed a scheme of subregional autonomy within a united Sudan. Both northern and southern representatives disagreed strongly on whether the South should be considered a unit (the southern preference) or divided along provincial lines (the northern preference); there was broad agreement, however, on the distribution of powers between the center and the subregion. These proposals set appropriate guidelines for the final settlement. Thus the document on subregional self-government presented by Abel Alier to the negotiators at Addis Ababa was based largely on earlier work by this twelve-person committee.[45]

The regimes of Muhammed Ahmed Mahgoub (1965–66 and 1967–69) and Sayed Sadiq el-Mahdi (1966–67) represented a temporary break in the progress toward a North-South settlement by retreating from the liberal-minded guidelines of the twelve-person committee on subregional autonomy. Mahgoub, a highly educated person who identified closely with Arab religion and culture, rejected the conciliatory approach adopted by the framers of the twelve-person committee report and launched a new effort to crush the Anya-Nya insurgency by means of force. Furthermore, with the accession of el-Mahdi to the premiership in 1966, the official stance on southern issues changed little. The new regime was intent on encouraging an Islamic revival and increasingly influenced by the small but influential Islamic Charter Front, so it urged the adoption of an Islamic constitution. Abel Alier observed that southern politicians found the idea of an Islamic constitution repugnant and therefore withdrew from the constitutional drafting commission in December 1968.[46]

With the war continuing and proving costly and these regimes unable to offer a way out of the impasse, it is not surprising that the military, led by Nimeiry, decided to intervene. Nimeiry favored a new political effort at reconciliation with the South and offered the goal of subregional autonomy within the framework of a united Sudan. He announced plans in June 1969 to broaden the amnesty for southern opposition elements; initiate an intensive social, economic, and cultural program in the South; appoint a minister of southern affairs; and train southerners for positions of responsibility. In the prenegotiation period that followed, Nimeiry remained firmly committed to reaching a political settlement. He authorized the implementation of the subregional autonomy plan, a task that was undertaken separately by southern intellectuals and by Gaafar Mohamed Ali Bakheit, the minister of local government, and Sayed Abdel Rahman Abdullah, the former chairman of the twelve-person committee and later deputy minister of local government. Both implementation plans were similar in that they proposed to maintain the unity of the South, to give the head of the subregion the status of a minister, to have a subregional assembly and executive, and to allow the subregion the power to raise money by levying taxes. In brief, there was considerable continuity in the process. The recommendations of the roundtable and the twelve-person committee influenced the negotiations at Addis Ababa in 1971–72, narrowing differences and facilitating agreement upon the final terms.

One important element was the willingness of both parties to engage in an ongoing process of reciprocal concessions. This went beyond a tit-for-tat relationship and was evidence of a joint commitment to search for a settlement. A prime example of such reciprocal concessions involved the agreements by the Nimeiry regime and the SSLM on the conditions for entering into negotiations. The government asked that southern representatives be individuals who had influence over those actually involved in the fighting and that negotiations be conducted within the framework of subregional autonomy of the South within one Sudan.[47] In turn, the SSLM required that negotiations take place in an independent, non-Arab, African country and that an African leader be used as a mediator. The SSLM also asked that the Sudanese government recognize the Anya-Nya as the sole southern Sudanese bargaining party.[48] It is significant that each of the two parties agreed to the conditions that the other party set before the negotiations, thereby demonstrating that both were serious about embarking upon the negotiation process.

Besides these compromises, which were critical for initiating talks, at least three other major accommodations surfaced during the negotiations. First, northern representatives contended that Arabic should be the country's only official language, acknowledging that the development of local languages was a part of the national culture and heritage but arguing that the existence of more than one official language could prove divisive. Southerners sought to make English the official language of the Southern Region, fearing that non-Arabic-speaking southerners might later be at a disadvantage when seeking government positions. The issue was resolved when both sides agreed that Arabic would be the official language for Sudan and English the principal language for the Southern Region.[49]

Second, the government wanted a single national army controlled by central authorities, whereas the SSLM argued that there should be three armies: one for the North, one for the Southern Region (composed of Anya-Nya troops), and a third army to guard Khartoum, which would be controlled by the central government and made up equally of northerners and southerners.[50] This proved to be a very contentious issue, but a minimally satisfactory formula was finally devised whereby the military units in the Southern Region would consist of a unified force made up of 6,000 Anya-Nya and 6,000 northern troops. This formula met the government's objective of establishing one national force and addressed the SSLM's concern regarding the incorporation of Anya-Nya contingents into the army.

Third, some southern politicians favored the South's secession from the North, although others had sought a federal structure to link the two subregions. The North, meanwhile, entered the negotiations urging that the South be given a limited subregional autonomy. Mutual adjustments led to an agreement whereby the southern provinces of Bahr el Ghazal, Equatoria, and Upper Nile constituted a self-governing unit within Sudan. As Mohamed Omer Beshir observed: "In this way the unity of the country had been confirmed, thus meeting the wishes of the Northerners. At the same time, the wishes of the Southerners were met by having their own legislature and executive agencies."[51]

Reciprocal concessions between the contending parties proved to be an important process-related variable because they demonstrated that the sacrifices entailed in an agreement would not be unilateral. After seventeen years of prolonged warfare, no single action could be expected to create trust on the part of an adversary party nor to legitimate the entire negotiation process. However, the concessions that were made did serve to create a history of positive responses between the two groups and to build a network of relationships between them. Through reciprocal concessions, each party was able to test the negotiation process at various stages and to receive concrete evidence of its rival's political will to reach and implement a settlement. Moreover, the leadership of each coalition could use the concessions of their opponents to strengthen its position among its own constituents.

As part of the negotiation process, reciprocal concessions also encouraged participants to alter their perceptions of each other. Increasing interactions between the parties during the negotiations and the give-and-take of concessions prompted an evolution from essentialist perceptions to something more pragmatic in nature and more conducive to bargaining outcomes. For example, the North's agreement to negotiate with the SSLM outside Sudan accorded a certain degree of legitimacy to the southern movement, because it met one of the southern politicians' demands and also because it placed the parties on somewhat more diplomatically equal terms. Another example of evolving perceptions is to be found in a statement by Leopoldo J. Niilus, WCC director of the Council of Churches on International Affairs: "During the still secret but formal negotiations the government party had no objections to the—what were technically and politically 'rebels'...— calling itself the SSLM, the south Sudan *Liberation Movement*! What is even more, that was the formal treatment given to it by the government delegates all along the negotiations!"[52]

Although essentialist perceptions were altered during the negotiations, the changes remained within certain parameters. For example, negotiations could not have occurred had the southern coalition insisted on secession. Once the southern politicians agreed to the government's "one Sudan" condition, the parties then diverged on interests rather than principles. Interests proved to be negotiable because both sides were willing to make concessions. By acknowledging tacit limits and recognizing that some principles were nonnegotiable, the negotiations could move forward and issues were circumvented that might have led to deadlock.

I have already mentioned some of the important roles played by the WCC and AACC, such as promoting contacts between groups. These unofficial mediators also helped to encourage concessions by both parties at Addis Ababa, by offering formulas for the delegates to discuss, reminding each party of the dilemmas and political constraints faced by its opponents, recalling what was at stake when the negotiations grew heated, and slowing the pace of the negotiations when it became prudent to do so. The mediators and the tone they set for the negotiations may have also helped to alter perceptions. When the agreement was reached at the conference on the composition of the army, Canon Burgess Carr stood to pray, crying as he did so. According to others present, one of the generals in the northern delegation cried as well, admittedly remorseful for the slaughter that had taken place over the years.[53]

Several groups and individuals had attempted to mediate the conflict before the interchanges at Addis Ababa. Among these were private organizations such as the Movement for Colonial Freedom (MCF), based in London and affiliated with the British Labour party. The MCF, under the leadership of its secretary-general, Barbara Haq, attempted to use its good offices in 1970 to bring about a reconciliation between exiled southerners and the Sudanese government. This effort came to naught, however, for the MCF issued a press release and Haq later wrote an article that were both viewed by southerners as biased in favor of the government, leading them to end their relations with the organization.

Given the history of repeated mediation efforts, why were the WCC and AACC able to succeed where others had failed? The answer is partly that the WCC-AACC mediators' presence on the scene and their familiarity with the conflict enabled them to gain the trust of both contending parties. The confidence of the North was based in part on the fact that the AACC's 1966 report, "Mission to the Sudan," had been sympathetic to its position. Strategically speaking, this trust became important later, because the government's consent and participation were necessary to the negotiations.

Some southerners were put off by the 1966 report, but their trust was gradually restored by the mediators' willingness to meet with them in Uganda under the auspices of the Kampala committee and the Makerere group and because the AACC was an African organization that included leading Africans such as Burgess Carr and Kodwo Ankrah. Moreover, the willingness of the mediators to provide the SSLM with funds for travel and lawyer's fees, thus enabling southern leaders to participate more effectively in the negotiations, probably reassured them that the WCC and AACC were not inherently biased in favor of the North's position.

In addition, the WCC and AACC appear to have been able to play the role they did because of the nonstate nature of their organizations. Leopoldo Niilus phrased it this way:

There is no government which could call in bodies like the UNO or the OAU to "intermediate" between it and its "rebels." For to do so would be to give to the rebels formal status, parallel to that of the government. However, bodies like the WCC and the AACC, which can give no diplomatic *status* to anybody can be made use of, *provided*, of course, that they are understood to be objective and *informed* enough and not suspected of having their own stake to interfere in a Nation's internal affairs.[54]

As private, activist bodies with relatively limited resources, the WCC and AACC were not in a position to coerce or threaten the state or insurgent movement. This was probably another reason that the two sides trusted them and decided to allow them the leeway necessary to promote the peacemaking process.

That the WCC and AACC were private organizations with unofficial status was very important to advancing the negotiations. Once the government had sufficient political will to embark on the negotiation process, northern officials were able to turn to the WCC and AACC, who were already on the scene, to facilitate the process. Doing so meant the negotiation process would not be publicly subjected to pressures from other states or international organizations and that the government did not have to accord the southern coalition more legitimacy than it was initially prepared to give. The unofficial status of the mediators, combined with the nonthreatening manner in which they handled the negotiations, allowed the antagonists to gradually move away from their prenegotiation stances without losing face.

Having noted the significant role played by the unofficial mediators in advancing the Sudanese negotiations, however, I should not overstate their contributions. Because of the nondiplomatic status of these organizations and their general inability to use effective pressures and incentives, the WCC and AACC had a limited ability to overcome the stalemates that occurred during the negotiations at Addis Ababa. Even though they were able to enhance communication, help to build a consensus, draft possible agreements, facilitate reciprocal concessions, and draw the actors' attention to issues on which agreement existed, they were unable to guarantee any agreements reached, and they were in no position to enforce them.[55] Because the WCC and AACC had only limited power to make credible threats or to coerce the parties involved, once a stalemate occurred in the negotiations, they lacked sufficient leverage to persuade the parties to compromise. In fact, a deadlock did arise over the future of the army, and neither side would agree to make any concessions on this issue. The WCC and AACC, unable to do more, then turned to an arbitrator, Emperor Haile Selassie of Ethiopia.

The emperor played a unique role during the negotiations, coming to the fore only after other efforts had failed to keep the negotiations on track. Although Haile Selassie was willing to have the contending parties meet under his auspices, he insisted that his role not be considered as that of a mediator. The WCC and AACC were advised that they could refer only to the emperor's *"good offices, under his auspices."*[56]

The emperor's stance on this issue may have stemmed from his fear that self-determination movements in his own country (particularly in Eritrea) would use this precedent to pressure him to submit their conflicts to mediation. Nevertheless, when an impasse was reached on the military-security question at Addis Ababa, Canon Burgess Carr persuaded the emperor to use his good offices to attempt to settle the matter. The emperor met separately with the northern and southern delegations. Although recommending that the SSLM accept the principle of a unified army with a single command structure, he also suggested that half (6,000) of the armed forces to be deployed in the South be recruited from the Anya-Nya and half from the North. He is reported to have said that such a mixed force "would most probably go a long way to reassure Southerners of their physical safety and equal place in the country."[57] Moreover, the emperor gave his personal guarantee against any repression or reprisals against Anya-Nya returnees in case the South reached an agreement on the military issue.[58] Southerners were disappointed that their primary objective—an independent southern unit—was not met, but they viewed the emperor's proposed insurance incentives in a most positive light. In the end, the emperor's recommendation led to concessions by both coalitions; neither side was prepared to antagonize him by opting for their first preferences.

The emperor's formula for splitting the differences was one that the literature on third-party mediation might well have suggested. Why did a proposal put forth by Emperor Haile Selassie move the negotiations out of stalemate when the efforts of the WCC and AACC had failed? The answer appears to lie in the emperor's status as a head of state, possessing a substantial amount of implied coercive capacity. As such, he could threaten the parties involved with certain consequences should they fail to agree on the issue at hand. The emperor could alert the Nimeiry government that the SSLM might need external assistance again if the northern coalition proved recalcitrant or else no longer allowed

Sudanese refugees to remain in Ethiopia, thereby flooding Sudan with refugees that it was ill equipped to handle. In turn, the agreement that the emperor had signed with Nimeiry pressured the southerners to reach a settlement with the Sudanese government; dwindling military supplies would affect the firepower of the Anya-Nya and, in the long term, might also weaken the unity of the southern coalition itself.

In brief, the emperor, backed by the power of a state active in the region, was in a very favorable position to influence the two parties to the conflict, thereby helping to overcome hostile perceptions at a critical point in the negotiations. State and private third parties cooperated in an effective manner, with the emperor backstopping the private, unofficial mediators at critical junctures, and this yielded impressive results: the parties moved from adversarial relations to a more pragmatic, bargaining encounter.

The Failure of Implementation

The successful negotiations between the Nimeiry regime and the SSLM at Addis Ababa in 1972 brought an end to the first Sudanese civil war. To be sure, suspicions remained very much alive on both sides, but the agreement did provide some basic rules of relations for the following decade. Sudan therefore enjoyed a period of relative peace, under a rather centralized and unstable system of governance. The intrastate system of conflict management resulting from the Addis Ababa negotiations could well have provided the foundation for long-term national reconciliation and a self-enforcing system of decentralization and power sharing. However, this was not to be, for the pragmatism shown during the negotiations was not carried over into the implementation stage. Instead, the hegemonic preferences of the ruling coalition overwhelmed the restraints incorporated in the country's arrangement on subregional autonomy, causing grave insecurity among southerners and the collapse of the new conflict management system.

According to the provisions of the Addis Ababa agreement and the follow-up Southern Provinces Regional Self-Government Act of 1972, the Southern Region (including the provinces of Bahr el Ghazal, Equatoria, and Upper Nile) constituted a "self-governing region" within a united, socialist Sudan. A High Executive Council and People's Regional Assembly were created for the Southern Region, with the authority to handle specified subregional subjects, particularly the preservation of public order, internal security, efficient administration, and the promotion of economic, social, and cultural development. The subregional authorities were empowered to establish a separate budget and to levy duties and taxes.

The leading position of the central government in center-subregional relations was never in doubt. The central government was given exclusive authority to deal with a variety of matters (defense, external affairs, currency, communications, customs and foreign trade, immigration, educational planning, and public audit), and the president of the republic was also given broad authority to manage relations between the central ministries and the subregional organs. The People's Regional Assembly could decide, by a two-thirds majority, to request that the president postpone the enactment of any law that adversely affected the welfare and interests of the citizens of the Southern Region; however, the president had to accede to such a request. Under the 1973 constitution, central-subregional relations remained ambiguous, and Nimeiry took advantage of this by intervening in subregional elections and making economic decisions without referring to southern authorities.[59]

Shortly after the Regional Self-Government Act was put into effect, Nimeiry appointed a Provisional High Executive Council, headed by Abel Alier, to act as the subregional government for an eighteen-month transition period. A series of other steps intended to reassure the South followed quickly. Lagu was commissioned a major general in the Sudanese army, and three southerners were appointed to the central government. The Nimeiry regime cooperated with neighboring governments and the UN High Commissioner for Refugees to repatriate, resettle, and rehabilitate one-half million or more refugees living in the bush or abroad, and Nimeiry integrated 10,000 SSLM troops into the People's Armed Forces, the police, and prison forces.[60]

A financially strapped state such as Sudan, which had just experienced a brutal civil war, would have had difficulty healing the wounds of the past under any circumstances; yet, for all the anger and resentment within and between these parties, the transition to peace proved as smooth as could be expected. Conditions were created for norms and rules of interaction to emerge among politicians in the future. That this failed to occur is a commentary not so much on the peacemaking process of 1971–72 as on the shortsightedness of President Nimeiry and his government as they sought to align themselves with northern-based sectarian parties and fundamentalist elements, including the Muslim Brotherhood.[61]

Evidence of Nimeiry's reconsideration of the extent of southern autonomy began to emerge soon after the initial transition period. Although the 1973 elections to the Regional Assembly in the South augured well, some were concerned about Nimeiry's efforts to assure Alier's nomination as the official candidate of the Sudan Socialist Union for the presidency of the High Executive Council. Although many have concluded that Alier, who had played an important role in the Addis Ababa negotiations, would probably have been elected anyway, Nimeiry's intercession as president of the party was an embarrassment that weakened Alier's position. At least as serious was the harm done to the spirit of Addis Ababa.[62]

Southerners also expressed general disappointment over the level of central expenditures allocated for developmental purposes and for the rebuilding of the war-devastated infrastructure in the South.[63] By the mid-1970s, they saw worrisome signs indicating that the Nimeiry regime was not fully committed to reconciliation. In the eyes of militant Sudanese leaders—most notably John Garang de Mabior, the leader of the Sudan People's Liberation Movement–Sudan People's Liberation Army (SPLM-SPLA)—Nimeiry backtracked from his earlier position and took a series of actions that pointed to a shift in regime priorities away from accommodation. The result was most destructive of the Addis Ababa compromise and led to a flare-up of guerrilla warfare.[64] The most significant of these "provocations," as Garang describes them, were the Nimeiry government's decision to build a 175-mile canal between Jonglei and Malakal to save water for use in northern Sudan and Egypt (feared by southerners because of its drying effects in the swampy Sudd area); Nimeiry's alteration of southern electoral processes and inter-vention in southern executive and legislative affairs (including the dis-solution of legally constituted bodies); proposed changes of the border between North and South (removing certain mineral-rich and prime agricultural lands from southern control); and the decision to locate a refinery to process oil extracted in the South at Kosti in the North, rather than the site in the South recommended by the southern Regional Assembly.[65]

Two of Nimeiry's policies were particularly provocative. In a major bid in 1983 to gain support from some key northerners, Nimeiry imposed Islamic *Sharia* law upon the country as a whole.[66] *Sharia* law, which applies traditional punishments (including whippings, stonings, and amputations) in specified cases as a means of deterrence, is strongly opposed by southerners and also by many northerners who view it as a harsh legal system that violates the human rights and cultural autonomy of the largely non-Muslim peoples of the South.[67] All three of the southern Regional Assemblies passed resolutions in 1983 and 1984 rejecting a proposed amendment to the Sudan constitution that would impose *Sharia* law and urging that, in any event, the law not be applied to non-Muslim peoples. By late 1984, Nimeiry was under pressure from Western governments as well as leaders in the Southern Sudan and in Eastern Africa, so he backtracked a bit, declaring that he was suspending the further use of *Sharia* law.[68] But the announced suspension was not a decision to cease applying Islamic law to non-Muslims; this left southerners apprehensive about their future in a politically centralized Sudanese state.

Moreover, Garang and many southerners viewed Nimeiry's determination to redivide the South into three subregions as an effort to weaken the South and an "abrogation" of the Addis Ababa provision to maintain the South as a single entity.[69] The redivision of the South followed an earlier decision by the Sudanese government to decentralize and devolve limited powers, under the Regional Government Act of 1980, to five new subregional governments in the North. With this in place, Nimeiry was eager to extend the decentralization policy to the South, thereby increasing his influence over rival elements and his access to oil revenues in the subregion.[70] Toward this end, Nimeiry received strong encouragement from Vice President Lagu, the champion of the smaller ethnic (non-Dinka) peoples in Equatoria Province. Lagu argued that administrative decentralization was necessary to promote cultural distinction, stability, and progress in the South. He struck out forcefully against what he described as Dinka domination: "The truth... is that many of the leaders of the Dinka tribe have chosen to mark time [on] the issue of decentralisation so as to effect the spread of members of their tribe in all areas of the South, and thereby guaranteeing themselves the control of any government formed at any level."[71]

Other southern politicians were quick to challenge Lagu's stance on redivision. One booklet described the proposals as "nakedly tribal[istic]" and a threat to the unity and integrity of the Southern Region.[72] Although Nimeiry initially made preparations for a referendum on the issue, as provided in the guidelines set out at Addis Ababa, he abandoned these preparations as conflict between the pro- and antidivisionists became intense, and in June 1983 he decreed that the South be split into three subregions. "By that act," Bona Malwal writes, "he took the 'final' step which in effect totally abrogated the 1972 Self-Government Act for the South which had embodied the Addis Ababa Agreement."[73]

Step by step, then, Nimeiry subverted the very agreement he had helped to create. His motives were unclear, although his desire to strengthen his coalitional base in the North appears to have been a primary factor. As Nimeiry's financial and political base of support shrank, he tended to be increasingly responsive to the demands made by Islamic fundamentalist elements in the North for *Sharia* laws and the redivision of the South.[74] Ominous signs of southern discontent soon became evident; a new guerrilla movement that took on the name Anya-Nya II, implying the rebirth of the pre–Addis Ababa agreement insurgent force, emerged as a serious challenge in 1983, soon to be overtaken by Garang's SPLA. Nimeiry became isolated and broadly unpopular and was overthrown by his defense minister, General Abdel Rahman Siwar el-Dahab, in April 1985.

The takeover by el-Dahab and the assumption of power by his legally elected successor, former prime minister Sadiq el-Mahdi, in May 1986 did little to restore the spirit of Addis Ababa. As the peace agreement came apart, leaders on both sides turned again to the military option, with the cruelest of consequences for civilians in the South. The fighting intensified as Garang's forces grew and wrested control over much of the rural areas and as the Sudanese army, supported by well-armed tribal militias, fought to extend its hold over the area. Sadiq el-Mahdi showed little willingness to accommodate basic southern demands. He did compromise on the issue of redivision, urging that Equatoria be accorded a special status within a reunited South, and took steps to soften (but not to abrogate) the system of *Sharia* law. Garang rejected such compromise measures as insufficient and ruled out meaningful negotiations with Khartoum until the el-Mahdi regime would agree to end the application of *Sharia* laws, adopt a secular constitution, and restructure the country's political system.[75] While el-Mahdi and Garang became locked into diametrically opposed positions regarding the government's commitment to an Islamic state, the Opposition Democratic Unionist party leader, Muhammad Uthman al-Mirghani, entered into negotiations with Garang, reaching an agreement in November 1988.[76] Under the terms of this accord, the implementation of *Sharia* law would be put on hold, the state of emergency lifted and a cease-fire declared, and a national constitutional conference established.[77]

With el-Mahdi's fall from power in 1989, Brigadier General Omar Hassan Ahmed al-Bashir assumed control in a coup d'etat and called for a "revolution of national salvation." The new military junta, which had close links to the Muslim Brotherhood, immediately suspended the constitution, dissolved political parties, and replaced hundreds of civil servants with National Islamic Front (NIF) members.[78] The signs were menacing in terms of government relations with southern Sudan. The new administration and its allies, resolved upon applying *Sharia* law throughout the country, had misgivings over earlier efforts to negotiate an end to the civil war and were determined to find a military solution to the southern problem. The war in the South quickly took a turn for the worse.

By 1992, the Sudanese army, aided by new military supplies and advisers from abroad, managed to achieve a series of victories in the South. Not only were southern forces outgunned by the rejuvenated Sudanese army, but they became divided among themselves, into Garang's mainstream SPLM-SPLA and the breakaway SPLA-United, led by Riek Machar and Lam Akol. Mediatory efforts by the Nigerians in 1992 and the Americans in 1993 to reconcile these opponents failed, and in April 1996 Machar and Commander Kerubino Kuanyin Bol, whose troops are fighting the mainstream SPLA in the northern Bahr El Ghazal, signed a "political charter" with the ruling NIF regime.[79]

Efforts in 1994 by the Intergovernmental Authority on Drought and Desertification (IGADD), a loose regional organization of eastern African states, did bring about a Declaration of Principles upholding the principles of national unity (based upon principles of multiparty democracy and secularism) and the right of self-determination. These principles were accepted by the SPLM-SPLA factions but rejected by the NIF authorities.[80] The NIF regime remained unresponsive to the East African states' mediatory initiative until October 1996, when, at a meeting in Nairobi with Kenyan president Daniel arap Moi, the Sudanese minister for peace, Colonel Mohamed el Amin Khalifa, called for a resumption of the peace process under the auspices of the regional body, now named the Intergovernmental Authority on Development (IGAD). Optimism rose as Sudanese authorities made it clear that their delegation would not set any preconditions and would be prepared to negotiate on the basis of the 1994 Declaration of Principles. Moi thereupon recommended that the Sudanese government formally call for a resumption of the peace process at a meeting of IGAD in Djibouti scheduled for December. Hopes were soon dashed, however, because when the Djibouti meeting took place, the NIF regime made no commitments to resume the peace process.[81] For the time being, essentialist perceptions and nonnegotiable demands appear to have triumphed and the country's conflict management system as it affects the South is in a state of collapse. New mediation efforts seem imperative, but few mediators seem to have the political will and the capacity to intervene and enforce a peace agreement.

Conclusion

At this point it is useful to examine the kinds of coercive and noncoercive incentives that were at the disposal of both domestic and international actors in Sudan in the 1970s. At the outset, two important points should be mentioned. First, in this case the domestic state actor (the Sudanese government) put forward more important incentives than did the external third-party intermediaries. Several possible explanations for the state's leading role in offering inducements can be made. The conflict remained largely insulated from cold war politics; the governments had the political resources at their disposal to offer both symbolic and substantive incentives to the hard-pressed insurgents; and other countries lacked any incentive to intervene, except to extend humanitarian relief. Most important, the Sudanese state viewed its civil conflict as an internal matter and jealously guarded itself, for the most part, against intrusive forms of external interference. It did work with nonstate mediators, but mainly on its own terms and when it suited its purposes. The unofficial mediators' lack of resources made them more acceptable to the rival parties but gave them only a limited capacity to offer meaningful incentives to help the parties change their preferences and reach a peace accord.

Second, a coalition of conflict management agents was critically important, because it combined the strengths of an unofficial mediator (the WCC-AACC) in facilitating the acceptance of some common norms and in communicating between the adversaries following the breakdown of the conflict management system with the leverage exercised by a state actor (Emperor Haile Selassie). The WCC-AACC team did achieve results in conveying information, gaining acceptance for a negotiating process, and encouraging the parties to reach an agreement. In the final analysis, however, the team's success in concluding an accord was dependent upon the timely intercession of a state leader (Emperor Haile Selassie). The emperor's ability to intervene at timely junctures and use appropriate pressures and incentives proved critical in terms of surmounting the obstacles to a peaceful outcome at Addis Ababa.

Because of the intensity of civil wars and the nonnegotiable quality of the demands and counterdemands made by the state and the insurgent movement, it is not surprising that fiscal incentives were generally of limited significance. The Sudanese government announced plans in June 1969 to initiate an intensive social, economic, and cultural program for the development of the South; these, however, represented rather intermittent purchase initiatives, and the overlap with insurance incentives should be apparent. Instead, among the noncoercive incentives in the internal realm, it was the insurance category that proved critical. Embattled insurgents, fearing retribution, need reassurance about their future status in a reunited country. Where the state is prepared to bargain tacitly, giving affirmations and guarantees, the easing of anxieties over reintegration can be anticipated.

In the period before the Addis Ababa agreement of 1972, President Nimeiry, seeking a political solution to the conflict, made several gestures intended to promote southern confidence. He replaced Joseph Garang as minister of state for southern affairs with Abel Alier, a moderate spokesman intent upon protecting southern rights. He also announced plans to broaden the amnesty for southern opposition elements. And, most important, he proposed that the South be given a degree of subregional autonomy within a unitary Sudanese state.

Later, at Addis Ababa, the plan for a conflict management system that included subregional autonomy was fleshed out more fully. Not only did the 1972 agreement define the South as a "self-governing region" within a united, socialist Sudan, but it made English the principal language of the Southern Region and established both a High Executive Council and People's Regional Assembly for this subregion. The subregional government was given the authority to raise taxes and was assigned a specific list of administrative responsibilities. During the implementation phase that followed, the Nimeiry administration showed good faith by commissioning Joseph Lagu a major-general in the Sudanese army; integrating 10,000 SSLM troops into the People's Armed Forces, police, and prison forces; and appointing three southerners to the central cabinet in Khartoum. During the initial period, the effect of these measures was to restore the faith of many southerners about their reintegration into Sudan, thus setting up a basis for a partial return to regularized rules of relations.

At the international level, Emperor Haile Selassie, while acting as arbitrator in the Sudanese peace negotiations, offered insurance incentives to the South by giving his personal guarantee against any reprisal or repression of Anya-Nya returnees, should the Addis Ababa agreement result in a merging of the two armies. By combining status with power (that is, an ability to affect the course of the civil war in neighboring Sudan), the emperor was in a strong position to overcome southern fears and therefore to promote credible commitment. In such cases, external guarantors can provide an indispensable incentive for minority group cooperation by holding out the promise of protection in the event that the state backslides on its agreement.

Finally, a sharp contrast between the unofficial and official third-party actors was evident regarding the use of incentives to facilitate the peace process. The WCC-AACC team was effective as a communicator and even as a conciliator, yet it was prudent not to overstep its boundaries, choosing to leave the manipulation of pressures and the use of incentives to the governments themselves and to other international actors. As Adam Curle remarks, unofficial mediators "can exert no pressure, make no threats, offer no promises; and they cannot bargain."[82]

States, however, were not so constrained. Emperor Haile Selassie reached an agreement with Nimeiry to close the Ethiopian line of access to the insurgents in the South, thereby pressuring the SSLM to negotiate with the Sudanese government, and the emperor could also use coercive diplomatic incentives to force the two sides to make concessions regarding the future composition of the army. As head of state, the emperor had substantial political resources at his disposal to threaten the two parties with mutually damaging consequences if they failed to reach a compromise on the issue.

Ironically, as Robert Harrison Wagner theorizes, the negotiated agreement in Sudan proved to be unsteady and insecure, while military victory elsewhere, as, for example, in the Nigerian civil war of 1966–70, has led to the restoration of a relatively stable intrastate conflict management system in the period that followed.[83] Tragically, Sudan's Nimeiry, a key champion of a political solution before the Addis Ababa agreement, took steps soon after the implementation process began that undercut the limited power-sharing system of conflict management he had helped to create. Then, as he became isolated and in need of new coalition partners in his northern base, he initiated several policies in the early 1980s that contravened the spirit and terms of the peace settlement. The South felt betrayed, and guerrilla actions mounted rapidly. Nimeiry's sabotage of the agreement polarized the society, undermining the fragile norms of relations that had been slowly developing within the elite.

That the conflict cycle has gone full circle clearly has grave ramifications for contemporary Sudan. In the period that followed the collapse of the Addis Ababa agreement, cynicism and distrust came to prevail, creating a kind of "negotiating fatigue" that inhibited subsequent public and private efforts to mediate the conflict. With the mounting costs of hegemonic rule and the renewed civil war, Sudan's leaders may find it extremely difficult to build support for conciliatory moves within their heterogeneous constituencies. If simple reciprocative acts are no longer sufficient to move the negotiating process along under the prevailing circumstances, then something more may be necessary to break Sudan out of its current stalemate, such as sanctions on military equipment, partition, or a strategy of graduated and reciprocated initiatives in tension reduction (GRIT) involving a series of conciliatory moves by one of the antagonists (preferably the state, as the stronger actor) or a third-party intervener. Clearly, the costs of inaction by a weak state may in time compel a reconsideration of current policy preferences.

9

Mediators' Uses of
Pressures and Incentives

Internal conflicts almost always have implications for
regional stability.... Policy options do exist, and these
options...have not been optimally utilized.

MICHAEL E. BROWN

Not all ethnic situations are inherently dangerous. So long as mutual fears remain low, there is little risk that normal competition will degenerate into deep enmity and possible violence. Conflicts among ethnic groups and between the state and ethnic actors first become a problem when political elites, determined to maintain or increase their power, seek to manipulate latent identity group consciousness to advance their own interests and the perceived interests of their group. Their ability to manipulate the political symbols of identity politics does not take place in a vacuum. It is facilitated by the consciousness that communal peoples have of their affinities to others, regardless of whether these identities are recent or have a long history and whether collective memories of exploitation and persecution are accurate or not. The desire for inclusion becomes a matter of overriding importance, providing group members with the security and sense of purpose they need to live in a world of strangers. At times, this urge for inclusion may become so strong that many members will willingly subordinate their material interests, safety, and moral values for the well-being of the collectivity.[1]

I must stress that state and ethnic elites have often responded to their political environment by competing with each other according to well-understood rules. When they abide by the rules of the political game, they adopt ethnic strategies that make politics more manageable both for themselves and for their clients. To enhance the opportunities for such collaboration, these political elites have used a variety of structural incentives to keep conflicts at manageable levels, such as polyarchy, inclusive coalitions, proportional allocations, balanced recruitment, guarantees of autonomy, and electoral mechanisms to ensure representativeness.

South Africa's 1993 interim constitution applied a package of proportional representation, subregional autonomy, electoral, and power-sharing incentives that went far toward assuring racial and ethnic minorities that they did not need to act violently to secure their future. The result was constructive; it encouraged moderation and discouraged deviant behavior among these minorities.[2] When a political entrepreneur goes against the structure of these agreed-upon incentive systems, however, such an action can involve what David Baldwin calls an "opportunity cost": denying a desired distribution of gains in an effort to avoid a worse alternative.[3] As such confidence-building mechanisms become accepted, a transition may take place from isolated acts of reciprocity to what Adam Przeworski describes as a "self-enforcing" regime where "all the relevant political forces find it best to continue to submit their interests and values to the uncertain interplay of the institutions."[4] In such a polyarchical context, reciprocity becomes "diffuse" (communitywide), and stable and persistent patterns of bargaining among groups can develop over time.[5]

More menacingly, as ethnic leaders pursue their separate interests by "playing the ethnic card" among peoples who are conscious of their ethnic identity, they can entrap their constituents (and themselves) in a deadly encounter from which there may be no escape. Fearful of collective insecurity unless the group hangs together and takes precautionary measures, the ethnic group acts aggressively toward its neighbor. Thus, even though the antagonists and the society at large would benefit from mutual cooperation, the defection of leaders from such action (with support from their group members) can preclude joint problem solving. The strategy of defection may well be effective for mobilizing the elite's ethnic following, but in the event of a stalemate, it occurs at great cost to the society at large.

In worst-case situations, when leaders and their constituents perceive their political and strategic goals to be incompatible with those of their adversary and they become entrapped in a situation of ungovernability, conflict can escalate to a dangerous level. The appraisal of rival groups inevitably involves a historical and cultural appraisal or stereotyping, but it becomes part of the calculus that one actor makes about another's threatening or nonthreatening intentions. The logical outcome of such intense confrontations may be state collapse, where state and ethno-regional elites are caught up in the escalating conflict and lose the capacity for effective communitywide governance. Each side (assuming the actors are unified) may be loath to compromise, fearing that their opponents will perceive their concessions as a sign of weakness. People on both sides come to believe that neither party can prevail in the conflict, and thus they recognize the existence of a mutually hurting stalemate. In best-case circumstances, such a stalemate can provide the incentive to change preferences toward ones that are mutually beneficial to both parties.

Leaders in such a situation have an incentive to pull back from the threat of extended conflict and negotiate with their rivals. This becomes the basis for a possible political settlement (as I have examined in the chapters on Sudan, Zimbabwe, South Africa, and, in certain periods, Angola).[6] In these instances, the African state could reform its intrastate conflict management system and recognize that the major actors are better off with an agreement to cooperate than with no agreement at all.

Because state and ethnic leaders may pursue their interests to the logical end, however, irrespective of the consequences for their constituents and the society at large, the mutually hurting stalemate may become endurable. In such a situation, a political spoiler, such as Jonas Savimbi during the breakdown of the Bicesse accords (see chapter 5), may perceive the breaking of connections to be preferable to either political accommodation or the implementation of the contract. Ethnic entrepreneurs' fear that their opponents will take advantage of any cooperative moves by cheating creates incentives to sever connections and to use force preemptively. The political entrepreneurs' desire to increase group security, combined with a lack of reliable information about their adversaries' intentions and an inability to make a reliable commitment, produces an environment of distrust. In some cases this fuels an arms race and makes a preemptive strike preferable to a wait-and-see policy. When this worst-case scenario materializes, efforts to promote the security of any one actor will leave all actors with a heightened sense of insecurity (hence the existence of a "security dilemma").[7]

With suspicions of treachery rising on all sides, all actors feel increasingly insecure and retreat into their subethnic, ethnic, or national containers, and the trap ensnaring them all is sprung (examples include post-Bicesse Angola and Sudan after 1982). Until a restructuring of regimes takes place, ordinary people can find security only within the narrower confines of a ministate, and this protection exposes them to retaliation from members of competing groups or within-group factions. In these circumstances, key tasks for third parties are to communicate between the adversaries, enforce salvageable contracts, and assist in the development of effective conflict management systems. Such efforts may help to reduce the potential for misunderstanding and increase the likelihood of credible commitment.

Mediation

In essence, conflict management involves avoiding a collapse in the norms of encounter and encouraging actors to shift their preferences (their rank ordering of outcomes) before a stalemate, thus enabling them to engage in cooperative activities. "The object of our policy," Harvard negotiation specialist Roger Fisher contends, "is to cause someone else to make a decision. To do so we must alter the decision or the consequences of making it and of not making it so that they will now see the total choice in a favorable light."[8] This can be accomplished partly by carefully structuring state-societal relations to raise the costs of breaking the agreed-upon rules of encounter. Here, internal structural incentives, created and maintained most effectively by a strong and responsive state, can have a critical role in confidence building. Such incentives encourage the parties to reevaluate their actions *before* undercutting the reciprocities and negotiating processes that provide for a civil society.[9]

Ideally, it is the polyarchical African state that can be most effective in maintaining regular relations among ethnic groups and between itself and these groups. As long as the state remains responsive to the legitimate demands of various interests (such as in South Africa following the 1994 transition to nonracial majoritarian rule), an authoritative state actor, if it exists, can play a positive role by mediating between rival internal parties, provided, of course, that the state is not captured by one of the competing ethnic-based interests.[10] A strong, responsive state can afford to facilitate the coalition of moderate elements, because, as Daniel Brumberg writes, such a state is in a favorable position to forge "implicit pacts between reformists in the state."[11]

Unfortunately, this ideal situation has rarely prevailed in Africa or elsewhere. Many African states are soft and lack the capacity to regulate the actions of societal leaders and groups. They are unable to ensure that the legitimate demands of group leaders are channeled along predetermined lines. As a consequence, many states cannot coordinate rival ethnic interests using structurally determined incentives. Moreover, for every Nelson Mandela, there are scores of leaders who have failed to display a sufficient understanding of minority feelings of uncertainty. Clearly, if regularized rules of relations are to survive in divided societies, leaders must emphasize the notion of fairness toward major interests. In this respect, democracy should be interpreted quite broadly, embracing the measures and principles of governance that inspire confidence among political minorities. Prominent among such confidence-building (or trust-inducing) measures, as noted in chapter 2, are provisions for power sharing, decentralization, cultural autonomy, respect for traditional authorities, proportional subregional allocations, balanced civil service and military recruitment, competitive election systems, and demilitarization. Unless state and societal interests can deal effectively with these issues, serious conflict will probably emerge over time.

Internal structural incentives may be necessary but are not always sufficient to deal with the difficult organizational tasks at hand. Tensions can mount when the state acts repressively, social connections deteriorate, or ambitious elites play the ethnic card. In such a deteriorating context, external third-party interveners may attempt to help the antagonistic groups extricate themselves from an impending security dilemma by clarifying potential misperceptions, employing incentives to change actor preferences, and providing guarantees against aggressive group behavior. During the cold war, the superpowers acted as ethnic buffers, influencing their allies to limit ethnic conflicts.

As the post–cold war world became an accepted reality, it opened up new possibilities for ethnic violence. Francis Deng notes: "Although the end of the Cold War has removed this aggravating external factor [of superpower intervention], it has also removed the moderating role of the superpowers, both as third parties and as mutually neutralizing allies."[12] Given the destruction of life and property that followed in such countries as Liberia and Somalia, the international community had little alternative but to become directly involved in the management of Africa's internal conflicts.[13] In internal wars, where intrastate systems of conflict management have broken down and conflicts have become intense, some form of international third-party conciliation or mediation may prove to be a determining option. The presence of a third party can make it possible for the antagonists to engage in reciprocal interchanges under the aegis of an intermediary, who sometimes is in a position to reassure the parties that their adversary will not renege on commitments, especially during the difficult implementation process. In this situation, the actors are more inclined to internalize the prohibitions against destructive behavior, thus reducing the temptation to defect. Moreover, by reframing the issues in contention and making use of a package of external pressures and incentives, the third-party actor may be able to alter the distribution of gains and encourage rival internal disputants to accept lower-order preferences, thereby reducing the incompatibilities dividing them.

The question is, What can realistically be expected of third-party initiatives under current circumstances? International mediation is, at best, a difficult undertaking. In cases of state-ethnic or intercommunal negotiations, the process of conflict management is further complicated by the issue of state jurisdiction over its own internal affairs. African leaders have long been determined to deny any form of international legitimacy to their ethnic rivals; only recently have they come to consider any limits on their sovereign jurisdiction.[14] In light of this resistance, it is not surprising that the majority of the civil wars in this century have ended by means of military victory and capitulation and not by mediation (see chapter 1).

The circumstances within which mediators must operate are clearly critical in determining their success or failure. Mediatory skill and leverage are both viewed as important to a negotiated end to a conflict, although this study has placed a greater emphasis upon the context in which a mediator operates and the resources that third-party actors can use to influence the behavior of the parties, as I set out in the first proposition of chapter 1. U.S. Assistant Secretary of State Chester A. Crocker's skill and resolve were significant factors in the international negotiations in Angola, but more critical were such situational factors as a mutually hurting stalemate, the change in great-power perceptions that followed the advent of the Soviet Union's new political thinking, and the pressures and incentives that the great powers brought to bear.

Political and military leverage reflect not only the capacity of the third-party intervener to influence outcomes, but also the intensity of the conflict. Thus, President A. Milton Obote of Uganda was able to bring the Rwenzururu negotiations to a close on his own, because the issues at stake were not deeply divisive and the involvement of side payments proved to be sufficient (see chapter 4). In Angola, however, external leverage needed to be quite extensive, because the parties made non-negotiable demands and, for a long time, shunned compromise and credible commitment (see chapter 5).

The purpose of mediation is to help the parties reach an agreement and create a new conflict management system or bring about a return to an effective one. To this end, mediators must use the resources at their disposal (moral stature, ability to communicate, and above all, pressures and incentives) to speed up the process of "ripening." As practicing diplomat Chester Crocker attests, "the peacemaker needs power and leverage to be effective."[15] A return to regularized rules of relations can happen after capitulation, as in Nigeria following the Biafran war, but this was a unique event, partly attributable to the magnanimity shown by the victors. In most cases, however, the return to routinized relations will not happen on its own. Third-party initiatives, unofficial or official, will most likely be essential to facilitate the making and, in some cases, enforcing of the contracts during the implementation stage.

Depending upon the context, this can also involve efforts to overcome information failures, enabling the adversaries to gain reliable intelligence about their rival's intentions (whether totalist or pragmatic) and possibly (if pragmatic) to be able to make credible commitments.[16] The third-party actor can then try to narrow the differences and, when either a strong state or international organization is involved, push the process ahead through a combination of pressures, incentives, enforcement, and guarantees. As my various case studies have indicated, private mediators often enjoy certain advantages in communicating between the adversaries under difficult circumstances. When "muscle" becomes essential to surmount an impasse or to enforce the terms of a bargain, however, state and interstate initiative can be indispensable, primarily because only states have the necessary leverage to induce the parties to accept new alternatives.

The External Mediator's Capacity to Manipulate

In the cases discussed in this volume, one key variable for facilitating an externally guided agreement appears to be the status and power of the third-party actor. The range of possible mediators (or coalitions of mediators) and their capacity to change the peace process through combinations of coercive and noncoercive incentives is striking (see chapter 1). When a decolonizing state is prepared to mediate between internal parties (as Britain was in Ghana, Kenya, and Zimbabwe), or when the great powers change their preferences and perceptions and cooperate to press the disputants to reach a compromise (as in the Angola-Namibia accords of 1988), the prospects for successful conflict management are enhanced.[17]

Provided that a great power such as the United States remains committed to managing the conflict (and this cannot be assumed), it usually pays a proportionately smaller cost to put a sanction into effect than would a regional or smaller power. When medium and smaller powers— lacking the political and economic resources to orchestrate the process leading up to a settlement—undertook the task of mediation, weak, ineffective leadership did complicate a change of preferences on cooperation (for example, President Mobutu Sese Seko's abortive Gbadolite effort to act as a go-between in the Angolan negotiations). Middle-range powers and regional and international organizations can play an important mediatory role and may, in some cases, have an incentive to bear the greater costs of sanctions. In many cases, however, they will be reluctant to incur such costs, thus making their participation in a coalition with a great power or powers opportune at this period in history.

The mediation process at the time of Africa's decolonization was unique because of the enormous influence that external actors could bring to bear on the various internal parties.[18] One key participant in the Lancaster House negotiations on Zimbabwe stated that the British-led effort was more like arbitration (with its firm third-party control over the negotiations) than mediation. In this instance, the colonial third-party actor, Great Britain, determined to extricate itself once and for all from its difficult entanglement in Zimbabwe's internal affairs, was able to bring "real leverage" to bear on the disputant parties, partly as a consequence of Commonwealth and frontline state backing (see chapter 6).[19] The official mediator was well placed to lead the disputant parties toward a settlement. British Foreign Secretary Lord Carrington, determined to maintain control over the process at Lancaster House, effectively used his central position at the meetings to control the agenda, determine the seating arrangements, cajole and threaten the delegations regarding critical points of contention, impose deadlines, solicit outside diplomatic support to pressure the negotiating parties, offer financial incentives, and dispatch a governor and a monitoring force.[20]

The process of arriving at a decolonization bargain has not always proceeded smoothly, however. Two of the worst-case scenarios took place in Algeria and Angola, where contested legitimacies and threatening intergroup perceptions led to some of the most destructive confrontations in modern Africa. In Algeria, a long and brutal colonial war finally ended with France's negotiation of a cease-fire, a transition to independence at Evian in March 1962, and the exodus of many of the *pieds noirs* (French settlers) from the country. As Alistair Horne commented, regarding the fate of the Evian agreements, most of the provisions remained "a dead letter, overtaken by events for one reason or another."[21]

Unlike the Evian agreements, the 1975 Alvor accord—negotiated at the time of decolonization by the representatives of Portugal, the Popular Movement for the Liberation of Angola (MPLA), the National Union for the Total Independence of Angola (UNITA), and the National Front for the Liberation of Angola (which disappeared as a major force in the 1980s)—preceded the heavy fighting in Angola. The Alvor accord provided for an interim coalition government and elections, provisos that were canceled out by later events.

From independence in November 1975 to the signing of the Angola-Namibia agreements of December 1988, the civil war among Angola's nationalist movements was exacerbated by the ties that these nationalist groups maintained with various external powers (see chapter 5). By January 1991 there were reports of significant progress on a peace plan, including an agreement in principle on such issues as the cease-fire, the timing of multiparty elections, and the stationing of armed forces during these elections. With strong backing from the major powers, the Portuguese mediators gained leverage and were able to overcome the remaining differences over the recognition of UNITA's legitimacy and the process of military integration. Although the resulting Bicesse accords were undercut by Jonas Savimbi's defection following the first round of the 1992 elections, the combined strength of a capable UN mediator and a supporting cast of state go-betweens brought about an end to the renewed civil war. The shaky Lusaka protocol of 1994 reaffirmed the Bicesse accords but modified them by including insurance incentives for Savimbi's UNITA on the decentralization of provincial police responsibilities and power sharing at both the political center and the subregions.

The same coalitional dynamics were also evident in Mozambique, where several medium and smaller powers, with encouragement from the United States, interceded in the conflict between the Frente de Libertaçao de Moçambique (Frelimo) government and the Mozambique

National Resistance (Renamo) insurgency. In August 1989 a formal effort to mediate the civil war took place in Nairobi, with Presidents Daniel arap Moi of Kenya and Robert Mugabe of Zimbabwe serving as the cochairs of the meetings. However, the Nairobi talks soon lost their impetus. Renamo demanded recognition as a precondition for participating in the negotiations; Frelimo sought the government's recognition as the valid ruling authority in the country.[22] The gap between adversaries remained wide, and the mediators (allied as they were with one of the local rivals) lost the confidence of the opposing party.

In such circumstances, a new third-party intermediary that would be acceptable to both sides became essential. The Kenyans and Zimbabweans remained active diplomatic players, but by late 1990 they gave over the reins to Roman Catholic emissaries (the archbishop of Beira and members of the Catholic lay organization Sant' Egidio), acting jointly with representatives of the Italian Foreign Ministry. The private and public third-party actors made an effective team, because the Italian government had friendly relations with the Mozambican government and Archbishop Gonçalves had long maintained close contacts with Renamo leader Afonso Dhlakama. U.S. support for the peace process, particularly in the areas of technical and military advice, was critical.[23]

The rounds of negotiations that took place in Rome in the ensuing period resulted in some important accomplishments: an October 1992 agreement setting forth a complicated arrangement for a cease-fire, the withdrawal of Zimbabwean and Malawian troops from the country, the restriction of government and Renamo forces to specified assembly points, the demobilization of certain units and the inclusion of the remainder in an integrated army, the holding of multiparty elections in late 1993 (later extended to the fall of 1994), and the creation of an International Joint Verification Commission to monitor the cease-fire arrangement. The Italian government played an important role at this stage: by offering financial incentives, Italy was able to overcome Renamo's hesitations about signing the cease-fire agreement.[24]

The United Nations Operation in Mozambique (ONUMOZ) sent a significant observer force to the area and generously funded the transition process (learning from the implementation failure in Angola after the collapse of the 1992 presidential election process); however, it proved difficult to implement the timetables on demobilization, disarmament, and the unification of armies. Renamo negotiators sometimes failed to turn up for meetings, and their forces reportedly violated the Rome accord occasionally by cutting the railway lines alongside the two corridors.[25] Implementation of the peace accord required continuing pressures and incentives by UN Special Representative Aldo Ajello in coalition with an ambassadorial-level standing committee of third-party states, particularly because Renamo—composed of disparate and somewhat autonomous elements—was difficult to unite behind its leader for bargaining purposes. In deep conflict situations such as that in Mozambique, cooperation among antagonistic interests clearly requires determined mediatory leadership and the use of packages of positive and negative incentives to influence the preferences of the parties. Mediation by a strong state actor can contribute to an effective third-party effort, provided that it combines a determination to bring the conflict to a successful close with a willingness to shoulder the costs of intervention.

The role of ONUMOZ in Mozambique points to the central dilemma of mediation in the 1990s: state go-betweens are increasingly reluctant to assume burdensome responsibilities on their own in areas of the world regarded as peripheral to their main interests. At the same time, initiatives by international organizations, such as the UN, the Organization of African Unity, or, at the regional level, the Economic Community of West African States (ECOWAS) Ceasefire Monitoring Group and the Intergovernmental Authority on Development, are necessary to fill the void but in many instances are insufficient. International organizations, as assemblages of states, have an interest in the peaceful settlement of conflicts; however, their interests tend to reflect those of the great powers, who provide much of the financial and logistical support for UN-coordinated actions. Many resent the dominance of the great powers, however, which undercuts organizational unity of purpose. Despite this heavy dependence on great-power support, UN officials have acted as third-party facilitators in several African internal conflicts, but, with the possible exceptions of South Africa, Angola, Namibia, and Mozambique, the UN's record has been disappointing.

The UN possesses some important symbolic and political resources of its own, most notably its ability to legitimate parties and outcomes and to threaten or use sanctions and military force. In general, it seems reasonable to conclude that the UN's inherent fiscal and military weaknesses limit its ability to play the role of a strong mediator.[26] Given its political legitimacy, however, it can exercise "soft power."[27] It can recognize actors, sponsor sanctions, give entry to financial institutions, and authorize the dispatch of peacekeeping units, but its lack of access to adequate and predictable sources of revenue and its inability to raise a military force of its own severely hamper its ability to maintain the peace.

Because of the UN's organizational and resource problems, it lacks leverage and cannot provide effective packages of positive or negative incentives to alter the preferences of leaders engaged in civil war. "These U.N. weaknesses are perceived by disputants," notes Saadia Touval. "Parties are likely to doubt that U.N. promises of assistance or threats of punishment will actually be fulfilled."[28] The UN can play a critically important role in the implementation of peace agreements, but its efforts are hampered by its uncertain ability to gain a consensus among its state members to act decisively to prevent the outbreak of violence or hasten the process of ripening. In the case of UN military action in the Congo in the early 1960s, UN legitimacy, combined with the resources of a great power, proved to be a potent force for changing the preferences of key actors on the ground. Such forceful actions, however, can overextend the UN's organizational capacity and thereby weaken and undermine a political body that is critically important for other purposes, such as taking significant symbolic actions, keeping the peace, and implementing agreements.

The Structure of Incentives

When both parties to a conflict can see some advantage to be gained from a conciliatory approach, there may be room for a mediator to manipulate the situation to facilitate a settlement. Through changes in the distribution of gains, the mediator can seek to use combinations of carrots and sticks to influence the adversaries' assessments of their interests.[29] The third-party actor may transmit information or help to bring about a change in the ranking of preferences, thus possibly causing the rivals to reevaluate their interests and, with that, their behavior at the negotiating table.

Mediators hope that the cumulative effect of a package of positive and negative inducements will lead at least one of the parties to accept their second preference and, therefore, to bring about some degree of mutual cooperation. "To overcome problems of organizing collective action," Jack Snyder remarks, "successful cooperation requires a push from some powerful provider of incentives to cooperate, and the creation of institutions that coordinate the participants' expectations and actions." But, he notes, once these institutions are in place, a cooperative regime and its institutions may create habits and constituencies that make them self-perpetuating.[30] In other words, pressures and incentives assist the negotiating process by creating a context in which new institutions and choices can shape the distribution of actor preferences.

Where profound ethnic insecurities exist, how much scope does a strong mediator have to manipulate incentives? To what extent do such inducements enable the mediator to offer benefits for cooperation and to raise the costs of defection significantly? Which of these incentives have contributed most to a mediator's leverage? When one of the parties concludes that military victory or capitulation is possible, as in the Nigerian civil war, this party certainly has only a limited incentive to negotiate a compromise; thus an external mediator can have only marginal influence. The use of mediator pressures and incentives becomes critical when a relative equality of military power exists, making third-party intervention potentially promising.[31]

One can anticipate that third parties will prefer noncoercive incentives in light of their low cost, expected impact, and ability to promote friendly responses from the rival actors.[32] Hence it makes sense for mediators to apply incentives sequentially, moving from noncoercive to coercive ones. Certainly, in their effect on the distribution of preferences the lines between these incentives are blurred; in practice, the threshold between making rewards contingent and threatening deprivation is very unclear. In many cases, the most effective means of encouraging adversaries to alter preferences is to apply combinations of incentives.[33] In South Africa, for example, both carrots and sticks were necessary to induce the apartheid regime to alter its policies, with sanctions alerting the white-led regime to the likelihood of future carrots and sticks unless it shifted preferences toward greater comity. Then, as the change to majority rule approached, the likelihood of gaining acceptance for the interim 1993 constitution was increased when the negotiators agreed to include a package of provisions for power sharing, quasi-federalism, market mechanisms, civil service guarantees, proportional representation, and a bill of rights. The particular mix of incentives must be appropriate to each situation, taking into account such factors as regime patterns, political memories, respect for the legitimacy of identity group cultures, strategic interactions, and the intensity of social conflict. In chapter 4, I examined the effectiveness of six types of incentives on a disaggregated basis; I nonetheless recognize that, in practice, a statesperson-mediator will want to combine these for maximum effect.

When assessing the appropriateness of specific incentives for altering the preferences and behavior of rival actors, I will examine the applicability of the various types of incentives for such factors as ease of application, impact on institutions, and the ability to promote a friendly response toward the mediator. Other situational variables, including the intensity of the conflict, the depth of distrust and uncertainty, and the negotiability of demands, will also be taken into account. The main consideration here is what is needed to accomplish the task (to alter preferences and induce compromise) and at what cost. As Arild Underdal writes regarding the notion of cost, "Failure or inefficiency can be measured as the extent to which a given negotiation process incurs higher transactions costs than necessary to accomplish whatever it accomplishes."[34] In the final analysis, incentives are likely to prove useful only where the parties are receptive. Purchase incentives made a difference in Mozambique, but would not have in South Africa. And no amount of incentives are likely to budge China from Tibet or India from Kashmir.

Coercive and Noncoercive Incentives

I should distinguish between coercive and noncoercive incentives at the outset, in terms of their ability to encourage the disputants to shift their preferences and thereby to promote agreement among them. When I analyze the consequences of using these incentives, the effects on the parties to the conflict and the third-party actor will be taken into account. All of the parties have interests: they can all reap benefits from a settlement, but if the negotiations collapse, all parties will suffer a variety of negative effects, including loss of status and prestige.

Both coercive and noncoercive incentives seek to alter behavior in a cooperative direction, but they differ in their costs of application and their anticipated effect upon recalcitrant local actors. Noncoercive incentives extend benefits or rewards for compliance by a targeted actor, whereas coercive incentives punish or threaten to punish such an actor to bring it into line with preferred types of political behavior. The first set of incentives is obviously easier to apply and may well elicit a positive response to the third-party intervener from the target state or movement.

In all cases, the promised rewards and threatened punishments must be credible ones. Mediators cannot expect incentives to alter actor preferences unless they are backed up by considerable political and material resources. When offering material rewards or security guarantees— particularly with respect to legitimacy incentives—a mediator (or coalition of mediators) must be able to make a credible commitment. Similarly, threats of force must be viewed as credible. Unless the target country or insurgent movement believes that noncompliant behavior will result in predictable consequences, that actor may resist responding in a conciliatory manner.[35]

The ease of applying noncoercive incentives also has implications for their sequencing. Because economic, security, and legitimacy incentives tend to exhibit less conflictive structures for distributing gains than do coercive incentives, it is logical for third-party actors to start by using these reward systems. They can then turn to more costly punishments when rewards prove ineffective and a higher structure of benefits is required (see table 9-1).[36] Even the strongest mediator will be reluctant to become militarily embroiled in a costly conflict between state and insurgent groups, not only because of the fiscal expenditures involved but also because of anticipated hostilities from identifying with one side or the other.

Noncoercive Incentives

Noncoercive incentives seek to change the behavior of target groups by using a variety of rewards to make cooperation a preferred course of action. As anticipated, the cases examined in this volume point to a predilection on the part of mediators to turn initially to noncoercive incentives, using high-profile coercive incentives only when no other appropriate course of action is available.

PURCHASE. Purchase incentives reward groups and individuals with tangible resources for acting cooperatively on peace initiatives. By extending additional resources to a party or parties, the intermediary attempts "to transform a constant-sum dispute (characterized by outcomes that are acceptable to one party at the exclusion of the other) into a nonconstant-sum exchange (in which mutually acceptable outcomes are possible.)"[37] In the African cases, purchase incentives were evident in several of the negotiation efforts. As shown in chapter 4, in the internal negotiations between the Ugandan government and the Rwenzururu movement, a package of material side payments and administrative appointments proved sufficient to conciliate the insurgent leaders and to end their demands for secession. Financial incentives also were among those involved in the transfer of land to the KwaZulu government just before the 1994 election in South Africa and were important for gaining Renamo's agreement to a cease-fire in Mozambique; foreign donors reportedly committed $19 million to transform Renamo from a guerrilla organization into a political party.[38]

TABLE 9-1. *External Mediator Types and Incentive Strategies in Selected African Conflicts*[a]

Incentive strategy	Unofficial	Colonial official	Mediator type			
			Third-party official			
			Super-power	Medium power	International organization	State
Noncoercive						
Purchase			Rhodesia, 1976 (–)	Mozam-bique, 1992 (+)		Rwenzu-ruru, 1982 (+)
Insurance	Biafra (–)	Ghana (+)		Sudan, 1972 (+)	Angola, 1994 (+)	
	South Africa, 1994 (+)					
Legitimation			Namibia, 1981 (–)	Angola, 1994 (+)		
Coercive						
Pressures			Rhodesia, 1977 (–) Angola, 1988 (+)	Rhodesia, 1979 (+) Uganda, 1985 (–)		
Sanctions			South Africa 1986 (+) Rhodesia, 1965 (+)		Liberia, 1992 (–) Burundi, 1996 (–)	
Force					Congo, 1962 (+) Liberia, 1993 (–) Somalia, 1993 (–)	

a. A plus indicates success; a minus indicates failure.

As shown in table 9-1, aspects of purchase also figured significantly in the land issue in the independence negotiations in Rhodesia/ Zimbabwe. When I questioned several participants in the negotiations regarding the significance of these payoffs for facilitating the Zimbabwe agreement, their assessments of the importance of these inducements differed considerably. British negotiator Robin Renwick described the Anglo-American financial incentives on land resettlement as "reassuring" and "psychologically helpful," but not really critical, whereas A. M. Chambati, who was an active and influential participant in the negotiation process, characterized these incentives as "very important." In Chambati's view, the conference could have broken down over this issue, and the external offer on the land question "led to movement" at the Lancaster House conference.[39]

These purchase incentives proved to be critical in moving seemingly intractable conflicts toward peaceful outcomes. Because these distributions of gains concentrate on divisible issues, they are easy to apply and relatively low in political cost.[40] By making use of these tangible side payments, a mediator gains some leverage over the parties, provided, of course, that securing tangible resources continues to remain important to them.

In the cases I have mentioned, purchase was clearly a factor in overcoming resistance to a settlement. Nevertheless, side payments do have their problems: First, in most cases, a third party is unlikely to extend side payments indefinitely. A mediator cannot be expected to reward a claimant over a long period, so new conflicts can arise between the mediator and a disappointed recipient of side payments. Second, purchase incentives, with their heavy emphasis upon tangible rewards, do little to create trust and confidence.[41] Other values, including community, security, loyalty, status, and prestige, are also critical in an intense state-ethnic encounter, and these are difficult to deal with by means of purchase incentives.[42] And third, supplying or denying resources is not necessarily adequate for managing conflict. The lack of resources in Sudan has not, in itself, led to a winding down of this conflict, and the extension of resources to Angola has actually *increased* the level of violence. Purchase incentives have contributed to a settlement in some instances, yet in others a third party must do considerably more than advance tangible resources to a resistant party.

INSURANCE. Those using insurance incentives seek to structure political relations so that politics will seem less threatening to one or more parties. They seek to enhance group security to build confidence in future intergroup relationships. Unlike purchase incentives, insurance incentives involve both nonmaterial and material goods. In dealing with such indivisible and inexchangeable issues as group security and status, honor, face, self-esteem, and identity, mediators must make an extended effort to come to grips with these emotional and psychological aspects of politics to address the full gamut of issues in contention.

Because it is impossible to split the difference on these questions, the mediator can either resort to intangible or symbolic rewards or use structural incentives that anticipate group anxieties before the outbreak of mass violence. Alternatively, the mediator must manage the security dilemma after collective violence has occurred and group perceptions have hardened, using such means as security guarantees, mutual vetoes, power sharing, the *regroupement* of ethnic populations, partition, and separate sovereignties.[43]

In the period before mass violence, one can reasonably expect incentives relating to either gaining power (elections) or sharing power (inclusive coalitions) within a state to be most critical when coping with political minorities' fears of being excluded from decisionmaking.[44] Thus Nigeria's 1993 constitution and subsequent laws contained a package of incentives intended to allay the fears of minorities regarding the possibility of their exclusion from the halls of state power. These incentives included provisions for two-party elections, party zoning, the requirement of a broad national majority to elect a president, federalism, and balanced recruitment to fill high government positions.

In coping with the next level of group anxieties, insurance incentives can also make use of several other mechanisms to depoliticize conflict, including official or unofficial arrangements providing for governments of national unity, proportional representation, guidelines to ensure fairness in subregional allocations, decentralization, bills of rights, and protection for the judiciary. During the transition period in South Africa, various "sunset clauses" also guaranteed the continued employment of civil servants and provided amnesty for military and other security personnel. Such measures seek to overcome mutual fears and suspicions by using disincentives to discourage abusive behavior. These protections of group interests may trigger a backlash, however, where the majority expresses resentment at efforts to block genuine change.

In the postindependence period, many of these structural incentives have helped to make internal conflicts more manageable. As I have shown in chapter 6, on negotiating decolonization in Zimbabwe, and in a book on racial bargaining in Kenya, assurances that a transition would include fair elections, political participation, and constitutional protections (particularly on land transfers and political representation) were important to both racial and ethnic minorities.[45] In South Africa, as I analyzed in chapter 7, the mediation effort orchestrated by Kenya's W. A. Okumu during the final days before the 1994 elections successfully prevailed upon the Inkatha Freedom party leader, Chief Mangosuthu

Buthelezi, to accept insurance incentives regarding the Zulu king's future status. African National Congress negotiators made these concessions to encourage Buthelezi to agree to the new constitutional protections and to participate in the elections. Provisions in the interim constitution for power sharing, proportional representation, and a decentralized administrative system (although not specifically designed along ethnic lines) also provided security incentives for South Africa's minorities.[46] It is certainly not surprising, as table 9-1 shows, to find insurance centrally important in an ethnic-related conflict, for group insecurity is often the critical factor in mobilizing ethnic supporters behind their leaders.

When insurance incentives fail to allay the security fears of political minorities within the state and when violence threatens or has actually occurred, international third-party intervention may become essential for restoring regularized state-society relationships. At this point, diplomatic incentives can play a role in reassuring beleaguered political minorities about their security. Thus, in response to the demands of the Ashanti-based National Liberation Movement for minority safeguards in Ghana in 1954–57, the British government gained concessions from the Nkrumah government regarding the political autonomy of the subregions, constitutional restrictions on an energetic executive branch, and entrenched clauses on the amendment of the basic law. These concessions eased Ashanti fears temporarily, thus enabling the British to maintain the momentum leading to the transfer of power. The 1972 Addis Ababa agreement's emphasis on the political autonomy of the Southern Region of Sudan is another example of diplomatic efforts to reassure minorities about their security concerns.

Deep-seated security fears of the Federal Military Government (FMG) and northern domination contributed substantially to the Biafran decision to attempt to secede from Nigeria in 1967. To seek to meet these anxieties, federal officials assured the Biafrans that, once they renounced secession, the FMG would be willing to leave security in the Igbo heartland in the hands of a totally Igbo police force under the control of an Igbo commissioner of police.[47] And in Zimbabwe, Commonwealth observers and military monitors lent an air of impartiality during the period leading up to the country's general elections, as did the UN election monitoring groups in South Africa, Namibia, Angola, and Mozambique in the years that followed. In other cases, such as Rwanda and Burundi, where widespread terror and mass killing have created a security dilemma among demographically intermingled peoples, it may be extremely difficult for external interveners to induce people to restore the political connections of the past. Hence ethnic war freezes loyalties and perceptions and leads diplomats and scholars (reluctantly) to offer such extreme alternatives as population transfers, de facto autonomy, and independent statehood. For example, Chaim Kaufmann concludes:"Once ethnic groups are mobilized for war, the war cannot end until the populations are separated into defensible, mostly homogeneous regions."[48]

In brief, because minority security fears are to be expected in a world of weakening connections and rules of encounter, insurance incentives can be a critically important resource in the hands of mediators intent on promoting a consensus for enduring agreements. This is inevitably an emotionally charged issue, which makes insurance incentives difficult to apply and keep in place. Unless all groups, minorities as well as majorities, will have a secure position in the new order, there is little reason to hope that agreements will survive the first crisis, and the failure of such guarantees can cause poisonous political memories to become embedded, affecting the relations between local antagonists for decades.

LEGITIMATION. International legitimacy is derived from the judgment of other governments and movements regarding the claims made by a particular set of elites about their right to govern; it is a frail but highly consequential resource for insurgent movements (UNITA, Renamo) and governments (South Africa under apartheid). Norman Uphoff contends that granting legitimacy can be likened to extending political credit. "Legitimacy," he writes,"is not so much traded for other resources as it is granted or accorded in keeping with the beliefs people have about what is right and proper, when procedures or outcomes meet normative expectations."[49]

To be effective in making conflict more manageable, a third party must interact continuously with the major parties to a dispute. Such contacts by an external actor have the effect of extending a measure of legitimacy to states or insurgent movements. Established governments court the support of other states, but they also resist any dealings by state or international organizations with insurgents who are viewed as being under their jurisdiction. State elites, jealously guarding their territorial domain, often regard the very act of negotiating directly with an insurgent movement as strengthening their opponents at their own expense in terms of loss of international status and control.

Thus the FMG felt uplifted by U.S. State Department recognition and support.[50] At the same time, the Nigerian government sought to insulate Biafra from contacts with external powers and the OAU and deeply resented countries that extended diplomatic recognition to the Biafran regime. Similarly, in Mozambique, government negotiators reportedly insisted in May 1991 that the peace process not raise doubts about the legitimacy of their regime.[51] It is potentially very costly for third parties to intervene in the relations between state and insurgents by conferring political legitimacy on the latter; the external actors' future contacts with a state elite still in power may be jeopardized in the process.

When a pariah state (apartheid South Africa) or movement (UNITA, Renamo) seeks the endorsement of the international community, then legitimacy can be used either as a powerful incentive or disincentive for cooperation. The inclusion of a pariah may involve great potential international and domestic risks for a third-party actor, precisely because these moves can be interpreted as "appeasing the devil." South Africa's illegal occupation of Namibia created a source of leverage that the Contact Group (representatives of Great Britain, France, West Germany, Canada, and the United States), the United States acting on its own, and the UN could use to induce South Africa to reconsider its domestic and international strategies. Apartheid South Africa, yearning for international acceptance, was tempted to consider Namibia's independence as being in its own larger economic and diplomatic interests. In due course, apartheid itself was abandoned, at least partly because of South Africa's perceived need to end international exclusion.

Similarly in Angola, legitimacy incentives figured in Savimbi's calculus on agreeing to the Lusaka protocol in 1994. By 1994 Savimbi was internationally isolated and his armies were faring poorly; legitimacy incentives then became a means of facilitating his agreement to the protocol. Following appeals by the international mediators (the UN, with U.S. diplomats active in the wings) for help in promoting a settlement, Nelson Mandela did agree to invite Savimbi to visit South Africa, thereby extending a measure of credibility to the largely excluded guerrilla leader. This initiative (along with Savimbi's growing sense of military vulnerability) may have contributed to his decision to negotiate in earnest at Lusaka.

Legitimacy incentives, then, are powerful tools in the hands of a mediator. For the OAU and UN, with their financial difficulties and lack of military capabilities, legitimacy incentives perhaps represent their strongest mechanism; they can affect a target country's behavior by including or excluding certain of its citizens from international contact, something that has proven to be a powerful reward or punishment for those who did or did not deviate from internationally accepted norms. Yet these legitimacy incentives can be potentially costly to a third-party actor if they are perceived to sacrifice the moral high ground for the sake of peace at any price. Such incentives must therefore be employed skillfully and responsibly if they are to advance cooperation without embarrassment to either the granter or the grantee.

Coercive Incentives

In general, mediators are more reluctant to use coercive than noncoercive incentives, because the use of force tends to involve higher political and economic costs and is more difficult to apply. Not only do coercive incentives usually require greater commitment from the external actor, but they can also earn the intermediary lasting enmities. Unlike their noncoercive counterparts, which reward rival parties for acting cooperatively, coercive incentives seek to alter behavior through the use of punishments, thereby imposing heavy costs on recalcitrant actors. Such incentives can involve various threats or the use of limited force. The threat of coercion is important, according to Max Neiman, "not simply because it is one way of trying to influence people's behavior, but also because it provides the basis for inflicting retribution on noncomplying individuals."[52]

Various sticks (including condemnation, diplomatic pressure, delegitimation, sanctions, and peace enforcement) act as instruments in the hands of strong mediators who seek to change actors' preferences to promote cooperative behavior. Such coercive means are appropriate for dealing with intense ethnic conflicts, but their effectiveness often depends upon a greater resoluteness on the part of the implementing powers than can realistically be anticipated. Somalia and Bosnia stand as reminders of the limits on coercive third-party action in such encounters; in both cases, an element of peacekeeper fatigue was apparent when local elites refused to acquiesce and pursue a policy of reconciliation.

At heart, the problem of "coercive ripening" involves marshaling sufficient force to encourage the disputants to alter their perceptions and, as Louis Kriesberg contends, "change the environment of the antagonist so that it will be more likely to yield."[53] Coercive incentives can sometimes contribute to constructive change, as they have in South Africa; in other instances, however, such incentives can prove costly and ineffective, especially when they lead to passive aggressiveness and counter-strikes (for example, Aidid's attacks on UN peacekeeping units in Somalia in 1993–94). Not only do coercive measures have limited effectiveness for inducing adversaries to change their preferences,[54] but also the long-term stability of an agreement based on the threat or actual use of force will probably remain in doubt because of the political memories carried over from this experience and the perception of the new benefits resulting from changed interactional patterns. The initial temptation to overcome a stalemate by threatening or attempting to take decisive military action is strong; however, a cautious and well-informed assessment may at times seem advisable, for coercion can prove costly and may be ineffective in influencing the antagonists to act constructively.

PRESSURES. In recent years, it has become increasingly accepted that states have a right to intervene in the affairs of other states to ensure respect for minimal international norms regarding human rights and to promote the peaceful resolution of conflicts. Sovereignty entails responsibility, and it cannot legitimately be used as a refuge for abusive leaders. In light of these changing norms on international action, states have used various diplomatic means to pressure errant countries to alter their behavior along more constructive lines. Third-party actors have protested violations (in Sudan and Kenya in 1993); closed embassies (Amin's Uganda); shut down military bases (South Africa); imposed a temporary cessation of bilateral aid projects (Uganda; Nigeria in 1994); aligned themselves politically with state or insurgent groups (U.S.-UNITA); recognized the legitimacy of internal parties (Biafra); and provided military equipment to one party in a civil war (USSR-Angolan government; U.S.-Ethiopian government; U.S.-UNITA). Significantly in this regard, the World Bank and International Monetary Fund reportedly conditioned further funds to the government of former president Juvenal Habyarimana in Rwanda on its signing the Arusha peace agreement with the Rwandan Patriotic Front insurgents and beginning the process of implementation.[55] Many of these diplomatic pressures are relatively easy to employ, thus making them attractive for symbolic as well as substantive purposes. To the extent that third parties have a significant ongoing relationship with a target state or insurgency, they will be in a better position to use their leverage constructively.

Certainly, the use of diplomatic leverage by third-party actors has at times had a subtle but perceptible influence on the behavior of targeted elites. However, such threats are often most effectively employed in a veiled, somewhat ambiguous manner if they are used to motivate leaders to change their practices regarding conflict resolution or human rights. The incentive to act emerges as the targeted elite seeks to avoid the perceived costs arising from its resistance to change, and to do so, preferably, without losing face.

One complicated use of diplomatic incentives to bring about a change of preferences occurred during U.S. Secretary of State Henry A. Kissinger's negotiations with Prime Minister Ian Smith regarding the transition to majority rule in Rhodesia. From Kissinger's standpoint, no dominant community was likely to accept a transition from minority to majority rule without an element of coercion. Kissinger therefore acted indirectly to alter the distribution of gains in an effort to bring about a major shift in elite preferences. He had two meetings with South African Prime Minister John Vorster in Europe before confronting Smith in Pretoria in September 1976; Kissinger indicated to Vorster that if he wanted his cooperation he would have to help him with the Rhodesian negotiations. Vorster was intent on gaining political legitimacy from engaging in open talks with the U.S. secretary of state, so he agreed in Europe that he would indicate to Smith his preparedness to terminate railroad traffic from South Africa to Rhodesia unless the Rhodesian leader agreed to Kissinger's terms. Vorster subsequently told Kissinger that he definitely *had* advised Smith of his position on this matter.[56] Such pressures no doubt contributed mightily to Smith's capitulation in Pretoria.

Other uses of diplomatic incentives, albeit less dramatic, were evident in many of Africa's peace negotiations (see table 9-1). In Rhodesia, for example, the Lancaster House incentives offered to the various local parties on the franchise, the integration of military forces, and the land question must be viewed against the backdrop of powerful international pressures from the Mozambicans and others who were pushing Robert Mugabe to accept a negotiated transition. In the deliberations at Lancaster House, Carrington's "principal bargaining lever" was his threat to accept a so-called second-class solution (that is, a settlement including the moderate African nationalists and possibly Zimbabwe African People's Union leader Joshua Nkomo).[57] Robin Renwick, a key British negotiator at Lancaster House, has said that Britain did actually intend to recognize moderate African nationalist leader Abel Muzorewa if the all-party talks failed to result in an agreement; hence, the threat of a second-class solution was a credible one. There was a need to put pressure on the Patriotic Front in order to reach agreement, he noted, and the second-class solution was useful for fulfilling this requirement.[58] The participants took the threat seriously. Conference participant A. M. Chambati remarked candidly that the threat represented bargaining leverage that provided a major incentive for Mugabe to settle.[59] Taken in conjunction with the pressures mounted by the heads of the frontline states (particularly President Samora Machel of Mozambique), the cumulative effect was to influence Mugabe's ordering of preferences, inducing him to choose a settlement and general elections over a continuance of the guerrilla war and possible destabilization of the region.

Diplomatic incentives also played a significant role in Angola's international negotiations. The linking of Cuban troop withdrawal from Angola with Namibian independence initially gave the South Africans increased room to maneuver; however, by the late 1980s, this linkage tied them to a diplomatic formula that left them little option but to accept the outcome of the 1988 negotiations over Angola and Namibia. Pressures were also brought to bear on the Angolan government during the international negotiations over the Angola-Namibia accords. The United States pointedly delayed processing Angola's application to the International Monetary Fund, possibly intending thereby to give Luanda a "nudge ... toward greater flexibility in the negotiations."[60]

Other examples could be cited, such as U.S. President George Bush's unwritten understanding that, if the South African government failed to enact political reforms by early 1990 (including the termination of the ban on the ANC, the release of political prisoners, and the lifting of the state of emergency), he would not veto any further sanctions bills passed by Congress.[61] However, it should now be clear that coercive incentives can indeed be used to offer opportunities for diplomats and mediators alike to influence the behavior of target states and insurgent movements. In general, states can manipulate these coercive incentives in the most effective manner, and it seems reasonable to contend that strong states with enormous resources at their disposal have a clear advantage when employing these diplomatic incentives to accelerate the ripening process.

SANCTIONS. Economic or trade sanctions have been defined as "measures in which one country (the initiator) *publicly* suspends a major portion of its trade with another country (the target) to attain *political* objectives."[62] Such sanctions, to be credible, must hold out the prospect of ongoing deprivation well into the future, and this often requires a coalition of state actors. Such coalitions frequently find it politically necessary to make minimalist demands on the target government or insurgent movement, and this then leads to an extended process involving risks of defection among the initiating states.

The political and punitive effects of economic sanctions are relevant here. As incentives for inducing parties to change their behavior regarding the peace process, the various forms of economic statecraft have a long and rather mixed history. The means vary widely, including limited and specific threats to end trade privileges; denying the availability of technical knowledge and trained personnel; blocking access to export supplies, credits, and guarantees; and invoking comprehensive mandatory sanctions. Precisely because mandatory economic sanctions represent a more forceful form of pressure on targeted actors (compelling them to shift their preferences or face the consequences of trade restrictions), such forms of punishment are ranked higher in terms of effectiveness than diplomatic pressures. Mandatory economic sanctions tend to be more difficult to agree upon and to implement than their diplomatic counterparts. When these sanctions are enacted, they indicate the initiators' resolve to win concessions from the targeted elite.

Economic sanctions are a rather crude tool that can prove to be ineffective (for example, the 1992 ECOWAS sanctions against Charles Taylor's National Patriotic Front of Liberia) and difficult to calibrate; thus they can be hurtful to friend and foe alike (as in South Africa). In some cases, these sanctions can even promote a backlash effect as constituents rally around their beleaguered leaders. These unanticipated consequences make it unwise to anticipate too many concessions to the initiators; however, although caution is warranted, deep cynicism about the consequences of using these policy instruments is not. In Africa's postindependence experience, some proposals for economically punishing measures have come to naught, but others have shown "modest success" in inducing either target countries or insurgent movements to change their preferences.[63] Clearly, the tough economic sanctions against Burundi put in place by the eastern African countries in 1996 imposed severe costs on the Tutsi-dominated government of Major Pierre Buyoya, causing him to assure the mediator, former Tanzanian President Julius Nyerere, that the Burundi regime was prepared to negotiate with the pro-Hutu Conseil National pour la Defense de la Democratie on the restoration of parliamentary government.[64] Although little movement took place in the negotiations, the summit of regional heads of state held in Arusha, Tanzania, in April 1997 relaxed the embargo to alleviate the harsh effects of the sanctions on the public.[65]

The application of economic sanctions by foreign governments, banks, industrial firms, and civil associations also had a modest impact on the preferences of the white-led governments in Rhodesia and South Africa (see table 9-1). These external actors became increasingly prepared to use coercion to advance the process of regime change, raising the costs of doing business in the present and resulting in lost opportunities. Perhaps more significant were the psychological effects of external disapproval and marginalization implicit in the sanctions imposed by Western governments. White elites in southern Africa, who exhibited a declining belief in the future under a system of white dominance, began to identify more and more with mainstream thinking and to adopt a more cooperative stance on proposals for reform. The impact of economic sanctions was modest, however, both because there were many defections and partial defections among the coalition of initiators and because the trade sanctions had only minimal economic effects on the dominant white elite. In both cases, however, the economic integration of these countries into the world market eventually made them vulnerable to external pressures.

In Zimbabwe, international sanctions (and particularly the threats of such actions) were critical to the negotiation process, for they isolated white Rhodesians and raised the costs of *not* reaching an agreement. Although some industries, such as textiles, metal products, and nonmetallic mineral products, managed to grow despite sanctions, the general climate for business was adversely affected. Thus a unilateral declaration of independence "tax" estimated at between 6 and 10 percent was in effect; Rhodesian exports such as tobacco were harmed by international sanctions; and the price of imports such as gasoline became relatively expensive.[66] Smith responded to the negative incentive; he reasoned, as University of Zimbabwe Professor R. H. F. Austin phrased it, that he would lose something if he did not reach an agreement.[67] Moreover, sanctions did have an important symbolic impact: the regime of Ian Smith was ostracized as "a moral leper in the international community."[68] Sanctions must be viewed in terms of their total impact—social, psychological, and economic—over the long term.[69] By denying a regime legitimacy, sanctions leave it isolated and empower the opposition. Seen in these terms, sanctions no doubt contributed to the white regime's belief, in the late 1970s, that any agreement was preferable to no agreement (especially because it seemed unlikely that Smith could do better under any future British government than that of Margaret Thatcher).

In South Africa, sanctions were also viewed as a coercive inducement calculated to encourage a change of leadership preferences in a more cooperative direction.[70] U.S. Representative Howard Wolpe, a leader in the struggle to enact the Comprehensive Anti-Apartheid Act of 1986, sought to tighten sanctions to "increase significantly the costs the white minority regime must bear for its repression and its inhumanity."[71] Wolpe and his colleagues realized that sanctions alone could not bring down the South African regime, but by raising the cost of the status quo, sanctions could place heavy pressures on white leaders and possibly induce them to alter their preferences. Not only were the sanctions themselves incentives for constructive change, but they also involved an implicit stick: unless the government acted to release political prisoners, make sufficient progress toward reform, repeal apartheid laws, and encourage positive change, it could expect that the international community would put new sanctions into effect. For OAU Secretary-General Salim Salim, sanctions were one element of the combined internal and external pressures that were "instrumental in compelling the apartheid authorities to accept the principle of negotiation."[72]

North American, European, and African economic sanctions did not, by themselves, explain South African President F. W. de Klerk's change of heart about cooperating with the African majority, but they no doubt made a difference.[73] International pressures limited South Africa's long-term political and economic options, denying it political legitimacy, access to international banking facilities to fund its external debts (estimated at $22 billion), and entrance into key markets for goods, technology, and services. Yet it is difficult to be precise about the impact of sanctions on the country's economic growth potential. Annual economic growth rates fell from a level of 5.8 percent in the 1960s to 1.4 percent for the period between 1983 and 1988, but this was hardly sufficient to satisfy the reasonable expectations of a black population increasing at a rate of nearly 3 percent a year. Average incomes, meanwhile, were estimated to be 15 percent lower than they would have been without sanctions and disinvestment.[74]

The foreign ban on new loans and investment and the net outflow of capital (about $12 billion in 1984–88) were indeed damaging, yet it is also important to note that real exports (in particular, coal and manufacturing items) nonetheless rose substantially during these years.[75] In general, then, one can conclude that trade sanctions took a toll on the economy by imposing added costs and limiting the potential for eco-

nomic growth; moreover, the political and psychological cos[
extensive. By isolating the dominant whites and making them i[
tional pariahs, sanctions provided a kind of shock therapy f[
entrenched whites, encouraging them to consider new options that
altered the existing discriminatory policies on race relations.[76] Initially,
the government fought back by creating a section in the Foreign
Ministry to manage the counterattack; later, when this effort failed and
the costs of maintaining the status quo outweighed the benefits of negotiating a cooperative solution, the de Klerk government went to the
bargaining table to attempt to work out a joint solution to the problems.
The cumulative effect of economic sanctions over an extended period
clearly contributed to the process of coercive ripening.

FORCE. In general, as table 9-1 and the general literature on third-party
mediation indicate, "Force is not an effective way to induce an adversary
to yield many of the objectives sought by a party to a conflict."[77] Thus,
in Somalia, the American-led international humanitarian intervention
and peace enforcement initiative of 1992 and 1993 proved largely ineffective in disarming the combatants and restoring regularized rules of
relations among the militia leaders. Similarly, in Liberia, successful military action by an enlarged Economic Community of West African States
Ceasefire Monitoring Group (ECOMOG) force induced Charles Taylor
and the other militia leaders to accede to the new reality. In July 1993,
they signed the Cotonou agreement and then several follow-up agreements, only to see the implementation of the cease-fire and plans for the
disarming the militias prove ineffective. For the ethnic and subethnic
militia leaders in both countries, a security dilemma remained in place;
for a limited time the external interveners could alter the balance of
forces on the ground and push the combatants to the bargaining table,
but (as also seen in Bosnia following the NATO air strikes) they could
not shift the preferences of the rival factions in the direction of a cooperative outcome.[78] Again, incentives had demonstrable results only
where the local parties were receptive.

One African exception in terms of coercive military ripening, however, occurred over the reintegration of Katanga into the Congo in
the early 1960s. In this case, the Congolese government and UN and
U.S. officials remained convinced that forceful pressures provided an
indispensable incentive for Moise Tshombe to back down from his
secessionist plans. Here again, the expectation of future sanctions

was as important as the imposition of the initial ones. Ghana's Robert Gardiner, who headed the UN operation in the Congo, contended that "there must be [an] available reserve of force to convince Tshombe to negotiate."[79] Congolese Prime Minister Cyrille Adoula felt that Tshombe should not be allowed to have his way simply because of a fear of using force.[80] A continuation of UN military action might be desirable, he argued, although he expressed a concern that the UN might break off the engagement after a short period. Under such circumstances, the pressure on Katanga would cease, and "there would be no incentive for them to give in to UN."[81] On the American side, U.S. Under Secretary of State George Ball, commenting on the impact of coercive pressures, observed in a telegram that the "Tshombe offer should be looked upon as having been modified by firm policy UN has been following with full support USG [U.S. Government] and GOC [Government of Congo]."[82] Thus coercive pressures exerted over an extended period by these actors in the Congo drama played a critical role in altering Tshombe's commitment to a separatist course.

At the outset, UN military contingents represented anything but overwhelming force to the Katangan gendarmes. UN forces acted rather indecisively in the first rounds of the Katanga conflict (Operations "Rumpunch" and "Morthor") in September 1961, when they sought to arrest Tshombe, Minister of Interior Godefroid Munongo, and several other Katanga ministers, occupy the Elisabethville radio station and post office, and neutralize foreign mercenaries fighting for Katanga.[83] Then, in December 1961, the UN force responded to Katangan military provocations by taking armed action to restore freedom of movement in the area and to gain control of Elisabethville and the airport, using air power in support of military maneuvers on the ground. The December offensive acted in a coercive manner to convince the Katanga administration that their reintegration into the Congo was in their own best interests. The UN military triumph provided an incentive for Tshombe to recognize the unity of the country and the authority of the central government, as enshrined in the Kitona agreement in December. This agreement required another round of fighting between the UN forces and the Katangan gendarmes in December 1962, but again UN military superiority was demonstrated conclusively when its units occupied key points throughout the province.

In the rather unusual case of Katanga, limited military force succeeded in bringing Tshombe back from the precipice of secession;

Tshombe was unable to get his own way, but this provided a context in which his second-favorite option, mutual cooperation, could surface. Military action can certainly prove counterproductive and can lead to mutual defection and guerrilla action; in this instance, however, Tshombe's essential pragmatism led to a more moderate ordering of preferences.

Incentives during the Implementation Stage

As I set forth in the second proposition of chapter 1 and explored in my analyses of Angola, Zimbabwe, and Sudan, implementation has proved to be very much a part of the prenegotiation and negotiation processes. Actors' assessments of the expected benefits influence their thinking about whether to cooperate or defect when the agreement is put into effect.[84] The assessments of African leaders and their resulting decisions to either cooperate or defect have varied widely. Although peace agreements were successfully consolidated in Zimbabwe, Namibia, and apparently Mozambique, where democratic elections lent an air of legitimacy to the transition process, they led to failure and a collapse of state-society relations in Rwanda, Burundi, Angola (1975 and 1992), and Sudan. Success in overcoming the security dilemma and creating regularized societal relations or bringing about their return clearly entailed an enormous international commitment on the part of a coalition of mediators. Such a coalition has frequently combined UN or regional peacekeepers (for example, ECOMOG in Liberia) and peace builders with the active financial, logistical, military, and monitoring support of great powers. When the strengths of the UN or regional organizations (in terms of political legitimacy) coincide with those of the great powers (in terms of resources), it is likely that sufficient incentives and pressures can be brought to bear on the antagonists to deter their defection. Such third parties can raise the costs of breaking agreements by monitoring the implementation process, highlighting any violations of the intentions of the signers, and focusing an international spotlight on any breaches that may occur.[85] The UN's careful monitoring of the military forces and the election process in Namibia increased the parties' incentives to abide by the terms of the peace agreement.

Sometimes, as in Namibia and the Congo, the UN, with its repertoire of symbolic rewards, and a great power, with a capacity for providing substantive benefits, can combine to wield considerable leverage at the implementation stage. Provided that the third-party commitment is credible, external monitoring and enforcement can influence the behavior of the actors, enabling them to make short-term commitments to an agreement as well as to the long-term process of security building (that is, viewing peace as an extended and interconnected experience).[86] Because demobilization and force restructuring leave both state and insurgent armed forces highly vulnerable during the transition period following the signing of a peace agreement, third parties often play a significant role in enforcing the terms of an accord. To the extent that they can prevent cheating and the reoccurrence of fighting, they contribute in an important way to the move from deadly strife to stable, regularized relations.

When assessing the record of implementation by international organizations and great powers, I am struck by the generally mixed pattern of performance thus far.[87] With respect to the preparedness of international organizations to intervene with sufficient capabilities to establish or return to an effective conflict management system following civil war, the record of the international community has been less than satisfactory, partly because of an unwillingness or inability to commit sufficient financial resources and personnel to monitoring. On the one hand, as in Namibia in 1989, the UN Transition Assistance Group (UNTAG) successfully guided the transition process to a peaceful conclusion. This proved to be a complex change, involving considerable expenditure of resources and the exercise of effective international control over Namibia's progress toward independence. UNTAG monitored the South African–appointed administrator-general and his government at the central and subregional levels and sought to ensure that the elections were conducted in a free and fair manner. The UN secretary-general's special representative, Martti Ahtisaari, effectively defused a crisis at the early stages of the operation—the premature incursion of South West Africa People's Organization (SWAPO) troops—that could have resulted in renewed hostilities. UNTAG, attempting to build public confidence in the transition process, had substantial financial resources and personnel at its disposal. UNTAG leverage therefore proved sufficient to ensure a relatively smooth transition to democratic elections and a peaceful transfer of power.

By contrast, the UN's entrance onto the scene in Angola and its management of the transition process there seemed lacking in leverage and commitment. In accordance with the tripartite agreement reached in

December 1988, a phased withdrawal of Cuban and South African military forces from Angola did take place somewhat in advance of the scheduled dates (see chapter 5). In implementing these arrangements, the Security Council authorized a verification mission (UNAVEM I) to monitor the redeployment and withdrawal of Cuban troops. UNAVEM I was composed of sixty military observers from ten countries and was given a limited mandate to monitor the transition process of thirty-one months.

With the transition process in place leading to external disengagement, pressure soon mounted on the MPLA and UNITA to reach an internal settlement. The Bicesse accords of May 1991 established a cease-fire, provisions for elections, the integration of military forces, and the establishment of a Joint Political-Military Commission (including the MPLA, UNITA, the UN, Portugal, the United States, and the Soviet Union) to oversee the transition. Over the course of 1991, influenced by continued U.S. and Soviet diplomatic pressures, the Bicesse process was institutionalized. It produced an agreement on a transition that would result in new elections, allowing UNITA to compete as a political party.

The Angolan government requested that the secretary-general ensure UN participation in the verification of the accords, including the cease-fire, demobilization of the UNITA forces, a reduction in MPLA troops, and monitoring of the elections. The new mission, named UNAVEM II, was authorized by the Security Council to observe and verify the elections and to provide technical assistance to the newly formed Angolan electoral commission. UNAVEM II, totaling 450 blue-helmeted soldiers and police and 400 civilian observers, operated on a mandate that continued until the elections on September 29 and 30, 1992. However, because UN budgets were stretched thin by operations in Somalia, Bosnia, and Cambodia, UNAVEM II was allocated a mere $100 million.

By all accounts, the Angola transition process teetered on the brink of failure from the outset. Only half of the 120,000 troops on both sides were demobilized by the time of the presidential election, and those soldiers who did enter the assembly points were clearly not elite forces. The elections, when they were finally held, were certified by the international observers to be substantially "free and fair." Because victorious MPLA leader José Eduardo dos Santos had received less than 50 percent of the vote, a run-off election was required. UNITA's Jonas Savimbi was unwilling to accept the likely prospect of a defeat in a second election, so he cried foul, claiming the first round to be fraudulent, and defected. UNITA's officers and men withdrew from the unified army and returned to the bush, and a savage civil war resumed, causing some of the heaviest casualties thus far.

Clearly, the UN peacekeeping effort floundered partly because of continuing distrust on both sides and because of the lack of a viable political process acceptable to the main parties. Another important factor was that the UN mission was badly understaffed and underfunded and therefore unable to oversee the implementation of the agreement. In contrast to the successful UN operation in Namibia, the UNAVEM II effort seemed grossly inadequate. Namibia, a country of 1.4 million people, saw a UN operation composed of 4,650 people at a cost of $367 million, whereas in Angola, a country of 5.7 million, roughly one-third of these resources were available.[88] Whether a larger UN operation could have corralled the recalcitrant UNITA leader into accepting defeat at the polls remains a matter of speculation, but most observers fault the UN for its failed attempt to implement the Bicesse accords "on the cheap."

Moreover, the UN Security Council mandate and the instructions to the secretary-general's special representative, Margaret Joan Anstee, were ambiguous and imprecise. As a consequence, Anstee was uncertain whether she had the authority—and the support of the great powers in the Security Council—to delay the elections until after the demobilization of forces and the creation of a unified army had been completed. The dependency of the UN and other international organizations upon the backing of the great powers became painfully evident in Angola, because in this case the UN was shown to lack the necessary political, economic, and military resources of its own to pressure the adversaries to stick to the rules of the game during the critically important presidential elections. When a spoiler such as Savimbi refuses to demobilize and abide by the election results, there is little that a weak third-party actor can do, unless it is backed by strong and determined state actors in the region and in the world at large.

Subsequently, the United States and other countries, learning from past failures, gave more generous backing to the UN Angola Verification Mission III (UNAVEM III), which was set up to oversee the implementation of the 1994 Lusaka protocol. The result was a broad-based UNAVEM III operation that backed demobilization, the reintegration of the army, de-mining, the return and support of refugees, and development and reconstruction. In contrast with the small UN outlays of the 1991–92 period, the 1996 commitment involved 7,000 troops and military observers and cost $1 million a day.[89] In sum, it is as important during the implementation phase as it is during the negotiation phase for mediators to be prepared to use their leverage to overcome defections and a possible breakdown in state-society relations, or else an enduring stalemate is likely to materialize.

Conclusion: Shifting Forms of Mediator Leverage

This book has shown that in attempting to create an effective conflict management system within the countries of Africa, a mediator needs both leverage and legitimacy to make effective use of incentives. A strong and responsible *internal* state mediator can use leverage to structure incentives so as to minimize insecurity and prevent intense conflict from occurring. When civil wars arise, a strong *external* state mediator, often in coalition with allied states, may be necessary to accelerate the process of ripening and to assist in implementing the peace. Particularly when dealing with violent encounters involving issues of individual and group security, external state mediators (alone or in a coalition of other state mediators) will be more favorably situated to achieve their objectives when they are accepted as valid third-party actors and when they are able to bring substantial resources to bear on the target state or movement. Obviously, when working with suspicious and hostile adversaries, a powerful state actor (or actors) has distinct advantages in combining pressures and incentives to facilitate a settlement. For example, the ability of the British foreign secretary, Lord Carrington, to mediate an international settlement in Rhodesia/Zimbabwe was enhanced by the formal acceptance of his intermediary role and by the very considerable resources he could bring to bear, in collaboration with the Commonwealth and African frontline states, on the parties to the dispute. Strong international organizations can also be well placed to facilitate peace agreements. For this reason, it is also important to invest in the leverage that the United Nations can bring to bear on deviant behavior, keeping in mind the useful role it has played in overseeing the implementation of the Lusaka protocol on Angola and the peace agreements in Namibia and Mozambique.

But the characteristics that signified a strong mediator in the context of the cold war differ from the qualities that are likely to be prominent in the twenty-first century. The need to have a third party capable of applying noncoercive and coercive incentives will remain constant, but the nature of the mediation process can be expected to change significantly in the years ahead. External access to African countries became more complicated as the process of formal decolonization came to an end and economic and social linkages between the West and Africa weakened. Now the great powers lack the justification to intercede on their own in Africa's internal disputes, and Western publics are fatigued with costly and protracted interventions. Moreover, with passing years, the strategic interactions among groups within Africa's countries have become more complex as the number of contending factions have multiplied and the stakes at issue have increased. Where central government authority weakens and distrustful militia leaders in such countries as Liberia and Somalia exhibit an overriding concern with their security and the survival of their group, the intensifying confrontation has new and difficult implications for the creation of effective conflict management systems.

This shift in strategic interactions raises a key question for today's statespersons and observers: how can they build mediator capacity that is relevant to a changing African political environment? The old order is an insufficient and unreliable safety net; powerful external actors have largely remained on the sidelines as ethnic brutality and genocide have appeared in Rwanda, Burundi, Liberia, and the Democratic Republic of the Congo. New investments in mediator capacity are therefore necessary to deter ambitious and unscrupulous leaders who might manipulate ethnic identities in a destructive manner, some of which have the potential of spreading across international borders (for example, the spread of warfare from Liberia to Sierra Leone in the early 1990s). Aside from occasional external interventions (such as the French-led foray into Rwanda in 1994), three main options exist at this time: increased external support for African regional initiatives, greater backing for United Nations peacekeeping efforts, and the Clinton administration's proposed African Crisis Response Force (ACRF).

All of these represent state-based coalitions that are capable of using noncoercive and coercive incentives to deal with the possible breakdown of conflict management systems in African countries. They share a concern with confidence building and the need to reassure vulnerable and insecure peoples about their place in the evolving regional order. At the same time, they differ in terms of their inspiration and vision and in their commitment to control "the factors which produce legitimate fear, both the underlying unchanging realities and the rules or norms according to which the conflict is waged."[90]

Certainly, the more centralized and externally encouraged initiatives are most liable to encounter difficulties in building interethnic trust. Because the permanent ACRF would involve 10,000 African troops and cost an estimated $40 million a year, it seems most likely to encounter both African resistance over the mandate, leadership, and autonomy of the force and Western caution regarding future financial obligations. Although African countries seem more likely to respond positively to the more neutral, accountable, and relatively well-paid United Nations peacekeeping initiatives (such as the UN Observer Mission in Liberia), even here problems of organizational leadership and purpose can be anticipated.

Rather, it is the African regional diplomatic and peacekeeping initiatives that would seem to hold out the greatest hope for increased mediatory leverage in a world community marked by withdrawal and a lack of commitment to ensuring the maintenance of constructive systems of managing conflict. The confrontations in Sierra Leone and Burundi are two examples of positive African responses to specific crises. Côte d'Ivoire's foreign minister, Amara Essy, with the backing of countries in the region, successfully mediated an agreement in 1996 between the government of Sierra Leone and an insurgent force, the Revolutionary United Front. This success at mediation proved short-lived, however, because Sierra Leonean army officers overthrew the civilian government of President Ahmed Tejan Kabbah in 1997 and set off a new crisis in the region. In Burundi, former president Julius Nyerere of Tanzania, as noted above, has mobilized the eastern African countries to exert heavy pressure on the Buyoya regime in Burundi, imposing a punishing oil embargo and sanctions on trade. Regional organizations such as the Economic Community of West African States and the Intergovernmental Authority on Development have also attempted to take on the internal crises in Liberia and Sudan, respectively. Such African initiatives can bring pressures and incentives to bear because of the legitimate concerns that these third parties have with moving regional confrontations toward stable outcomes.

Because these African efforts to manage conflict come at the very time when the West is leaning toward disengagement, they should be viewed as a creative means of developing new and practical forms of third-party intervention. But these African regional initiatives, based largely on states with limited economic resources, cannot be expected to achieve their conflict management objectives unassisted. New coalitions are therefore required. Such collaborations can bring together

African legitimacy and purpose with the industrialized countries' financial and logistical strengths and thereby create a potentially influential third force to deal with future challenges. To develop this new collaboration, however, it is vital that current leaders in the industrialized countries pave the way by preparing their publics now for a new, more understanding involvement with Africa's affairs.

Notes

Epigraphs

Sources for the epigraphs at the beginning of each chapter are as follows: Chester A. Crocker, *High Noon in Southern Africa: Making Peace in a Rough Neighborhood* (Norton, 1992), p. 474; Russell Hardin, *One for All: The Logic of Group Conflict* (Princeton University Press, 1995), p. 9; Samuel P. Huntington, *The Third Wave: Democratization in the Late Twentieth Century* (University of Oklahoma Press, 1991), p. 28; William B. Quandt, *Camp David: Peacemaking and Politics* (Brookings, 1986), p. 336; Barry R. Posen, "The Security Dilemma and Ethnic Conflict," in Michael E. Brown, ed., *Ethnic Conflict and International Security* (Princeton University Press, 1993), p. 110; Louis Kriesberg, "Introduction: Timing Conditions, Strategies, and Errors," in Kriesberg and Stuart J. Thorson, eds., *Timing the De-escalation of International Conflicts* (Syracuse University Press, 1991), p. 14; Nelson Mandela, *Long Walk to Freedom* (Little, Brown, 1994), p. 533; Christopher R. Mitchell, "Conflict Resolution and Civil War: Reflections on the Sudanese Settlement of 1972," Working Paper 3 (George Mason University, Center for Conflict Analysis and Resolution, 1989), p. 19; and Michael E. Brown, "The Causes and Regional Dimensions of Internal Conflict," in Brown, ed., *The International Dimensions of Internal Conflict* (MIT Press, 1996), p. 572.

Chapter 1

1. Robert Axelrod, *The Evolution of Cooperation* (Basic Books, 1984).

2. Donald Rothchild, *Racial Bargaining in Independent Kenya: A Study of Minorities and Decolonization* (London: Oxford University Press, 1973), chap. 1. For a somewhat similar process in the Zimbabwe independence negotiations, see Jeffrey Herbst, "Racial Reconciliation in Southern Africa," *International Affairs,* vol. 65 (Winter 1988-89), pp. 43-54.

3. Mancur Olson, *The Rise and Decline of Nations: Economic Growth, Stagflation, and Social Rigidities* (Yale University Press, 1982), p. 37.

4. Donald Rothchild, "Ethnic Inequalities in Kenya," *Journal of Modern African Studies,* vol. 7 (December 1969), pp. 689-711.

5. As used here, a pattern of relations refers to a "regular occurrence" that can be observed, not an institution. See Lewis A. Coser, *The Functions of Social Conflict* (Free Press, 1956), p. 34.

6. I. William Zartman, "Conflict Reduction: Prevention, Management, and Resolution," in Francis M. Deng and I. William Zartman, eds., *Conflict Resolution in Africa* (Brookings, 1991), pp. 306-07.

7. Walter L. Barrows, "Ethnic Diversity and Political Instability in Black Africa," *Comparative Political Studies*, vol. 9 (July 1976), pp. 162-66. To understand the process of direct bargaining and third-party mediation, race will be subsumed under the broader category of ethnic stratification patterns. Although the social boundaries tend to be wider in a racially stratified society such as South Africa or colonial Rhodesia than in the ethnically stratified societies of black Africa, the two forms of stratification nonetheless share many characteristics and can be regarded, for the purposes of this book, as congruent. See Gerald D. Berreman, "Race, Caste, and Other Invidious Distinctions in Social Stratification," *Race*, vol. 13 (April 1972), p. 388.

8. See Barry R. Posen, "The Security Dilemma and Ethnic Conflict," *Survival*, vol. 35 (Spring 1993), p. 28; and Robert Jervis, "Cooperation under the Security Dilemma," *World Politics*, vol. 30 (January 1978), p. 172.

9. Russell Hardin, *One for All: The Logic of Group Conflict* (Princeton University Press, 1995), p. 22.

10. Warren Weinstein, "Conflict and Confrontation in Central Africa: The Revolt in Burundi, 1972," *Africa Today*, vol. 19 (Fall 1972), p. 27. See also René Lemarchand, *Burundi: Ethnocide as Discourse and Practice* (Cambridge: Cambridge University Press, 1994), chap. 1.

11. Review essay by Alex de Waal, "The Genocidal State," *Times Literary Supplement*, July 1, 1994, p. 3, which summarizes a paper by Tim Allen in Katsuyoshi Fukui and John Markakis, *Ethnicity and Conflict in the Horn of Africa* (Ohio University Press, 1994).

12. David A. Lax and James K. Sebenius, *The Manager as Negotiator: Bargaining for Cooperation and Competitive Gain* (Free Press, 1986), p. 339.

13. Robert D. Putnam, "Diplomacy and Domestic Politics: The Logic of Two-Level Games," *International Organization*, vol. 42 (Summer 1988), pp. 433-35.

14. Donald L. Horowitz, *Ethnic Groups in Conflict* (University of California Press, 1985), pp. 22-23. I leave for later a discussion of "ranked" (that is, politically and morally unequal) ethnic systems, although I recognize that in eastern and southern Africa during colonial times such systems were of great significance.

15. On this overlap, see Brian Weinstein, "Social Communication Methodology in the Study of Nation-Building," *Cahiers d'études Africaines*, vol. 4, no. 4 (1954), pp. 572-73.

16. Tessilimi Bakary, "Elite Transformation and Political Succession," in I. William Zartman and Christopher Delgado, eds., *The Political Economy of Ivory Coast* (Praeger, 1984), p. 28.

17. For an example of ongoing subregional-cultural dominance that is less influenced by the intervening factor of colonial overrule, see Paul Henze, *Rebels and Separatists in Ethiopia: Regional Resistance to a Marxist Regime* (Santa Monica, Calif.: Rand, 1986), pp. 14-16.

18. Low decisional costs occur when a limited array of groups is engaged in the process of decisionmaking. The result is to reduce the organizational costs of arriving at decisions. See James M. Buchanan and Gordon Tullock, *The Calculus of Consent* (University of Michigan Press, 1962), p. 111; and Mancur Olson, *The Logic of Collective Action* (Harvard University Press, 1965), p. 42.

19. On the "soft" state, see Gunnar Myrdal, *Asian Drama: An Inquiry into the Poverty of Nations,* vol. 2 (New York: Twentieth Century Fund, 1968), pp. 895-900; and Goran Hyden, "Problems and Prospects of State Coherence," in Donald Rothchild and Victor A. Olorunsola, eds., *State versus Ethnic Claims: African Policy Dilemmas* (Boulder, Colo.: Westview, 1983), pp. 73-74. On the colonial state's hegemonic imperative, see Crawford Young, *The African Colonial State in Comparative Perspective* (Yale University Press, 1994), p. 100.

20. Christian Coulon, "Senegal: The Development and Fragility of Semi-democracy," in Larry Diamond, Juan J. Linz, and Seymour Martin Lipset, eds., *Democracy in Developing Countries: Africa* (Boulder, Colo.: Lynne Rienner, 1988), p. 145. Also see Lucy C. Behrman, *Muslim Brotherhoods and Politics in Senegal* (Harvard University Press, 1970), p. 58; and Lucy E. Creevey, "Muslim Brotherhoods and Politics in Senegal in 1985," *Journal of Modern African Studies,* vol. 23 (December 1985), p. 718.

21. At the most the colonial secretary, Mr. Lennox-Boyd, "envisaged the formation of a decentralized federation of local parties." Quoted in Mordechai Tamarkin, "A Failure in the British Colonial Counter-Revolution to Mau Mau: The Case of Moderate African Politics in Nakuru," *Asian and African Studies,* vol. 18 (November 1984), p. 232. Also see George Bennett and Carl Rosberg, *The Kenyatta Election: Kenya 1960-1961* (London: Oxford University Press, 1961), pp. 33, 37.

22. Young, *The African Colonial State,* pp. 235-36.

23. Obafemi Awolowo, *The People's Republic* (Ibadan, Nigeria: Oxford University Press, 1968), pp. 62, 72; also see Obafemi Awolowo, *Path to Nigerian Freedom* (London: Faber and Faber, 1947), chap. 5. For an example of divide-and-rule politics in French Africa during colonial times, see René Lemarchand, "Chad: The Misadventures of the North-South Dialectic," *African Studies Review,* vol. 29 (September 1986), pp. 30-32.

24. Dunstan M. Wai, "Geoethnicity and the Margin of Autonomy in the Sudan," in Rothchild and Olorunsola, *State versus Ethnic Claims,* p. 307. On the role of indirect rule in controlling change, see Beverly Grier, "Contradiction, Crisis, and Class Conflict: The State and Capitalist Development in Ghana Prior to 1948," in Irving L. Markovitz, ed., *Studies in Power and Class in Africa* (New York: Oxford University Press, 1987), p. 38.

25. See Donald Rothchild, "Rural-Urban Inequities and Resource Allocation in Zambia," *Journal of Commonwealth Political Studies,* vol. 10 (November 1972), p. 225.

26. Maxwell Owusu, *Uses and Abuses of Political Power: A Case Study of Continuity and Change in the Politics of Ghana* (University of Chicago Press, 1970), p. 121.

27. On this harmony of interest, see Johan Galtung, "A Structural Theory of Imperialism," *Journal of Peace Research,* vol. 8, no. 2 (1971), p. 84; and Colin

Leys, *Underdevelopment in Kenya: The Political Economy of Neo-Colonialism, 1964-1971* (University of California Press, 1975), pp. 8-27.

28. Donald Rothchild, "Majimbo Schemes in Kenya and Uganda," in Jeffrey Butler and A. A. Castagno, eds., *Boston University Papers on Africa: Transition in African Politics* (New York: Praeger, 1967), pp. 294-95; and Donald Rothchild, "On the Application of the Westminster Model to Ghana," *Centennial Review,* vol. 4 (Fall 1960), p. 477.

29. Michael E. Brown, "Introduction," in Brown, ed., *The International Dimensions of Internal Conflict* (MIT Press, 1996), p. 17.

30. Michael Bratton and Nicolas van de Walle, "Toward Governance in Africa: Popular Demands and State Responses," in Goran Hyden and Michael Bratton, eds., *Governance and Politics in Africa* (Boulder, Colo.: Lynne Rienner, 1992), pp. 50-51.

31. Michael Bratton and Nicolas van de Walle, *Democratic Experiments in Africa: Political Transitions in Comparative Perspective* (Cambridge: Cambridge University Press, forthcoming), table 6.1.

32. Terry Lynn Karl, "Petroleum and Political Pacts: The Transition to Democracy in Venezuela," in Guillermo O'Donnell, Philippe C. Schmitter, and Laurence Whitehead, eds., *Transitions from Authoritarian Rule: Latin America* (Johns Hopkins University Press, 1986), p. 217.

33. On the potential dangers of forming elite contracts (or pacts), see Horowitz, *Ethnic Groups in Conflict,* pp. 574-76.

34. See the data in Bakary, "Elite Transformation and Political Succession," p. 36; and J. F. Medard, "La regulation socio-politique," in Y. A. Faure and J. F. Medard, eds., *État et Bourgeoisie en Côte-d'Ivoire* (Paris: Karthala, 1982), p. 75.

35. Timothy D. Sisk, "The Violence-Negotiation Nexus: South Africa in Transition and the Politics of Uncertainty," *Negotiation Journal,* vol. 9 (January 1993), p. 91. For a fuller discussion of this point, see his *Democratization in South Africa: The Elusive Social Contract* (Princeton University Press, 1995), pp. 200-48.

36. Terry Lynn Karl, "Dilemmas of Democratization in Latin America," *Comparative Politics,* vol. 23 (October 1990), p. 11.

37. Kenyan political scientist Meddi Mugyenyi called for the adoption of "minimalist democracies" in "Development First, Democracy Second: A Comment on Minimalist Democracy," in Walter O. Oyugi and others, eds., *Democratic Theory and Practice in Africa* (Portsmouth, N.H.: Heinemann, 1988), pp. 185-87.

38. Larry Diamond, "Issues in the Constitutional Design of a Third Nigerian Republic," *African Affairs,* vol. 86 (April 1987), p. 219.

39. Alfred Stepan, *Rethinking Military Politics: Brazil and the Southern Cone* (Princeton University Press, 1988), p. 137. Also compare Frances Hagopian, "'Democracy by Undemocratic Means'? Elites, Political Pacts, and Regime Transition in Brazil," *Comparative Political Studies,* vol. 23 (July 1990), pp. 147-70; and Terry Lynn Karl and Philippe C. Schmitter, "Modes of Transition in Latin America, Southern and Eastern Europe," *International Social Science Journal,* vol. 128 (May 1991), pp. 269-84.

40. The findings of the cross-national literature give some support for this link between repression and internal wars and rebellions. See Ekkart Zimmermann, "Macro-Comparative Research on Political Protest," in Ted Robert Gurr, ed., *Handbook of Political Conflict: Theory and Research* (Free Press, 1980), p. 210.

41. Michael Holman, "Short of Everything—Including Hope," *Financial Times,* July 31, 1981, p. 13.

42. Horowitz, *Ethnic Groups in Conflict,* pp. 166-75.

43. Claude Ake, "Explaining Political Instability in New States," *Journal of Modern African Studies,* vol. 11 (September 1973), p. 356. By political exchange, I mean the combination of material benefits, information, status, legitimacy, and other resources by state or societal groups to promote the consent of others to public policy or its implementation. Robert H. Salisbury, "An Exchange Theory of Interest Groups," *Midwest Journal of Political Science,* vol. 13 (February 1969), pp. 1-32.

44. I. William Zartman, "Introduction: Posing the Problem of State Collapse," in Zartman, ed., *Collapsed States: The Disintegration and Restoration of Legitimate Authority* (Boulder, Colo.: Lynne Rienner, 1995), pp. 1-11.

45. Howard Raiffa, *The Art and Science of Negotiation* (Belknap Press of Harvard University Press, 1982), pp. 210-14.

Chapter 2

1. Jack Snyder, "Averting Anarchy in the New Europe," *International Security,* vol. 14 (Spring 1990), p. 30.

2. Donald L. Sparks, "Economic Trends in Africa South of the Sahara, 1996," in *Africa South of the Sahara, 1997* (London: Europa Publications, 1997), p. 11.

3. *Africa Research Bulletin,* Political, Social and Cultural Series, vol. 33 (June 4, 1996), p. 12546.

4. Claude Ake, *Democracy and Development in Africa* (Brookings, 1996), p. 158.

5. *Africa Research Bulletin,* Political, Social and Cultural Series, vol. 31 (October 1994), pp. 11599-601.

6. Edward E. Azar, "The Theory of Protracted Social Conflict and the Challenge of Transforming Conflict Situations," in Dina A. Zinnes, ed., *Conflict Processes and the Breakdown of International Systems,* vol. 20, no. 2 (University of Denver, Graduate School of International Studies Monograph Series in World Affairs, 1983), p. 92.

7. Compare with Donald L. Horowitz, *Ethnic Groups in Conflict* (University of California Press, 1985), p. 104.

8. For an earlier discussion of these issues, see Donald Rothchild, "Interethnic Conflict and Policy Analysis in Africa," *Ethnic and Racial Studies,* vol. 9 (January 1986), p. 86; and Donald Rothchild, "State and Ethnicity in Africa: A Policy Perspective," in Neil Nevitte and Charles H. Kennedy, eds., *Ethnic Preference and Public Policy in Developing States* (Boulder, Colo.: Lynne Rienner, 1986), pp. 15-61.

9. Howard Adelman and Astri Suhrke, *Early Warning and Conflict Management* (Copenhagen: Joint Evaluation of Emergency Assistance to Rwanda, 1996), pp. 16-17.

10. See René Lemarchand, "Revolutionary Phenomena in Stratified Societies: Rwanda and Zanzibar," *Civilisations*, vol. 18, no. 1 (1968), p. 47; Horowitz, *Ethnic Groups in Conflict*, p. 186; and Donald Rothchild, *Racial Bargaining in Independent Kenya* (Oxford University Press, 1973), chap. 5.

11. On the demands of religious organizations in Nigeria, see Donald Rothchild, "Conclusion: Management of Conflict in West Africa," in I. William Zartman, ed., *Governance as Conflict Management: Politics and Violence in West Africa* (Brookings, 1997), pp. 197-237.

12. In relationship to the total population, the survey I administered showed the Fanti and Ga-Adangbe to be significantly overrepresented, although the northerners were underrepresented. Others, such as the Ashanti, Boron, Akim-Akwapim, Nzima, and Ewe, showed no statistically significant variance from proportionality. See Donald Rothchild, "State-Ethnic Relations in Middle Africa," in Gwendolen M. Carter and Patrick O'Meara, eds., *African Independence: The First Twenty-Five Years* (Indiana University Press, 1985), p. 85.

13. See Donald Rothchild, "Middle Africa: Hegemonial Exchange and Resource Allocation," in Alexander J. Groth and Larry L. Wade, eds., *Comparative Resource Allocation* (Beverly Hills: Sage Publications, 1984), pp. 173-75.

14. Dunstan M. Wai, "Geoethnicity and the Margin of Autonomy in the Sudan," in Donald Rothchild and Victor A. Olorunsola, eds., *State versus Ethnic Claims* (Boulder, Colo.: Westview, 1983), p. 320 (emphasis added).

15. George Tsebelis, *Nested Games: Rational Choice in Comparative Politics* (University of California Press, 1990), p. 173.

16. Important examples of these general explanations of ethnic conflict include Harold Issacs, "Basic Group Identity: The Idols of the Tribe," *Ethnicity*, vol. 1 (April 1974), pp. 15-41; Ali A. Mazrui, *Post Imperial Fragmentation: The Legacy of Ethnic and Racial Conflict*, vol. 1, no. 2 (University of Denver, Studies in Race and Nations, 1969); Karl W. Deutsch, "Research Problems on Race in Intranational and International Relations," in George W. Shepherd Jr. and Tilden J. LeMelle, eds., *Race among Nations: A Conceptual Approach* (Lexington, Mass.: Heath Lexington Books, 1970), pp. 123-52; Karl W. Deutsch, "Social Mobilization and Political Development," *American Political Science Review*, vol. 55 (September 1961), pp. 493-514; and Samuel P. Huntington, *Political Order in Changing Societies* (Yale University Press, 1968).

17. Adam Przeworski, *Democracy and the Market* (Cambridge University Press, 1991), p. 33.

18. For a more extended summary of these findings, see Donald Rothchild, "Collective Demands for Improved Distributions," in Rothchild and Olorunsola, eds., *State versus Ethnic Claims*, pp. 172-98. See also Anthony Oberschall, "Communications, Information, and Aspirations in Rural Uganda," *Journal of Asian and African Studies*, vol. 4 (January 1969), p. 48.

19. Joan M. Nelson, *Access to Power* (Princeton University Press, 1979), p. 241.

20. Manfred Halpern, "Changing Connections to Multiple Worlds," in Helen Kitchen, ed., *Africa: From Mystery to Maze* (Lexington, Mass.: Lexington Books, 1976), pp. 15-17.

21. In an important discussion of the possibilities of negotiating national identity, a political psychologist, Herbert C. Kelman, states that national identity has "many of the earmarks of a 'non-negotiable' item, for both normative and empirical reasons;" however, he holds to his basic proposition that national identity "is an appropriate subject for negotiation." "Negotiating National Identity and Self-Determination in Ethnic Conflicts: The Choice between Pluralism and Ethnic Cleansing," address to the 5th International Conference on Social Justice Research, University of Nevada, Reno, June 27, 1995, pp. 15-16.

22. Donald Rothchild and Alexander J. Groth, "Pathological Dimensions of Domestic and International Ethnicity," *Political Science Quarterly,* vol. 110 (Spring 1995), pp. 69-82.

23. Horowitz, *Ethnic Groups in Conflict,* p. 196.

24. Leo Kuper, *The Pity of It All: Polarization of Racial and Ethnic Relations* (University of Minnesota Press, 1977), pp. 122, 271.

25. Manfred Halpern, "Choosing between Ways of Life and Death and between Forms of Democracy: An Archetypal Analysis," *Alternatives,* vol. 12 (January 1987), p. 13.

26. René Lemarchand, *Burundi: Ethnocide as Discourse and Practice* (Cambridge University Press, 1994), p. 81.

27. René Lemarchand, *Selective Genocide in Burundi,* Report 20 (London: Minority Rights Group, 1974), p. 18. On the processes of diffusion, see Stuart Hill and Donald Rothchild, "The Impact of Regime on the Diffusion of Political Conflict," in Manus I. Midlarsky, ed., *The Internationalization of Communal Strife* (London: Routledge, 1993), chap. 9.

28. Horowitz, *Ethnic Groups in Conflict,* pp. 22-23.

29. Quoted in *Weekly Review* (Nairobi), February 3, 1980, p. 3.

30. On Somalia's claim to the Ogaden as a nonnegotiable issue in the 1970s, see Jeffrey A. Lefebvre, *Arms for the Horn: U.S. Security Policy in Ethiopia and Somalia 1953-1991* (University of Pittsburgh Press, 1991), p. 213.

31. Robert H. Jackson and Carl G. Rosberg, "Why Africa's Weak States Persist: The Empirical and the Juridical in Statehood," *World Politics,* vol. 35 (October 1982), pp. 12-16.

32. Chaim Kaufmann, "Possible and Impossible Solutions to Ethnic Civil Wars," *International Security,* vol. 20 (Spring 1996), pp. 136-75.

33. The United Republic of Tanzania, *Tanzania Government's Statement on the Recognition of Biafra* (Dar es Salaam: Government Printer, 1970), p. 1.

34. See, for example, Organization of African Unity, *No Genocide* (Lagos: Federal Ministry of Information, 1968), pp. 6-11.

35. On "totalist" perceptions, see Donald Rothchild, "Hegemonial Exchange: An Alternative Model for Managing Conflict in Middle Africa," in Dennis L. Thompson and Dov Ronen, eds., *Ethnicity, Politics, and Development* (Boulder, Colo.: Lynne Rienner, 1986), pp. 87-89; Robert Jervis, *Perception and Misperception in International Politics* (Princeton University Press, 1976); Noel

Kaplowitz, "Psychopolitical Dimensions of International Relations:The Reciprocal Effects of Conflict Strategies," *International Studies Quarterly,* vol. 28 (December 1984), pp. 377-81; and Alexander Dallin and Gail W. Lapidus, "Reagan and the Russians: U.S. Policy toward the Soviet Union and Eastern Europe," in Kenneth A. Oye, Robert J. Lieber, and Donald Rothchild, eds., *Eagle Defiant: United States Foreign Policy in the 1980s* (Little, Brown, 1983), pp. 206-09.

36. For several excellent discussions of zero-sum mind-sets in Africa, see René Lemarchand, *Rwanda and Burundi* (London: Pall Mall Press, 1970), pp. 169, 179, and *Selective Genocide in Burundi,* p. 8. Also see Kuper, *The Pity of It All;* and Thomas P. Melady, *Burundi: The Tragic Years* (Maryknoll, N.Y.: Orbis Books, 1974), p. 72.

37. Anthony D. Smith, *State and Nation in the Third World: The Western State and African Nationalism* (St. Martin's Press, 1983), p. 93. Among the theories of violence, see James B. Rule, *Theories of Civil Violence* (University of California Press, 1988); Ted Robert Gurr, *Why Men Rebel* (Princeton University Press, 1970); Anthony Oberschall, *Social Conflict and Social Movements* (Prentice-Hall, 1973); and Timothy D. Sisk, "The Violence-Negotiation Nexus: A Framework for Analysis," paper prepared for the Norwegian Nobel Institute Seminar Series, Oslo, Norway, November 9, 1995.

38. Lemarchand, "Revolutionary Phenomena in Stratified Societies," p. 47.

39. Quoted in Lemarchand, *Rwanda and Burundi,* pp. 169, 179 (originally in Supplement to *Jya Mbere,* November 27, 1959, p. 3). Also see Kuper, *The Pity of It All.*

40. Melady, *Burundi: The Tragic Years,* p. 72. Also see René Lemarchand, *Burundi: Ethnocide as Discourse and Practice* (Washington: Woodrow Wilson Center Press, 1994), pp. 29, 59-60.

41. David A. Lake and Donald Rothchild, "Containing Fear: The Origins and Management of Ethnic Conflict," *International Security,* vol. 21 (Fall 1996), pp. 41-75; Barry R. Posen, "The Security Dilemma and Ethnic Conflict," in Michael E. Brown, ed., *Ethnic Conflict and International Security* (Princeton University Press, 1993), pp. 103-24; and Robert Jervis, "Cooperation under the Security Dilemma," *World Politics,* vol. 30 (January 1978), pp. 167-214.

42. Jane Perlez, "Under the Bougainvillea: Litany of Past Wrongs," *New York Times,* August 15, 1994, p. A6. See also Donatella Lorch, "Vicious Circle: Hate Returns to Haunt Those Who Cradled It," *New York Times,* July 17, 1994, p. E1.

43. Republic of Kenya, The National Assembly, *Report of the Parliamentary Select Committee to Investigate Ethnic Clashes in Western and Other Parts of Kenya 1992* (Nairobi: Government Printer, 1992).

44. Russell Hardin, *One for All: The Logic of Group Conflict* (Princeton University Press, 1995), p. 9.

45. "Mandela Calls on Right Wing to Reject Civil War," *Johannesburg Sunday Star,* September 26, 1993, p. 8, in Foreign Broadcast Information Service (FBIS), *Daily Report: Republic of South Africa,* September 28, 1993, p. 10.

46. For a more extended discussion of these conflict-regulating strategies, see Rothchild, "State and Ethnicity in Africa," pp. 38-50.

47. See the presidential address by Claude Ake to the Nigerian Political Science Association, reprinted in *West Africa,* May 25, 1981, p. 1162.

48. Dessalegn Rahmato, "Land, Peasants, and the Drive for Collectivization in Ethiopia," in Thomas J. Bassett and Donald E. Crummey, eds., *Land in African Agrarian Systems* (University of Wisconsin Press, 1993), pp. 283-84.

49. Terry Lynn Karl and Philippe C. Schmitter, "Modes of Transition in Latin America, Southern and Eastern Europe," *International Social Science Journal,* vol. 43 (May 1991), pp. 269-84. "Pacts," writes Timothy D. Sisk, "are mutual security agreements in which parties forswear the use of violence to achieve their aims in exchange for protection under agreed-upon rules of the political game." *Power Sharing and International Mediation in Ethnic Conflicts* (Washington: U.S. Institute of Peace Press, 1996), p. 81.

50. Charles E. Lindblom, *The Intelligence of Democracy* (Free Press, 1965), p. 68.

51. Przeworski, *Democracy and the Market,* p. 26.

52. James M. Buchanan and Gordon Tullock, *The Calculus of Consent* (University of Michigan Press, 1962), p. 111.

53. For this characterization of "directed democracy," see *Africa Demos,* vol. 1 (May 1991), p. 2; see also "Zimbabwe: An Opposition Emerges," *Africa Confidential,* vol. 33 (July 17, 1992), pp. 3-4.

54. Jennifer A. Widner, "Single Party States and Agricultural Policies: The Cases of Ivory Coast and Kenya," *Comparative Politics,* vol. 26 (January 1994), p. 129.

55. Sammy Smooha, "Control of Minorities in Israel and Northern Ireland," *Comparative Studies in Society and History,* vol. 22 (April 1980), p. 257. See also Percy C. Hintzen and Ralph R. Premdas, "Guyana: Coercion and Control in Political Change," *Journal of Interamerican Studies and World Affairs,* vol. 24 (August 1982), p. 352.

56. Frances Hagopian, "'Democracy by Undemocratic Means'? Elites, Political Pacts, and Regime Transition in Brazil," *Comparative Political Studies,* vol. 23 (July 1990), pp. 147-70.

57. Horowitz, *Ethnic Groups in Conflict,* pp. 598-99.

58. On the timing of democratization, see Michael E. Brown, "Introduction," in Brown, ed., *The International Dimensions of Internal Conflict* (MIT Press, 1996), p. 17.

59. Federal Republic of Nigeria, *Report of the Political Bureau* (Lagos: Federal Government Printer, 1987), p. 74.

60. Larry Diamond, "Introduction," in Larry Diamond, Juan J. Linz, and Seymour Martin Lipset, eds., *Democracy in Developing Countries: Africa* (Boulder, Colo.: Lynne Rienner, 1988), p. 28.

61. Donald L. Horowitz, *A Democratic South Africa?* (University of California Press, 1991), p. 34.

62. W. Arthur Lewis, *Politics in West Africa* (London: George Allen & Unwin, 1965), pp. 84-85.

63. Milton J. Esman, "The Management of Communal Conflict," *Public Policy,* vol. 21 (Winter 1973), p. 62.

64. Arend Lijphart, *Democracy in Plural Societies* (Yale University Press, 1977), p. 39.

65. Hussein M. Adam, "Somalia: Militarism, Warlordism or Democracy?" *Review of African Political Economy,* no. 54 (1992), p. 18. See also Rakiya Omaar, "Somalia: At War with Itself," *Current History,* vol. 91 (May 1992), p. 233.

66. Federal Republic of Nigeria, *Official Gazette*, vol. 76, no. 29, May 3, 1989 (Lagos: Federal Government Printer, 1989), secs. 131, 132.

67. This is not always the case. For example, Kenya's 1992 election rules, which provided that the president would have to obtain 25 percent of the vote in five out of eight provinces in order to be elected, was not an attempt to promote a sense of ethnic inclusiveness. Rather, it represented President Daniel arap Moi's effort to organize the rules to keep himself in power. Following the election, moreover, he continued the politics of exclusion, appointing only one Kikuyu and one Luo to the cabinet, and these were hardly the most prominent representatives of their communities.

68. For an African endorsement of proportional representation, see "The Kampala Document," in Olusegun Obasanjo and Felix G. N. Mosha, eds., *Africa: Rise to Challenge: Towards a Conference on Security, Stability, Development and Cooperation in Africa* (New York: Africa Leadership Forum, 1993), pp. 318-19.

69. Joseph Rothschild, *Ethnopolitics: A Conceptual Framework* (Columbia University Press, 1981), p. 165.

70. Timothy D. Sisk, "South Africa Seeks New Ground Rules," *Journal of Democracy*, vol. 4 (January 1993), p. 87.

71. "ANC Ends Crucial Meeting on Regionalism," South African Press Association, March 20, 1993, in FBIS, *Daily Report: Sub-Saharan Africa*, March 22, 1993, p. 11.

72. Colin Legum, "South Africa: The ANC's Major Concession towards Conceding a Federal-Type State," *Third World Reports*, T.P/3 (May 26, 1993), p. 1.

73. International Republican Institute, *Kenya: The December 29, 1992 Elections* (Washington, 1993), p. 37; and Joel D. Barkan, "Kenya: Lessons from a Flawed Election," *Journal of Democracy*, vol. 4 (July 1993), pp. 91-99.

74. Of course, the number of group representatives is not sufficient by itself. It is also important to assure proportional group influence and the authenticity of this representation. See Robert B. Mattes, "Beyond 'Government and Opposition': An Independent South African Legislature," *Politikon*, vol. 20 (December 1993), p. 76; and Lani Guinier, *The Tyranny of the Majority* (Free Press, 1994), p. 156.

75. "Mandela Rejects Power Sharing," South African Press Association, February 14, 1993, in FBIS, *Daily Report: Sub-Saharan Africa*, February 16, 1993, p. 15.

76. Ibid.

77. See Donald Rothchild, "Majimbo Schemes in Kenya and Uganda," in Jeffrey Butler and A. A. Castagno, eds., *Boston University Papers on Africa: Transition in African Politics* (New York: Praeger, 1967), pp. 291-318.

78. *Africa Research Bulletin*, Political, Social and Cultural Series, vol. 31 (October 1994), p. 11599.

79. See the *General Agreement of Mozambique, 1992*, p. 54; and Iraê Baptista Lundin, "Cultural Diversity and the Role of Traditional Authority in Mozambique," and Donald Rothchild, "The Debate on Decentralization in Africa: An Overview," in Donald Rothchild, ed., *Strengthening Local Initiative: Local Self-Governance, Decentralization, and Accountability* (Hamburg: Institute of African Affairs, 1994), chaps. 1, 8.

80. Federal Republic of Nigeria, *Report of the Political Bureau,* p. 80.

81. President Babangida told a conference on intergovernmental relations in Abuja that federalism "provided a unique medium for coping with certain problems in the country's association as ethnic groups which formed a new political community." *The Republic* (Lagos), January 19, 1993, p. 1.

82. Horowitz, *A Democratic South Africa?* p. 221.

83. Cameron McWhirter and Gur Melamede, "Ethiopia: The Ethnicity Factor," *Africa Report,* vol. 37 (September-October 1992), p. 33.

84. Marina Ottaway, "Nationalism Unbound: The Horn of Africa Revisited," *SAIS Review,* vol. 12 (Summer-Fall 1992), p. 123.

85. Billy Paddock, "Constitution to Be Redrafted: Bid to Break Deadlock on Regional Plan," *Business Day* (Johannesburg), July 29, 1993, p. 1.

86. *Constitution of the Republic of South Africa, 1993,* Act 200, 1993, *Government Gazette,* vol. 343, no. 15466 (Cape Town, January 28, 1994), secs. 125-59 and Schedule 6.

87. Tim Cohen, "Regions May Still be Tied to Central Govt's Purse Strings," *Business Day* (Johannesburg), August 2, 1993, p. 4.

Chapter 3

1. Charles E. Lindblom, *Politics and Markets* (Basic Books, 1977), p. 139.

2. On other markets of political exchange, see Donald Rothchild, "State-Ethnic Relations in Middle Africa," in Gwendolen M. Carter and Patrick O'Meara, eds., *African Independence: The First Twenty-Five Years* (Indiana University Press, 1985), pp. 82-91.

3. Martin Shubik, *Games for Society, Business and War* (New York: Elsevier, 1975), p. x.

4. George Tsebelis, *Nested Games: Rational Choice in Comparative Politics* (University of California Press, 1990), pp. 173-74; and Brian Barry, "Political Accommodation and Consociational Democracy," *British Journal of Political Science,* vol. 5 (October 1975), pp. 484-86.

5. Manfred Halpern, "Changing Connections to Multiple Worlds," in Helen Kitchen, ed., *Africa: From Mystery to Maze* (Lexington, Mass.: D.C. Heath, 1976), p. 15.

6. This conforms to the intensity scales set out by Ted Robert Gurr in "A Causal Model of Civil Strife: A Comparative Analysis Using New Indices," *American Political Science Review,* vol. 62 (December 1968), pp. 1109-11.

7. Larry Diamond, "Class, Ethnicity, and the Democratic State: Nigeria, 1950-1966," *Comparative Studies in Society and History,* vol. 25 (July 1983), pp. 476, 487.

8. Letter from René Lemarchand to Donald Rothchild, January 2, 1988.

9. Shaheen Mozaffar, "Leadership Process and the Management of Ethnic Conflict in Africa," Working Paper 112, Boston University, African Studies Center, 1986, p. 14.

10. David Easton, "An Approach to the Analysis of Political Systems," *World Politics,* vol. 9 (April 1957), p. 389.

11. Donald Horowitz, "Democracy in Divided Societies," *Journal of Democracy,* vol. 4 (October 1993), p. 20.

12. *West Africa*, July 16, 1979, p. 1257.

13. John A. Marcum, "Angola: A Quarter Century of War," *CSIS Africa Notes*, no. 37 (December 21, 1984), p. 3.

14. As Foreign Minister Paulo Jorge explained in 1981, "We do not accept reconciliation of traitors and terrorists." Richard Deutsch, "Building an Africa Policy," *Africa Report*, vol. 26 (July–August 1981), pp. 44–47.

15. Ike Onwordi, "A Question of Race," *West Africa*, October 24-30, 1988, pp. 1984–85; and Lyse Doucet, "Mauritania: Fragile Politics," *West Africa*, January 19, 1987, pp. 110–11.

16. Dunstan M. Wai, "Geoethnicity and the Margin of Autonomy in the Sudan," in Donald Rothchild and Victor A. Olorunsola, eds., *State versus Ethnic Claims: African Policy Dilemmas* (Boulder, Colo.: Westview, 1983), p. 320.

17. Samuel Aru Bol, *Statement on the Southern Problem: The Position in the South to Date* (Khartoum: Sudan African National Union, 1968), p. 2.

18. Calculated from *Europa Year Book*, vol. 2, for 1959–88; *Africa Research Bulletin*, Political Series, vol. 26 (March 15, 1989), p. 9179; and Yehudit Ronen, "Sudan," in Ami Ayalon, ed., *Middle East Contemporary Survey 1989-1990*, vol. 13 (Boulder, Colo.: Westview, 1991), p. 617.

19. *Grass Curtain*, vol. 1 (April 1971), p. 28.

20. Regarding the links between the military junta and the National Islamic Front, see Abbashar Jamal, "Funding Fundamentalism: Sudan," *Review of African Political Economy*, no. 52 (November 1991), p. 104.

21. Jean Gueyras, "Doubts over Sudan's New Masters," *Manchester Guardian Weekly*, July 30, 1989, p. 13.

22. "The military," Pauline Baker wrote while President Botha was in control, "is at the center of the present decision-making structure, wielding more political power than ever through the State Security Council . . . and the National Security Management System." "South Africa: The Afrikaner Angst," *Foreign Policy*, no. 69 (Winter 1987–88), p. 76. See also Heribert Adam and Hermann Giliomee, *Ethnic Power Mobilized: Can South Africa Change?* (Yale University Press, 1979), p. 253.

23. Regarding the determination of the National party to advance "Afrikaner sectionalism," see Sampie Terreblanche, "A New Government," *Leadership Politics*, vol. 6 (1987), pp. 18–23.

24. Baker, "South Africa," p. 66.

25. I am indebted to Kenneth Grundy and Louis A. Picard for these data.

26. Richard A. Joseph, "Ethnicity and Prebendal Politics in Nigeria: A Theoretical Outline," paper prepared for the 1982 annual meeting of the American Political Science Association, p. 9. Also see his comments on ethnic balancing in Richard Joseph, *Democracy and Prebendal Politics in Nigeria* (Cambridge University Press, 1987), pp. 84–85.

27. Ladipo Adamolekun, *Sekou Touré's Guinea* (London: Methuen, 1976), pp. 130–31.

28. Gregory Kronsten, *Zaire to the 1990s: Will Retrenchment Work?* (London: Economist Intelligence Unit, 1986), p. 6.

29. Crawford Young and Thomas Turner, *The Rise and Decline of the Zairian State* (University of Wisconsin Press, 1985), pp. 150–51.

30. Southern Sudanese were generally unimpressed with the three ministers appointed to the cabinet in 1985; they were either not regarded as authentic representatives or were restricted to the less important ministries. *SUDANOW* (Khartoum), vol. 10 (May 1985), p. 6.

31. Goran Hyden, "Reciprocity and Governance in Africa," in James S. Wunsch and Dele Olowu, eds., *The Failure of the Centralized State* (Boulder, Colo.: Westview, 1990), chap. 11.

32. Howard Adelman and Astri Suhrke, *Early Warning and Conflict Management* (Copenhagen: Joint Evaluation of Emergency Assistance to Rwanda, 1996); see also Donald L. Horowitz, *Ethnic Groups in Conflict* (University of California Press, 1985), p. 630.

33. Adam Przeworski, *Democracy and the Market* (Cambridge University Press, 1991), p. 26.

34. Ali A. Mazrui, *Violence and Thought* (London: Longmans, 1969), p. 147.

35. See Donald Rothchild and Michael Rogin, "Uganda," in Gwendolen M. Carter, ed., *National Unity and Regionalism in Eight African States* (Cornell University Press, 1966), pp. 345-51.

36. Nelson Kasfir, *The Shrinking Political Arena* (University of California Press, 1976), p. 180.

37. Colin Legum, ed., *Africa Contemporary Record 1981-82* (New York: Africana, 1981), pp. B299, B303.

38. Museveni's decision, in March 1989, to appoint seven non-Bantus and three Bantus as the military representatives to the National Resistance Council was described as an "eclectic outcome" by the *Indian Ocean Newsletter.* "Ethnically," it concluded, "this is a positive development." *Indian Ocean Newsletter,* no. 375 (March 25, 1989), p. 5. See also Michael Bratton, "Beyond the State: Civil Society and Associational Life in Africa," *World Politics,* vol. 41 (April 1989), p. 420.

39. See Tendayi Kumbula, "Zimbabwe: A Mandate for Mugabe," *Africa Report,* vol. 31 (September–October 1986), p. 73.

40. Masipula Sithole, "State Power Consolidation in Zimbabwe: Party and Ideological Development," in Edmond Keller and Donald Rothchild, eds., *Afro-Marxist Regimes: Ideology and Public Policy* (Boulder, Colo.: Lynne Rienner, 1987), p. 102.

41. James Mackay, "Zimbabwe: Dissidents Come Home," *New African,* no. 250 (July 1988), p. 19.

42. Richard W. Hull, "Overcoming Zimbabwe's Vulnerabilities," *Current History,* vol. 87 (May 1988), p. 197.

43. Robert H. Jackson, "Planning, Politics, and Administration," in Goran Hyden, Robert Jackson, and John Okumu, eds., *Development Administration: The Kenyan Experience* (Nairobi, Kenya: Oxford University Press, 1970), p. 177.

44. Naomi Chazan, "The Dynamics of Civil Society in Africa," paper prepared for the International Conference on Civil Society in Africa, Hebrew University, Jerusalem, January 5-10, 1992, p. 13.

45. Donald L. Horowitz, *A Democratic South Africa?* (University of California Press, 1991), p. 261; and Robert Axelrod, *The Evolution of Cooperation* (Basic Books, 1984), p. 129.

46. Peter Anyang' Nyong'o, "Democratization Processes in Africa," *CODESRIA Bulletin,* no. 2 (1991), p. 3. Also see Claude Ake, "Rethinking African Democracy," *Journal of Democracy,* vol. 2 (Winter 1991), p. 35.

47. John D. Holm, "Botswana: A Paternalistic Democracy," in Larry Diamond, Juan J. Linz, and Seymour Martin Lipset, eds., *Democracy in Developing Countries: Africa* (Boulder, Colo.: Lynne Rienner, 1988), p. 187.

48. Peter P. Ekeh, "The Structure and Meaning of Federal Character in the Nigerian Political System," in Peter P. Ekeh and Eghosa E. Osaghae, eds., *Federal Character and Federalism in Nigeria* (Ibadan, Nigeria: Heinemann, 1989), p. 32. Also see Osaghae, "The Federal Cabinet, 1951-1984," ibid., p. 131.

49. See Osaghae, "Federal Cabinet," pp. 150-51.

50. See Nosa Igiebor, "The Tug of Character," *Newswatch* (Ikeja), April 13, 1987, p. 27.

51. Daniel G. Matthews, "Nigeria 1985: An Interim Report," *CSIS Africa Notes,* no. 24 (February 29, 1984), pp. 3-4; and Larry Diamond, "Nigeria: The Coup and the Future," *Africa Report,* vol. 29 (March-April 1984), pp. 13-14.

52. *New African* (London), no. 218 (November 1985), p. 24.

53. "Nigerian Coup Attempt Defeated," *Financial Times,* April 23, 1990, p. 1; "In Coup-Prone Nigeria, 2 Halves Make a Crisis," *New York Times,* May 1, 1990, p. A15; and Paxton Idowu, "A Bloody Attempt," *West Africa,* April 30-May 6, 1990, pp. 696-97.

54. Federal Republic of Nigeria, *Report of the Political Bureau* (Lagos: Federal Government Printer, 1987), pp. 93, 126.

55. Constitution of the Federal Republic of Nigeria (Promulgation) Decree 1989, Supplement to Federal Republic of Nigeria, *Official Gazette,* vol. 76, no. 29, May 3, 1989 (Lagos: Federal Government Printer, 1989), p. A79.

56. Draft Constitution of the Federal Republic of Nigeria, vol. 1 (1995), sec. 172 (4).

57. Robert Melson and Howard Wolpe, "Modernization and the Politics of Communalism," *American Political Science Review,* vol. 64 (December 1970), p. 1124.

58. Robert H. Bates, "Modernization, Ethnic Competition, and the Rationality of Politics in Contemporary Africa," in Rothchild and Olorunsola, eds., *State versus Ethnic Claims,* p. 161.

59. Shubik, *Games for Society,* p. x.

60. Pierre du Toit, *State Building and Democracy in Southern Africa* (Washington: U.S. Institute of Peace Press, 1995), pp. 164-65.

61. Anne Shepherd, "South Africa: The Land Inequity," *Africa Report,* vol. 39 (January-February 1994), pp. 65-66.

62. Heribert Adam and Kogila Moodley, *South Africa without Apartheid: Dismantling Racial Domination* (University of California Press, 1986), p. 234.

63. Bruce McKenney, "Reconstructing Education for a New South Africa," *CSIS Africa Notes,* no. 131 (December 1991), p. 2.

64. Tim Niblock, *Class and Power in Sudan* (State University of New York Press, 1987), pp. 143-45.

65. B. Yongo-Bure, "Southern Sudan in Sudanese Development Policy 1946-1972," in Diana Rosenberg, ed., *The Role of the Southern Sudanese People*

in the Building of Modern Sudan (Juba,The Sudan: University of Juba, 1986), pp. 89–98.

66. Democratic Republic of the Sudan, *The Six Year Plan of Economic and Social Development, 1977/78-1982/83,* vol. 1 (Khartoum: Ministry of National Planning,April 1977), p. 49; and Wai,"Geoethnicity and the Margin of Autonomy," p. 320.

67. Jacob Alier Chol, "The North-South Relations in the Sudan:A Political and Economic Perspective," M.A. thesis, University of Manchester, 1983, pp. 55–56.

68. President Gaafar Nimeiri, *Speech on Main Features and Development Aspects of the Six Year Economic Development Plan, 1977/78-1982/83* (Washington: Sudanese Embassy, January 1977), p. 2; and People's Executive Councils' Budgets for FY 80/81, Ministry of Finance on National Economy, Democratic Republic of Sudan (n.d.).

69. B.Yongo-Bure,"Prospects for Socioeconomic Development of the South," in Francis Mading Deng and Prosser Gifford, eds., *The Search for Peace and Unity in the Sudan* (Washington:Wilson Center Press, 1987), pp. 36–38.

70. Christopher Clapham,"Centralization and Local Response in Southern Ethiopia," *African Affairs,* vol. 74 (January 1975), p. 73.

71. John W. Harbeson, *The Ethiopian Transformation* (Boulder, Colo.: Westview, 1988), p. 69.

72. Edmond J. Keller, *Revolutionary Ethiopia* (Indiana University Press, 1988), pp. 138–41.

73. Christopher Clapham, *Transformation and Continuity in Revolutionary Ethiopia* (Cambridge University Press, 1988), p. 150.The regime's emphasis on more egalitarian allocative patterns is in line with the findings on general distributional practices in Marxist-Leninist societies. See Alexander J. Groth,"Third World Marxism-Leninism: The Case of Education," *Comparative Education,* vol. 23, no. 3 (1987), p. 334.

74. Holm,"Botswana," p. 191.

75. Milton J. Esman,"The Management of Communal Conflict," *Public Policy,* vol. 21 (Winter 1973), p. 62.

76. This section draws substantially from Donald Rothchild,"Middle Africa: Hegemonial Exchange and Resource Allocation," in Alexander J. Groth and Larry L. Wade, eds., *Comparative Resource Allocation* (Beverly Hills: Sage Publications, 1984), pp. 167–76.

77. Clearly this small percentage of increase in allocations did little to improve a situation where there were only nine secondary schools in the province. Reportedly, these schools prepared only 150 O-level students a year, and not all of these were Somalis. *Africa Now,* vol. 24 (April 1983), p. 36.

78. Willard Johnson,"Introduction," in Ndiva Kofele-Kale, ed., *An African Experiment in Nation Building* (Boulder, Colo.:Westview, 1980), p. xvi; *Daily Times* (Lagos),August 21, 1980, p. 24; *West Africa,* October 25, 1982, p. 846; *Standard* (Nairobi), October 13, 1979, p. 23; Donald Rothchild, "Rural-Urban Inequities and Resource Allocation in Zambia," *Journal of Commonwealth Political Studies,* vol. 10 (November 1972), p. 228; Donald Rothchild,"Military Regime Performance: An Appraisal of the Ghana Experience, 1972-1978,"

Comparative Politics, vol. 12 (July 1980), p. 474; and *West Africa,* March 29, 1980, p. 1732.

79. Rothchild, "Middle Africa," p. 169; A. B. Amey and D. K. Leonard, "Public Policy, Class and Inequality in Kenya and Tanzania," *Africa Today,* vol. 26, no. 4 (1979), pp. 37-38; and Andrew Coulson, "Decentralization and the Government Budget," Working Paper, vol. 75, no. 6 (Dar es Salaam: University Research Project on Government Decentralization and the Management of Rural Development in Tanzania, 1975), pp. 40-41.

80. The line-of-rail provinces were Copperbelt (0.471) and Central (0.660); off the line of rail were Northern (1.002), Luapula (1.214), North-Western (1.463), Eastern (1.888), and Western (1.519). Southern Province's allocation was 1.420. Rothchild, "Middle Africa," p. 170; and Rothchild, "Rural-Urban Inequities," pp. 235-36. See also Dennis L. Dresang, "Ethnic Politics, Representative Bureaucracy and Development Administration: The Zambia Case," *American Political Science Review,* vol. 68 (December 1974), pp. 1613-14.

81. Quoted in Rothchild, "Rural-Urban Inequities," p. 238.

82. Rothchild, "Military Regime Performance," pp. 475-76.

83. Thomas M. Callaghy, "Lost between State and Market: The Politics of Economic Adjustment in Ghana, Zambia, and Nigeria," in Joan M. Nelson, ed., *Economic Crisis and Policy Choice* (Princeton University Press, 1990), pp. 257-319.

84. *People's Daily Graphic* (Accra), April 7, 1983, p. 1; and *West Africa,* October 25, 1982, p. 2765.

85. See Donald Rothchild and Emmanuel Gyimah-Boadi, "Ghana's Economic Decline and Development Strategies," in John Ravenhill, ed., *Africa in Economic Crisis* (Columbia University Press, 1986), pp. 276-79.

86. Edmond J. Keller, "The State, Public Policy and the Mediation of Ethnic Conflict in Africa," in Rothchild and Olorunsola, eds., *State versus Ethnic Claims,* p. 263. Also see Melson and Wolpe, "Modernization and the Politics of Communalism."

87. On this tactic, see Brian H. Tracy, "Bargaining as Trial and Error: The Case of the Spanish Base Negotiations, 1963-1970," in I. William Zartman, ed., *The Negotiation Process: Theories and Applications* (Beverly Hills: Sage Publications, 1978), pp. 194-98.

88. Ted Robert Gurr, "A Comparative Study of Civil Strife," in Hugh Davis Graham and Ted Robert Gurr, eds., *Violence in America* (New York: New American Library, 1969), p. 552. On the relationship between democracy and economic growth, see Jane Perlez, "Is Botswana a Model for Democracies in Africa?" *New York Times,* May 16, 1990, p. A6.

89. Arend Lijphart, *Democracy in Plural Societies* (Yale University Press, 1977), p. 75.

90. Ted Robert Gurr, *Minorities at Risk* (Washington: U.S. Institute of Peace Press, 1993), p. 136.

91. Daniel S. Geller, "The Impact of Political System Structure on Probability Patterns of Internal Disorder," *American Journal of Political Science,* vol. 31 (May 1987), p. 230. Also see Alvin Rabushka and Kenneth A. Shepsle, *Politics in Plural Societies* (Columbus, Ohio: Merrill, 1972), pp. 207, 217.

92. Donna Bahry and Brian D. Silver, "Intimidation and the Symbolic Uses of Terror in the USSR," *American Political Science Review,* vol. 81 (December 1987), p. 1089.

93. Further complicating this picture of incoherence is the possibility of conflict within one of the bargaining parties—what two writers describe, with reference to Southern Sudan, as "the emergence of a civil war within the civil war." Francis M. Deng and Larry Minear, *The Challenges of Famine Relief: Emergency Operations in the Sudan* (Brookings, 1992), p. 133.

Chapter 4

1. For data on the outcomes of civil wars, see Stephen John Stedman, *Peacemaking in Civil War: International Mediation in Zimbabwe, 1974-1980* (Boulder, Colo.: Lynne Rienner, 1991), pp. 5-7. Among other aggregate accounts of civil war termination, see Paul R. Pillar, *Negotiating Peace: War Termination as a Bargaining Process* (Princeton University Press, 1983); and Roy Licklider, "The Consequences of Negotiated Settlements in Civil Wars, 1945-1993," *American Political Science Review,* vol. 89 (September 1995), p. 684.

2. "De Klerk Reiterates Anti-Communist Positions," *Johannesburg SAPA,* May 2, 1991, in Foreign Broadcast Information Service (FBIS), *Daily Report: Republic of South Africa,* May 3, 1991, p. 1; and "Continental Alignments," *Africa Research Bulletin,* Political Series, vol. 26 (September 15, 1989), p. 9368.

3. On the earlier period, see Martin Doornbos, "Kumanyana and Rwenzururu: Two Responses to Ethnic Inequality," in Robert I. Rotberg and Ali A. Mazrui, eds., *Protest and Power in Black Africa* (Oxford University Press, 1970), pp. 1109-26.

4. "Ceremony Marks Tribal King's Acceptance of UPC," Kampala Domestic Service, August 18, 1982, in FBIS, *Daily Report: East Africa,* August 25, 1982, p. R3. Regarding this, I am also grateful to Nelson Kasfir and Martin Doornbos for interviews.

5. Arnold Wolfers, "Statesmanship and Moral Choice," *World Politics,* vol. 1 (January 1949), p. 182.

6. Saadia Touval, *The Peace Brokers: Mediators in the Arab-Israeli Conflict, 1948-1979* (Princeton University Press, 1982), p. 5.

7. On the benefits of being perceived as neutral in gaining the trust of the disputant parties, see Adam Curle, *Making Peace* (London: Tavistock, 1971), p. 221.

8. Russell J. Leng and Hugh G. Wheeler, "Influence Strategies, Success, and War," *Journal of Conflict Resolution,* vol. 23 (December 1979), p. 679.

9. This section makes extensive use of the game theory literature. In particular, see Martin Patchen, *Resolving Disputes between Nations: Coercion or Conciliation?* (Duke University Press, 1988); Glenn H. Snyder and Paul Diesing, *Conflict among Nations: Bargaining, Decision Making, and System Structure in International Crises* (Princeton University Press, 1977); Anatol Rapoport, "Exploiter, Leader, Hero, and Martyr: The Four Archetypes of the 2 x 2 Game," *Behavioral Science,* vol. 12 (1967), pp. 81-84; Anatol Rapoport and Melvin Guyer, "A Taxonomy of 2 x 2 Games," *General Systems,* vol. 11 (1966), pp. 203-13; and Robert Axelrod, *The Evolution of Cooperation* (Basic Books, 1984).

10. Snyder and Diesing, *Conflict among Nations,* p. 97 (emphasis in original).

11. Thomas C. Schelling, *The Strategy of Conflict* (Harvard University Press, 1960), p. 214.

12. Snyder and Diesing, *Conflict among Nations,* p. 89.

13. I. William Zartman, "Conflict Reduction: Prevention, Management, and Resolution," in Francis M. Deng and I. William Zartman, eds., *Conflict Resolution in Africa* (Brookings, 1991), p. 306.

14. Interview, E. Gibson Lanpher, Washington, June 25, 1987, p. 14.

15. I. William Zartman, *Ripe for Resolution: Conflict and Intervention in Africa* (Oxford University Press, 1985), p. 9.

16. Kenneth A. Oye, "The Domain of Choice: International Constraints and Carter Administration Foreign Policy," in Kenneth A. Oye, Donald Rothchild, and Robert J. Lieber, eds., *Eagle Entangled: U.S. Foreign Policy in a Complex World* (New York: Longman, 1979), p. 13; and Roger Fisher and William Ury, *Getting to Yes: Negotiating Agreement without Giving In* (Houghton Mifflin, 1981), p. 122.

17. On hastening ripe moments, see Chester A. Crocker, *High Noon in Southern Africa: Making Peace in a Rough Neighborhood* (Norton, 1992), pp. 471, 475; Richard N. Haass, *Conflicts Unending: The United States and Regional Disputes* (Yale University Press, 1990), p. 147; and Fen Osler Hampson, *Nurturing Peace: Why Peace Settlements Succeed or Fail* (Washington: U.S. Institute of Peace Press, 1996).

18. Donald L. Horowitz, "Making Moderation Pay: The Comparative Politics of Ethnic Conflict Management," in Joseph V. Montville, ed., *Conflict and Peacemaking in Multiethnic Societies* (Lexington, Mass.: Lexington Books, 1991), pp. 464, 471.

19. The role of the state and external enforcer is explored in David A. Lake and Donald Rothchild, "Containing Fear: The Origins and Management of Ethnic Conflict," *International Security,* vol. 21 (Fall 1996), pp. 41–75.

20. Inis L. Claude Jr., *Swords into Plowshares: The Problems and Progress of International Organization* (Random House, 1956), p. 244.

21. Harold Nicolson, *Diplomacy,* 3d ed. (Oxford University Press, 1963), p. 105.

22. See Jeffrey Davidow, *A Peace in Southern Africa: The Lancaster House Conference on Rhodesia, 1979* (Boulder, Colo.: Westview, 1984), p. 106. Also see Ronald J. Fisher, "Third Party Consultation: A Method for the Study and Resolution of Conflict," *Journal of Conflict Resolution,* vol. 16 (March 1972), pp. 76–77.

23. Jeffrey Z. Rubin, "The Timing of Ripeness and the Ripeness of Timing," in Louis Kriesberg and Stuart J. Thorson, eds., *Timing the De-Escalation of International Conflicts* (Syracuse University Press, 1991), p. 240 (emphasis in original).

24. Svenn Lindskold, "Trust Development, the GRIT Proposal, and the Effects of Conciliatory Acts on Conflict and Cooperation," *Psychological Bulletin,* vol. 85, no. 4 (1978), p. 772.

25. For an excellent discussion of the use of deadlines, see I. William Zartman, "Deadlock in Namibia," *SAIS Review,* vol. 5 (Summer–Fall 1985), pp. 256–57; and Zartman, *Ripe for Resolution,* pp. 240–41.

26. I. William Zartman and Johannes Aurik, "Power Strategies in De-Escalation," in Kriesberg and Thorson, eds., *Timing the De-Escalation*, p. 181.

27. Louis Kriesberg, "Noncoercive Inducements in U.S.-Soviet Conflicts: Ending the Occupation of Austria and Nuclear Weapons Tests," *Journal of Political and Military Sociology*, vol. 9 (Spring 1981), p. 2.

28. Touval, *Peace Brokers*, p. 327.

29. Jane Rosen and John Torode, "Cyprus Summit Talks Fail," *Manchester Guardian Weekly*, January 27, 1985, p. 7; and Alex Vines, "Mozambique: The Road to Peace (1982–1992)," paper prepared for the 1993 annual meeting of the African Studies Association, p. 33.

30. Jonathan C. Randal, "Algerian, Moroccan Leaders Meet," *Washington Post*, May 5, 1987, p. A21.

31. Cyrus Vance, *Hard Choices: Critical Years in America's Foreign Policy* (Simon and Schuster, 1983), p. 299.

32. On the commitment dilemma, see James D. Fearon, "Commitment Problems and the Spread of Ethnic Conflict," in David A. Lake and Donald Rothchild, eds., *Ethnic Fears and Global Engagement: The International Spread and Management of Ethnic Conflict* (Princeton University Press, forthcoming), chap. 5.

33. H. L. de Silva, "The Indo-Sri Lanka Agreement (1987) in the Perspective of Inter-State Relations," *Ethnic Studies Report*, vol. 10 (July 1992), pp. 10–17.

34. Arild Underdal, "Causes of Negotiation 'Failure'," *European Journal of Political Research*, vol. 11 (June 1983), p. 190 (emphasis in original).

35. *Counterspy*, vol. 5 (August–October 1981), p. 56.

36. On Mozambique, see Witney W. Schneidman, "Conflict Resolution in Mozambique," in David R. Smock, ed., *Making War and Waging Peace: Foreign Intervention in Africa* (Washington: U.S. Institute of Peace Press, 1993), p. 233.

37. Jeffrey Z. Rubin and Bert R. Brown, *The Social Psychology of Bargaining and Negotiation* (New York: Academic Press, 1975), pp. 130–31.

38. James Laue, "The Conflict Resolution Field: An Overview and Some Critical Questions," in W. Scott Thompson and others, *Dialogues on Conflict Resolution: Bridging Theory and Practice* (Washington: U.S. Institute of Peace, 1993), p. 22.

39. Svenn Lindskold and Russell Bennett, "Attributing Trust and Conciliatory Intent from Coercive Power Capability," *Journal of Personality and Social Psychology*, vol. 28 (November 1973), pp. 184, 186.

40. Alexander L. George, *Forceful Persuasion: Coercive Diplomacy as an Alternative to War* (Washington: U.S. Institute of Peace Press, 1991), p. 12.

41. Confidential interview, Nairobi, July 26, 1986; and "President Moi: Peacebroker," *Weekly Review* (Nairobi), December 20, 1985, p. 14. Also see Hilary Ng'weno, editorial, *Weekly Review*, January 3, 1986, p. 1.

42. Interview, Nairobi, July 26, 1986.

43. See Chester A. Crocker, "A Democratic Future: The Challenge for South Africans," U.S. Department of State, Bureau of Public Affairs, October 1, 1987, Current Policy no. 1009, p. 2.

44. Timothy D. Sisk, *Democratization in South Africa: The Elusive Social Contract* (Princeton University Press, 1995), pp. 82–84.

45. Lindskold and Bennett, "Attributing Trust," pp. 184-85.

46. *Congressional Record*, September 11, 1985, p. S23294.

47. James M. Lindsay, "Trade Sanctions as Policy Instruments: A Re-examination," *International Studies Quarterly*, vol. 30 (June 1986), p. 159. See also Leonard T. Kapungu, *The United Nations and Economic Sanctions against Rhodesia* (Lexington, Mass.: Lexington Books, 1973); Robin Renwick, *Economic Sanctions* (Harvard University, Center for International Affairs, 1981); and Harry R. Strack, *Sanctions: The Case of Rhodesia* (Syracuse University Press, 1978).

48. This conclusion was reached regarding the Rhodesian sanctions in Donald L. Losman, *International Economic Sanctions: The Cases of Cuba, Israel, and Rhodesia* (University of New Mexico Press, 1979), p. 116.

49. George F. Kennan, *American Diplomacy 1900-1950* (University of Chicago Press, 1951), p. 90.

50. Donald K. Petterson, "Somalia and the United States, 1977-1983: The New Relationship," in Gerald Bender, James S. Coleman, and Richard L. Sklar, eds., *African Crisis Areas and U.S. Foreign Policy* (University of California Press, 1985), pp. 198-201. See also Jeffrey A. Lefebvre, *Arms for the Horn: U.S. Security Policy in Ethiopia and Somalia, 1953-1991* (University of Pittsburgh Press, 1991), chap. 9.

51. Susan F. Rasky, "Reagan to Press Ahead on Aid to Angola Rebels," *New York Times*, December 11, 1985, p. 6.

52. On the U.S. government's preparedness to risk hostilities, see National Security Files, Congo Cables, Dean Rusk to American Embassy, Leopoldville, May 22, 1962, p. 1. U.S. Ambassador Edmund Gullion acted upon this immediately, informing Prime Minister Cyrille Adoula after consulting UN Representative Robert Gardiner. Ibid., Gullion to Secretary of State, May 30, 1962, p. 1 (John F. Kennedy Library).

53. Hussein M. Adam, "Somalia: Militarism, Warlordism or Democracy?" *Review of African Political Economy*, no. 54 (July 1992), p. 18.

54. John L. Hirsch and Robert B. Oakley, *Somalia and Operation Restore Hope: Reflections on Peacemaking and Peacekeeping* (U.S. Institute of Peace Press, 1995), pp. 162-63.

55. Ted Robert Gurr, "A Causal Model of Civil Strife: A Comparative Analysis Using New Indices," *American Political Science Review*, vol. 62 (December 1968), p. 1124.

56. Martin Patchen, "Strategies for Eliciting Cooperation from an Adversary: Laboratory and Internation Findings," *Journal of Conflict Resolution*, vol. 31 (March 1987), p. 182.

57. On the use of carrots and sticks to enforce deadlines, see Zartman, *Ripe for Resolution*, p. 224.

58. Charles E. Osgood, *An Alternative to War or Surrender* (University of Illinois Press, 1962). Also see Patchen, "Strategies for Eliciting Cooperation," pp. 171-77; Leng and Wheeler, "Influence Strategies," pp. 659-60, 680; and Svenn Lindskold and Michael G. Collins, "Inducing Cooperation by Groups and Individuals: Applying Osgood's GRIT Strategy," *Journal of Conflict Resolution*, vol. 22 (December 1978), p. 689.

59. Lindskold, "Trust Development," pp. 775-77.

60. See, for example, Lindskold and Collins, "Inducing Cooperation," p. 686; Patchen, "Strategies for Eliciting Cooperation," pp. 178-80; Leng and Wheeler, "Influence Strategies," pp. 676-81; and Marc Pilisuk and Paul Skolnick, "Inducing Trust: A Test of the Osgood Proposal," *Journal of Personality and Social Psychology,* vol. 8, no. 2 (1968), pp. 121-33.

61. Pilisuk and Skolnick, "Inducing Trust," p. 131.

62. John Paul Lederach, *Preparing for Peace: Conflict Transformation across Cultures* (Syracuse University Press, 1995).

Chapter 5

1. "Angola: Savage Battles," *Africa Research Bulletin,* vol. 30 (August 1-31, 1993), p. 11116.

2. John Marcum, *The Angolan Revolution,* vol. 2: *Exile Politics and Guerrilla Warfare (1962-1976)* (MIT Press, 1978), pp. 2-3.

3. Ibid., p. 56.

4. Telegram from the American Embassy in Kinshasa to U.S. Secretary of State, Washington, D.C., December 16, 1975, p. 2. Reproduced in Kenneth Mokoena, ed., *The Angola Crisis: The United States' Role* (Washington: National Security Archive, 1991).

5. The MPLA's intellectual Marxist ideology set the movement apart from the others and attracted support from such countries as Algeria, Congo-Brazzaville, and, in time, the Soviet Union. Agostinho Neto sought the support of many Western countries in the early 1960s but was unable to change the perceptions those governments had of the MPLA as a pro-Soviet movement. John A. Marcum, "The People's Republic of Angola: A Radical Vision Frustrated," in Edmond J. Keller and Donald Rothchild, eds., *Afro-Marxist Regimes: Ideology and Public Policy* (Boulder, Colo.: Lynne Rienner, 1987), p. 70.

6. Portugal's "native" policy in Angola classified an assimilado as an indigenous African who was considered to have assimilated Portuguese values, customs, and language to such an extent that he had become Portuguese, fully alienated from his ethnic group and village culture. In fact, such a person was normally paid lower wages than a white person. See Gerald J. Bender, *Angola under the Portuguese: The Myth and the Reality* (University of California Press, 1978), p. 103, fn. 38.

7. "Appendix I Documents: Major Program of Movimento Popular de Libertaçao de Angola (MPLA)," in Thomas Okuma, *Angola in Ferment: The Background and Prospects of Angolan Nationalism* (Boston: Beacon Press, 1962), p. 113.

8. BBC Monitoring Service, Summary of World Broadcasts, "Angolan Commentary Cites British Reports of Increased South African Aid to UNITA," ME/0557 (September 9, 1989), p. B/5.

9. Irving Kaplan, ed., *Angola: A Country Study,* 2d ed. (American University, 1979), pp. 127-28.

10. John Prendergast and David R. Smock, "Angola's Elusive Peace," *CSIS Africa Notes,* no. 182 (March 1996), p. 3.

11. The eventual "fading away" of the FNLA from the Angolan sociopolitical scene began with the routing of the FNLA on the outskirts of Luanda by MPLA and Cuban forces on November 10, 1975.

12. Emphasizing the role of ethnicity in the 1992 fighting, Savimbi stated: "It was not until 31 October and 1 November that the MPLA launched what we called tribal genocide." "Savimbi on UNITA Factions, Lusaka Protocol," Lisbon RTP-2 Television Network, January 11, 1995, in Foreign Broadcast Information Service (FBIS), *Daily Report:Angola,* January 13, 1995, p. 11.

13. Thomas Ohlson and Stephen John Stedman with Robert Davies, *The New Is Not Yet Born: Conflict Resolution in Southern Africa* (Brookings, 1994), p. 192.

14. "UNITA Accuses Government of 'Atrocities,'" Jamba Voz da Resistencia do Galo Negro, April 29, 1995, in FBIS, *Daily Report:Angola,* May 1, 1995, p. 12.

15. Arthur Jay Klinghoffer, *The Angolan War: A Study in Soviet Policy in the Third World* (Boulder, Colo.:Westview, 1980), p. 13.

16. Fred Bridgland, *Jonas Savimbi, A Key to Africa* (Edinburgh: Mainstream Publishing, 1986), p. 108.

17. I. William Zartman and Johannes Aurik, "Power Strategies in De-Escalation," in Louis Kriesberg and Stuart J. Thorson, eds., *Timing and De-Escalation of International Conflicts* (Syracuse University Press, 1991), p. 158.

18. Marcum, *Angolan Revolution,* p. 243.

19. On the allocation of ministries, see the Alvor agreement, art. 21, reprinted in Colin Legum, ed., *Africa Contemporary Record:Annual Survey and Documents, 1974-1975* (New York:Africana Publishing, 1975), p. C223.

20. Cable from Secretary of State, Washington, D.C., to American Embassy, Nairobi, January 12, 1984, p. 7 (National Security Archive); Information Memorandum, Chester A. Crocker to Deputy Secretary, March 8, 1984, p. 2 (National Security Archive); and U.S. Department of State, *United States Policy toward Angola,* document prepared for Senate Foreign Relations Committee, December 16, 1975, p. 2 (National Security Archive).

21. Briefing Memorandum from Chester A. Crocker to U.S. Secretary of State, September 22, 1982, p. 1 (National Security Archive).

22. Ibid., p. 3.

23. "Angola's War," *Africa Research Bulletin,* vol. 20 (January 15, 1984), p. 7071; see also Paul Van Slambrouck, "South Africa Hints It Is Willing to Talk with Rebels to Gain Cease-Fire in Angola," *Christian Science Monitor,* January 10, 1984.

24. BBC Monitoring Service, Summary of World Broadcasts, "South Africa and Angola and SWAPO," ME/7571 (February 20, 1984), p. B/2.

25. I. William Zartman, *Ripe for Resolution: Conflict and Intervention in Africa,* 2d ed. (Oxford University Press for Council on Foreign Relations, 1989), p. 225.

26. Fidel Castro pointedly denied any responsibility for the "mistakes" in strategic judgment at this juncture. See his quotation in Robert S. Jaster, "The 1988 Peace Accords and the Future of South-western Africa," *Adelphi Papers,* no. 253 (London: International Institute for Strategic Studies, Autumn 1990), p. 17.

27. U.S. Defense Intelligence Agency, *The 1987-88 Combat in Southern Angola: Lessons Learned* (n.d.), p. 13 (National Security Archive).

28. Gillian Gunn, "A Guide to the Intricacies of the Angola-Namibia Negotiations," *CSIS Africa Notes,* no. 90 (September 8, 1988), p. 12; see also Howard Wolpe, "Seizing Southern African Opportunities," *Foreign Policy,* no. 73 (Winter 1988-89), p. 61.

29. Obinna Anyadike, "Angola: Britain Hosts Secret Talks," *West Africa,* May 9, 1988, p. 833.

30. BBC Monitoring Service, Summary of World Broadcasts, "Angolan President Interviewed on Relations with USA," ME/8609 (July 2, 1987), pp. B/3-4.

31. "Diplomatic Solution for Angola?" *New African,* no. 244 (January 1988), p. 18.

32. Press Conference, Angolan Politburo member Juliano Matros. Telegram from U.S. Embassy, Lusaka, to Secretary of State, Washington, D.C., September 5, 1987, 03974 050922Z (National Security Archive).

33. BBC Monitoring Service, Summary of World Broadcasts, "Cuba-Angola Communique: Greater Flexibility on Southern Africa," ME/8639 (August 6, 1987), p. ii; BBC, "Angolan Commentary on 'Flexibility' of Its New Southern Africa Proposal," ME/8644 (August 12, 1987), p. B/6; and Gunn, "A Guide to the Intricacies," p. 7.

34. Robert Pear, "U.S. Making New Push for Angolan Pact," *New York Times,* April 15, 1988, p. A4.

35. Ray Kennedy, "Tit for Tat Threats Precede London Meeting on Angola," *Times* (London), May 2, 1988, p. 7.

36. "Angola-South Africa: Cairo Talks," *Africa Research Bulletin,* Political Series, vol. 25 (July 15, 1988), pp. 8900-02; and Gunn, "A Guide to the Intricacies," p. 11. On Soviet pressures on the Angolan government, see Chester A. Crocker, *High Noon in Southern Africa: Making Peace in a Rough Neighborhood* (Norton, 1992), p. 423; Jaster, "The 1988 Peace Accords," p. 29; Michael McFaul, "The Demise of the World Revolutionary Process: Soviet-Angolan Relations under Gorbachev," *Journal of Southern African Studies,* vol. 16 (March 1990), pp. 182-83; and Hella Pick, "Namibia Independence Pact Signed," *Manchester Guardian Weekly,* vol. 140 (January 1, 1989), p. 8. With respect to U.S. pressures on South Africa, see Crocker, *High Noon in Southern Africa,* p. 457.

37. Crocker, *High Noon in Southern Africa,* p. 394.

38. For the text of the Joint Declaration, see "Southwestern Africa: Ceasefire Agreement," *Africa Research Bulletin,* Political Series, vol. 25 (September 15, 1988), p. 8964.

39. John D. Battersby, "Less Optimism as Southern Africa Talks Resume," *New York Times,* September 8, 1988, p. A8; and Gunn, "A Guide to the Intricacies," p. 15.

40. "Southwestern Africa: Talks Stalled as Namibian Deadline Nears," *Africa Research Bulletin,* Political Series, vol. 25 (November 15, 1988), p. 9028.

41. ANC officials stated that five of their training camps in Angola were being closed; however, two others were described as farms and would be kept open to accommodate the needs of ANC civilians. James Brooke, "Angola Sanctuary Closing to Rebels," *New York Times,* January 10, 1989, p. A3.

42. Quoted in James Brooke, "Angola Says Rebels Still Hold Border in Southeast," *New York Times,* January 13, 1989, p. A17.

43. BBC, "Angolan Commentary Cites British Reports of Increased South African Aid to UNITA," p. B/5.

44. *Africa Research Bulletin,* Political Series, vol. 25 (November 15, 1988), p. 9028; and Gunn, "A Guide to the Intricacies," p. 15.

45. Warren Clark Jr., *National Reconciliation Efforts for Angola, a Statement before the Subcommittee on Africa of the House Foreign Affairs Committee, September 27, 1989* (Department of State, Bureau of Public Affairs, 1989), Current Policy no. 1217, p. 1.

46. BBC Monitoring Service, Summary of World Broadcasts, "Zairean Party 'Astonished' by UNITA Leaders' Reported Comments on Angolan Peace Process," ME/0532 (August 11, 1989), p. B/6.

47. BBC Monitoring Service, Summary of World Broadcasts, "Angolan President on Prospects for Zaire Summit; Issue of Savimbi's 'Voluntary and Temporary Retirement,'" ME/0490 (June 23, 1989), p. B/1.

48. "Angola: Peace Plan Unveiled," *Africa Research Bulletin,* Political Series, vol. 26 (June 15, 1989), p. 9285.

49. BBC Monitoring Service, Summary of World Broadcasts, "Zaire Summit: Agreement on Cease-Fire Reported between Angola Government and UNITA," ME/0491 (June 24, 1989). p. B/1.

50. Regarding the pressures placed on dos Santos to encourage him to attend the summit, see *Africa Confidential,* vol. 30 (July 7, 1989), pp. 3-4; and ibid.

51. "Angola: Ceasefire Accord," *Africa Research Bulletin,* Political Series, vol. 26 (June 15, 1989), p. 9316.

52. Quoted in Andrew Meldrum, "A Golden Handshake?" *Africa Report,* vol. 34 (July-August 1989), p. 35.

53. See "Southern Africa: Testing Time for the Crocker Plan," *Africa Confidential,* vol. 29 (October 7, 1988), p. 1; and James Brooke, "Angola Gives Hints of Willingness to Seek Political Solution to War," *New York Times,* January 28, 1989, p. 4.

54. Lisa Hopkins, "Is Peace Finally in Store for Angola?" *The Guardian* (New York), July 5, 1989, p. 21; Kenneth B. Noble, "For Angola Rebel, New Respectability," *New York Times,* June 26, 1989, p. A3; and Robert Pear, "Angola Cease-fire a Start, U.S. Says," *New York Times,* June 24, 1989, p. 3.

55. Herman J. Cohen, *Hearings before the Committee on Foreign Relations, United States Senate* (unedited, unofficial), May 3, 1989 (Washington: Alderson Reporting, 1989), p. 26.

56. Martin Lowenkopf, "If the Cold War Is Over in Africa, Will the United States Still Care?" *CSIS Africa Notes,* no. 98 (May 30, 1989), p. 5; and Robert Pear, "U.S. and Angola Discuss Forging Diplomatic Ties," *New York Times,* January 27, 1989, p. A3.

57. Cable from U.S. Secretary of State to the U.S. Embassy, Cairo, June 24, 1989, pp. 1-2 (National Security Archive).

58. The text of the Gbadolite declaration appeared in BBC Monitoring Service, Summary of World Broadcasts, "Angola: Text of Gbadolite Declaration," ME/0493 (June 27, 1989), p. B/1.

59. BBC Monitoring Service, Summary of World Broadcasts, "UNITA Leader Assesses Achievements of Gbadolite Summit," ME/0494 (June 28, 1989), p. B/1.

60. BBC Monitoring Service, Summary of World Broadcasts, "Angolan President Addresses Assembly Session on Peace Process and the Economy," ME/0538 (August 18, 1989), p. B/5.

61. See the interview with Herman J. Cohen, U.S. assistant secretary of state for African affairs, in Margaret A. Novicki, "Herman J. Cohen: Forging a Bipartisan Policy," *Africa Report*, vol. 34 (September-October 1989), p. 16.

62. BBC, "UNITA Leader Assesses Achievements of Gbadolite Summit," p. B/1.

63. Andrew Meldrum, "The Gbadolite Debacle," *Africa Report*, vol. 34 (September-October, 1989), p. 31.

64. BBC Monitoring Service, Summary of World Broadcasts, "Angola: UNITA Rejects Harare Communique: 'War Has Resumed,'" ME/0544 (August 25, 1989), p. B/1.

65. Clark, *National Reconciliation Efforts for Angola,* p. 2.

66. BBC Monitoring Service, Summary of World Broadcasts, "Angola: Savimbi's Speech at Start of UNITA Extraordinary Congress," ME/0574 (September 29, 1989), p. B/2.

67. Novicki, "Herman J. Cohen," p. 17.

68. At least five interest groups existed alongside one another within the MPLA in 1989. These included those backing dos Santos and his effort to achieve a political solution, the hard-line members who supported pro-Soviet principles, the pro-Cuban elements, the businessmen, and the *mestiços,* who feared the possible addition of UNITA members in government and party ranks. See *Africa Confidential,* vol. 30 (August 11, 1989), pp. 1-2.

69. Kenneth B. Noble, "Rebel Head Agrees to Angolan Truce," *New York Times,* December 4, 1989, p. A7.

70. In an August 25, 1990 interview, with the Lisbon weekly *Expresso,* dos Santos stated that Mobutu's role as mediator had "implicitly ended." Cable from the U.S. Embassy, Lisbon, to Secretary of State, Washington, D.C., August 27, 1990, p. 1 (National Security Archive).

71. Cable from U.S. Secretary of State, Washington, D.C., to American Embassy, Abidjan, May 8, 1990, p. 2 (National Security Archive).

72. Cable from the U.S. Embassy, Lisbon, to U.S. Secretary of State, Washington, D.C., May 30, 1990, p. 5 (National Security Archive).

73. Cable from U.S. Secretary of State, Washington, D.C., to all U.S. diplomatic posts, June 14, 1990, pp. 2-3 (National Security Archive).

74. Letter from James Baker to U.S. Senator George Mitchell, October 15, 1990, p. 1 (National Security Archive).

75. Briefing Memorandum from Herman Cohen to Secretary of State Baker, December 11, 1990, Attachment Tab 2 (National Security Archive).

76. Ibid., Talking Points, p. 1 (National Security Archive).

77. Herman J. Cohen, "Ceasefire and Political Settlement in Angola," *U.S. Department of State Dispatch,* vol. 2 (May 6, 1991), p. 328.

78. Interview with Stephen R. Weissman, Washington, April 26, 1995.

79. Shawn McCormick, "Angola: The Road to Peace," *CSIS Africa Notes,* no. 125 (June 6, 1991), p. 11.

80. "UNITA, Government Peace Accords Detailed," Luanda Domestic Service, May 3, 1991, in FBIS, *Daily Report: Angola,* May 3, 1991, p. 7, and "Luanda: Peace

Accord May Be Signed 2, 3 May," Luanda Domestic Service, April 30, 1991, in FBIS, *Daily Report:Angola,* May 1, 1991, p. 16.

81. By the time of the election, less than 10 percent of the planned army integration had taken place. See Witney W. Schneidman, "The West's Stake in Angola's Elections," *Christian Science Monitor,* September 21, 1992, p. 18.

82. By comparison, $430 million was provided for the peacekeeping and monitoring operation in Namibia. *Africa Confidential,* vol. 34 (March 5, 1993), p. 1.

83. Andrew Meldrum, "Angola: Hungry to Vote," *Africa Report,* vol. 37 (November-December 1992), p. 29; and Witney W. Schneidman, "Africa's Transition to Pluralism: Economic and Investment Implications," *CSIS Africa Notes,* no. 142 (November 1992), p. 2.

84. Margaret Joan Anstee, *Orphan of the Cold War: The Inside Story of the Collapse of the Angolan Peace Process, 1992-93* (St. Martin's, 1996), p. 237.

85. Ibid., p. 202.

86. Ibid., p. 277.

87. Meanwhile, Luanda Radio charged: "UNITA did not have the least interest in the elections. UNITA wanted and wants power at any cost." "Commentary Blames Savimbi's 'Excessive Ambition,'" Luanda Radio Nacional Network, October 15, 1992, in FBIS, *Daily Report: Angola,* October 15, 1992, p. 21. Regarding the unification of the government and UNITA armies before the elections, see *Peace Accords for Angola,* sec. VI (9), trans. by Department of State, Office of Language Services, LS no. 134967.

88. See Stephen John Stedman, "Spoiler Problems in Peace Processes," *International Security,* forthcoming.

89. "Savimbi Seeks Support for UN Peace Plan," Lisbon Radio Renascenca, November 12, 1992, in FBIS, *Daily Report:Angola,* November 12, 1992, p. 16.

90. Barbara F. Walter, "Domestic Anarchy and Civil War," Columbia University, Institute of War and Peace Studies, April 10, 1996, p. 20.

91. On the contention that military victories are more stable than negotiated settlements, see Robert Harrison Wagner, "The Causes of Peace," in Roy Licklider, ed., *Stopping the Killing: How Civil Wars End* (New York University Press, 1993), p. 263.

92. Desmond Davies, "A New Look at ... Conflict," *West Africa,* December 5-11, 1994, p. 2066. UNITA and other observers charged that the Angolan government used Executive Outcome to funnel 500 to 3,000 mercenaries into Angola; many of these were directly involved in military encounters with UNITA forces. "Spokesman on Possible Santos-Savimbi Meeting," BBC World Service, December 7, 1994, in FBIS, *Daily Report: Angola,* December 8, 1994, p. 10.

93. "Angola: The Militarists on Top," *Africa Confidential,* vol. 35 (February 18, 1994), pp. 6-7.

94. "Savimbi Addresses Nation on New Year's Eve," Jamba Voz da Resistencia do Galo Negro, January 1, 1995, in FBIS, *Daily Report:Angola,* January 3, 1995, p. 17; and "Savimbi Considers Peace Accord, Santos Meeting," *Liberation* (Paris), December 21, 1994, in FBIS, *Daily Report:Angola,* December 22, 1994, p. 23.

95. Lusaka Protocol, Annex 4, Agenda Item II.1, Military Issues (II), General Principles (2), November 15, 1994 (http://www.angola.org/politics/p_annex4.htm).

96. "Southern Africa: A New Deal in the Making," *Africa Confidential,* vol. 35 (November 18, 1994), p. 2.

97. Ohlson and Stedman, *The New Is Not Yet Born,* p. 126.

98. Confidential interview, Washington, D.C., December 1, 1994. It was also reported that the U.S. paid nearly one-third of UN costs in implementing the Lusaka protocol. Prendergast and Smock, "Angola's Elusive Peace," p. 6.

99. "Southern Africa: A New Deal in the Making," p. 1.

100. Mobutu sent a delegation to meet with Savimbi two days before the signing ceremony. Confidential interview, Washington, December 12, 1994.

101. David A. Lake and Donald Rothchild, "Containing Fear: The Origins and Management of Ethnic Conflict," *International Security,* vol. 21 (Fall 1996), pp. 41-75.

102. See the interview by Stephen Smith with Jonas Savimbi in *Liberation* (Paris), as reported in FBIS, *Daily Report: Angola,* December 22, 1994, p. 22. See also "Savimbi Calls Lusaka Accord 'Violation of International Law,'" *Lisbon Diario de Noticias,* January 10, 1995, in FBIS, *Daily Report: Angola,* January 12, 1995, p. 7.

103. Stephen John Stedman and Donald Rothchild, "Peace Operations: From Short-Term to Long-Term Commitment," *International Peacekeeping,* vol. 3 (Summer 1996), pp. 17-35.

104. "Angola: Slow, Painful," *Southern Africa Confidential,* supplement (April 12, 1996), p. 3.

105. "Angola: Gabon Meeting," *Africa Research Bulletin,* Political Series, vol. 33 (February 1-29, 1996), p. 12163.

106. Confidential interview, March 8, 1996.

107. "Angola: UN Commander Oversees Quartering of Government Troops," Luanda Radio Nacional Network, March 25, 1996, in FBIS, *Daily Report: Angola,* March 26, 1996, p. 5; and Prendergast and Smock, "Angola's Elusive Peace," p. 5.

108. "Angola: UNITA Updates Number of Selected, Quartered Soldiers," Jamba Voz da Resistencia do Galo Negro, November 28, 1996, in FBIS, *Daily Report: Angola,* November 28, 1996, p. 2; and "Angola: UNITA Official Hails Government Decision to Discuss Program," Luanda TPA Television Network, March 22, 1997, in FBIS, *Daily Report: Angola,* March 22, 1997, p. 7.

109. "UN Mediator Views Current Situation," Paris Radio France International, January 2, 1995, in FBIS, *Daily Report: Angola,* January 4, 1995, p. 12.

110. One participant in the mediation process considered linkage the "only available framework for a settlement." Charles W. Freeman Jr., "The Angola/Namibia Accords," *Foreign Affairs,* vol. 68 (Summer 1989), p. 133. See also Colin Legum, "Southern Africa: Analysis of the Peace Process," *Third World Reports,* L.B/1 (January 11, 1989), p. 6; and G. R. Berridge, "Diplomacy and the Angola/Namibia Accords," *International Affairs* (London), vol. 65 (Summer 1989), p. 471.

111. Sergio Trefaut, "UNITA Embarks on Electoral Campaign," Lisbon SEMA-NARIO, in FBIS, *Daily Report: Angola,* May 2, 1991, p. 16.

Chapter 6

1. John Day, "The Insignificance of Tribe in the African Politics of Zimbabwe Rhodesia," in W. H. Morris-Jones, ed., *From Rhodesia to Zimbabwe: Behind and Beyond Lancaster House* (London: Frank Cass, 1980), p. 86; and *Constitution, Bill to Provide for a New Constitution for Rhodesia,* A. B. 49, 1969 (Salisbury, Rhodesia: Government Printer, 1969), secs. 13 (2) (b), 18 (2).

2. Ken Flower, *Serving Secretly:An Intelligence Chief on Record, Rhodesia into Zimbabwe 1964-1981* (London:John Murray, 1987), pp. 104, 110. For data on the overwhelmingly Shona composition of ZANU, see the letters by Ndabaningi Sithole and Eddison J. M. Zvobgo, with their very different conclusions, in Goswin Baumhögger, ed., *The Struggle for Independence: Documents on the Recent Development of Zimbabwe (1975-1980)*, vol. 2: *Doc. 1-249 (December 1974-January 1977)* (Hamburg: Institute of African Studies, 1984), pp. 33-36.

3. Jeffrey Herbst, *State Politics in Zimbabwe* (University of California Press, 1990), p. 29.

4. Roger Martin, "Zimbabwe: A Status Report," *CSIS Africa Notes*, no. 92 (November 16, 1988) p. 2.

5. For an earlier example of this internal negotiation process, see Donald Rothchild, *Racial Bargaining in Independent Kenya: A Study of Minorities and Decolonization* (Oxford University Press, 1973).

6. W. Clay Hamner and Gary A.Yukl, "The Effectiveness of Different Offer Strategies in Bargaining," in Daniel Druckman, ed., *Negotiations: Social-Psychological Perspectives* (Beverly Hills: Sage Publications, 1977), p. 140.

7. After the UDI, Wilson added a sixth principle on the need to ensure that the white minority did not oppress the majority, or vice versa. This was later discarded by the Conservative government.

8. Interview with Roger J.A. Martin, Britain's deputy high commissioner in Harare, Zimbabwe, Princeton, N.J., March 25, 1987.

9. *Rhodesia. Relations between the Rhodesian Government and the United Kingdom Government November, 1965-December, 1966* (Salisbury, Rhodesia: Government Printer, 1966), p. 17. By contrast, Selwyn Lloyd, the Conservative party spokesman on Commonwealth affairs, called for "negotiations without preconditions." Robert C. Good, *U.D.I.:The International Politics of the Rhodesian Rebellion* (Princeton University Press, 1973), p. 153.

10. Great Britain, *Rhodesia: Documents Relating to Proposals for a Settlement 1966*, Cmnd. 3171 (London: Her Majesty's Stationery Office, December 1966), p. 126.

11. Good, *U.D.I.*, p. 193; Flower, *Serving Secretly*, p. 85; and Colin Legum, "Why Smith & Co Said 'No,'" *Observer* (London), December 11, 1966, p. 11.

12. Great Britain, *Rhodesia: Report on the Discussions Held on Board H.M.S. Fearless, October, 1968*, Cmnd. 3793 (London: HMSO, October 1968), p. 5.

13. Anthony Lewis, "Wilson and Smith Finish Talks without Agreement," *New York Times*, October 14, 1968, pp. 1, 15.

14. Great Britain, *Rhodesia: Proposals for a Settlement*, Cmnd. 4835 (London: HMSO, November 1971), p. 3. See also Martin Meredith, *The Past Is Another Country: Rhodesia: UDI to Zimbabwe* (London: Pan Books, 1979), p. 77.

15. *Rhodesia: Proposals for a Settlement*, p. 11.

16. Great Britain, *Rhodesia: Report of the Commission on Rhodesian Opinion under the Chairmanship of the Right Honourable the Lord Pearce*, Cmnd. 4964 (London: HMSO, May 1972), p. 112.

17. Flower, *Serving Secretly*, p. 99.

18. Regarding guerrilla-civilian relations, see Norma J. Kriger, *Zimbabwe's Guerrilla War: Peasant Voices* (Cambridge University Press, 1992), chap. 4.

19. Interview with J. M. Tongogara, the ZANU secretary for defense, in May 1978, as reported in Baumhögger, *Struggle for Independence,* vol. 2, p. 26.

20. Flower, *Serving Secretly,* p. 127.

21. David Martin and Phyllis Johnson, *The Struggle for Zimbabwe: The Chimurenga War* (London, Boston: Faber and Faber, 1981), p. 141.

22. Stephen John Stedman, *Peacemaking in Civil War: International Mediation in Zimbabwe, 1974-1980* (Boulder, Colo.: Lynne Rienner, 1991), pp. 49-52.

23. Meredith, *The Past Is Another Country,* p. 153. Another version concludes that South Africa supported majority rule within fifteen years. See M. Tamarkin, *The Making of Zimbabwe: Decolonization in Regional and International Politics* (London: Frank Cass, 1990), p. 51.

24. Baumhögger, *Struggle for Independence,* vol. 2, p. 10. Henry Kissinger reportedly told Smith that any constitutional proposals would need the approval of the frontline states of Botswana, Mozambique, Tanzania, and Zambia and, in September 1976, Angola. Robert S. Jaster, "A Regional Security Role for Africa's Front-Line States: Experience and Prospects," *Adelphi Papers,* no. 180 (London: International Institute for Strategic Studies, 1983), p. 5.

25. See the remarks by Foreign Secretary James Callaghan in *Parliamentary Debates,* Commons, 5th ser., vol. 908 (March 22, 1976), col. 29.

26. "Kissinger's African Trip," Duval Papers, Box no. 16 (Gerald R. Ford Library).

27. Donald Rothchild, "U.S. Policy Styles in Africa: From Minimal Engagement to Liberal Internationalism," in Kenneth A. Oye, Donald Rothchild, and Robert J. Lieber, eds., *Eagle Entangled: U.S. Foreign Policy in a Complex World* (New York: Longman, 1979), pp. 312-16.

28. Henry A. Kissinger, *Africa,* statement before the Senate Foreign Relations Committee, May 13, 1976, Department of State, Bureau of Public Affairs, PR 246, 1976, p. 4.

29. Henry A. Kissinger, *Southern Africa and the United States: An Agenda for Cooperation,* Lusaka, April 27, 1976, Department of State, Bureau of Public Affairs, PR 205, 1976, p. 3; and Kissinger, "Toward A New Understanding of Community," *Department of State Bulletin,* vol. 75 (October 25, 1976), p. 500.

30. *Africa Research Bulletin,* Political, Social and Cultural Series, vol. 134 (October 15, 1976), p. 4166; "Spare Us These Falsehoods," *Ghanaian Times* (Accra), April 29, 1976, p. 4; and "Vorster Confesses at Last: U.S. Forced Pretoria to Invade Angola," *Ghanaian Times,* May 11, 1976, pp. 1, 4.

31. Tim Patten, "Rhodesia: Vorster Warning," *The Star* (Johannesburg), November 1, 1976, p. 19.

32. Baumhögger, *Struggle for Independence,* vol. 2, p. 113. Meredith states that Kissinger sought to "induce" Vorster to align himself with the United States on the Rhodesian question "by suggesting that, if Vorster co-operated, South Africa would not find itself subjected to such a radical change in US policy as the Lusaka commitment implied." *The Past Is Another Country,* p. 223.

33. Nyerere and other African presidents reportedly were "infuriated" over Kissinger's claim to be engaging in diplomacy at Africa's invitation. See David Martin, "Secret Deal Would Get Rid of Smith," *Observer,* September 19, 1976, p. 1.

34. *Parliamentary Debates,* Commons, 5th ser., vol. 908 (March 22, 1976), cols. 30-31. For an American restatement of these principles, see letter from Jeanne W. Davis, staff secretary of the National Security Council, to Congressman Andrew Young, June 22, 1976, CO 124 (Gerald R. Ford Library).

35. Interview with former Secretary of State Henry Kissinger, Davis, California, October 21, 1987.

36. Colin Legum, *Southern Africa: The Year of the Whirlwind* (New York: Africana Publishing, 1977), pp. 36-37.

37. "Memorandum of Conversation between Dr. Henry A. Kissinger, Kenneth David Kaunda, and their delegations," State House, Lusaka, September 17, 1976, p. 12 (National Security Archive).

38. "Memorandum of Conversation between Balthazar Johannes Vorster, Dr. Henry A. Kissinger, and their delegations," American Ambassador's Residence, Pretoria, September 18, 1976, p. 4 (National Security Archive).

39. Arthur L. Gavshon, "Kissinger: AP News Analysis," September 25, 1976, FG 11, CO 135 (Gerald R. Ford Library); and interview with Martin Lowenkopf, deputy director, Bureau of Intelligence and Research of Office of Analysis for Africa, State Department, Washington, D.C., May 7, 1987.

40. Legum, *Southern Africa,* pp. 38-39.

41. Legum, *Southern Africa,* p. 39; Colin Legum and others, "Rhodesia: Why the Game Is Up," *Observer* (London), September 26, 1976, p. 8; and Meredith, *The Past Is Another Country,* p. 254.

42. Legum, *Southern Africa,* p. 39.

43. Telegrams from Kissinger to U.S. Embassy, Pretoria, 27255 211902Z, September 21, 1976, p. 1; and 27248 211358Z, September 21, 1976 (National Security Archive).

44. Telegram from U.S. Embassy, Pretoria to U.S. Embassy, Nairobi, 04309 221553Z, September 22, 1976, p. 2 (National Security Archive).

45. "Rhodesia Bargaining," *Times* (London), September 27, 1976, p. 13; see also "Kissinger Promises More Than He Can Perform," *Manchester Guardian,* October 3, 1976, p. 1.

46. Telegram from U.S. Embassy, Lusaka, to U.S. Secretary of State, Washington, D.C., Lusaka 02580 261531Z, September 26, 1976, p. 3 (National Security Archive).

47. Quoted in Stedman, *Peacemaking in Civil War,* p. 104.

48. Sithole had once been a leader, along with Mugabe, of ZANU, but the two had a falling-out while Sithole was in prison in the 1970s. The ZLC was formed in 1975 and left the once powerful Sithole very isolated.

49. Baumhögger, *Struggle for Independence,* vol. 2, p. 206.

50. *Africa Research Bulletin,* Political, Social and Cultural Series, vol. 13 (November 15, 1976), p. 4201.

51. *International Herald Tribune,* September 28, 1976, p. 1; also see the press briefing with spokesman Robert Funseth and U.S. Undersecretary William

D. Rogers in a telegram from U.S. Secretary of State to all African diplomatic posts, 240517, September 28, 1976 (National Security Archive).

52. Stedman, *Peacemaking in Civil War,* p. 121.

53. Baumhögger, *Struggle for Independence,* vol. 2, pp. 251-52.

54. Regarding Vorster's reluctance at this point to exert further pressure on Smith, see Martin Meredith, "Richard Mission Looks Doomed," *Sunday Times* (London), January 2, 1977, p. 6.

55. Cyrus R. Vance, *Hard Choices: Critical Years in America's Foreign Policy* (Simon and Schuster, 1983), p. 257.

56. Baumhögger, *Struggle for Independence,* vol. 3: *Doc. 250-476 (January 1977-March 1978),* p. 325.

57. Interview with U.S. Ambassador Donald F. McHenry, Washington, D.C., May 14, 1987.

58. Interview with U.S. Ambassador Stephen Low, Washington, D.C., May 19, 1987. See also Stephen Low, "The Zimbabwe Settlement, 1976-1979," in Saadia Touval and I. William Zartman, eds., *International Mediation in Theory and Practice* (Johns Hopkins University, School for Advanced International Studies, Foreign Policy Institute, 1985), p. 93.

59. Interview with U.S. Ambassador Stephen Low, Washington, D.C., May 19, 1987.

60. "Rhodesia—Proposals for a Settlement," *U.S. Department of State Bulletin,* vol. 77 (October 3, 1977), pp. 417-39.

61. Vance notes that Owen was "visibly upset" by reports that Carter had agreed, in private talks with Nyerere, on basing the Zimbabwe national army on the PF liberation forces. *Hard Choices,* p. 269.

62. Stedman, *Peacemaking in Civil War,* p. 138.

63. "Meeting held on Thursday September 1st 1977 at Mirimba House, Salisbury, between the Rev. Ndabaningi Sithole, his Delegation and the British Foreign Secretary Dr David Owen and the United States Ambassador to the United Nations Mr. Andrew Young" (Hoover Institution Archives).

64. Telegram from American Embassy, Vienna, to Secretary of State, Washington, D.C., 04122 200361Z, May 20, 1977 (National Security Archive).

65. Meredith, *The Past Is Another Country,* p. 320.

66. Baumhögger, *Struggle for Independence,* vol. 3, p. 511.

67. Vance, *Hard Choices,* p. 289.

68. Martin and Johnson, *Struggle for Zimbabwe,* p. 264.

69. Chengetai J. Zvobgo, "Rhodesia's Internal Settlement 1977-1979: A Record," *Journal of Southern African Affairs,* vol. 5 (January 1980), p. 28. On Muzorewa's desire to have an "army of his own," see Anthony Verrier, *The Road to Zimbabwe: 1890-1980* (London: Jonathan Cape, 1986), p. 188.

70. "Minutes of the Meeting between Dr. David Owen, Secretary of State for Commonwealth and Foreign Affairs, and the Rev. Ndabaningi Sithole, President of ZANU," London, February 20, 1978, p. 9 (Hoover Institution Archive).

71. "Minutes of the Second Meeting Between the Rev. Ndabaningi Sithole, the President of ZANU, and Dr. David Owen, the British Foreign Secretary," London, February 21, 1978 (Hoover Institution Archives).

72. Baumhögger, *Struggle for Independence*, vol. 4: *Doc. 477-695 (March 1978-February 1979)*, p. 533.

73. Interview with U.S.Ambassador Stephen Low,Washington, D.C., May 19, 1987.

74. I.William Zartman,"The Strategy of Preventive Diplomacy in Third World Conflicts," in Alexander L. George, ed., *Managing U.S.-Soviet Rivalry: Problems of Crisis Prevention* (Boulder, Colo.:Westview, 1983), p. 345.

75. Janice Gross Stein,"Getting to the Table:The Triggers, Stages, Functions, and Consequences of Prenegotiation," in Stein, ed., *Getting to the Table:The Processes of International Prenegotiation* (Johns Hopkins University Press, 1989), p. 244.

76. "The Art of Pre-Negotiation: Opening New Doors to Negotiations," *In Brief...*, no. 26 (Washington: U.S. Institute of Peace Press,January 1991), p. 1.

77. In particular, Fraser alerted Nyerere, Kaunda, and others that the British were prepared to support the idea of new Rhodesian elections. I am grateful to Richard A. Higgott for discussing with me Australia's role in the negotiations.

78. Baumhögger, *Struggle for Independence*, vol. 5: *Doc. 696-899 (February-September 1979)*, p. 1011.

79. Ronald J. Fisher,"Prenegotiation Problem-Solving Discussions: Enhancing the Potential for Successful Negotiation," in Stein, ed., *Getting to the Table*, p. 230.

80. Baumhögger, *Struggle for Independence*, vol. 5, p. 1017.

81. Interview with James G. Kamusikiri, Pomona, California, February 14, 1986.

82. Baumhögger, *Struggle for Independence*, vol. 5, p. 1020.

83. Michael Holman,"Mugabe Says 'Smith Regime' Must Go," *Financial Times,* August 8, 1979, p. 1; and John F. Burns, "Rhodesian Cabinet Weighs Lusaka Plan," *New York Times,* August 8, 1979, p. 3.

84. Jaster,"A Regional Security Role," p. 12.The fact that there was no separate white delegation pointed to the end of a direct racial bargaining encounter, although a tacit racial bargaining situation persisted. In the voting within the Muzorewa delegation, Smith was isolated by the use of a majority rule rather than a consensus rule. Interview with James Kamusikiri, Stanford, California, April 22, 1989.

85. Tamarkin, *Making of Zimbabwe*, p. 261.

86. Interview with Robin Renwick, London,July 4, 1986.

87. Interview with PF delegate A. M. Chambati, Harare, Zimbabwe, July 14, 1986.

88. Jeffrey Davidow, *A Peace in Southern Africa: The Lancaster House Conference on Rhodesia, 1979* (Boulder, Colo.:Westview, 1984), pp. 36-37; and Stedman, *Peacemaking in Civil War,* p. 169.

89. *Southern Rhodesia: Report of the Constitutional Conference, Lancaster House, London, September-December 1979*, Cmnd. 7802 (London: HMSO, January 1980), p. 6.

90. Ibid., p. 10.

91. David Adamson, "Nkomo Avoids Rushing into Confrontation," *Daily Telegraph* (London), September 12, 1979, p. 1.

92. *Rhodesia: Summary of the Independence Constitution,* Cmnd. 7758 (London: HMSO, November 1979).

93. David Adamson, "Turns on Muzorewa: Split on Safeguards for Whites," *Daily Telegraph* (London), September 17, 1979, p. 1.

94. Bridget Bloom and Michael Holman, "Carrington in Move to Save Rhodesia Talks," *Financial Times* (London), September 18, 1979, p. 1.

95. Bridget Bloom and Michael Holman, "Nkomo Says Front May Agree Reserved Seats for Whites," *Financial Times* (London), September 17, 1979, p. 1.

96. Quoted in Jaster, "A Regional Security Role," p. 15.

97. In fact, after independence, politicians did speak bitterly about the Lancaster House provisions on land and property rights as "entrenching inequality." Speech by Comrade Maurice Ngumbo at the University of Zimbabwe, Harare, July 15, 1986.

98. Jaster, "A Regional Security Role," p. 15 (emphasis in original).

99. Bridget Bloom and Martin Dickson, "Rhodesia Deadlock as Front Hedges on Draft Constitution," *Financial Times* (London), October 12, 1979, p. 1.

100. Interview with George Moose, Washington, D.C., June 30, 1987.

101. This paragraph is based on an interview with E. Gibson Lanpher, director of southern African affairs at the U.S. State Department, Washington, D.C., June 25, 1987.

102. Interview with former President Jimmy Carter, Atlanta, April 14, 1987.

103. Bridget Bloom and Michael Holman, "Constitution Agreed as Patriotic Front Makes Concessions," *Financial Times* (London), October 19, 1979, p. 1.

104. Baumhögger, *Struggle for Independence,* vol. 6: *Doc. 900-1050 (September-December 1979),* p. 1124.

105. Ibid., p. 1134; and Davidow, *A Peace in Southern Africa,* p. 70. Also see Flower, *Serving Secretly,* pp. 237-38.

106. Bridget Bloom and Michael Holman, "Showdown Likely on Rhodesia," *Financial Times* (London), October 27, 1979, p. 1.

107. United Kingdom, Constitutional Conference, Lancaster House, London, Summary of the Proceedings of the 24th Plenary Session, November 1, 1979 (National Security Archive).

108. UK, Constitutional Conference, Summary of the Proceedings of the 28th Plenary Session, November 7, 1979 (National Security Archive).

109. Bridget Bloom, "Compromise Sought in Rhodesia Talks," *Financial Times* (London), October 29, 1979, p. 1.

110. UK, Constitutional Conference, Conference Paper, 33d Plenary Session, November 15, 1979 (National Security Archive).

111. UK, Constitutional Conference, Summary of the Proceedings of the 34th Plenary Session, November 16, 1979, p. 2 (National Security Archive).

112. Stephen John Stedman, "Negotiation and Mediation in Internal Conflict," in Michael E. Brown, ed., *The International Dimensions of Internal Conflict* (MIT Press, 1996), pp. 342-43.

113. Jeremy Ginifer, *Managing Arms in Peace Processes: Rhodesia/Zimbabwe* (Geneva: United Nations Institute for Disarmament Research, 1995), pp. 4, 22.

114. UK, Constitutional Conference, Summary of the Proceedings of the 36th Plenary Session, November 20, 1979 (National Security Archive).

115. David A. Lake and Donald Rothchild, "Containing Fear:The Origins and Management of Ethnic Conflict," *International Security,* vol. 21 (Fall 1996), pp. 41-75.

116. UK, Constitutional Conference, Summary of the Proceedings of the 35th Plenary Session, November 22, 1979 (National Security Archive).

117. Interview with Robin Renwick, London, July 4, 1986.

118. James D. Fearon, "Commitment Problems and the Spread of Ethnic Conflict," in David A. Lake and Donald Rothchild, eds., *The International Spread of Ethnic Conflict: Fear, Diffusion, and Escalation* (Princeton University Press, forthcoming), chap. 5.

119. Bridget Bloom and Michael Holman, "Rhodesia Talks Close to Success—Thatcher," *Financial Times* (London), November 24, 1979, p. 1.

120. Baumhögger, *Struggle for Independence,* vol. 6, p. 1194.

121. Jaster, "A Regional Security Role," p. 16.

122. Stedman, *Peacemaking in Civil War,* p. 199.

123. Interview with Professor R. H. F. Austin, Harare, Zimbabwe, July 16, 1986.

124. UK, Constitutional Conference, Summary of the Proceedings of the 39th Plenary Session, December 5, 1979, p. 2 (National Security Archive).

125. Interview with Robin Renwick, London, July 4, 1986.

126. UK, Constitutional Conference, Summary of the Proceedings of the 44th Plenary Session, December 13, 1979 (National Security Archive).

127. Davidow, *A Peace in Southern Africa,* pp. 89-90; and Jaster, "A Regional Security Role," pp. 16-17.

128. Saadia Touval, "Managing the Risks of Accommodation," in Nissan Oren, ed., *Termination of Wars* (Jerusalem: Magnes Press, 1982), pp. 17-39.

129. Telegram from U.S. Secretary of State to U.S. Mission NATO, 246013, October 2, 1976, p. 5 (National Security Archive); and Memorandum of Conversation between Patrick Miles, the U.K. High Commissioner in Zambia, and Henry Kissinger, U.S. Secretary of State, in Lusaka, Zambia, September 16, 1976, p. 3 (National Security Archive).

130. Letter from Jeffrey Davidow to Donald Rothchild, November 3, 1986; and interview with E. Gibson Lanpher, June 25, 1987.

131. Interview with Henry Kissinger, Davis, California, October 21, 1987; and telegram from Kissinger to Nyerere, 252328, October 11, 1976 (National Security Archive). See also John de St. Jorre, *A House Divided: South Africa's Uncertain Future* (New York: Carnegie Endowment for International Peace, 1977), p. 74.

132. For an acknowledgment by Rhodesian transportation officials of rail congestion in South Africa following the Kissinger-Vorster meeting, see a reference to a *Times of Zambia* article of July 22, 1976, in a telegram from the U.S. Embassy, Lusaka, to U.S. Secretary of State Washington, D.C., 01879 241404Z, July 23, 1976, p. 2 (National Security Archive). See also Meredith, *The Past Is Another Country,* p. 242.

133. Flower, *Serving Secretly,* p. 153.

134. For further evidence of South Africa's gain in terms of legitimacy, it is useful to note President Gerald Ford's telegram to Vorster expressing appreciation for Vorster's "vision and the role which South Africa has played in making a peaceful settlement to the Rhodesian question possible." Telegram from Ford to U.S. Embassy, 238060, Pretoria, South Africa, September 25, 1976 (National Security Archive).

135. Interview with Professor R. H. F. Austin, Harare, Zimbabwe, July 16, 1986.

Chapter 7

1. "De Klerk Reiterates Anti-Communist Position," Johannesburg SAPA, May 2, 1991, in Foreign Broadcast Information Service (FBIS), *Daily Report: Sub-Saharan Africa*, May 3, 1991, p. 1; and "Organization of African Unity (OAU): Preconditions Agreed for Talks with Pretoria," *Africa Research Bulletin*, Political Series, vol. 26 (September 15, 1989), p. 9368.

2. Commonwealth Group of Eminent Persons, *Mission to South Africa: The Commonwealth Report* (Harmondsworth, England: Penguin Books, 1986), pp. 20, 103.

3. Princeton Lyman, "S. African Leaders Need Rededication to Democracy," AEF503 (July 30, 1993), pp. 4-5 (excerpts from Ambassador Lyman's July 22 address to the Institute for Multi-Party Democracy in South Africa).

4. Interview with Lloyd Vogelman, Johannesburg, South Africa, July 10, 1995.

5. Heribert Adam, "The Manipulation of Ethnicity: South Africa in Comparative Perspective," in Donald Rothchild and Victor A. Olorunsola, eds., *State versus Ethnic Claims: African Policy Dilemmas* (Boulder, Colo.: Westview, 1983), pp. 132-33; and Heribert Adam and Hermann Giliomee, *Ethnic Power Mobilized: Can South Africa Change?* (Yale University Press, 1979), p. 15.

6. Marina Ottaway, *South Africa: The Struggle for a New Order* (Brookings, 1993), pp. 159-67.

7. Joseph Lelyveld, "Mandela Plea to Curb Conflict Reported," *New York Times*, July 12, 1986, p. 3.

8. George P. Shultz, "The U.S. Approach to South Africa" (Department of State, Bureau of Public Affairs, July 23, 1986), Current Policy No. 854, p. 2; and Ronald Reagan, "Report to the Congress Pursuant to Section 501 of the Comprehensive Anti-Apartheid Act of 1986," *Weekly Compilation of Presidential Documents*, vol. 23 (October 5, 1987), pp. 1110-16.

9. Heribert Adam and Kogila Moodley, *South Africa without Apartheid: Dismantling Racial Domination* (University of California Press, 1986), p. 203.

10. Noel Kaplowitz, "Psychopolitical Dimensions of International Relations: The Reciprocal Effects of Conflict Strategies," *International Studies Quarterly*, vol. 28 (December 1984), pp. 377-79.

11. Stephen John Stedman, "Negotiation and Mediation in Internal Conflict," in Michael E. Brown, ed., *The International Dimensions of Internal Conflict* (MIT Press, 1996), p. 347; also see Donald Rothchild and Alexander J. Groth, "Pathological Dimensions of Domestic and International Ethnicity," *Political Science Quarterly*, vol. 110 (Spring 1995), pp. 69-82.

12. Commonwealth Group, *Mission to South Africa*, p. 103.

13. See ibid., Annex 7, pp. 131, 175-76. Also see "Sanctions Breach International Law, Says Botha," *Manchester Guardian Weekly*, August 24, 1986, p. 7.

14. Allister Sparks, "Why Botha Went into Reverse," *Manchester Guardian Weekly*, vol. 135 (August 24, 1986), p. 16.

15. Interviews, Pauline Baker, Washington, May 15, 1987, and General Olusegun Obasanjo, Washington, October 15, 1989.

16. "Howe's SA Mission Waste of Time—PM," *Herald* (Harare), July 11, 1986, p. 1.

17. I. William Zartman, *Ripe for Resolution: Conflict and Intervention in Africa* (Oxford University Press, 1985), p. 9.

18. "Foreign Minister Discusses Swaziland Talks," Johannesburg Television Service, April 28, 1986, in FBIS, *Daily Report: Middle East and Africa*, May 1, 1986, p. U6. The U.S. Congress took a similar position on the issue of violence; thus, the Comprehensive Anti-Apartheid Act of 1986 asserted that "it is the sense of the Congress that a suspension of violence is an essential precondition for the holding of negotiations." P. L. 99-440, p. 1092.

19. Malcolm Fraser and Olusegun Obasanjo, "What to Do about South Africa," *Foreign Affairs*, vol. 65 (Fall 1986), p. 156.

20. African National Congress, *ANC Call to the People: From Ungovernability to People's Power* (Lusaka: African National Congress, 1986), p. 1.

21. African National Congress, "Statement of the National Executive Committee of the African National Congress on the Question of Negotiations," Lusaka, October 9, 1987, p. 4.

22. "APLA Fights On: PAC Rejects Negotiations," *Azania Combat* (Azania People's Liberation Army), vol. 1 (1986), p. 4.

23. "Comment: The Deception of the Botha-Malan Junta," *Solidarity* (Black Consciousness Movement of Azania), (February 1986), pp. 2-3; and Commonwealth Group, *Mission to South Africa*, p. 175.

24. For a discussion of these constraints on negotiation in South Africa in the 1980s, see Donald Rothchild, "From Exhortation to Incentive Strategies: Mediation Efforts in South Africa in the Mid-1980s," in Edmond J. Keller and Louis A. Picard, eds., *South Africa in Southern Africa: Domestic Change and International Conflict* (Boulder, Colo.: Lynne Rienner, 1989), pp. 25-48.

25. "SA Has Capacity and Will to Break ANC," *South African Digest*, May 30, 1986, p. 467.

26. Interview with Robin Renwick, London, July 4, 1986. Also see Jeffrey Davidow, *A Peace in Southern Africa: The Lancaster House Conference on Rhodesia, 1979* (Boulder, Colo.: Westview, 1984), pp. 115-21.

27. John W. Burton, "The Procedures of Conflict Resolution," in Edward E. Azar and John W. Burton, eds., *International Conflict Resolution: Theory and Practice* (Boulder, Colo.: Lynne Rienner, 1986), p. 105.

28. Robert Jaster, "South Africa's Narrowing Security Options," in Jaster, ed., *Southern Africa: Regional Security Problems and Prospects* (St. Martin's Press, 1985), p. 37.

29. Howard Raiffa, *The Art and Science of Negotiation* (Harvard University Press, 1982).

30. Wimpie de Klerk, as quoted in Allister Sparks, *Tomorrow Is Another Country: The Inside Story of South Africa's Road to Change* (New York: Hill and Wang, 1995), p. 95.

31. Timothy D. Sisk, *Democratization in South Africa: The Elusive Social Contract* (Princeton University Press, 1995), p. 82. On Nelson Mandela's important meeting with President Botha while in jail, see Nelson Mandela, *Long Walk to Freedom* (Little, Brown, 1994), pp. 478–81.

32. On calls for a deadlock-resolving actor, see United Nations, Security Council, *Report of the Secretary-General on the Question of South Africa*, S/24389 (August 7, 1992), p. 18.

33. "Article Reassess Breakdown of Codesa Talks," *The Star* (Johannesburg), July 23, 1992, p. 22, in FBIS, *Daily Report: Sub-Saharan Africa*, July 24, 1992, p. 12.

34. "ANC's Mandela Addresses UN Security Council," Johannesburg SAPA, July 16, 1992, in FBIS, *Daily Report: Sub-Saharan Africa*, July 16, 1992, p. 7.

35. Sisk, *Democratization in South Africa*, p. 109.

36. *National Peace Accord*, p. 27. This accord, agreed to on September 14, 1991, was enacted into law by the South African Parliament, Act 135 of 1992. As of June 1993, the full complement of eleven subregional and sixty-five local committees was functioning and another thirty to forty local committees were planned. See Timothy D. Sisk, "South Africa: The National Peace Accord and the International Community" (Washington: United States Institute of Peace, 1993), p. 1.

37. United Nations, Security Council, Resolution 765 (July 16, 1992), sec. 4.

38. "Government Responds to UN Recommendations," Johannesburg SAPA, August 13, 1992, in FBIS, *Daily Report: Sub-Saharan Africa*, August 13, 1992, p. 10. Before this, the UN high commissioner of refugees had been active in South Africa, assisting refugees to return home. Because of the professional and non-partisan way the high commission had conducted its affairs, it had broken the ice and made it easier for the South African government to accept UN monitors. While the government was not opposed to UN monitors, it took pains to make it clear that it did not think that there was a need for formal mediation by an external actor. See the statement by Constitutional Development Deputy Minister Tertius Delport in "Delport Sees No Need for Formal Outside Mediation," Johannesburg SAPA, July 8, 1992, in FBIS, *Daily Report: Sub-Saharan Africa*, July 8, 1992, p. 5.

39. United Nations, Security Council, "Report of the Secretary-General on the Question of South Africa," S/24389 (August 7, 1992), p. 18.

40. United Nations, Security Council, Resolution 772 (August 17, 1992).

41. Interview, Hannes Siebert, Washington, April 29, 1993.

42. Angela King, "'Free and Fair,'" *Track Two*, vol. 2 (November 1993), p. 11.

43. Interview, Chris Spies, Washington, June 9, 1993.

44. United Nations, Security Council, "Report of the Secretary-General on the Question of South Africa," p. 18.

45. "South Africa: Stalemate?" *Africa Research Bulletin*, Political Social and Cultural Series, vol. 31 (March 1–31, 1994), p. 11360.

46. "IFP's Buthelezi Urges Postponement of Election," Johannesburg SAPA, March 29, 1994, in FBIS, *Daily Report: Sub-Saharan Africa*, March 30, 1994, p. 3.

47. "South Africa: Election Hurdles," *Africa Research Bulletin*, Political, Social and Cultural Series, vol. 31 (February 1-28, 1994), p. 11329.

48. "Election Date Not Part of Mediation," Johannesburg SAPA, April 13, 1994, in FBIS, *Daily Report: Sub-Saharan Africa*, April 13, 1994, p. 15.

49. "The Constitutional Process," *Information Update*, Consultative Business Movement no. 15 (July 29, 1994), p. 3.

50. Henry A. Kissinger, "South Africa's Strength: A Bias for Moderation," *Los Angeles Times*, May 15, 1994, p. M2.

51. "The Constitutional Process," p. 4.

52. Kaizer Nyatsumba, "Deal 'an African Solution,'" *The Star* (Johannesburg), April 20, 1994, p. 3.

53. Consultative Business Movement, *Information Update*, p. 4.

54. Chris Whitfield, Esther Waugh, and Helen Grange, "Back on the High Road," *The Star* (Johannesburg), April 20, 1994, p. 1.

55. "IFP-ANC-Government Memorandum of Agreement," Johannesburg SAPA, January 19, 1994, in FBIS, *Daily Report: Sub-Saharan Africa*, April 20, 1994, p. 9.

56. Patti Waldmeir, "God—and Realpolitik—Bring in Buthelezi," *Financial Times*, April 20, 1994, p. 9.

57. Steven Friedman, "Yesterday's Pact: Power Sharing and Legitimate Governance in Post-Settlement South Africa," *Policy: Issues and Actors*, vol. 7 (September 1994), p. 4. Also explored during an interview with Steven Friedman, Johannesburg, South Africa, July 10, 1995.

58. Adrian Guelke, "Dissecting the South African Miracle: African Parallels," *Nationalism and Ethnic Politics*, vol. 2 (Spring 1996), p.149.

59. "South Africa: The Succession Taboo," *Africa Confidential*, vol. 36 (May 12, 1995), p. 2.

60. Estelle Randall and Farouk Chothia, "'Secret' Land Deal Cedes KwaZulu/Natal Land to Zulu King," *Weekly Mail and Guardian* (Johannesburg) (May 20-26, 1994), p. 2, in FBIS, *Daily Report: Sub-Saharan Africa*, May 23, 1994, p. 8.

61. Bill Keller, "Secret Zulu Land Transfer Poses First Crisis for Mandela," *New York Times*, May 24, 1994, p. A3.

62. "Move to Defuse Zulu Land Row," *The Citizen*, May 24, 1994, p. 1, as reported in the *Daily News Bulletin* (Embassy of South Africa, Washington), May 24, 1994.

63. Joseph S. Nye Jr., "Soft Power," *Foreign Policy*, no. 80 (Fall 1990), p. 168.

64. David A. Lake and Donald Rothchild, "Containing Fear: The Origins and Management of Ethnic Conflict," *International Security*, vol. 21 (Fall 1996), pp. 41-75.

65. On the difficulty of appeasing spoilers, see Stedman, "Negotiation and Mediation in Internal Conflicts," pp. 369-71.

66. See Andrew Reynolds, ed., *Election '94: South Africa: The Campaigns, Results and Future Prospects* (St. Martin's Press, 1994).

Chapter 8

1. Adam Curle, *Making Peace* (London:Tavistock, 1971), p. 243.

2. Nelson Kasfir, "Southern Sudanese Politics since the Addis Ababa Agreement," *African Affairs*, vol. 76 (April 1977), p. 165.

3. Saadia Touval and I.William Zartman, "Introduction: Mediation in Theory," in Touval and Zartman, eds., *International Mediation in Theory and Practice* (Boulder, Colo.:Westview, 1985), p. 14. See also L. N. Rangarajan, *The Limitation of Conflict:A Theory of Bargaining and Negotiation* (London: Croom Helm, 1985), p. 267.

4. *First Population Census, 1955/56* (Khartoum: Ministry of Social Affairs, 1958), p. 23.

5. Godfrey Morrison, *Eritrea and the Southern Sudan:Aspects of Wider African Problems*, Report no. 5, new ed. (London: Minority Rights Group, 1976), p. 11. See also Edgar O'Ballance, *The Secret War in the Sudan: 1955-1972* (London: Faber and Faber, 1977), p. 151; and Hizkias Assefa, *Mediation of Civil Wars:Approaches and Strategies: The Sudan Conflict* (Boulder, Colo.:Westview, 1987), pp. 70-71.

6. Karl Deutsch, "Research Problems on Race in Intranational Relations," in George W. Shepherd Jr. and Tilden J. LeMelle, eds., *Race among Nations:A Conceptual Approach* (Lexington, Mass.: Heath, Lexington Books, 1970), p. 123.

7. Republic of the Sudan, *Commission of Inquiry into the Disturbances in the Southern Sudan during August 1955* (Khartoum: Ministry of Interior, 1956), p. 17.

8. Francis M. Deng, *War of Visions: Conflict of Identities in the Sudan* (Brookings, 1995), pp. 11-12.

9. On the delay in the rise of southern political organizations, see Mohamed Omer Beshir, *The Southern Sudan: From Conflict to Peace* (London: C. Hurst, 1975), pp. 45-49.

10. International Labour Office, *Growth, Employment and Equity: A Comprehensive Strategy for the Sudan* (Geneva: International Labour Organization, 1976), pp. 199, 289.

11. Dunstan M. Wai, *The African-Arab Conflict in the Sudan* (New York: Africana Publishing, 1981), p. 37.

12. Robert O. Collins, *African-Arab Relations in the Sudan*, paper prepared for the 1985 annual meeting of the Middle East Studies Association, p. 5.

13. International Labour Office, *Growth, Employment and Equity*, p. 128.

14. O'Ballance, *Secret War in the Sudan*, p. 151.

15. John Howell, "Horn of Africa: Lessons from the Sudan Conflict," *International Affairs*, vol. 54 (1978), p. 427.

16. Douglas James Amy, "Environmental Mediators: An Alternative Approach to Policy Stalemates," *Policy Sciences*, vol. 15 (August 1983), p. 354.

17. O'Ballance, *Secret War in the Sudan*, p. 142; and Beshir, *Southern Sudan*, p. 105.

18. Quoted in Conflict Research Society, "Intermediary Activity and the Southern Sudanese Conflict: Draft Report of a Symposium Held at the

Richardson Institute on November 21st and 22nd 1973" (London: Conflict Research Society, November 1973), p. 2.

19. O'Ballance, *Secret War in the Sudan*, pp. 132-35.

20. Conflict Research Society, "Intermediary Activity and the Southern Sudanese Conflict," pp. 2-3. Robert O. Collins noted that Lagu was working out of Equatoria and the Israelis built air strips in eastern Equatoria, but their main diplomatic and organizational channels came out of Entebbe in neighboring Uganda, so that it would be natural for them to work with Lagu and the Equatorians, rather than the Nilotes, who were far to the north and really not involved. I wish to express my appreciation to Robert O. Collins for his comments on this subject.

21. O'Ballance, *Secret War in the Sudan*, p. 158.

22. I. William Zartman, *Ripe for Resolution*, updated ed. (Oxford University Press, 1989), p. 268.

23. O'Ballance, *Secret War in the Sudan*, p. 116.

24. Howell, "Horn of Africa," p. 426.

25. Conflict Research Society, "Intermediary Activity and the Southern Sudanese Conflict," p. 20.

26. Quoted in Assefa, *Mediation of Civil Wars*, p. 153.

27. Ibid., p. 72; and "Sudan: Political Anatomy of the South," *Africa Confidential*, vol. 12 (October 15, 1971), p. 1.

28. Letter from Dwain C. Epps to Canon Burgess Carr, August 6, 1971 (Geneva: WCC Archives). On the loneliness of Alier's position at the bargaining table at Addis Ababa, see Bona Malwal, *People and Power in Sudan: The Struggle for National Stability* (London: Ithaca Press, 1981), p. 145.

29. At the time, some of the Anya-Nya commanders believed that the tide of the war was turning in their favor. See "Sudan: Political Anatomy of the South," p. 3.

30. Letter from Joseph Lagu to Mading de Garang, October 30, 1970 (Geneva: WCC Archives), p. 1.

31. Ibid.

32. Kodwo E. Ankrah, "Sudan: The Church and Peace," *Africa*, no. 9 (May 1972), p. 63 (emphasis added); and "Sudan: [Report of the] 1st Mission by SSLM European Representatives to Africa, Trip Beginning August 7, 1971, August 30, 1971" (Geneva: WCC Archives), p. 2.

33. Cecile Eprile, *War and Peace in the Sudan, 1955-1972* (London: David and Charles, 1974), p. 144. Eprile points out that other sources find these figures conservative and have estimated the number of refugees overseas at 250,000 or more.

34. See letter from Jan Orner to L. J. Niilus, March 25, 1971 (Geneva: WCC Archives), p. 2.

35. Memorandum from D. C. Epps to L. J. Niilus, August 6, 1971, on a "Visit to Sudan and Southern Sudanese leadership" (Geneva: WCC Archives).

36. The symposium on Intermediary Activity and the Southern Sudanese Conflict held at the Richardson Institute in Geneva (November 1973) claimed that the United States pressured Nimeiry to reach a settlement; see Conflict Research Society, "Intermediary Activity and the Southern Sudanese Conflict," p. 21.

37. Memorandum from Kodwo E. Ankrah to Dr. Alan A. Brash, October 26, 1971. This memorandum contains a section on "Notes of Discussion with His Excellency Abel Alier, Vice President and Minister for Southern Affairs Held at his Office on October 22, 1971" (Geneva: WCC Archives), p. 7.

38. Ankrah, "Sudan: The Church and Peace," p. 61.

39. Undated document in WCC Archives, Geneva. The four-page document appears to be the minutes of a meeting between WCC members Leopoldo Niilus, Dwain Epps, Theresa Scherf, Jan Orner, and Kodwo Ankrah and Sudanese-in-exile Mading de Garang and Arthur Akuien. Ankrah's statement to de Garang and Akuien is "you make it easier if…you can solve internal problems in your camp, if you can bring them together to see the situation" (p. 3).

40. Unsigned letter bearing names of Reverend A. Brash and Mr. D. C. Epps, July 20, 1971 (Geneva: WCC Archives).

41. Conflict Research Society, "Intermediary Activity and the Southern Sudanese Conflict," p. 23.

42. Maureen R. Berman and Joseph E. Johnson, eds., *Unofficial Diplomats* (Columbia University Press, 1977).

43. On the process at work in the Sudanese negotiations, see Assefa, *Mediation of Civil Wars*; Wai, *African-Arab Conflict in the Sudan*, chap. 8; and Kodwo Ankrah, "In Pursuit of Peace in the Sudan," *Study Encounter*, vol. 8, no. 2 (1972), pp. 1-11.

44. The results of the 1965 roundtable conference are reprinted in Dunstan M. Wai, ed., *The Southern Sudan: The Problem of National Integration* (London: Frank Cass, 1973), pp. 208-09.

45. See Abel Alier, *Southern Sudan: Too Many Agreements Dishonoured* (Exeter, England: Ithaca Press, 1990), p. 63; see also "Notes of Discussion with His Excellency Abel Alier."

46. Abel Alier, "The Southern Sudan Question," in Wai, ed., *Southern Sudan*, p. 25.

47. "AACC Follow-up of Reconciliation and Relief Initiatives in the Sudan," p. 2. These are notes on the May 25, 1971, meeting between the AACC and "the involved parties" in Kampala, Uganda (Geneva: WCC Archives).

48. Letter from Joseph Lagu to Mading de Garang, October 30, 1970.

49. "The Addis Ababa Agreement on the Problem of South Sudan," *Grass Curtain*, vol. 2 (May 1972), p. 18.

50. "Minutes of the Third Session of the Conference on the Southern Sudan Held in Addis Ababa on February 18, 1972, between the Sudan Government on the One Hand and the Southern Sudan Liberation Movement (SSLM) on the Other" (Geneva: WCC Archives).

51. Beshir, *Southern Sudan*, p. 110.

52. Leopoldo J. Niilus, "Peace in the Sudan: Reflections on Questions for a Written Interview from Mrs. Barbara Hampton," March 12, 1973, p. 12 (Geneva: WCC Archives) (emphasis in original).

53. Assefa, *Mediation of Civil Wars*, p. 142.

54. Niilus, "Peace in the Sudan," p. 10 (emphasis in original.)

55. Conflict Research Society, "Intermediary Activity and the Southern Sudanese Conflict."

56. Communication from Leopoldo Niilus to Dwain Epps, Addis Ababa, February 17, 1972 (Geneva: WCC Archives), p. 4 (emphasis in original).

57. Alier, *Southern Sudan*, p. 112.

58. Assefa, *Mediation of Civil Wars*, p. 141.

59. Douglas H. Johnson, *The Southern Sudan*, Report no. 78 (London: Minority Rights Group, 1988), p. 5.

60. Tristram Betts, *The Southern Sudan: The Ceasefire and After* (London: Africa Publications Trust, 1974), pp. 2-3; and Sayed Abel Alier, *Peace and Development in the Southern Region* (Khartoum: Ministry of Culture and Information, 1976), p. 4.

61. Deng, *War of Visions*, p. 12.

62. "Southern Sudan," *Africa Confidential*, vol. 15 (February 22, 1974), p. 7.

63. Dunstan M. Wai, "Geoethnicity and the Margin of Autonomy in the Sudan," in Donald Rothchild and Victor A. Olorunsola, eds., *State versus Ethnic Claims: African Policy Dilemmas* (Boulder, Colo.: Westview, 1983), p. 320. See also Andrew Deng, "Political Power and Decentralization in the Sudan," *Decentralization and Development Review*, no. 1 (Spring 1981), p. 7.

64. See Colonel/Dr. John Garang de Mabior, *Appeal to the Sudanese People on the Founding of the Sudan People's Liberation Army (SPLA) and Sudan People's Liberation Movement (SPLM)* (SPLM/SPLA, March 3, 1984), p. 5, reprinted in Mansour Khalid, ed., *John Garang Speaks* (London: KPI Ltd., 1987), pp. 19-25.

65. Jon Tinker, "Sudan: The Ecology and Economics of the Jonglei Canal," *Weekly Review* (Nairobi), April 28, 1978, p. 34; Garang, *Appeal to the Sudanese People*, p. 5; interview with Abel Alier in "Nine Years: An Evolving Miracle," *SUDANOW*, vol. 6 (March 1981), pp. 13, 14; Khalid, ed., *John Garang Speaks*, p. 21; and "Sudan: Ruffles All Around," *Africa Confidential*, vol. 22 (November 25, 1981). p. 1.

66. Alexis Heraclides, "Janus or Sisyphus? The Southern Problem of the Sudan," *Journal of Modern African Studies*, vol. 25 (June 1987), p. 227. There were various signs that the majority of the Sudanese people, Muslim as well as non-Muslim and upper class as well as lower class, preferred the old Sudanese penal and civil codes to the *Sharia* law. I wish to thank Robert O. Collins for his observations on this matter.

67. "Return to Roots," *SUDANOW*, vol. 8 (November 1983), pp. 8-11; "Sudan: Southern Rebels Hold Upper Hand," *Africa News*, vol. 24 (February 11, 1985), p. 7; Deng, *War of Visions*, p. 171; "Sudan: Opposition Grows to Sudan's Harsh Islamic Law," *New African*, no. 204 (September 1984), pp. 34-35; and John Garang de Mabior, "Brief Background to the Sudanese Conflict" (Southern Sudan General Headquarters: Sudan People's Liberation Movement and Sudan People's Liberation Army, January 15, 1993), p. 1.

68. See "Letter from the Editor," *Weekly Review* (Nairobi), June 1, 1984, p. 1; and David B. Ottaway, "Sudan Backtracks on Muslim Law," *Manchester Guardian Weekly*, vol. 131 (October 7, 1984), p. 15.

69. Khalid, ed., *John Garang Speaks*, p. 22.

70. Khalid Medani, "Sudan's Human and Political Crisis," *Current History*, vol. 92 (May 1993), p. 205.

71. Joseph Lagu, *Decentralisation:A Necessity for the Southern Provinces of the Sudan* (Khartoum: Samar P. Press, 1981), pp. 3, 7.

72. See Solidarity Committee of the Southern Members 4th People's National Assembly, Omdurman, *The Redivision of the Southern Region:Why It Must be Rejected* (Juba, Sudan: Nile Press, n.d.), p. 6.

73. Bona Malwal, *The Sudan:A Second Challenge to Nationhood* (NewYork: Thornton Books, 1985), p. 34.

74. Jean Gueyras, "Oil Holds Promise for Sudan," *The Guardian*, November 13, 1983, p. 14.

75. Garang describes SPLA-SPLM as a "vanguard movement for the liberation of the whole Sudanese people," not a separatist movement in the South alone. See Khalid, ed., *John Garang Speaks*, p. 22.

76. On Sadiq el Mahdi's "reluctance" to place a freeze on the application of the *Sharia* laws, see Medani, "Sudan's Human and Political Crisis," p. 206.

77. Francis Mading Deng, "War of Visions for the Nation," *Middle East Journal*, vol. 44 (Autumn 1990), p. 603.

78. Riad Ibrahim, "Factors Contributing to the Political Ascendancy of the Muslim Brethren in Sudan," *Arab Studies Quarterly*, vol. 12 (Summer–Fall 1990), p. 37; and Yehudit Ronen, "Sudan," in Ami Ayalon, ed., *Middle East Contemporary Survey 1989-1990*, vol. 13 (Tel Aviv University Press, 1991), p. 616.

79. "Sudan: Nothing to Celebrate," *Africa Confidential*, vol. 33 (July 31, 1992), p. 3; and "Machar and Kuanyin Finally Join Forces With NIF Against the South," *Sudan Democratic Gazette*, no. 72 (May 1996), p. 6.

80. Francis M. Deng, "Mediating the Sudanese Conflict:A Challenge for the IGADD," *CSIS Notes*, no. 169 (February 1995), pp. 5-6.

81. "NIF Regime Highlights Mistaken Stance of Some of the Friends of IGAD," *Sudan Democratic Gazette,* no. 80 (January 1997), p. 6.

82. Curle, *Making Peace*, p. 225.

83. Robert Harrison Wagner, "The Causes of Peace," in Roy Licklider, ed., *Stopping the Killing: How Civil Wars End* (New York University Press, 1993), p. 263.

Chapter 9

1. Russell Hardin, *One for All: The Logic of Group Conflict* (Princeton University Press, 1995).

2. Concerning proportional representation as a critical factor in the Inkatha Freedom party's calculus regarding participation in the 1994 elections in South Africa, see Timothy D. Sisk, "Electoral System Choice in South Africa: Implications for Intergroup Moderation," *Nationalism and Ethnic Politics*, vol. 1 (Summer 1995), p. 195.

3. David A. Baldwin, "Power and Social Exchange," *American Political Science Review*, vol. 72 (December 1978), p. 1232.

4. Adam Przeworski, *Democracy and the Market: Political and Economic Reforms in Eastern Europe and Latin America* (Cambridge University Press, 1991), p. 26.

5. Robert O. Keohane, "Reciprocity in International Relations," *International Organization*, vol. 40 (Winter 1986), p. 20; and Alexander L. George, "Strategies for Facilitating Cooperation," in Alexander L. George, Philip J. Farley, and Alexander Dallin, eds., *U.S.-Soviet Security Cooperation:Achievements, Failures, Lessons* (Oxford University Press, 1988), p. 703.

6. Regarding the mutually hurting stalemate as an incentive to negotiate, see Stephen John Stedman, "Conflict and Conflict Resolution in Africa:A Conceptual Framework," in Francis M. Deng and I.William Zartman, eds., *Conflict Resolution in Africa* (Brookings, 1991), p. 384.

7. Margaret Joan Anstee, the UN secretary-general's special representative for Angola, has stated that her greatest fear before the 1992 elections was "the level of mistrust each of the parties showed about the other's actions and intentions, leading them to adopt defensive positions of an escalating nature that could all too easily tip over into offensive action." *Orphan of the Cold War:The Inside Story of the Collapse of the Angolan Peace Process, 1992-93* (St. Martin's Press, 1996), pp. 155-56. See also David A. Lake and Donald Rothchild, "Containing Fear:The Origins and Management of Ethnic Conflict," *International Security*, vol. 21 (Fall 1996), pp. 41-75; Barry R. Posen, "The Security Dilemma and Ethnic Conflict," *Survival*, vol. 35 (Spring 1993), p. 28; and Robert Jervis, "Cooperation under the Security Dilemma," *World Politics*, vol. 30 (January 1978), p. 172.

8. Roger Fisher, *International Conflict for Beginners* (Harper and Row, 1969), p. 49.

9. Victor Azarya, "Civil Society and Disengagement in Africa," in John W. Harbeson, Donald Rothchild, and Naomi Chazan, eds., *Civil Society and the State in Africa* (Boulder, Colo.: Lynne Rienner, 1994), pp. 83-100.

10. See Donald Rothchild, "Social Incoherence and the Mediatory Role of the State," in Bruce E. Arlinghaus, ed., *African Security Issues: Sovereignty, Stability and Solidarity* (Boulder, Colo.:Westview, 1984), pp. 99-125.

11. Daniel Brumberg, "Some Thoughts on Fundamentalist Utopias and the Question of Democratic Transitions," paper prepared for conference on Regime Change and Democratization in Comparative Perspective, University of California at Los Angeles, May 19-21, 1994, p. 11.

12. Francis M. Deng, "Africa and the New World Dis-Order," *Brookings Review*, vol. 11 (Spring 1993), p. 34.

13. Raymond F. Hopkins, "Anomie, System Reform, and Challenges to the UN System," in Milton J. Esman and Shibley Telhami, eds., *International Organizations and Ethnic Conflict* (Cornell University Press, 1995), p. 87.

14. Boutros Boutros-Ghali, *An Agenda for Peace: Preventive Diplomacy, Peacemaking and Peacekeeping* (New York: United Nations, 1992), p. 9. See also the chapters by Olusegun Obasanjo, Ibrahim Gambari, and Solomon Gomes in Edmond J. Keller and Donald Rothchild, eds., *Africa and the New International Order* (Boulder, Colo.: Lynne Rienner, 1996); and Francis M. Deng and others, *Sovereignty as Responsibility: Conflict Management in Africa* (Brookings, 1996).

15. Chester A. Crocker, *High Noon in Southern Africa: Making Peace in a Rough Neighborhood* (Norton, 1992), pp. 471, 474; and Richard N. Haass,

Conflicts Unending: The United States and Regional Disputes (Yale University Press, 1990), p. 147.

16. James D. Fearon, "Commitment Problems and the Spread of Ethnic Conflict," in David A. Lake and Donald Rothchild, eds., *The International Spread of Ethnic Conflict: Fear, Diffusion, and Escalation* (Princeton University Press, forthcoming).

17. Thomas A. Kochan, "Step-By-Step in the Middle East from the Perspective of the Labor Mediation Process," in Jeffrey Z. Rubin, ed., *Dynamics of Third Party Intervention: Kissinger in the Middle East* (Praeger, 1981), p. 125.

18. See Donald Rothchild, *Racial Bargaining in Independent Kenya: A Study of Minorities and Decolonization* (Oxford University Press, 1973), pp. 103-45.

19. Interview with Robin Renwick, London, July 4, 1986.

20. For a discussion of Lord Carrington's directed mediation at Lancaster House, see Jeffrey Davidow, *A Peace in Southern Africa: The Lancaster House Conference on Rhodesia, 1979* (Boulder, Colo.: Westview, 1984), pp. 115-21.

21. Alistair Horne, *A Savage War of Peace: Algeria 1954-1962*, rev. ed. (Penguin Books, 1987), p. 521.

22. Interview, Nairobi, March 1, 1991; and Witney W. Schneidman, "Conflict Resolution in Mozambique: A Status Report," *CSIS Africa Notes*, no. 121 (February 28, 1991), p. 6.

23. Cameron Hume, *Ending Mozambique's War: The Role of Mediation and Good Offices* (Washington: United States Institute of Peace Press, 1994).

24. Alex Vines, "Mozambique: The Road to Peace (1982-1992)," paper prepared for the 1993 annual meeting of the African Studies Association, p. 33; see also Hume, *Ending Mozambique's War*, p. 93.

25. For confirmation of this by the International Joint Verification Commission, see "Renamo Wants to Resume Talks with Government," Maputo Domestic Service, March 9, 1991, in Foreign Broadcast Information Service (FBIS), *Daily Report: Sub-Saharan Africa*, March 11, 1991, p. 20.

26. For a listing of the major "deadbeat" countries in terms of the regular UN and peacekeeping UN budgets, see Chantal de Jonge Oudraat, "The United Nations and Internal Conflict," in Michael E. Brown, ed., *The International Dimensions of Internal Conflict* (MIT Press, 1996), p. 498.

27. Joseph S. Nye Jr., "Soft Power," *Foreign Policy*, no. 80 (Fall 1990), p. 168.

28. Saadia Touval, "Why the U.N. Fails," *Foreign Affairs*, vol. 73 (September-October 1994), p. 52.

29. Jeffrey Z. Rubin, "Introduction," in Rubin, ed., *Dynamics of Third Party Intervention*, p. 5; and Malvern Lumsden, "The Cyprus Conflict as a Prisoner's Dilemma Game," *Journal of Conflict Resolution*, vol. 17 (March 1973), p. 17.

30. Jack Snyder, "Averting Anarchy in the New Europe," *International Security*, vol. 14 (Spring 1990), p. 30.

31. George Modelski, "International Settlement of Internal War," in James N. Rosenau, ed., *International Aspects of Civil Strife* (Princeton University Press, 1964), p. 143.

32. Jeffrey Z. Rubin and Bert R. Brown, *The Social Psychology of Bargaining and Negotiation* (New York: Academic Press, 1975), pp. 285-87.

33. Louis Kriesberg, "Introduction: Timing Conditions, Strategies, and Errors," in L. Kriesberg and Stuart J. Thorson, eds., *Timing the De-Escalation of International Conflicts* (Syracuse University Press, 1991), p. 14.

34. Arild Underdal, "Causes of Negotiation 'Failure,'" *European Journal of Political Research*, vol. 11 (June 1983), p. 184.

35. Alexander L. George, *Forceful Persuasion: Coercive Diplomacy as an Alternative to War* (Washington: United States Institute of Peace Press, 1991), pp. 4-5.

36. Robert Axelrod and Robert O. Keohane, "Achieving Cooperation under Anarchy: Strategies and Institutions," *World Politics*, vol. 38 (October 1985), pp. 231-32.

37. Rubin, "Introduction," p. 27.

38. Bill Keller, "Mozambican Opposition Rejects Election," *New York Times*, October 28, 1994, p. A6. See also Hume, *Ending Mozambique's War*, p. 44; and Thomas Ohlson and Stephen John Stedman, *The New Is Not Yet Born: Conflict Resolution in Southern Africa* (Brookings, 1994), p. 115.

39. Interviews with Robin Renwick, London, July 4, 1986, and A. M. Chambati, Harare, Zimbabwe, July 14, 1986.

40. Rubin and Brown, *Social Psychology of Bargaining*, p. 137.

41. Kenneth Kressel, "Kissinger in the Middle East: An Exploratory Analysis of Role Strain in International Mediation," in Rubin, ed., *Dynamics of Third Party Intervention*, p. 244.

42. I. William Zartman and Saadia Touval, "Conclusion: Mediation in Theory and Practice," in Touval and Zartman, eds., *International Mediation in Theory and Practice* (Boulder, Colo.: Westview, 1985), p. 263; and George I. Balch, "The Stick, the Carrot, and Other Strategies: A Theoretical Analysis of Government Intervention," *Law and Policy Quarterly*, vol. 2 (January 1980), p. 52.

43. Rubin and Brown, *Social Psychology of Bargaining*, pp. 136-37. See also Donald L. Horowitz, *Ethnic Groups in Conflict* (University of California Press, 1985), p. 224.

44. Donald L. Horowitz, "Incentives and Behavior in the Ethnic Politics of Sri Lanka and Malaysia," *Third World Quarterly*, vol. 11 (October 1989), p. 33.

45. Rothchild, *Racial Bargaining in Independent Kenya*, p. 118.

46. Moreover, in early 1994 Mandela conceded to conservative Afrikaners the right of setting up a "Volkstaatraad" or homeland council.

47. Walter Martin, Notes of a meeting at Quaker House, Friday, February 23, 1968, with Ambassador J. T. F. Iyalla, William Huntington, and Walter Martin, February 26, 1968 (American Friends Service Committee Archives).

48. Chaim Kaufmann, "Possible and Impossible Solutions to Ethnic Civil Wars," *International Security*, vol. 20 (Spring 1996), p. 150.

49. Norman Uphoff, "Distinguishing Power, Authority and Legitimacy: Taking Max Weber at His Word by Using Resources-Exchange Analysis," *Polity*, vol. 22 (Winter 1989), p. 310.

50. Michael S. Strah, "An Ethical Analysis of United States Involvement in the Nigerian/Biafran Conflict," Ph.D. thesis, Boston University, 1984, pp. 406, 484, 488.

51. Hume, *Ending Mozambique's War*, p. 61.

52. Max Neiman, "The Virtues of Heavy-Handedness in Government," *Law and Policy Quarterly*, vol. 2 (January 1980), p. 25.

53. Louis Kriesberg, "Noncoercive Inducements in U.S.-Soviet Conflicts: Ending the Occupation of Austria and Nuclear Weapons Tests," *Journal of Political and Military Sociology*, vol. 9 (Spring 1981), p. 3.

54. See ibid., p. 13; Rubin and Brown, *Social Psychology of Bargaining*, p. 286; Roger Fisher, "Negotiating Power: Getting and Using Influence," *American Behavioral Scientist*, vol. 27 (November–December 1983), p. 152; and David Wendt, "The Peacemakers: Lessons of Conflict Resolution for the Post–Cold War World," *Washington Quarterly*, vol. 17 (Summer 1994), p. 170.

55. Confidential letter, January 26, 1995.

56. Interview with U.S. Secretary of State Henry A. Kissinger, Davis, California, October 21, 1987.

57. Davidow, *A Peace in Southern Africa*, p. 39.

58. Interview with Robin Renwick, London, July 4, 1986.

59. Interview with A. M. Chambati, Harare, Zimbabwe, July 14, 1986.

60. Gillian Gunn, "A Guide to the Intricacies of the Angola-Namibia Negotiations," *CSIS Africa Notes*, no. 90 (September 8, 1988), p. 7.

61. "South Africa: Washington Issues an Ultimatum," *Africa Confidential*, vol. 30 (October 20, 1989), pp. 1–2.

62. James M. Lindsay, "Trade Sanctions as Policy Instruments: A Re-examination," *International Studies Quarterly*, vol. 30 (June 1986), p. 154 (emphasis in original).

63. Ambassador Donald F. McHenry asserts that the threatened use of sanctions against South Africa in April 1977 regarding Namibia's independence "opened the door for mediation." Interview, Washington, May 14, 1987.

64. Frederick Ehrenreich, "Burundi: The Current Political Dynamic," paper prepared for U.S. Institute of Peace Conference on Burundi (Washington, December 8, 1996); and "Burundi: Arusha Summit Decides to Maintain Embargo," *Africa Research Bulletin*, Political, Social and Cultural Series, vol. 33 (October 1–31, 1996), p. 12438.

65. "Arusha Summit Partially Lifts Embargo," *Africa Research Bulletin*, Political, Social and Cultural Series, vol. 34 (April 1–30, 1997), p. 12654.

66. Interview with Roger J. A. Martin, British deputy high commissioner in Harare, Zimbabwe, Princeton, N.J., March 25, 1987. See also Donald L. Losman, *International Economic Sanctions: The Cases of Cuba, Ireland and Rhodesia* (University of New Mexico Press, 1979), pp. 88, 107, 109.

67. Interview with R. H. F. Austin, Harare, Zimbabwe, July 16, 1986.

68. David A. Baldwin, *Economic Statecraft* (Princeton University Press, 1985), p. 192; and Losman, *International Economic Sanctions*, p. 112.

69. See the assessment of Johan Galtung, "On the Effects of International Economic Sanctions with Examples from the Case of Rhodesia," *World Politics*, vol. 19 (April 1967), pp. 409–10.

70. Regarding the goal of sanctions as compliance with the demands for a change of regimes, see Richard Stuart Olson, "Economic Coercion in World

Politics: With a Focus on North-South Relations," *World Politics*, vol. 31 (July 1979), p. 475.

71. *Congressional Record*, August 11, 1988, p. H 6879.

72. "Salim Comments," Kampala Domestic Service, September 8, 1990, in FBIS, *Daily Report: Sub-Saharan Africa*, September 11, 1990, p. 1.

73. Before Nelson Mandela's trip to Europe and North America in June 1990, de Klerk asked the ANC leader to mute the appeal for continued international sanctions. Mandela rejected this request, declaring that "in our view sanctions remained the best lever to force him to do more." Nelson Mandela, *Long Walk to Freedom* (Little, Brown, 1994), p. 507.

74. "How Do South African Sanctions Work?" *The Economist*, October 14, 1989, pp. 45-46; and Lynda Schuster, "S. Africa's Foreign Policy Game Plan," *Christian Science Monitor*, November 17, 1988, p. 10.

75. "Challenges Facing Constitutional Negotiations," *Cape Times* (Capetown), in FBIS, *Daily Report: Sub-Saharan Africa*, July 24, 1990, p. 15.

76. Douglas G. Anglin, "Ripe, Ripening, or Overripe? Sanctions as an Inducement to Negotiations: The South African Case," *International Journal*, vol. 45 (Spring 1990), p. 369.

77. Kriesberg, "Noncoercive Inducement," p. 13.

78. David Owen, *Balkan Odyssey* (Harcourt Brace, 1995), p. 336.

79. Telegram from Edmund Gullion to U.S. Secretary of State, no. 2803, May 11, 1962, pp. 1-2 (John F. Kennedy Library).

80. U.S. Department of State, "Memorandum of Conversation: Congo," February 5, 1962, p. 4 (John F. Kennedy Library). On this occasion, Adoula also remarked, "We have to be ready to 'brandish the hammer.'"

81. Telegram from Dean Rusk to U.S. Embassy, Leopoldville, Congo, no. 1409, February 8, 1962, p. 3 (John F. Kennedy Library).

82. Telegram from George Ball to Leopoldville, Congo, December 14, 1961, p. 2 (John F. Kennedy Library).

83. Helpful discussions of the military encounters in Katanga appear in Ernest W. Lefever, *Crisis in the Congo: A United Nations Force in Action* (Brookings, 1965); Indar Jit Rikhye, *Military Adviser to the Secretary General: U.N. Peacekeeping and the Congo Crisis* (St. Martin's, 1993); Conor Cruise O'Brien, *To Katanga and Back: A UN Case History* (Simon and Schuster, 1962); and United Nations, *The Blue Helmets: A Review of United Nations Peacekeeping*, 2d ed. (New York: Department of Public Information, 1990).

84. Alexander L. George, "Incentives for U.S.-Soviet Security Cooperation and Mutual Adjustment," in George, Farley, and Dallin, eds., *U.S.-Soviet Security Cooperation*, p. 643.

85. Virginia Page Fortna, "Success and Failure in Southern Africa: Peacekeeping in Namibia and Angola," in Donald C. F. Daniel and Bradd C. Hayes, eds., *Beyond Traditional Peacekeeping* (St. Martin's, 1995), p. 283.

86. Stephen John Stedman and Donald Rothchild, "Peace Operations: From Short-Term to Long-Term Commitment," *International Peacekeeping*, vol. 3 (Summer 1996), pp. 17-35.

87. On the variables of success and failure in UN peacekeeping and peacebuilding efforts, see Donald Rothchild and Timothy Sisk, "The Role of

Peacekeeping in African Transitions: April 1990 to March 1992," in Colin Legum, ed., *Africa Contemporary Record*, vol. 23 (New York: Holmes and Meier, forthcoming).

88. "Angola: The Toothless Watchdogs," *Africa Confidential*, vol. 34 (March 5, 1993), p. 1.

89. "Angola: Christopher's Visit Said 'Marred' by Savimbi's Nonappearance," *Johannesburg Mail and Guardian*, October 18, 1996, in FBIS, *Daily Report: Sub-Saharan Africa*, October 18, 1996, p. 4; and "Angola: Peacekeeping Extended," *Africa Research Bulletin*, Political, Social and Cultural Series, vol. 33 (December 1-31, 1996), p. 12504-05.

90. Howard Adelman, "Towards a Confidence Transformational Dynamic," in Gabriel Ben-Dor and David B. Dewitt, eds., *Confidence Building Measures in the Middle East* (Boulder, Colo.: Westview, 1994), p. 317.

Index